AF478350

FIRST TO FIGHT

Dedicated to those who fought in Vietnam
to serve their country.

BOB BREEN

The Battery Press
Nashville

First published in USA in 1988 by
The Battery Press, Inc.
P.O. Box 3107 Uptown Station
Nashville, Tennessee 37219

Eighth in the Vietnam War Series

ISBN: 0-89839-126-1

Library of Congress Catalog Card Number: 88-71387

Printed in Malaysia

Contents

Maps

The maps and sketches have been drawn as accurately as possible by John Essex-Clark, IRAR's operations officer. He wishes to say that he could only do today what his shaky hand and incomplete memory helped by old fold-worn, silver-fished, battered, crackling maps with smudged markings coupled to an overly-cryptic commander's diary would allow. He apologises if any platoon, company battery or troop was not where he put them on paper but adds 'So what, often most of us didn't know exactly where we were either!'

Glossary

AATTV   Australian Army Training Team — Vietnam
Acclimation   Adjustment of the body to a new climate and surroundings (US)
Acclimatisation   Adjustment of the body to a new climate and surroundings (Aust)
AIF   Australian Imperial Forces
Airborne   Military units that are able to be deployed by parachute
Airmobile   Military units that are able to be deployed by helicopter
AK47   7.62 millimetre Russian-made assault rifle carried by Viet Cong
'All the Way'   Motto used by US Paratroopers
ANZAC   Australian and New Zealand Army Corps, formed in World War I
ANZUS   Australia, New Zealand and US Treaty 1951
Aussie   Slang for an Australian or Australian-made
BAR   8 millimetre Browning Automatic Rifle (US)
Base bludgers   Military personnel who do not go on combat operations (Aust)
Basic load   Standard amount of ammunition carried on operations (US)
Battalion   Tactical grouping of about 1000 men (US), 800 for Australian units
Bde HQ   Brigade headquarters
B52   US heavy bomber
BHQ   Battalion headquarters
'Big Red One'   US 1st Infantry Division nickname
Biscuit   Australian term for a 'cookie'
BMS   Below medical standard
Bloke   Australian term for a man or male, equivalent to American term 'guy'
Body count   The number of enemy dead counted after combat
Booby trap   Explosive charge initiated when an attached mechanical device is disturbed
Brigade   Tactical formation of about 3000 to 5000 men
'Bug out'   US Slang for military retreat from a fire fight
Bunker   Dug-in fortification with firing ports or slits
Canister shot   Tank round that fires thousands of anti-personnel darts
Casevac   Casualty evacuation
'Cattle trucks'   Nickname for semitrailers used to transport troops to and from the tarmac at Bien Hoa Airbase
Cavalrymen   Members of the US 101st Airborne Division

CBU   Cluster Bomb Unit — a bomb which breaks up into several smaller bombs
CH47 Chinook   Medium lift helicopter
Civic action   Military operations focusing on assistance to the civilian population
Claymore mine   Anti-personnel, above-ground, explosive device, initiated remotely through an electric cable, which fires thousands of ball bearings in an arc
Command-detonated mine   Mine initiated remotely by electric cable
Company   Tactical grouping of about 100 men (Aust), 150 for US company
Company position   Location of a company while stationary
COMUSMACV   Commander US Military Assistance Command — Vietnam
CRW   Counter-Revolutionary Warfare
CS gas   'Tear' gas
CSM   Company Sergeant Major (Aust)
Digger   Australian member of the 1 RAR Group; also general term for Australian soldiers
Dust off   Aero-medical evacuation by helicopter (US)
Eagle flight   Military unit flown in helicopters seeking enemy (US)
Esky   Australian brand name for a container filled with ice to keep drinks cool
FAC   Forward Air Controller — an individual who co-ordinates the use of fire support delivered from the air
Fire and movement   The combination of the fire of weapons from one group covering the movement of another group in combat
Firepower   The combination of the fire of direct and indirect weapon systems employed by military forces
Fire support base   Location of headquarters, artillery and logistic units supporting a military operation
Flare   Device which burns brightly when fired to provide illumination by night and act as a signal by day
FO   Forward Observer — an individual who co-ordinates the use of artillery fire support
Fortified position   Location where obstacles have been erected and installations constructed which can withstand the effects of direct and indirect firepower and permit the optimum use of weapons
Free Fire Zone   Area in which all personnel are considered to be enemy and all types of military ammunition and ordnance can be used
FSB   Fire Support Base Location of artillery, mortars and forward headquarters during operations
FSCC   Fire Support Co-ordination Centre
GP boots   General Purpose calf-length leather boots (Aust)
GPMG M60   7.62 millimetre General Purpose Machine Gun (US)
Gunner   Term for an artilleryman, member of artillery corps (Aust)
Harbour   Australian term for a temporary defensive position
H and I   Harrassing and Interdictory artillery fire
'Hog'   Nickname for helicopter gunship (US)
HMAS   Her Majesty's Australian Ship
HQ AAFV   Headquarters Australian Army Force — Vietnam located in Saigon
Hutchie   Australian one or two-man plastic military tent
HP35   9 millimetre Browning Automatic Pistol
Kiwi   New Zealand member of the 161 Field Battery Royal New Zealand Artillery; also general slang term for a New Zealander
LCT   Landing Craft Tank
Local Force   Viet Cong units operating near the homes of their soldiers

LZ   Landing Zone for helicopters

M26   Fragmentation hand grenade (US)

M48   US Patton tank

M56 SPAT   90 millimetre Self Propelled Anti-Tank Weapon (US)

M60 GPMG   7.62 millimetre General Purpose Machine Gun (US)

M72   60 millimetre Anti-Armoured Weapon — rocket fired from the shoulder (US)

M79   40 millimetre hand-held grenade launcher (US)

M106 SPM   107 millimetre Self Propelled Mortar (US)

M203   40 millimetre hand-held grenade launcher fitted to an M16 Automatic Rifle (US)

Main Force   Viet Cong units and formations organised and trained for conventional and unconventional warfare in 6000-man divisions, 2000 men regiments, 600 man battalions

Mention-in-Despatches (MID)   British Imperial award to all ranks for meritorious service and/or valour while on active duty

MFC   Mobile Fire Controller — an individual who co-ordinates the fire of mortars

Mighty Mite   Air pump used to blow smoke or CS gas into tunnel complexes

Military Cross (MC)   British Imperial award to officers for valour in combat

Military Medal (MM)   British Imperial award to ranks other than officers for valour in combat

Mine   An explosive, normally encased, designed to destroy or damage vehicles or designed to wound, kill or otherwise incapacitate personnel. It may be detonated by the action of its victim (see Booby trap), by the passage of time or by controlled means (see command-detonated mine)

Mortar   A muzzle-loaded weapon with either a rifled or smooth bore. It normally has a shorter range than a howitzer and normally employs a higher angle of fire

National Servicemen   Australian term for conscripts or draftees

NATO   North Atlantic Treaty Organisation

NCO   Non-Commissioned Officer

NLF   National Liberation Front (often synonymous with Viet Cong) — political cadre commanding Viet Cong military units

NVA   North Vietnamese Army — formed and trained in North Vietnam

OMC   9 millimetre Owen Machine Carbine (Aust)

Paratrooper   Member of US 173rd Airborne Brigade (Separate); also general term for airborne-trained soldier

Platoon   Tactical grouping of about 30 soldiers (Aust) 45 for US platoons

PRC-25   Portable radio of US make, short range, very high frequency

Purple Heart   US medal awarded for being killed or wounded on operations

PWLH   Prince of Wales Light Horse Regiment (1APC Troop) attached under command of 1RAR

Queenslanders   Those born in the northern Australian state of Queensland

RAR   Royal Australia Regiment — battalions of the RAR are abbreviated thus: 1 RAR, 2 RAR, 3 RAR and so on

Recoiless rifle   A weapon capable of being fired from a ground mount or vehicle, and capable of destroying vehicles including tanks

Reconnaissance by fire   Tactical technique of firing into suspected enemy locations rather than sending troops to investigate. This technique was employed by US troops to force hidden enemy to move and reveal their positions.

RAA   Royal Australian Artillery

Regional Forces   South Vietnamese para-military units

RMO   Regimental Medical Officer

RNZA   Royal New Zealand Artillery

ROAD   Reorganization Objective Army Divisions (US). This programme reorganised US formations into groupings of different corps with specific operational capabilities.

RRU   Radio Research (or Relay) Unit

RSL   Returned Services League (Aust) same as US Legion

RVN   Republic of Vietnam (South Vietnam)

Sappers   Members of the Australian 3 Field Engineer Troop, also general term for military engineers

SEATO   South East Asian Treaty Organisation

Section   Smallest tactical grouping in the Australian Army of about ten men (equivalent to a US Army squad)

Separate   When written in brackets after a US Army formation like the 173rd Airborne Brigade it meant the unit or formation was organised for independent operations

Shell scrape   Rectangular hole about 30 centimetres deep, large enough for one man to take cover below ground level (Aust)

Sig   Short for signaller, a soldier who operates radio communications equipment (Aust) same as US RTO (Radio Telephone Operator)

Silent registration   Recording of data for laying guns or mortars onto a target using a map and not adjusting fire on the ground

Silver Star   US military award for bravery

'Sky Soldiers'   Nickname for members of the 173rd Airborne Brigade

'Slick'   Nickname for helicopter carrying troops

SLR   7.62 millimetre Self Loading Rifle carried by Australian soldiers

'Snake Pit'   Nickname for place where helicopters would arrive and depart at Bien Hoa Airbase

Spec 5   Specialist rank 5 — US Army rank equivalent to Australian sergeant

Special Forces   Units trained for unconventional warfare

Splintex   Artillery anti-personnel round which fires small darts

'Stand down'   Order given to end a period of full alert

'Stand to'   Period of time where Australian units go on to full alert. Typically occurs at first and last light each day but may be ordered when enemy is suspected of being in the area.

TAOR   Tactical Area of Responsibility. Area of terrain allocated to formations and units to dominate and deny to the enemy.

'The Herd'   Nickname for the 173rd Airborne Brigade(Separate)

Troopers   Members of 1 Armoured Personnel Carrier Troop, Prince of Wales Light Horse Regiment; also general nickname for armoured corps soldiers

Tropic Lightning   US 25th Infantry Division nickname

TS boots   Tropical Stud boots — circa World War II (Aust)

UHID or UHIB   Utility Helicopter ID or IB model

'Up-the guts'   Slang for direct attack on the enemy after contact without employing flanking manoeuvres

VC   Viet Cong — military arm of the National Liberation Front. Initially these were South Vietnamese units opposed to the Saigon Government. After taking heavy casualties they were reinforced by North Vietnamese.

Victoria Cross   Highest award for gallantry in the British Imperial system of awards

VNAF   Vietnamese National Air Force (South Vietnamese)

'Wheel'   Australian nickname for military officer or boss

Foreword

By Lieutenant General Sir Thomas Daly KBE, CB, DSO

Although Australia had been represented in Vietnam since 1962 by the Army Training Team, a group of professionals which was already enriching the pages of Australian military history, the First Battalion, Royal Australian Regiment was, as the title of this volume suggests, our first homogeneous fighting unit to enter the conflict. It had fought under my command in Korea, so apart from anything else I have a very personal interest in Colonel Breen's account of its service in Vietnam.

The First Battalion arrived in the theatre of operations in less than an ideal state of readiness. It had recently undergone a major reorganisation which saw the appointment of a new commanding officer and a substantial infusion of inexperienced young officers. As is so often the case, military requirements had taken second place to political expediency and in consequence little time was available for the multiplicity of administrative tasks needed before embarkation and none at all for the intensive training so necessary before engaging in a hazardous campaign in an unfamiliar and treacherous environment. Fortunately, it possessed a solid core of experience gained from operations in Malaysia which was to stand it in good stead. In addition, its American ally was able to supply certain modern weapons and equipment of which it was deficient.

This was not a new experience. It had all happened before, perhaps most recently with the commitment of the Third Battalion to the Korean conflict. Unfortunately, as a nation we have sometimes been slow to learn the lessons of history but we have in the past had the good fortune to have been able to call upon allies to repair our deficiencies. This will not always be the case and indeed, an important aspect of current defence policy is the development of a capacity for self reliance. However unless policy is converted to practice in rather less than the distant future, we are likely in an emergency to be caught short once more.

Colonel Breen has researched his subject with remarkable thoroughness. He describes in graphic detail the arrival of the Australians in Bien Hoa and the problems encountered in being absorbed into an alien organisation—the elite US 173rd Airborne Brigade—which differed not only in equipment and tactical doctrine but more importantly in operational philosophy. That this was successfully accomplished speaks volumes for the tough diplomacy of the Australian battalion commander and for the tolerance and understanding of his American brigade commander.

The account of the operations which follows is of intense interest. Throughout the many actions at various levels, the story is one of courage, initiative and leadership. Leaders at all levels were constantly faced with a need for quick and sound decisions involving life and death, often in desperate circumstances as units came up against an elusive and mostly invisible enemy in the steaming heat of the thick bush. Perhaps even worse was the passive enemy, the hidden mines and booby traps which claimed their victims with terrible effect.

During my service as the Australian Army's Chief of the General Staff from 1966 to 1971, I made many visits to the war zone. I was only too well aware of the immense difficulties confronting our troops as they sought to find and defeat a largely unseen enemy, of the hardships they endured and the casualties they were suffering. Not since World War I had our troops been engaged in such continuous operations over so long a period of time with so little relief. The maintenance of morale during such exhausting and often unrewarding operations was no mean feat nor was it assisted by the disgracefully biased reporting by sections of the press, by the efforts of misguided fellow countrymen who sought to provide aid and comfort to the enemy or worst of all by the actions of a few contemptible, cowardly creatures who endeavoured through anonymous telephone calls to terrorise the wives and children of men serving in Vietnam. Yet in spite of it all, the ordinary soldier doggedly stuck to his task. As one digger said to me—and he was typical of many: 'I haven't time to worry about what those bastards do or say, I am more concerned with doing my job and staying alive'. Over the years, the sordid consequences of the abandonment of Vietnam to the northern communists have become vividly apparent and a more mature appraisement of the war has emerged.

Colonel Breen lists a series of lessons culled from the experiences of the 173rd Airborne Brigade in 1965–66. The lesson which stands out above all others both for ourselves—and our allies—is that never again should we engage in a war unless we intend to bring it to a successful conclusion. A determined enemy can be defeated only when his will and capacity to fight have been destroyed. A defensive or piecemeal strategy, no matter how actively pursued, can never be decisive. In Vietnam, because of political constraints, the North's centres of power were inviolate while its forces in the South after suffering a defeat such as the 1968 Tet debacle were free to retire into sanctuaries beyond the demilitarised zone, or into Laos and Cambodia, to rest and refit prior to launching further attacks. In these circumstances, the best result that could have been hoped for would have been a stalemate as in Korea, but there it had been achieved only with the aid of a continuing American presence. The hypocrisy of the Paris agreements in 1973, the ultimate betrayal, precluded such a result in Vietnam.

I still have an intense feeling of frustration concerning the ultimate outcome of the Vietnam war. The death and mutilation of so many fine young men, all to so little purpose, cannot but fail to affect deeply anyone who gives serious thought to this unrewarding campaign. If, as a nation we are to espouse a cause, let it be one in which we believe, not one that can be switched off like a television soap opera if one has grown weary of the storyline. In wars, of whatever magnitude, men will die and their lives are far too precious to be dependent on the vagaries of a political weathervane.

Colonel Breen's book is a factual account of operations conducted by the First Battalion and its parent formation, the US 173rd Airborne Brigade. It does much to offset the lurid and sensationalised description of the Vietnam War which have, over the past few years, provided sanguinary entertainment in cinemas and living rooms the world over. At the same time, it does not spare the reader the inevitable horrors that war entails. It is a valuable addition to the sparse store of reliable information available to the general public and deserves to be widely read.

Thomas Daly
1988

Preface

There are few books on Australian military operations in the Vietnam War and none comparing the tactics of Australian and US infantry units. In this book I tell the story of the only Australian infantry battalion and New Zealand gun battery to have ever fought under the operational control of a US Army formation. This unique experiment in ANZUS co-operation has given me the opportunity to write about the combat operations of the first US, Australian and New Zealand army units to fight in the Vietnam War—operations characterised by differences rather than similarities. The challenges faced by the Paratroopers, Diggers and Kiwis of the 173rd Airborne Brigade (Separate) were faced again and again by units of their respective armies that followed them. This tri-national brigade set precedents for the way the Vietnam War was fought by the allies.

In some ways the 173rd and later the US 1st Infantry Division had achieved all that could have been achieved in stalemating the military situation around Saigon by June 1966. The 173rd hunted the Viet Cong relentlessly for twelve months and were victorious in seven provinces in the III Corps area. By June 1966 the two Viet Cong Main Force Divisions that had threatened Saigon early in 1965 were on the run, having suffered calamitous personnel and materiel losses. The Saigon Government, however, was not strong enough militarily or politically to take advantage of the breathing space the lives of young Americans, Australians and New Zealanders had given them in 1965–66. All that came after was fruitless attrition which killed off the southern-born Viet Cong and opened the door for the North Vietnamese to overwhelm their southern neighbours. By Tet 1968 the Viet Cong, heavily reinforced with North Vietnamese personnel, arms and equipment, were able to mount a military offensive which became the political turning point for the withdrawal of allied ground forces from Vietnam.

The Paratroopers, Diggers and Kiwis of the 173rd fought as they had been trained and used their past combat experience as guidance for fighting the Viet Cong. The Americans of the 173rd brought an attacking attitude and willingness to use firepower to Vietnam and the Australians and New Zealanders of the 1 RAR Group brought the stealth and patience of the Malayan Emergency. They were all in the midst of a war that was nothing like their past experiences: there were no frontlines, no territorially-based campaigns that permanently won areas from the enemy, no restoration of political control to an allied government, no time to remain in an area and discover enemy patterns and no guarantee that the enemy was not being informed of the location and duration of allied operations.

The lessons for those who may have to plan allied military interventions into Asia in the future are significant because little will have changed. The training of US, Australian and New Zealand Army units will be the same, the firepower available will be even more lethal, and the approach to bringing the enemy to battle will be identical. The intervention by US forces into Grenada in the early 1980s showed that the US Armed Forces still have an attacking attitude and a willingness to use firepower. The Australian Army now trains for low level threat contingencies in the north west of Australia and the emphasis is still on small-scale operations, stealth and patience.

This book has taken a few years to write and has involved the efforts of many individuals. In 1977 I completed a short dissertation comparing the tactics employed by 1 RAR in Vietnam to those developed during the Malayan Emergency. I am grateful to Lieutenant Colonel Ian Ahearn, the Commanding Officer of 1 RAR at the time, and Professor John Legge of Monash University for their assistance with this early research. I did not resume work on the book until 1984 because of commitments to my military career and post-graduate studies in instructional technology at Florida State University. In that year Principal Chaplain Gerry Cudmore AM (RL), representing a group of 1 RAR veterans, asked me to write a short history for a forthcoming twentieth anniversary reunion commemorating the 1 RAR Group's deployment to Vietnam in 1965.

By the time of the reunion in June 1985 I had completed a useful but incomplete draft and the 1 RAR veterans had concurred with my proposal to continue writing to produce a comprehensive history. During my year at the Australian Command and Staff College I wrote a further draft. After reviewing this draft, Lieutenant Colonel David Horner, my editorial adviser, and Lieutenant Colonel Sandy McQuarrie, my Canadian Directing Staff, identified the draft's lack of depth, breadth and balance. After picking up and dusting off my ego and self-confidence, I applied for sponsorship to travel on service aircraft to the US to make up these deficiencies. Sponsored by Major General Keith Kirkland AO (RL) and Major General Peter Day in Australia and Major General Ellis Williamson

(Ret) in the US, I gained access to 173rd Airborne Brigade records and returned to Australia with the makings of a more interesting book. I am grateful to Second Lieutenant George Farris for his hospitality and assistance in Washington DC.

With timely encouragement and editorial advice from John Iremonger of Allen & Unwin, the final manuscript was completed at the end of 1987. Of the many 1 RAR Group veterans who assisted me, the most prominent were Brigadier Peter Arnison, Brigadier John Essex-Clark (RL), Brigadier John Hooper CBE (RL), Colonel Ian McFarlane (RL), Colonel Alex Preece MVO, DSO (RL), Lieutenant Colonel John Dwyer AM (RL), Lieutenant Colonel Bill Kaine MBE, Major Tom Buckley (RL), Major John MacNamara (RL), Major Peter Rothwell (RL), Major Clive Williams (RL), Jack Currie MBE, Lex McAulay and Carey McQuillan. Colonel Alan Hutchinson provided the material for 105 Field Battery, Royal Australian Artillery and Lieutenant Steve Newman for 161 Field Battery, Royal New Zealand Artillery.

Of those mentioned above I wish to further acknowledge Major General Ellis Williamson (Ret), the commander of the 173rd in 1963–66, without whom I would not have gained access to US Army records and for his personal efforts to have the veterans of the 1 RAR Group awarded the US Meritorious Unit Commendation in retrospect when it was discovered that they had been left off the General Order awarding this decoration to the 173rd and its assigned and attached units for the Brigade's achievements in 1965–66, Brigadier John Essex-Clark (RL) for his advice, personal records and battle maps, Lex McAulay for the letters he wrote while in Vietnam and sustained assistance over ten years, Lieutenant Colonel Bill Kaine MBE, for his co-ordination, advice, encouragement and compilation of the nominal role, and Carey McQuillan for his sustained encouragement over the years and compilation of the glossary, honours and awards, and index. Finally I wish to thank Jeanette Muirhead, the staff in the keyboard section at Command and Staff College, Glenda Tarrant and Dorothy Stubbs, for word-processing the drafts over the years, Kay and Dareth Flavell for processing the index, and Ian Webb for the cover illustration.

Writing this book has been an experience akin to mental marathon running. Sometimes it has not been easy to find the time or the concentration to keep researching and writing. However, over the book's gestation I have made many new friends, learnt a great deal about war and have met many Vietnam veterans who have contributed immeasurably to my military education and personal development.

Bob Breen
Sydney 1988

1 The ANZUS connection

ANZUS was a mutual defence treaty signed in 1951 between Australia, New Zealand and the US. In 1965 the spirit of this treaty appeared as a trinational brigade. However, this was not the first time that Australian Diggers, New Zealand Kiwis, and the US GIs had fought alongside each other.

On 4 July 1918 the scene was set for an historic battle near the town of Hamel in France. For several weeks Major General George Bell's US 33rd Infantry Division had been training with Lieutenant General Sir John Monash's Australian Army Corps to gain experience in trench warfare. The date for the start of the Battle of Hamel (US Independence Day) had been selected because of its significance to the US troops. Platoons of Americans had been assigned under command of the battle-hardened Australian battalions.

The Battle of Hamel was a stunning victory for the Australians who had employed tanks successfully and used unprecedented techniques of deception and manoeuvre to surprise the Germans about the time, place and strength of the attack. Casualties among the Australian and US troops had been low and the numbers of German casualties and prisoners of war in the thousands. Monash was delighted with the performance of the Americans:

> Among other aspects of this battle which was worthy of mention is the fact that it was the first occasion in the war that American troops fought in an offensive battle. The contingent of them who joined us acquitted themselves most gallantly and were ever after received by the Australians as blood brothers—a fraternity which operated to great mutual advantage.[1]

The mutual advantage of this relationship was to be renewed in the Pacific Campaign against the Japanese in World War II. There were several occasions when Australian and US commanders combined units.

And, once again, US infantry units were sometimes placed under the command of experienced Australian infantry formations.[2]

After the defeat of Japan, the Australian Government sought assurances from the US Government that US military forces would remain in Asia to prevent a resurgence of Japanese military power. These requests resulted in the signing of the ANZUS Treaty in 1951. The Australian and New Zealand people were told that the ANZUS Treaty would be the cornerstone of Australia's and New Zealand's security. It was underwritten by a significant US military presence in Asia as a forward line of defence.[3]

Significantly, the ANZUS Treaty was signed partly to offset Australian and New Zealand concern that the peace treaty with Japan was too lenient and partly in recognition of Australia's and New Zealand's prompt commitment of military forces to the Korean War in support of the US policy of direct military intervention under the United Nations flag. Australian Prime Minister Robert Menzies had been the first head of government to offer military units for service in South Korea.

The Korean War changed the arrangements of the Pacific Campaign for combining Australian and US military units and formations. US units now greatly outnumbered Australian and New Zealand units. The Australian and New Zealand Governments sent small volunteer ground forces which fought as part of a British Commonwealth Brigade which later became the British Commonwealth Division.

The conservative Australian and New Zealand Governments set an important precedent by offering military forces to accompany the United Nations into South Korea in 1950. This was the beginning of a policy of warning of the threat of Communism and calling for a determined stand by allies against the spread of this ideology in Asia, while keeping defence appropriations low, introducing limited conscription and deploying token regular forces to fight Communist guerillas in South-East Asia.[4]

The formation of the South-East Asian Treaty Organization (SEATO) in 1954 gave expression to the simple logic of Cold War politics in the US, Australia and New Zealand. The North Atlantic Treaty Organization (NATO) represented the unity of free nations opposing the spread of Russian Communism in Europe; SEATO would represent the unity of free nations opposing the spread of Chinese Communism in South-East Asia. The defeat of the French in the First Indochina War and the loss of North Vietnam to Communism in 1954 had been a shock because the US geopolitical objective had been to contain international Communism within its then existing borders. Prime Minister Robert Menzies and his New Zealand counterparts in the 1950s and early 1960s defined international politics as the forces of the Free World led by the US against the

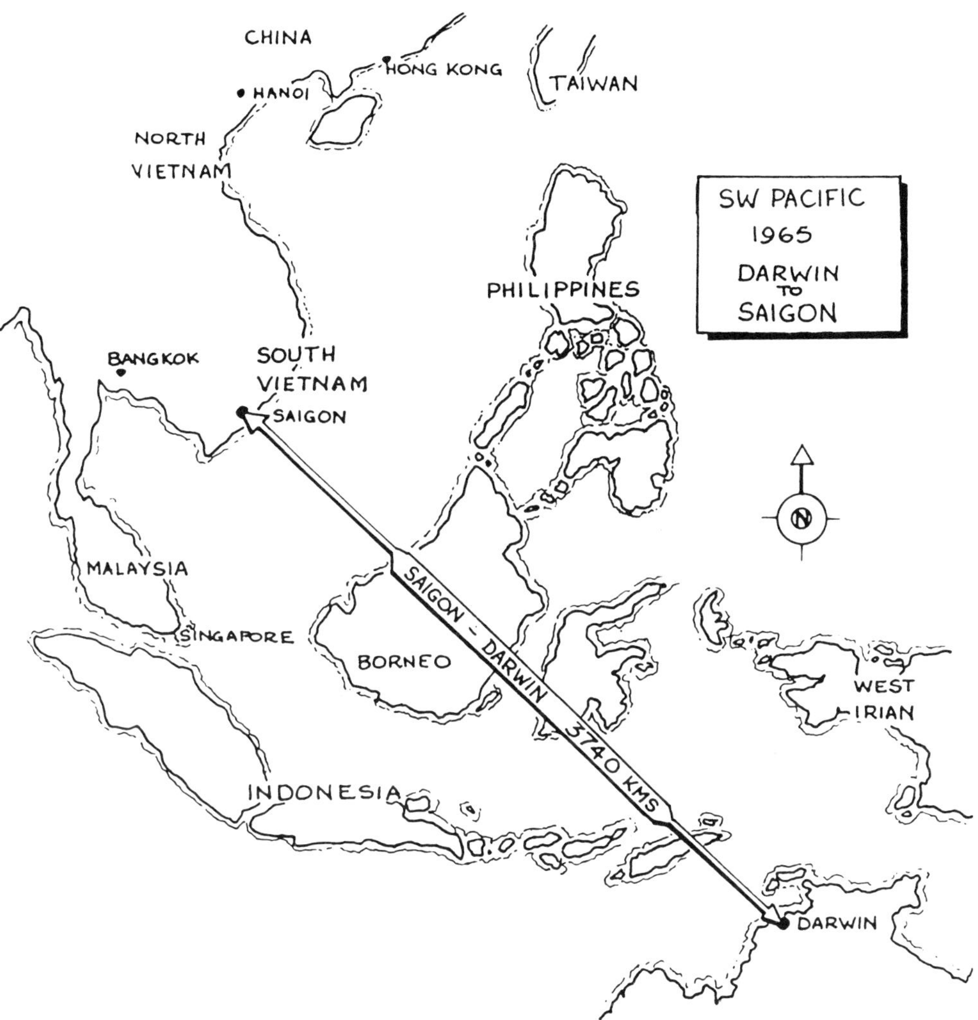

forces of the Communist Bloc led by the Soviet Union and the People's Republic of China.

The nature and implications of Communist expansion were often expressed in terms of President Eisenhower's domino theory. This theory drew the analogy of a number of dominoes stacked side by side in a manner in which if one domino fell it would start a chain reaction pushing the other dominoes over. The dominoes symbolised the countries of Asia. Eisenhower contended that if one of these nations fell to the forces of

Communism, all would fall eventually as the momentum of revolution increased.

Within the context of stopping the 'dominoes' falling and defending well forward against Communism in support of allies, Australian and New Zealand defence force units frequently participated in military exercises conducted under the auspices of SEATO and the ANZUS Treaty. In addition, Australian and New Zealand Army units fought continuously on twelve-month and two-year rotations for seventeen years from 1949 until 1965 against Communist-led military forces in the South-East Asian region. They fought alongside British and Malayan formations in the Malayan Emergency during the period 1955–60 and had stationed military forces in Malaya to enhance security. In 1963 Australian and New Zealand infantry battalions and supporting gun batteries were deployed with British forces to Borneo to counter the incursions of Indonesian raiders into the states of the newly formed Federation of Malaysia. At that time the Sukarno Government in Indonesia had established ties with the Soviet Union and Indonesia had a two million-strong Communist party. In 1962 Australian Army advisers had been deployed to Vietnam as part of the US Military Advisory Command—Vietnam (MACV). In 1964 short-range transport aircraft were added to Australia's commitment in Vietnam.

The brunt of the Australian Army representation in these undeclared, limited wars was met by the Royal Australian Regiment (RAR). In 1948 the Australian Government raised three regular infantry battalions. These were the First, Second and Third Battalions of the RAR (1 RAR, 2 RAR and 3 RAR). These three battalions were rotated continuously on twelve-month and two-year operational tours of duty against Communist-led military forces. Typically, during this period of forward defence against Communism, Australian infantry units were supported by New Zealand gun batteries and served alongside New Zealand infantrymen.[5]

The traditions of Australians and New Zealanders fighting alongside and in support of each other had started in 1915 on the Gallipoli Peninsula during the ill-fated campaign by Britain and British dominion forces to seize the Dardanelles in Turkey. The raising of the Australian and New Zealand Army Corps brought to the traditions of the two countries involved their most historic military acronym: ANZAC (pronounced annzak). The ANZAC tradition was forged and imprinted on the national consciousness of these two remote dominions of the British Commonwealth by the shared adversities of World War I. Forty per cent of all Australian men aged between eighteen and 45 years (417 000) had enlisted in the First Australian Imperial Force. Of the 330 000 who served in theatres of war, almost 60 000 were killed and 160 000 wounded. By 1918 43 per cent of all men of military age in New Zealand had enlisted

(120 000). Of those who enlisted, 105 000 served overseas in the theatres of war. Almost 19 000 men were killed or died within five years of their wounds and 50 000 were wounded.[6]

By January 1965 one of South-East Asia's most important 'dominoes' was about to fall. The Government of the Republic of Vietnam was in trouble. On 28 December 1964 the Viet Cong 9th Division had concentrated in one place for the first time and seized the Catholic village of Binh Gia south east of Saigon. Using tactics established against the French in the First Indochina War, units of this division ambushed and virtually destroyed two Army of the Republic of Vietnam (ARVN) battalions and their accompanying armoured and mechanised forces sent to relieve Binh Gia. Having held the village for four days and inflicted these defeats, the regiments of the 9th Division dispersed intact to their jungle bases. This victory at divisional level marked the turning point of the war in South Vietnam from the unconventional guerilla phase to the general offensive phase.

Eight days before this military humiliation there had been another unsettling coup in Saigon as factions wrestled for political supremacy. The political progress of the previous months had been illusory; there was no certainty that this government would last any longer than its predecessors. Further north, three North Vietnamese regular infantry regiments were marching south to participate in a final campaign to bring about the reunification of Vietnam under Communist control.

General William Westmoreland, Commander of MACV, assessed that South Vietnam was on the brink of military and political collapse.[7] The year 1965 was one of momentous decisions and military commitments. The choice for US policymakers was simple: allow South Vietnam to collapse under the weight of its own internal political instability and pressure from the Viet Cong, or intervene, and at least buy more time for the Saigon Government.

For the first three months of 1965 most of the South Vietnamese Army was tied down in static security—defensive and demoralised. Terrorist attacks on US personnel and installations increased; several Special Forces compounds and servicemen's billets were bombed or mortared. Ambush continued to be the preferred tactic for the Viet Cong. In the Mang Yang Pass in the Highlands, ARVN Ranger units and Civilian Irregular Defence Group troops suffered heavy casualties in an extensive area ambush. The French Group Mobile 100 had been massacred in the same area in 1954.

In February 1965 President Lyndon Johnson authorised Admiral Ulysses S. Grant Sharp, the Commander in Chief of the Pacific Area, to bomb selected targets in North Vietnam. Westmoreland was directed to use US fighter-ground-attack aircraft to support ARVN operations. On 22

South Vietnam in 1965

February Westmoreland requested the urgent dispatch of a force of US Marines to protect Da Nang Airbase where many of the aircraft used to bomb North Vietnam were based. On 8 March 1965 two battalions of Marines crossed the beach at Da Nang. In May these were reinforced and became the III Marine Amphibious Force of 8000 men.[8] On 30 March terrorism against Americans culminated in the detonation of a truck full of explosives outside the US Embassy in Saigon. The US Deputy Ambassador lay seriously injured among the dead and wounded.

President Lyndon Johnson, justifying his decision to increase the use of US military forces, stated:

> Our purpose, our objective there [Vietnam] is clear, that purpose and that objective is to join in the defence and protection of the freedom of a brave people who are under an attack that is controlled and that is directed from outside their country. We have no ambition there for ourselves. We seek no dominion. We seek no conquest. We seek no wider war. But we must all understand that we will persist in the defence of freedom, and our continuing actions will be those which are justified and those that are made necessary by the continuing aggression of others. These actions will be measured fitting and adequate. Our stamina and the stamina of the American people is equal to the task.[9]

In Australia the Menzies Government had anticipated the need to intervene in Vietnam and had decided in November 1964 to introduce a selective two-year period of National Service for 20-year-old males whose birthdays occurred on days selected in a ballot. The RAR was to be increased from four (4 RAR had been raised in 1964) to six battalions within twelve months, and then to nine battalions within two years. Conscription would give Menzies the infantry battalions and ancillary units to deploy to South-East Asia in support of any further US military initiatives in Vietnam and to back up Australian forces operating in the Malay Peninsula and Borneo. Sometime in December 1964 the Australian Government offered the US Government an infantry battalion for service in South Vietnam.[10]

On 23 March 1965 the Australian Minister of External Affairs, Paul Hasluck, made a parliamentary statement which supported US use of military force in South Vietnam and the bombing of North Vietnam:

> If the United States did withdraw, the same conflict would be renewed somewhere else. Within a brief period the struggle now taking place in South Vietnam would be shifted to Thailand. If there was an abandonment of Thailand, it would shift to Malaysia—to Indonesia, to Burma, to India and further. Nothing would be ended and no stability would be achieved by yielding in South Vietnam.[11]

On 1 April 1965 the US National Security Council met to discuss strategy in Vietnam. They reviewed the situation and received assessments from Ambassador Maxwell Taylor and Defense Secretary Robert MacNamara and a 'Commander's Estimate of the Situation' from Westmoreland.[12] The Joint Chiefs of Staff backed their commander in Vietnam and recommended the deployment of two US divisions and a Korean division. The Korean deployment would symbolise the similarities between the Vietnamese situation in 1965 and that of Korea in 1950. Taylor and MacNamara did not favour deployment of US ground troops in a direct counter-insurgency role. They argued for an enclave strategy which would guarantee the security of major installations and limit US involvement to local defence. President Johnson decided to proceed cautiously and did not authorise the troop build up requested by Westmoreland. He supported the enclave strategy and authorised the deployment of more Marine battalions and support troops. Using the same rationale as for the protection of Da Nang, the 173rd Airborne Brigade (Separate) of the Pacific Area Reserve was ordered to deploy to Bien Hoa Airbase on a 60-day temporary assignment. At this meeting, the possibility of more allies joining in the military intervention into Vietnam was also investigated.

Amidst a roll call of cautious and reluctant allies, Australia stood out as supportive of direct military intervention and enthusiastic about the commitment of substantial US ground forces to South Vietnam. Prime Minister Menzies had already backed up this encouragement with the offer of an infantry battalion group to fight alongside US ground forces in South Vietnam.

The document formalising the meeting of 1 April had authorised the use of Marine units based at Da Nang to act in a mobile counter-insurgency role within 80 kilometres of the airbase. This was a pivotal document because it set the precedent for offensive operations by US ground forces. However Ambassador Taylor was concerned when the Joint Chiefs of Staff applied pressure for a rapid build up of forces beyond the limits set by the meeting of 1 April. MacNamara organised another staff meeting for 20 April 1965 in Honolulu to clarify the situation.

The meeting in Honolulu was divided along similar lines to that on 1 April. On one hand, President Johnson, Ambassador Taylor and Defense Secretary MacNamara favoured an enclave strategy in which US troops would defend key installations freeing ARVN units to build up and once again go on the offensive. Admiral Earl Wheeler, Chairman of Joint Chiefs of Staff, Admiral Sharp and General Westmoreland contended that the best defence was offence and favoured rapid deployment of US units to Vietnam in time to conduct search and destroy operations with ARVN units against the Viet Cong. Westmoreland anticipated correctly that there would be a summer monsoon offensive by the Viet Cong which would aim to seize the Central Highlands and split South Vietnam in two. It was agreed finally to increase the commitment of group troops to seventeen maneouvre battalions, and concurrence was given for the deployment of up to 7000 allied troops. The 1st Air Cavalry Division was ordered to deploy to the Central Highlands, the 101st Airborne Division to Cam Ranh Bay and the 1st Infantry Division to Hau Nghia Province north east of Saigon. On 13 April 1965 the Australian Government's offer of an infantry battalion group was accepted.[13]

On 29 April 1965 Prime Minister Menzies rose solemnly and stated to a half-empty House of Representatives:

> The takeover of South Vietnam would be a direct military threat to Australia and all the countries of South and South East Asia. It must be seen as part of a thrust by Communist China between the Indian and Pacific Oceans . . . The Australian Government is now in receipt of a request from the Government of South Vietnam for further military assistance. We have decided—and this has been in close consultation with the Government of the United States—to provide an infantry battalion for service in South Vietnam.[14]

Ten years later Professor R. G. Neale using Department of Foreign Affairs files revealed the circumstances and motives for the commitment of the battalion group to Vietnam:

> Australian military assistance to South Vietnam was not at any time in response to a request for defence aid from South Vietnam as a Protocol State to SEATO as a treaty organization . . . It would then appear that, the offer of the battalion having been made by Australia first to the United States, the two Governments together (with the United States predominating) subsequently arranged for the formal request from South Vietnam . . . The provision of military aid was decided upon for political reasons and was in support of a fundamental of Australian policy towards South Vietnam, which was to ensure the long term defence interests of Australia . . . This was a policy developed in Australia independently of any outside pressure. The cornerstone of this policy was a compelling necessity to commit the power of the United States into the Asian area and thus to commit her to a practical guarantee of active support to Australia through the ANZUS and SEATO treaties.[15]

The Menzies Government's policy was successful. In a letter to Menzies, dated 29 April 1965, President Johnson said:

> I am delighted at the decision of your Government to provide an infantry battalion for service in South Vietnam at the request of the Government of South Vietnam. This action simply underscores the full co-operation and understanding that has existed between our two Governments . . . More broadly, this action proves again the

deep ties between our two countries in the cause of world peace and security.[16]

On 5 May the first element of the 173rd Airborne Brigade flew into Bien Hoa Airbase north of Saigon. Initially the deployment of the Marines to Da Nang and the Paratroopers to Bien Hoa were to be temporary measures to meet the specific requirement to defend those two important installations. As a result of the Honolulu meeting of 20 April the deployments were to be the first stage of a build up of US ground forces. Westmoreland assessed that the well-equipped, confident and experienced Viet Cong formations could not be defeated by ARVN units alone. He had contingency plans for the deployment of several US divisions with more to follow if the bombing of North Vietnam did not convince the Hanoi Government to stop their sponsorship of the insurgency in South Vietnam.[17]

Initially there was some indecision about whether the Australian battalion should be deployed under the operational control of the 101st Airborne Division, which was due in Cam Ranh Bay in July, or the 173rd, which had arrived at Bien Hoa.[18] The 173rd was probably decided upon because it only had two airborne battalions and would find a third battalion useful for its new ground-based role.

Brigadier General Ellis 'Butch' Williamson, the Commanding General of the 173rd, stated:

> I received no political instructions about the Australians being
> assigned to my outfit, I had been chairing a seven-nation military
> committee in Germany for two years before raising the Brigade in
> Okinawa in 1963. As a commander in the Pacific Area Reserve, I
> had conducted exercises with or had to gain the co-operation of
> about 15 armies in the Asian area. I had worked in Korea with
> Turkish, Ethiopian and French units. I needed no political
> instructions on how to foster troops from other nationalities. The
> Australians had a good reputation for jungle fighting. I was glad to
> have them aboard.[19]

Williamson was a tough, 47-year-old professional soldier who had risen from the rank of private to command the US 20th Infantry Regiment in the later months of World War II at 27 years of age. He had been wounded three times in combat and had been awarded five Silver Stars and three Bronze Stars for valour. Further decorations for valour had been presented to him from the governments of France, Belgium, Great Britain and Korea.

Meanwhile, on 25 April 1965 back in Australia, ten days before the 173rd arrived at Bien Hoa Airbase and four days before Menzies made his announcement of their deployment, 1 RAR was providing a Guard of Honour in Canberra for the commemoration of the fiftieth anniversary of the landings at Gallipoli in the Dardanelles. This ANZAC Day ceremony in the nation's capital was special because the road leading to the Australian War Memorial was to be opened and named ANZAC Parade. Veterans from World War I and World War II, including a few score veterans from the Gallipoli Campaign, marched up ANZAC Parade, and a memorial service was held. These veterans of Australia's most famous expeditionary forces, the First Australian Imperial Force (1914–18) and the Second Australian Imperial Force (1939–45), did not realise that the young soldiers standing on parade in front of them would constitute Australia's next expeditionary force. They also did not know these men too would fight alongside New Zealanders and give fresh life to the ANZAC tradition. 'We have proposed to the Republic of Vietnam that we will contribute an artillery battery', stated the New Zealand Prime Minister Keith Holyoake. 'This unit will take its place with Australian forces, alongside whom New Zealanders have stood before in the tradition of ANZAC in resisting aggression.'[20]

Thus the scene was set for a tangible demonstration of the tenets of the ANZUS Treaty and a renewal of the ANZAC tradition. However another lesser known tradition was being revived. On that ANZAC Day in 1965 if a veteran of the 7th Australian Infantry Division had been asked about the operation at Nadzab in Papua New Guinea in 1943 he might have recalled the Division having under its operational control a regiment of young US paratroopers. These paratroopers belonged to the 503rd Parachute Infantry Regiment which was the lineal ancestor of the airborne battalions of the 173rd, and a battalion of volunteers from the 7th Division were the lineal ancestors of 1 RAR. The assignment of 1 RAR to the 173rd renewed a US and Australian association from the Pacific Campaign against the Japanese. Bien Hoa was the second airfield where the airborne battalions of the 173rd were to join Australian infantrymen on operations.

2 The deployment

The 173rd Airborne Brigade was trained as a strategic fire brigade to 'Get in, get the job done and get out.' 1 RAR was experienced in sustained platoon-sized jungle operations. The scale, intensity and nature of the Vietnam War in 1965 meant that US and Australian military attitudes were on a collision course.

Early in 1965 1 RAR was not fully manned and equipped for operations in South-East Asia. Resources for training were insufficient. 'Live' firings of individual and crew-served weapons in tactical settings were infrequent due to ammunition shortages. These deficiencies extended to blank ammunition, defence stores such as wire and steel pickets, suitable training areas, road transport and helicopters for tactical exercises.[1] 1 RAR was designated to be on a high level of readiness but did not have the resources to maintain itself at that level.

Since 1964 1 RAR had been the AMBROSE battalion. This meant that it would be the first Australian unit committed to operations in South-East Asia to meet a number of contingencies in conjunction with other member nations of SEATO. Plan AMBROSE involved the deployment of 1 RAR to a sector of the Mekong River in Thailand to defend against an invasion of Thailand by Vietnam, should Vietnam become a predatory Communist power.[2] Thailand was to be one of Eisenhower's dominoes which would not be allowed to fall. Events had overtaken this contingency: South Vietnam, not Thailand, was to be the defended domino.

In March 1965, just over two months before deployment to Vietnam, command passed to Major Ivan 'Lou' Brumfield who was promoted to Lieutenant Colonel and ordered to reorganise 1 RAR to become a smaller streamlined battalion of about 800 men. For several years the Battalion had been organised according to the US Army's pentomic concept (means organised in tactical groupings of five); the Australian Army version was the pentropic organisation. This meant that 1 RAR was organised into five rifle companies. The previous Commanding Officer, Colonel Don

Dunstan (later Sir Donald Dunstan, Chief of the General Staff and Governor of South Australia), had commanded a battalion of about 1500 men and a large inventory of weapons, vehicles and equipment.

Brumfield was a tough operator with a sharp, quick wit. He graduated from the Royal Military College in 1947 and joined 67th Australian Infantry Battalion before it was redesignated 3 RAR. He saw operational service in Korea and, after several regimental and staff appointments, taught in tactics at the Royal Military College from 1961 until 1964. He joined the pentropic 1 RAR in 1964 as an operations officer. The task ahead of this newly promoted 38-year-old Commanding Officer was demanding. He had been told in great secrecy on 25 February 1965 that 1 RAR might be deployed to South-East Asia in a few months. He had to reorganise the Battalion, write new Standing Operating Procedures, train his men in the new procedures and prepare them for war, without telling them that war was probably only weeks away. Secrecy had to be maintained because of the politically sensitive issue of Australian military involvement in Vietnam. It was a constant source of frustration to the handful of officers in 1 RAR who knew of the deployment.

Without the professionalism and dedication of Brumfield and his subordinates, the deployment could have been a disaster. After the announcement of Australia's involvement on 29 April 1965, resources and co-operation were more plentiful. However, time had run out for pre-embarkation training and detailed administrative planning.

Captain Tom Buckley, a veteran Quartermaster, tried in vain to build up the Battalion's stock holdings. He examined the entitlements of the unit under Plan AMBROSE and requested that stocks be loaned for the period that 1 RAR was AMBROSE force. He intended that the stocks issued on loan could be put into crates immediately and would become 'permanent issue' when it was announced that the unit was to be deployed to Vietnam. His plan did not succeed as no-one in the supply organisations had been told of the pending deployment and there was no authorisation for 1 RAR to be issued items from war stocks. Despite requests from Brumfield that something should be done about this ridiculous situation, it was not until after the official announcement on 29 April that the Battalion received top priority for issues of weapons, vehicles and equipment. By that time only four weeks remained before deployment.[3] Buckley's wide administrative experience, patience and military wisdom were fully tested.

Major Mal Lander, the Second-in-Command, and Captain Ron Ducie, the Adjutant, were responsible for manning the Battalion. Captain Michael Naughton, a medical officer, recalled later, '5 RAR was raped of its personnel and this caused ill feeling particularly as 1 RAR's task had not been announced. As I understand it from Ron Ducie, 5 RAR co-operation was full and unqualified when the picture was clarified.'[4] It was not until after the official announcement that priority was given to 1 RAR for manpower. This resulted in an influx of personnel in the final weeks before embarkation which caused further administrative problems and increased the disruption caused by the recent reorganisation.

Of interest was the number of individuals, including officers, warrant officers and non-commissioned officers (NCOs), who applied for posting from the unit after the announcement. Others reported medical ailments that would prevent them from going to Vietnam. However, for every one of these men who decided against going, there were dozens seeking to join 1 RAR and take the risks of war.

The medical preparation of the Battalion was a shambles. Captain Michael Naughton, who assisted with the medical checks at the time, recalled:

> Many personnel who were BMS [below medical standard] for infantry service had been retained in 1 RAR and, as is so often the case, many were efficient clerks and storemen, well-liked characters and, being bumped out at the last minute by the doctors left an unfortunate taste in the mouth . . . The Medical Platoon consisted of an RMO [Regimental Medical Officer], who was ready for retirement and had already set up lucrative civilian commitments, a Sergeant Medical Assistant, six Corporal Medical Assistants and the Band; great blokes, good musicians but hopeless medical assistants/ stretcher bearers . . . at least we were lucky in having intelligent and well motivated men.[5]

The RMO did not go to Vietnam with 1 RAR. Another RMO left the Battalion soon after arrival at Bien Hoa suffering from a chronic ear condition. His place was taken by Captain Michael Naughton, the Senior Australian Medical Officer in Saigon until Captain Peter Haslau, the RMO of the newly-formed 5 RAR, could be flown in from Australia. Thus the Battalion had four RMOs in three months. The members of the Band were to receive medical training in Vietnam but not before their inadequate training was exposed.

The operational preparation of 1 RAR was co-ordinated by Major John Essex-Clark, the Officer Commanding Support Company who later became known as the S3 or Operations Officer. He recalled later:

> I attended a meeting with Lou Brumfield and Mal Lander on 26 February 1965. At that conference I was directed to write SOPs [Standing Operating Procedures] for our initial operations in Vietnam . . . At that time we were not sure where or how we would be fighting, but we thought it would be similar to Malaya, but with a greater concentration of force against a more aggressive enemy. This was a major change from our training as a pentropic battalion when

we had concentrated on conventional warfare and had done little preparation for CRW [Counter Revolutionary Warfare]. There was no modern doctrine or pamphlets available. There were no precedents for us to follow! So I used my imagination, current readings, old books and my experience in UW [Unconventional Warfare] . . . I spent many a long night trying to anticipate operations in Vietnam and studying, inter alia, Tanham's 'Communist Revolutionary Warfare', Praeger's 'The Guerrilla and How to Fight Him', Fall's 'Street Without Joy', the British 'ATOM' [Anti-Terrorist Operations—Malaya], pamphlets and articles on the war in Vietnam in the US Service magazines.[6]

Four new rifle company commanders were appointed during this reorganisation and, of the twelve rifle platoon commanders, eight had graduated less than six months before from the Officer Cadet School, Portsea. Ironically, their peers from the more prestigious Royal Military College, Duntroon (equivalent to the US Military Academy, West Point), had received first priority for choice of battalion in the Regiment after graduation. Most had elected to go to the newly raised 4 RAR which was to be the next battalion deployed to Terendak Barracks in Malaysia. It was to be Portsea graduates who would not only see overseas service first, but would also be the first to lead their platoons in a new war.

Each rifle company was commanded by a Major. Under him were three platoons commanded by subalterns (First or Second Lieutenants) with a Platoon Sergeant as Second-in-Command. Platoons were made up of three sections or squads of about ten men, each commanded by a Corporal with a Lance Corporal as Second-in-Command. These sections were to bear the brunt of the first contacts with the enemy. Each consisted of two scouts armed with 9 millimetre Owen Machine Carbines (later they were issued Colt M16 Automatic Rifles), a gun group of three men who operated a belt-fed 7.62 millimetre General Purpose Machine Gun M60 and a rifle group of four men armed with 7.62 mm Self Loading Rifles. This platoon organisation meant that the platoon commander could manoeuvre three sections, and section commanders could manoeuvre three groups.

Very rarely was a fully manned platoon to go out on operations. Typically, seven men or less would constitute a section on operations: one scout, section commander, gun group and two riflemen. Thus it was to be common for a platoon to number about 24 instead of its intended establishment of one officer and 33 men. Additional weapons to be carried by the platoon after arrival in Vietnam were the M26 Grenade used to throw at the enemy, the M72 Light Anti-Tank weapon to fire at fortifications, and the M79 Grenade Launcher which could fire a grenade out to 375 metres. 1 RAR was to incorporate five new weapons into its inventory within six months of arrival in Vietnam.

The only chance Brumfield had had to train his men in the field after the reorganisation had been early in April on exercise SKY HIGH II in the Gospers area north of Sydney. Live ammunition could not be used in the training area. Blank ammunition was in such short supply that the machine gunners had to use World War I gas rattles to simulate the firing of their weapons. Riflemen carried only a third of their combat load of ammunition as blank ammunition. Only four UHIB helicopters were available to familiarise soldiers in heliborne transport.[7]

Most officers had no recent experience in employing the indirect fire of artillery and mortars or calling for airstrikes. Two months after the exercise, 1 RAR was conducting sophisticated airmobile operations involving hundreds of helicopters and the employment of the firepower of artillery, helicopter gunships and fighter ground attack aircraft. Imagination and initiative can overcome some shortages of training resources but the fact remains that 1 RAR was not given the opportunity nor the resources to prepare for war. However the men of 1 RAR persevered; they did not dwell on the situation and accepted the deficiencies as being the norm.[8]

Many of the adverse effects of the reorganisation were offset because most officers, warrant officers, NCOs and soldiers knew each other well. The Royal Australian Regiment had only been made up of three battalions and one rifleman-training unit since it was formed in 1948. The continuity of the Battalion was in its warrant officers and NCOs who had been soldiers, corporals and sergeants together. Some of them like Staff Sergeant 'Dinky' Dean and Sergeant 'Stitches' Fife had been with the unit since its formation. Others like Company Sergeant Majors Ron 'The Grey One' Pincott, Harold Smith, Jack Cramp and Jack Currie had served on and off with 1 RAR for ten to fifteen years.

In those days, battalion life consumed the time of its members. Single soldiers lived in the long wooden barrack blocks, a section of ten men to a room, each with a bed, a wardrobe and a steel trunk. Most of them could not afford a car and their most expensive belonging was a transistor radio. Pay was spent on beer, cigarettes and nights out with fellow soldiers ostensibly looking for female companionship. In reality, females were often shunned in favour of a night 'on the grog' with the mates discussing the football, the cricket and, above all, the goings on in the Battalion.[9]

Young single officers were the same. Their lives revolved around leading their platoons and socialising with their peers. They received guidance from experienced platoon sergeants who, without undermining the authority of their young commanders, maintained discipline and 'sorted out' soldiers who erred in their ways. Later the pressures of war would test these relationships to breaking point or forge them into ones of lifelong mutual respect.

Thus, 1 RAR was a tightly knit group of professionals whose previous service together gave them cohesion in spite of the recent reorganisation. Fortunately there was also a large number of men who had completed an operational tour of duty in Malaya hunting for Communist terrorists. This experience helped to offset the lack of pre-embarkation training. The experienced 'old hands' maintained the standards and were able to indoctrinate the correct attitudes for war in young soldiers and assist their young officers. The presence of experienced men also contributed to the self-confidence of 1 RAR in the rush of the last weeks before deployment.

Jo Gullett wrote of his experiences as a soldier and an infantry officer in World War II:

> An effective battalion in being, ready to fight, implies a state of mind—I am not sure it is not a state of grace. It implies a giving and a taking, a sharing of almost everything—possessions, comfort, affection, trust, confidence, interest. It implies a certain restriction, and at the same time a certain enriching and widening of the human spirit. It implies doing a hundred things together—marching to the band, marching all night long, being hungry, thirsty, exhausted, filthy; being near but never quite mutinous. It involves not the weakening but the deferment of other bonds and interests; the acceptance that life and home are now with the battalion. In the end it is possible to say 'the battalion thinks' or 'the battalion feels'; and that is not an exaggeration.[10]

1 RAR was a battalion which fitted Jo Gullett's description.

The preparations for deployment were conducted during a period of intense political controversy. Prime Minister Menzies faced the explosive issue of sending conscripts to Vietnam. Conscription for overseas military service had caused deep divisions among Australians during both World Wars. Across Parliament Menzies faced Arthur Calwell, the leader of the Australian Labor Party: ' . . . on behalf of all of my colleagues of Her Majesty's Opposition, I say that we oppose the Government's decision to send 800 men to fight in Vietnam. We oppose it firmly and completely.'[11] The Government was not deterred. The intake of National Servicemen was doubled to ensure the Army could maintain its commitments to Australia's forward defence policy.

Brumfield recalled the feelings of the unit at the time:

> In my view, the battalion did not think much about the politics of their deployment to Vietnam. We were professional soldiers and accepted the commitment to Vietnam as another job against the Asian Communist. Most of us had been to Malaya during the Emergency. Vietnam did not appear to be very different at the time, except that the situation was worse and the Americans, not the British, were involved . . . Frankly, we read nothing to suggest that the vast majority of the Australian people were not fully behind us.

The election in 1966 seemed to confirm this. I suppose in the final analysis, we looked forward to the sheer adventure, challenge and competition of the whole thing. That was the feeling in April 1965.[12]

The political controversy contributed to an atmosphere of secrecy and isolation at the Holsworthy Camp in Sydney as the men of 1 RAR and their families prepared for the prospects of war and separation from loved ones. Adding to the tension, threatening, obscene letters and telephone calls were received in increasing numbers by families as the days passed. Security patrols by Military Police through married quarter areas increased.

While the men of 1 RAR completed their final preparations, the situation in Vietnam worsened.[13] Despite evidence of increased offensive activity from ARVN forces using US air power to support their operations, US analysts were uneasy during the first few days of May. On 11 May a Viet Cong regiment captured the town of Song Be, the provincial capital of Phuoc Long Province. One thousand South Vietnamese rangers with their 40 US advisers were routed and five US advisers were killed. Those advisers who survived complained of the lack of courage displayed by the South Vietnamese against their Communist opponents. After occupying the town for seven hours, the Viet Cong were forced to retreat under heavy aerial bombardment. The roads around Saigon were being continually cut and damaged by Viet Cong engineers. Security on Highway 1 to the north could not be guaranteed by day or night.

Heavy rains stalled ARVN operations until the end of May but allowed the Viet Cong to concentrate undetected near Quang Ngai City on the Central Coast. After destroying a battalion of the ARVN 51st Regiment based west of the city, the Viet Cong assembled for an attack on the city itself. Ignoring advice from his US advisers to withdraw and break out, the commander of the 51st Regiment rashly joined battle. Three US advisers and 26 ARVN soldiers were all that was left of 51st Regiment by the end of the day. The next day a battalion of ARVN Rangers was ambushed trying to break into the city. They attacked their opponents time after time and the next morning their bodies were strewn around a small hill which had been the scene of ferocious fighting. 'Bodies of 75 Rangers from one elite Vietnamese unit were found on one slope. The men died making repeated charges against the guerillas.[14] In all, ARVN had lost over 1000 of its best troops in these battles. Once again the Viet Cong held a provincial capital. Worse was to come.

On the day Quang Ngai City fell, major towns in Darlac, Pleiku and Phu Bon Provinces were attacked. The capitals of these provinces were overrun, resulting in heavy losses to ARVN forces. Another ARVN battalion was almost wiped out to the last man. There were reports of tactical stupidity and cowardice among ARVN commanders. Fortunately for the

South Vietnamese the concentration of Viet Cong regiments and fine weather coincided. US air power saved the province by forcing the Viet Cong to disperse.

These reports of whole battalions being massacred caused concern among the families of men in 1 RAR. The men themselves had been briefed on the characteristics and tactics of the Viet Cong by Australian and US intelligence personnel. The Viet Cong were portrayed as ruthless and hitherto successful jungle fighters as well as a conventional opponent.

> We got this briefing from a Yank major and some Australian Intelligence Corps people. The Viet Cong were made out to be super human. I would say that some of the blokes did not feel too good when the briefing finished. A fairly tense atmosphere was broken when RSM 'Macca' McKay stood up to dismiss us after the officers had left. He said, 'Don't believe half that shit men. Remember the Viet Cong are the market gardeners and we are the professional soldiers.'[15]

Unlike Brumfield who had two and a half months to reorganise his battalion to fit an establishment invented by staff officers, 'Butch' Williamson was given two and a half years to experiment with the organisation of his brigade until he was satisfied it was ready to do its job. The US Army had discarded the concept of organising units into tactical groupings of five (pentomic) in 1963 and raised lighter scaled formations based on principles of air mobility and firepower. One of the first units raised under the Reorganization Objective Army Divisions (ROAD) organisation was the 173rd Airborne Brigade. The ROAD concept involved units being raised as a combination of capabilities of units from different corps.[16] Using this concept of formations being a mix of units and sub-units with specific capabilities, a number of separate non-divisional brigades were raised for specific strategic missions.

Early in 1963 Colonel 'Butch' Williamson was called to the Pentagon in Washington and told:

> The United States Army is looking to the future. You are to organize, equip and train a unique unit. You will form a type of unit that the US Army has never seen before. It will be a separate airborne brigade on the island of Okinawa. In time it will become the Pacific Area 'Fire Brigade'. Congratulations, Brigadier General . . . I was told to search for perfection in speed and flexibility in all operations, I was to go ahead and try new ideas and record those things that worked and discard everything that did not work well or did not contribute toward the mission at hand. The 173rd had to have the capability to deploy quickly to a number of strategic locations around the Pacific basin and co-operate with the armed forces of several allied nations. However, most large-scale exercises were conducted with the armies of South Korea, Taiwan

and the Philippines and, contingency plans were co-ordinated within the structure of SEATO.[17]

By 1965 the 173rd was transportable in the aircraft available from the US Pacific Command. The Brigade had two airborne battalions, an artillery battalion equipped with 105 millimetre howitzers and a supply battalion as its major units, and a number of specialised sub-units which contributed to the Brigade's firepower, mobility and logistic capabilities. These sub-units included a motorised cavalry troop equipped with recoiless rifles and twin M60 machine guns mounted on jeeps and an armoured company equipped with M56 90 millimetre Self Propelled Anti Tank guns (known as SPATs), M106 107 millimetre Self Propelled Mortars and enough Armoured Personnel Carriers (APCs) to lift one rifle company. In all, the 173rd was made up of 133 officers, three warrant officers and 3394 NCOs and enlisted men.[18]

The raising of the 173rd and such formations as the 1st Air Cavalry Division and the Special Forces Groups (known as the Green Berets) had created a great deal of interest throughout the US Army. Thousands of young men volunteered for service in these units. The 173rd attracted many of the Class of 1962 from the US Military Academy, West Point, and dozens of top quality NCOs and soldiers. The high proportion of West Point graduates and specially selected NCOs and soldiers made the 173rd one of the US Army's elite airborne formations.

The 173rd benefited from its isolation from mainland US. The new combination of units and sub-units had a chance to develop as a brigade and concentrate on training and teamwork. Equally, the families of the Paratroopers lived in the same married quarter areas and shared schools, commissaries and entertainment venues. Soon infantry, artillery, engineer, armoured, signals and logistical units put their corps affiliations second to their identity as Paratroopers of the 173rd. The famous airborne espirit de corps predominated. Paratroopers saluted their officers and bellowed out, 'All the Way, Sir!' The officers would return the salute with just as loud a reply of, 'Airborne!'[19]

As a result of two quite different situations, the 173rd earned two nicknames. The first was earned in Taiwan during an exercise involving several large-scale parachute jumps. The local citizens gathered and began calling the men of the 173rd 'Tien Bien' which when translated meant 'Sky Soldiers'.[20] Williamson eagerly perpetuated this title. The Brigade's literature and Williamson's Combat Commander's Notes began to talk of his Paratroopers as Sky Soldiers. The other nickname sprang from the habit of one of the early company commanders of the Brigade playing the theme song of a popular television series *Rawhide* as a cue for his men to assemble for morning parades. The *Rawhide* theme evoked images of cattle being driven on a trail drive and that company, and eventually the whole Brigade, began to be called 'The Herd'.[21] The adoption of the nickname was helped along by members of the 3rd Marine Division who were also based in Okinawa.

The proximity of the proud Marines contributed to the 173rd bonding as a formation. A fierce rivalry developed between the Paratroopers and the Marines over the familiar question of, 'Who were the roughest and toughest fighting men on Okinawa, if not the entire US Armed Forces?' There were many formal sporting contests during the week and informal brawls on Saturday nights to keep the answer to the question unresolved and the competition keen.

The initial deployment of the 173rd in May 1965 conformed with its role of Pacific Area Reserve. They were given a 60-day assignment to protect the Bien Hoa Airbase. The Brigade was deployed by air and sea from Okinawa on 5 May 1965 and forward elements were in position defending a large sector of the perimeter twelve hours later. However, the ARVN defeats in Quang Ngai Province and the general deterioration of the military situation in Vietnam in May confirmed Westmoreland's assessment that US units would be needed to engage Main Force Viet Cong units. The role of the 173rd was intended to change from defensive to offensive as soon as Westmoreland could obtain authorisation from Washington.[22]

For this intended offensive role, large numbers of utility helicopters were made available to enhance the 173rd's mobility and close fire support. As a parachute brigade, the 173rd had not trained extensively with helicopters before and had not developed and practised tactics to incorporate them into their operations. The first manoeuvres using helicopters were chaotic. Throughout May the Paratroopers practised the tactics of airmobile warfare for the first time.[23]

The 173rd was organised to support its operations with heavy firepower. An analogy would be a fire brigade whose success or failure depends on its reaching the fire quickly and being able to produce large quantities of water to douse the flames. The success of the 173rd as a strategic reserve depended on its ability to deploy quickly and win a military contest. For example, typical missions could be to conduct a counter attack to capture an area held by an enemy force or secure an area about to fall into enemy hands. Large quantities of firepower would be needed to achieve initial shock action, to surprise the enemy before and during the assault, and to defend against enemy attack. Thus, the use of firepower was basic to the Brigade's operating procedures.

The vulnerability to ground fire of helicopters flying at low altitudes contributed to the requirement for defensive and pre-emptive firepower. This vulnerability could mean tactical disaster for a battalion being in-

Paratroopers of the 173rd conducting an airmobile assault. They planned to get into Vietnam, get the job done and get out. They felt the Viet Cong would not be able to withstand their air mobility, aggression and firepower.

serted for operations. Casualties would be heavy if landing zones were covered by enemy weapons. Hence, landing zones and their periphery were subjected to heavy bombardment before the arrival of the troop-carrying helicopters. Any suspicious areas which could conceal the enemy were also subjected to precautionary bombardment and strafing.

The scale and intensity of the operations in Vietnam at the time prompted commanders to use firepower to overcome manpower shortages. Viet Cong regiments were still destroying heavily armed ARVN battalions who were now supported by artillery and air firepower. The fate of the 51st Regiment in Quang Ngai City on 11 May was a recent reminder of the Viet Cong's lethality. The 173rd had no reason to discard the tactics of firepower in face of such a threat and being outnumbered.

The 173rd was the first US Army ground force unit to be deployed to Vietnam and could not afford to be defeated. Heavy casualties in the 173rd would have given the Viet Cong the political victory which could reverse US policy. Thus, the pre-emptive use of firepower to avoid taking casualties was emphasised in May 1965 and throughout the next twelve months. Finally, no commander would discard the means for victory and keeping his men alive. Williamson envisaged using rapid manoeuvre and firepower to defeat Viet Cong regiments which might attack and outnumber the Brigade.

While the 173rd continued their training, the Diggers of 1 RAR began their journey to join them. At 1 a.m. on 28 May 1965 the converted aircraft carrier HMAS *Sydney* slipped through Sydney Heads escorted by the destroyers HMAS *ANZAC* and HMAS *Duchess*. Aboard were Bravo Company, elements of Support and Administration Companies, the men and vehicles of the First APC Troop (Prince of Wales Light Horse), the First Australian Logistic Supply Company, press correspondents Pat Burgess, Graham Connolly, Alan Ramsay, Creighton Burns and Garry Barker, and most of the force's vehicles, equipment and stores.

There had been no emotional farewells—no scenes of soldiers kissing tearful wives, mothers, sisters or girlfriends in the midst of a noisy crowd of well-wishers. The group had embarked after an almost stealthy move by buses and closed trucks from Holsworthy. As the correspondents were to report later, the Diggers were solemn and tense as they lined up and embarked in the dead of the night. Two wives, who rushed to the headland at Watsons Bay, were interviewed by a press team sent there to take a photograph of the departure. One wife mournfully reflected, 'There they go, now we begin the letter writing.'[24] 'My wife is expecting our first baby any minute,' 21-year-old Private Paul Slattery told reporters at the time. 'She was already in St Margaret's Hospital, Darlinghurst, when I left. Of course I hated to leave her, but she understands how important this is.'[25]

Like many improvised troop ships before her, HMAS *Sydney* could only provide cramped and uncomfortable living conditions for its passengers. However, morale among the soldiers was high and the co-operation with the sailors was good. Chaplain Gerry Cudmore reported that the purpose of the journey had a good steadying influence on everyone. He was a robust young Catholic priest from Melbourne who became very popular among the soldiers of the 1 RAR Group. His aim was to provide the men with every opportunity for spiritual reflection and to understand the evils of Communism. During the trip, he presented 50 hours of instruction on the subjects of the necessity of character and character development, and the philosophy and history of Communism. Religious services conducted daily were well attended.[26] Gerry Cudmore had done a good job of putting the fear of God and the fear of Communism into the soldiers aboard HMAS *Sydney*.

Despite the crowded conditions, a rigorous training program was undertaken aboard ship. Two physical training instructors provided training in unarmed combat and conducted muscle-toughening exercise sessions. Lectures on minor tactics and map reading were conducted by the officers. Vietnamese language training was conducted by Warrant Office Alex Craig from the Intelligence Corps who had completed twelve months in South Vietnam with the Australian Army Training Team—

General William C. Westmoreland, Commander of the US Military Assistance Command–Vietnam greets Warrant Officer Jack Currie, Support Company 1 RAR, on arrival in Vietnam. Corporal Bill Clifton, Assault Pioneer Platoon, sees some humour in it all in the background.

Vietnam (AATV) in 1963–64. Range practices were a daily event and comprised shooting at balloons and beer cans half filled with water dropped over the stern. Training was interspersed with recreational activities such as volleyball and deck hockey. A Race Day, Revue and an elaborate 'Crossing of the Line' ceremony provided moments of humour. At night the men were shown films and issued their daily ration of one 26 ounce (740 millilitre) bottle of beer.

The remainder of the Battalion moved by air during the period 1–10 June 1965 in a chartered Qantas 707 jet operating out of Richmond Airforce Base near Windsor, New South Wales. This shuttle service was secret but provision had been made for the families of the soldiers to exchange last farewells at the airbase before departure. Captain David Paul recalled later that in his aircraft there was not a sound during take off. The men were very subdued as they saw Sydney disappear to the south.[27]

As each company arrived, the early morning trip took them through the crowded, petrol-hazed streets of Saigon, out into the clean, green countryside, along the newly completed highway to the east, over the great new bridges spanning the Dong Nai and Saigon Rivers, into dusty Bien Hoa, around the perimeter track and to the abandoned US gun positions which were to be the centre of the Battalion's area.

They climbed out onto a cleared rubber plantation covered with waist-high kunai grass interspersed with knee-high stumps of rubber trees. The tropic sun beat down on them as they moved about what was to be their home for a year. They would construct a town there, almost entirely by their own efforts. The town would consist of streets and company-sized suburbs, drainage, electricity (for some), hygienic arrangements, law and order, administration, entertainment and medical facilities; but there would be no women, no Vietnamese and no civilians. This would be a home base for the fraternity of soldiers—a tribal village of quiet hunters.

As the Diggers settled in, the battles in Quang Ngai Province were being fought. On 1 June news of the massacre of the 51st ARVN Regiment became known. The battles for the other provincial towns had already begun. At Darlac, Pleiku, Phu Bon and Le Thanh the Viet Cong repeated the tactics of overrunning a town and then setting up ambushes for relief forces. Five ARVN battalions had been rendered ineffective for further duty. In this climate, the 173rd was put into a defensive posture to ensure the security of Bien Hoa Airbase against attack. In November 1964 several millions of dollars worth of aircraft had been destroyed during a mortar attack and there were reports of Viet Cong artillery pieces again being deployed to the river bank within range of the airbase.[28]

Before the arrival of the Battalion there had been friction between Major John Essex-Clark, who led the 1 RAR reconnaissance party, and Brigadier General Williamson. Williamson had allocated an area about 150 metres by 150 metres to the Australians for their base camp. The area was of similar size to those occupied by each of the two airborne battalions of the Brigade but did not conform to Australian concepts of the area required for a battalion defensive position. The Paratroopers were accommodated in neat rows of tents which were being replaced progressively by permanent huts. An earthen bund incorporating several sand-bagged sentry positions had been bulldozed up around these camp areas.

Essex-Clark recalled:

> The area Williamson allotted to us on Thursday 27 May was a small patch of young rubber trees about 600 m from the 2/503rd [pronounced Second Five-oh-Third]. It was insecure and indefensible, had covered approaches for the enemy, the rubber would need to be tapped by the local Vietnamese, and in the wet would have remained muddy and dripping, mosquito-ridden and

Lieutenant Colonel Lou Brumfield (left), Commanding Officer of 1 RAR, pictured with Colonel David Jackson, Commander of the Australian Army Force–Vietnam. The tough diplomacy of these two officers ensured that the Australians were allowed to fight as they had been trained.

miserable, and in the dry would have no cooling breezes. I asked for what appeared to them to be a 'great open prairie' previously used by an artillery battery. It was on a reverse slope to observation from the Viet Cong on the north bank of the Dong Nai River. I was told it was not sensible and to go and see what the 2/503rd had done.[29]

The impasse was sorted out by Brigadier David Jackson, Commander of the Australian Force Vietnam, who impressed upon Williamson the need for the Australians to have a defensive position which conformed to their tactical doctrine. 1 RAR was given the 'prairie'.

A second clash had occurred over the period required for the Battalion to acclimatise. The Paratroopers had already seen action at Vung Tau and Xuan Loc, and Williamson was keen to commit the Australians to combat soon after arrival. Essex-Clark had asked for two weeks after the Battalion arrived for the Australians to train, get used to operating with the Brigade and adjust to the hot, humid weather. After arguing that the Australians were fit, came from a hot country and should be eager to kill the Viet Cong, Williamson relented and told Essex-Clark that he expected 1 RAR to be ready for combat a week after the last company arrived on 20 June.[30]

On 2 June, Brumfield had conferred with the officers of the 173rd and, after a wet and muddy night in a forward command post, inspected the Battalion's defensive position sited by Essex-Clark whose concept was to develop mutually supporting strong points which could be manned by the minimum number of troops when the Battalion was on operations. Between these points he planned extensive wire fortifications. Any enemy assault attempting to penetrate between the strong points would be channelled and caught in a cross fire of several machine guns and by the wire entanglements. This defensive layout was for 'Australian eyes only' and even 'Butch' Williamson, who was given a helicopter reconnaissance of the area later, was confounded by the apparent complexity of the configuration. In fact, it was a very simple layout allowing mutual fire support between the minimum number of machine guns to cover the barbed wire fences and entanglements. To prevent easy enemy fire control and registering of targets in the area from observation points on the Dong Nai River, Brumfield ordered the felling of all large trees on the forward slopes of the position, siting permanent patrol positions well forward. Vietnamese military and civilian personnel were not permitted in the area for the next twelve months. This contrasted with the remainder of the Brigade area which was frequented freely by Vietnamese civilians employed in domestic duties.[31]

Brumfield drew up a training program which would rotate key personnel from each Australian rifle company with instructors from the Brigade. Subject areas for combined training included 'Role of donor

'Are you sure this thing comes back?' Brigadier General Ellis 'Butch' Williamson, Commanding General of the 173rd Airborne Brigade, pictured with a boomerang presented to him by Lieutenant Colonel Lou Brumfield. This was not the only thing Williamson found unusual about the Australians he had under operational control.

country in RVN counter-insurgency', 'US organisation and mission (including rural reconstruction)', 'ARVN organisation', 'Ambush and counter ambush', 'Selected lessons learned in RVN', 'Survival, escape and evasion', 'Artillery and air support procedures', 'Airmobile operations with Iroquois (platoon and company drills)' and 'Mines and booby traps'. Each company was allocated from eleven in the morning until seven in the evening for their own acclimatisation, development of the defensive position and other training.[32]

Soon after arrival, the Australians re-earned their traditional title of 'Diggers'. In the pouring rain and mud, Brumfield had shown the company commanders to their defensive areas and digging had started immediately. The Americans were amused at the appearance of the grimy, saturated Australians dressed in baggy green pants, large tropical stud boots and floppy bush hats amidst a complex of fighting trenches. This attire was in sharp contrast to their own crisply starched fatigues, smart airborne 'baseball' caps, polished combat boots and colourful badges of rank and unit shoulder patches. 1 RAR was offered the red, white and blue 173rd Airborne Brigade patch to wear but Brumfield declined in favour of maintaining the traditional drab green Australian military forces shoulder patch.[33] Williamson was reported to have said when he observed the baggy Australian uniforms and their long-barrelled, semi-automatic, wood-stocked rifles that the Australians seemed to be dressed for a safari rather than military operations.

Second Lieutenant Clive Williams wrote on 5 June:

> Well I have now been at Bien Hoa three days—it is a really lousy place, no mod cons [modern conveniences] or anything. Quite a few of the soldiers are feeling the heat. I have had a healthy headache for the last two days. The Yanks here wear really gaudy uniforms with great big badges—compared to us, they look like Christmas trees . . . Last night there was torrential rain. My tent got blown down in the strong winds so I got my clothes wet through. We seem to be permanently wet here though mainly due to perspiration. Our main worry at present is attacks by mortars and artillery.[34]

On 1 RAR's right flank was the 2/503rd. On the left was the Brigade's Cavalry Troop. At night these units left electric lights on and often fired flares forward of their positions. The Viet Cong observing from a distance would have seen a mass of lights, and a black patch: the Australian perimeter. Each night Australian patrols left the position in search of any Viet Cong who may have tried to close in on the position or set up mortars to bombard the airbase and defensive areas. Like all newly arrived units in a theatre of operations, nothing was left to chance.

In the areas in which 1 RAR was to operate the climate was equatorial tropical monsoon which means hot and humid with temperatures varying from 26°C average in January (equivalent of winter) to 29°C average in April (equivalent of early summer). The summer monsoon, coming in off the South China Sea, would bring torrential rains from May to October. Rainfall in Saigon, for example, would be 1500 millimetres average per annum whereas in the Highlands it could go up to 2500 millimetres and more. In the dry season from November to April, the dust from the helicopters or a motor convoy could be thick and choking whereas, in the wet season, the ground would be transformed into foul-smelling, grey compost and sucking mud.

When the Battalion arrived from the winter in Sydney, the rains of the summer monsoon had started, the humidity was very high and the temperatures by midday were around 40°C. A period of acclimatisation was essential. The Paratroopers were already acclimatised having been in Vietnam for four weeks and come from a hot Okinawa summer.

The early monsoon rains exposed some errors of judgment in the siting of the Brigade's minefields and latrine areas. Hundreds of light-weight, small plastic anti-personnel mines (call Dingbats) began to float. This resulted in the Brigade Headquarters area, surrounded by sloping hills where minefields had been placed during initial occupation, being 'seeded' by floating 'Dingbats'. The worst problem was that the latrines, sunk in neighbouring paddy fields, were afloat as well and effluent also made its way to Brigade Headquarters. Needless to say, the Brigade Headquarters Company was relocated.[35]

Initially, Australian officers and NCOs joined the Paratroopers on patrol. It was soon realised that the US and Australian attitudes to patrolling were opposite. The situation could have been described as the meeting of two very different military cultures. The Paratroopers patrolled in a manner which invited contact with the enemy. In a way, the smoking, talking and wearing of the bright red, white and blue airborne shoulder patch amounted to saying to the Viet Cong, 'You know where we are. Take us on, and pay the price.' On the other hand, the Australians patrolled silently and were careful not to give away their location. They were saying to the Viet Cong, 'You will never know exactly where we are, but we will find you and kill you.'

Veteran Warrant Officer Jack Cramp told reporters:

Our patrols do not fire off ammo or shoot up flares like the Yanks— they listen and move quietly, we haven't fired a shot or sent up a flare yet. The Americans think we are mad. It seems to me though, that all they're doing is letting the Viet Cong know where they are. I guess we have a bit to teach them.[36]

Another Australian was quoted as saying, 'It was a bit too bloody dangerous. They [Paratroopers] talk and smoke and generally set themselves up as pretty good targets. The Americans are good blokes but not when they are on patrol.'[37]

Despite the different operating methods the Diggers and Paratroopers liked each other. Proof of the growing comradeship was the bartering and swapping of personal items of clothing and equipment. The Australian canvas shower bucket, the famous slouch hat, the blow-up mattress for sleeping on, large ammunition pouches and plastic two-man tents were sought after by the Paratroopers. Several pairs of US combat boots could be swapped for one shower bucket. At this time the Americans could only shower by making a trek to the 173rd Engineer Company. In the hot, humid conditions, frequent cold showers brought welcome relief. The erection of one's personal shower facility, adorned with the Aussie shower bucket, became a status symbol.

Until HMAS *Sydney* arrived, the Australians had to make do with the Brigade's shower facilities. They were showered in batches—undress in

*Lieutenant Bill Giles enjoy-
ing the benefits of the personal shower offered by the
Aussie canvas shower
bucket.*

one area; take soap into an enclosure ringed by overhead shower nozzles;
water controlled by an attendant—get wet, soap up, then water on for one
minute to rinse; leave in a batch, whether unsoaped, finished rinsing or
not; dry, dress and leave. The Diggers had never seen or experienced
anything like it. At least with a bucket they felt they had some personal
control.[38]

In many ways the Paratrooper was younger but similar to his Australian counterpart. The average age was 18 and a half: half man/half boy,
unmarried and self-sufficient with few material possessions. He had an
old car, a radio and, before posting to Okinawa and Vietnam, a girlfriend.
He, like the young Digger, smoked and drank because it was the thing to
do. Often he could not spell or write well but could strip and assemble his
rifle in seconds, dig a hole when required and give first aid. 'He can do the

work of two civilians for half the pay of one and find ironic humour in it all. He has learned to use his hands as weapons and his weapon as hands', wrote journalist Tom Tiede. 'He can save a life and most assuredly take one.'[39]

On 10 June the Diggers stopped training, cleaned up and, leaving men to secure the defensive position, were transported to Saigon for their official welcome by the South Vietnamese Government. The regimental atmosphere of the occasion was broken when tiny Vietnamese women dressed in national costume attempted to place Hawaiian-style lais around the necks of the tall soldiers wearing their wide-brimmed slouch hats. General Westmoreland was pleased with the inclusion of Australians under his command. 'These men are professionals, an elite corps, an asset to any army.'[40]

Major General Nguyen Van Thieu, the Minister of National Defence (later President of South Vietnam), addressed the assembled Australians with the following words:

> We are sure that you come here with the noble purpose of contributing to the restoration of peace in Vietnam. However we believe that the peace that we and our allies are fighting for is a peace in Honour with our victory over Communism and not the kind of shameful peace that 11 years ago the French Colonialists accepted. That peace came about with the complicity of the communists. I am certain that gallant allied combatants such as you and our mature Vietnamese Armed Forces of today will not sacrifice in vain in order to bring about a cowardly defeat. Thus, in order to defeat the communists, we must at the same time annihilate them by force . . .[41]

The next day a battle started which was to set the scene for offensive operations by the 173rd later in the month. The Viet Cong attacked the Special Forces compound at Dong Xoai in Phuoc Long Province and, after killing or wounding almost everyone in the garrison, laid siege to the camp. Once again the Viet Cong waited patiently for relief forces. Elite ARVN units were deployed into the area. The pattern of Viet Cong slaughter of fellow South Vietnamese was repeated. The 7th ARVN Airborne Battalion was never heard of again and a Ranger Battalion was overrun. The Viet Cong occupied the town. All twenty US advisers attached to ARVN units in the area were either killed or wounded.[42]

After discussions with Westmoreland, 'Butch' Williamson flew to the outskirts of Dong Xoai and spoke with General Phong, the commander of the ARVN 15th Division which was assembling to recapture the town and relieve its beleaguered garrison. 'The stench of death was all over the place,' wrote Captain Wayne Downing, Williamson's aide.

Williamson's discussions resulted in the 1/503rd (pronounced First

Five-o-Third) and a battery of US guns being deployed to Phuoc Long 20 kilometres south of Dong Xoai. They were to act as the Divisional reserve for General Phong. For the first time in the Vietnam War, US ground troops were about to be committed to fight Main Force Viet Cong formations.[43]

By 13 June three Viet Cong regiments (about 6000 men) had concentrated in the area ready to overrun the survivors holding out in the Special Forces compound. General Phong attacked after massive preparatory artillery and air strikes had pounded the Viet Cong positions. His regiments took heavy casualties and the Viet Cong retreated under the weight of direct and indirect firepower. Dong Xoai was reoccupied and the garrison relieved. The US Paratroopers remained in Phuoc Long for several more days but were not committed.

The battle of Dong Xoai marked the peak of the Viet Cong summer monsoon offensive. US analysts assessed that five ARVN regiments and nine other separate battalions were 'non-effective'. Other units were being reinforced with trainees who had not completed their recruit courses. The ARVN had been fought to a standstill and been bled of trained personnel. There would be no new battalions for six months to face the North Vietnamese regiments marching to the south.[44] The scope of the Viet Cong attacks confirmed that divisional-sized operations were possible and, with the arrival of North Vietnamese reinforcements imminent, a general offensive was likely.

Westmoreland wrote to his commander, Admiral Sharp:

> So far the VC have not employed their full capabilities in this campaign . . . They are capable of mounting regimental-size (approximately 2000 men) operations in all four ARVN Corps areas, and at least battalion-sized attacks in virtually all provinces . . . ARVN forces on the other hand are already experiencing difficulty in coping with this increased VC capability. Desertion rates are inordinately high. Battle losses have been higher than expected. In order to cope with the situation outlined above, I see no course of action open to us except to reinforce our efforts in SVN [South Vietnam] with additional US or Third Country forces as rapidly as is practical during the critical weeks ahead. Additional studies must continue and plans developed to deploy even greater forces, if and when required, to attain our objectives or counter enemy initiatives. Ground forces deployed to selected areas along the coast and inland will be used both offensively and defensively. US ground troops are gaining experience and thus far have performed well. Although they have not engaged the enemy in strength, I am convinced that US troops with their energy, mobility and firepower can successfully take the fight to the VC. The basic purpose of the additional deployments recommended below is to give us a substantial and

hard hitting offensive capability on the ground to convince the VC that they cannot win.[45]

Even as the battle at Dong Xoai had raged, a political coup had taken place in Saigon. On 12 June 1965 Nguyen Cao Ky, commander of the South Vietnamese Air Force, leading a clique of fellow service officers, had overthrown the civilian government of Prime Minister Quat. Once again South Vietnam had reached a point of political and military collapse. The new military junta had a precarious hold on power and the ARVN was demoralised. The South Vietnamese had nothing more to offer and no new forces to deploy against the Viet Cong. The arrival of the North Vietnamese in the northern provinces and the Highlands would probably mark the final weeks of the war. The time had come for US ground forces to break out of their enclaves around Da Nang and Bien Hoa Airbases and go on the offensive.

On 24 June 1965, Westmoreland ordered the 173rd to show its 'muscle'. 'Butch' Williamson was to deploy the entire brigade and clear the south-eastern approaches to the Bien Hoa Airbase. The operation was called the Anderson Approach by Brumfield after Colonel Anderson of Headquarters ARVN III Corps, who had assessed the south-eastern approach as the Viet Cong's most likely choice for ground attack.[46] (Later in the Vietnam War this approach was indeed used to attack the headquarters of the US II Field Force which had been sited there.[47])

That morning helicopters were parked in six long 'taxi ranks'. The three battalions of the Brigade were to be lifted at the same time in the biggest helicopter deployment of the Vietnam War to date. As the rotor blades started turning, air and artillery strikes were pounding five landing zones 10 kilometres away. Prowling helicopter gun ships were already at work strafing anything that moved. Above the long lines of helicopters, fighter ground attack aircraft loitered in the sky waiting for their turn to participate in this grand show of military force.

For the Australians, airmobile operations on this scale were new. From Brumfield down, they had much to learn from the Americans about large scale command, control and communications, artillery and close air support, armoured, APC and infantry operations, rapid 'on the march' orders (called fragmentary orders or when given at the last minute before taking off in a helicopter, 'skid briefings') and helicopter resupply.

Patrolling commenced after airmobile assaults by each company of the Brigade. Contact with the Viet Cong was fleeting, although none so fleeting as an incident involving Private Ross Mangano of Major Ian McFarlane's B Company, who slid down a small embankment and came face to face with a Vietnamese youth armed with a Thompson sub-machine gun. The mutual shock and surprise caused both to scurry away without firing a shot. Mangano's killer instinct had not yet developed. A quick platoon sweep through a nearby camp of seven huts failed to find the startled sentry or any of his companions.[48] There were several other incidents of brief, but inconclusive contact with individual Viet Cong. Most were probably scouts left behind to observe the movements of the Australians. 1 RAR finished the operation clearing a route for the move of the Brigade's logistic elements. It was hot dry work and most soldiers had run out of water. All looked forward to a cool drink on return to the airbase.

The move back to the defensive position at Bien Hoa began that afternoon. Transport from the tarmac of the airbase to the Brigade's defensive position was in high-sided semitrailers quickly dubbed by the Diggers as 'cattle trucks'. Each trailer held 50–60 soldiers, who stood up shoulder to shoulder in cramped conditions. Fortunately the trip was short. One of these 'cattle trucks', carrying members of Major Jim Tattam's C Company, rumbled into the Company's position and began to slow down near the kitchen. The scene was one of laughing and joking—some in the showers—some lining up for hot fresh food—others arriving. Clusters of soldiers were listening to a radio relay of the South African–Australian Rugby Union Test being played in Brisbane.[49]

On the way in, the occupants had called out to those already enjoying a cool shower not to use up all the water or there would be trouble. One of these light-hearted exchanges had been between Private Mick Bourke and one of his platoon commanders from the previous year, Second Lieutenant Bill Kaine, who now commanded 8 Platoon. Kaine, who had just arrived at the shower, jokingly mocked Bourke for not being smart enough to have caught an earlier truck.[50]

Standing near the front of the truck was Second Lieutenant John 'Lofty' Dwyer, the Platoon Commander of 7 Platoon. He had graduated from the Officer Cadet School, Portsea, in June 1964. In July of that year he had joined Charlie Company as a fresh-faced, gangly 20 year old. His first few days in the company had their lighter moments. At 201 centimetres (6 feet 7 inches), Dwyer was the tallest man in the Battalion. The Company Commander at the time, Major Mal Lander, had ordered Second Lieutenant Bill Kaine, one of Dwyer's fellow platoon commanders, to show him around the Battalion and make the appropriate introductions: Kaine at 163 centimetres (5 feet 4 inches) tall and the shortest man in the Battalion. The two had become very close friends despite the laughter and ribbing they received. Before leaving for Vietnam they had spent several afternoons at the Randwick Racecourse. Dwyer used his height to check the prices and call the bets. Kaine would then use his lack of height to squeeze through the legs of the other punters and put the bets on.[51]

Near Dwyer were two members of his platoon, Privates Billy Carroll and Arie Van Valen. Each had decided that the quickest way to get to the showers was to jump over the side of the truck rather than wait for the 40 soldiers in front of them to exit by the rear ramp. Everyone was chattering about the prospects of a shower, a good meal, a beer or two and a good sleep. As the truck stopped, a cook called out that a 'cold brew' was available. There were a few shouts of jubilation and encouragement as soldiers began to clamber over the side of the truck.[52]

As Billy Carroll went over the side, the pin of one of the grenades attached to his webbing snagged and was pulled out. He did not notice the striker lever spring loose as his mates scrambled over the side with him and they all hit the ground. Two steps later, the grenade detonated and Carroll's lifeless torso was thrown over the top of the truck.[53] Arie Van Valen and Mick Bourke were thrown several metres and lay unconscious with shocking wounds. Nine others, including two Americans, also lay wounded or staggered around stunned and bleeding from gaping wounds.

One soldier told journalist Alan Ramsay, at the time:

> It happened so suddenly I don't think many of the blokes knew just what hit them. The blast occurred near the front of the truck. The American driver was badly hit. Blood was splattered over the right front wheel of the truck, the cabin was smashed and soaked in blood. The windscreen was shattered and upholstery pitted and torn with slivers of steel.[54]

Most of those in the vicinity thought that the area was being mortared and hit the ground or the floor of the truck. When there were no more explosions, some looked up and saw the carnage. Bill Kaine sprinted towards the scene. When he reached the side of the truck where the grenade had gone off he had to fight back a massive wave of nausea before he could do anything. He recovered his composure and went to give first aid to the two Americans. The first was a signaller, who was lying over a rubber tree stump bleeding profusely from the face and the upper body. Kaine could see he was already dead. As Kaine reached the other American he heard him mumble, 'Leave me, I'm dead. Help someone else'. Kaine persevered and bound up the Paratrooper's wounds with the help of medical orderlies who were now arriving.[55]

Soldiers were by now running in from everywhere. Several men lay wounded in the showers; only seconds before they may have been feeling relieved at having survived their first major operation in Vietnam unscathed. It took only minutes for the first medical evacuation helicopters to arrive because members of Battalion Headquarters had observed the incident and called for every helicopter that was available. The message went out over Armed Forces radio that blood would be required at the Bien Hoa Hospital for the injured. Within a few minutes, donors had started to queue outside the hospital. The queue grew so long that many were turned away.[56]

The shock of the incident and the killing and maiming of members of his platoon did not affect John Dwyer until later that evening. He and his Platoon Sergeant, Sergeant 'Snow' Saville, shared a bottle of Bundaberg Over Proof Rum. He stated later, 'a half bottle of OP rum didn't cure it, but it was an effective medicine to slow one down till you came to grips with the situation.'[57]

Mick Bourke was 19 years old and had joined the Army on his seventeenth birthday. Billy Carroll was 21 years old and was married to 20-year-old Lorraine 'Mindy' Kirk. Mindy received the news of his death at his parents home in Dennington, Victoria, while cradling their six-month-old baby son.[58] Arie Van Valen died later in hospital. The American who had died only had fifteen days left to serve in Vietnam. The other Paratrooper, who had so selflessly directed Bill Kaine to help someone else, survived.[59]

A sad sequel to this incident was the added grief and financial burden which had to be borne by parents who wanted the bodies of Billy Carroll, Mick Bourke and Arie Van Valen returned to Australia for burial. Each family had to pay £300 ($600) to have their son's remains flown to Australia. A Sydney businessman Mr Ron Wiggins paid the money to assist the families of these soldiers to bring their sons home.[60] It had been a long-standing policy that deceased soldiers were buried at the nearest official war cemetery at government expense. For those who died in Vietnam, this meant burial at Terendak Barracks, Malaysia. The controversy of returning the bodies of soldiers killed in Vietnam for burial in Australia would become a national issue when Warrant Officer Kevin 'Dasher' Wheatley was killed in November 1965. The Defence Department refused to return his body to Australia for burial at government expense until there was extensive publicity in the media caused by a letter to the press from Wheatley's sister-in-law.

On 26 June 1965 Westmoreland was given permission to commit US troops to combat—'independent of or in conjunction with GVN [Government of Vietnam] forces in any situation in which the use of such troops is required by a GVN commander and when in COMUSMACV's [Westmoreland's] judgment, their use is necessary to strengthen the relative position of GVN forces.'[61]

As the 173rd returned from clearing Anderson's Approach on 26 June, orders were received from Westmoreland to deploy into War Zone D as soon as possible and search for and destroy Viet Cong units known to operate there. War Zone D was an area north and north east of Bien Hoa Airbase, about 60 kilometres wide running east–west and 35 kilometres long running north–south. It was an area of jungle-covered hills, unused paddy fields and derelict villages surrounded by secondary jungle. The inhabited villages in the area occupied small pockets of flat, arable land near the banks of the river.

War Zone D was named by the French Army in 1950 and had belonged to the Viet Cong and their predecessors, the Viet Minh, since the end of World War II. The French had failed to wrest the jungle areas from Viet Minh control, and, subsequently, South Vietnamese forces had failed to take the area from the Viet Cong. Politically, as well as militarily, a successful operation in War Zone D would be highly visible and advantageous to the prosecution of the war.

Williamson planned for the operation to start at dawn on 28 June. A wave of keen expectation swept through the Brigade. Everyone talks of 'getting into it'. 'There is a yearning for action,' wrote journalist Don Peterson at the time. 'A yearning to prove oneself. It is to be able to say one has been in a fire fight—what would it be like—to kill a man—watch others wounded and killed—be wounded—face death in the form of an enemy soldier?'[62]

3 The first forays

The first forays were in War Zone D. The Paratroopers were determined fighters, but allowed the Viet Cong to pick the time and place for battle. The Diggers aimed for tactical surprise, which resulted in a tactical stand off: the Viet Cong took no risks with the unpredictable Australians. And the Kiwi Gunners arrived, reviving the ANZAC tradition.

The literal translation of Bien Hoa is 'Land of Peaceful Frontiers'. Geographically, this translation was apt. Surrounding the sprawling town of Bien Hoa located 2 kilometres from the airbase was a checkerboard of rice paddies, market gardens, rubber plantations and, to the north and east, expanses of dense secondary jungle and primary rainforests. The Dong Nai River snaked in an almost lazy manner through the rich flat, farmland. The only hustle and bustle visible was the marketplace of Bien Hoa where vendors and customers haggled vigorously over the prices of agricultural produce. Elsewhere the pace of life was slow, repetitive and methodical. Bien Hoa Airbase was like a high-technology hornets' nest dropped into a quiet, green landscape.

The situation in Bien Hoa Province was typical of that in the other provinces surrounding the seat of government in Saigon. Behind the inscrutable faces of the people of 'The Land of Peaceful Frontiers' were deep fears about the future. The political and military organisations of the Viet Cong exploited their daily lives through determined cadre who lived with them in their villages and hamlets. At the same time, a seemingly distant government in Saigon sent tax collectors and corrupt local officials to prey upon their livelihoods.

Military operations by the ARVN were often characterised by harsh treatment of the peasants and an overdependence on firepower which caused civilian casualties. The conduct of the soldiers, who were not from the local district, alienated villagers and did nothing to attract support for a series of makeshift political regimes which, since the assassination of President Diem and his powerful family-based clique in 1963, had been subjected to a rapid succession of coups, counter-coups and violent protests.

The message for the people of Bien Hoa Province from the Viet Cong was simple and effective. They were promised a better future after the overthrow of the inefficient, ineffective and corrupt Saigon Government with its tax collectors, absentee landlords, venal local officials and bullying, thieving soldiers. The arrival of the 173rd was portrayed as an invasion by the Americans and their allied mercenaries to prop up an unworthy political order, continue the oppression of the Vietnamese people, and assist the ARVN in the destruction of the countryside with bombs and shells.[1]

In their propaganda, the Viet Cong described themselves as local freedom fighters who were overcoming their enemy's preponderance of military hardware and firepower with cunning and courage. The publications distributed to the villagers were full of highly romanticised stories of brave lightly armed individuals and small groups killing large numbers of 'puppet troops' and their imperialist US advisers in ambushes, assaults on outposts and through random sniping.[2] Indeed, the Viet Cong sold themselves to the people in a manner reminiscent in Western literature of the legendary exploits of Robin Hood and his Merry Men.

The Saigon Government had the task of building a country, an economy and a prosperous way of life for the South Vietnamese people. The inequities of Vietnamese society based on a thousand years of tradition and reinforced by a hundred years of French colonialism were not going to disappear in a decade. The Viet Cong had the simpler task of blaming all South Vietnam's ills on the Saigon Government and destroying every attempt that the Government, with the assistance of international aid, made to solve them.

A typical story of the growth of Viet Cong power was the fate of a dairy farm set up by the Australian Government in 1961 near Ben Cat, a village deep in War Zone D. The project had been funded from Australia's Colombo Plan which involved sharing technology with the countries of Asia and educating Asian students in Australia. Mr Wilfred Arthur, an Australian agricultural expert, was sent to Ben Cat to supervise the building of the farm and its stocking with prize Australian dairy cattle and modern dairying equipment.

In 1962 Arthur was kidnapped by guerillas and released later in exchange for a typewriter and an undisclosed sum of money paid by an official from the Australian Embassy in Saigon. By late 1963 all that was left of the project was a number of bullet-scarred buildings and rusting dairy machinery. The Viet Cong had started by sniping at Vietnamese employees and killing the cattle. Eventually, like vandals who are allowed to get away with initial acts of destruction, they overran the farm and destroyed everything. Final destruction came on 19 June 1965 when a B52 bombing raid pulverised the remaining buildings and shredded the surrounding vegetation. On the day the last remnants of an Australian effort to help South Vietnam through economic assistance were destroyed, 1 RAR became fully operational.[3]

Viet Cong military units were either Main Force or Local. The Main Force guerillas were cunning, well-disciplined, adequately trained and adept at jungle operations using stealth, rapid movement on foot and deception. They would attack vigorously and bravely when they had the initiative or assessed they would greatly outnumber their opponents.

> Ground is of no long term value to the VC and he will only stand and fight when he has us at a tactical disadvantage or to cover the evacuation of an important installation or larger unit. A quick assault on a VC position which he is willing to defend is likely to prove unprofitable . . . The Viet Cong has proved to be brave and aggressive when he has set the stage, but a reluctant soldier when surprised or on equal terms with his opponent.[4]

Main Force units, who were the revolutionary war equivalent of Western Regular Army units, operated from bases deep in jungle sanctuaries such as War Zones D and C, the Iron Triangle and the Ho Bo Woods. They would concentrate for specific operations and disperse to their bases afterwards. Their tactical doctrine was often expressed in simple maxims such as 'Four Quicks and a Slow' (quick approach, quick assault, quick reorganisation, quick withdrawal and slow preparation) and 'The Three Firsts' (first to open fire, first to occupy key terrain and first to assault). In many ways Viet Cong tactics were a series of set piece techniques rather than flexible, responsive manoeuvres. Viet Cong operational planning was fastidious, methodical and often involved detailed rehearsals. Combined with poor radio communications, this rigid, painstaking planning contributed to inflexibility in the execution of large-scale operations and an inability to adjust plans to allow for 'last minute' information.[5]

Viet Cong and North Vietnamese units were built on the basis of three-man cells, which formed the squads, platoons, companies, battalions and regiments. The three men lived, worked, travelled, fought and died together. The cell leaders reported to the squad leader, who reported to the platoon leader, and so on up the chain of command. Every aspect of daily activity, be it military, political, administrative or domestic, was supervised and controlled. If one of the three became a casualty, the others would evacuate him and his weapons.

> The enemy have a mystical method of whisking away their wounded at times during the thick of a fire fight . . . This includes

dead and wounded. He has been known to use wire loops around a casualty's feet or cloth straps around the (sic) body. He has also used locally-made meat hooks. Frequently, at short intervals after definite killing hits have been scored, bodies have disappeared.[6]

Sometimes dead and wounded were evacuated through well-camouflaged tunnel entrances into morgues and hospitals located below ground.

For twelve months US and Australian platoons would follow blood trails of seriously wounded or dead Viet Cong being dragged away by their companions to no avail because the red trails stopped suddenly or disappeared into impassable clumps of bamboo and other vegetation. Even if tunnel entrances were found, it was several months before techniques were developed to enter and destroy tunnels. However, the dependence of the Viet Cong on the use of tunnels, the extent of the tunnel complexes and the fact that tunnels were never effectively neutralised or denied to the Viet Cong was not fully understood until after the end of the Second Indochina War.

The Local Force guerilla was a farmer or villager who operated close to his home and family. If he was of military age, he hid in the vicinity of his home, visited his family, and worked for his livelihood only when it was safe to do so. The relationship between the Main Force and Local guerillas was very close. The Local guerillas were the 'eyes and ears' of the Main Force units who depended on the Local guerillas to keep them informed about the locations and movements of ARVN, US and Australian troops. While they maintained surveillance for Main Force unit commanders, the Local guerillas set booby traps, planted mines, sniped, and occasionally retrieved 60 millimetre mortars from concealed locations and conducted harassing missions. Of equal importance to the war effort, the Local guerilla assassinated or terrorised unco-operative local officials, school teachers and tax collectors as directed by the local political cadre, assisted in the indoctrination of fellow villagers and helped the functioning of Viet Cong's shadow government.

The logistic system of the Viet Cong was primitive but effective. Rather than having to carry large packs full of ammunition, rations, clothing and water like their US and Australian opponents, they would wear the minimum of webbing and carry small quantities of ammunition, food and water. Their sources of resupply were dispersed in local villages and hamlets, and in caches of supplies and in base or transit camps concealed throughout the jungle and in tunnel complexes. The Viet Cong had their supply system integrated into their areas of operation. The Paratroopers and Diggers carried several days' supplies and they were resupplied from outside their area of operations.

Viet Cong communications were rudimentary. Local guerillas provided much of the communication system by acting as couriers and providing intelligence information. Captured radio equipment was used for quicker communications. Viet Cong radio traffic was often intercepted by the specialist units and exploited. Australians found it disturbing that these intercepts confirmed that the Viet Cong had early warning of the Brigade's operations.[7]

The Viet Cong had infiltrated the ARVN.

With few exceptions, Viet Cong killed or captured have been in possession of documents, either of a military or personal nature, surrendered leaflets or commendation certificates and inevitably a wallet of photographs of himself, his male and female friends. Frequently there were photographs of himself in ARVN and/or Viet Cong uniform with a weapon. In some areas, eg Ben Cat, Viet Cong 'two timing' as ARVN have been encountered.[8]

... 10 per cent of all uniformed Vietnamese here, police, army etc are either Viet Cong or sympathizers ... The battalion did not kill or capture many VC [because] they had fled the area, probably tipped off by the South Vietnamese Army which, apart from a few units, appear to have 5% VC in its ranks.[9]

The Paratroopers and Diggers of the 173rd faced an opponent endowed with many military and political advantages. The Brigade was outnumbered by an enemy who could decide on the time and place for battle; an enemy who had prior information of the Brigade's intended areas of operations and knew the locations of Brigade units during the conduct of operations. The Main Force Viet Cong units were supported by an extensive political and military infrastructure at village and hamlet level. This infrastructure acted as their 'eyes and ears', means of resupply, and was also capable of causing demoralising casualties among the Americans and Australians through sniping, booby traps, mines and mortar fire. Guerillas could move freely in their areas of operations unencumbered by heavy personal loads of ammunition and supplies, 'disappear' into tunnel complexes and reappear on the surface later. They were also able to move more quickly, and evacuate an area, leaving behind snipers to delay any pursuing force.

The Viet Cong forces facing the 173rd were controlled and supported by a well-established political and military hierarchy. Strategic direction came from Hanoi and tactical direction from experienced commanders and cadre, many of whom had fought the French in the First Indochina War. The system of command, control and resupply encompassed all the provinces of South Vietnam and stretched back along the intricate routes of the Ho Chi Minh Trail. This complex, effective system functioned in a manner that any conventional Western army would envy, despite the US and South Vietnamese dominance in the air, capacity for rapid manoeuvre of ground forces and possession of immense firepower.

By 1965 Bien Hoa Province had been fully infiltrated by the Viet Cong. Bien Hoa Airbase was a Western military outpost in hostile territory. The violence perpetrated by the Viet Cong was designed to support political goals and not military objectives. Ambushes and assaults on military installations were selective and not intended as a systematic military campaign to take and hold ground for prolonged periods. Assassinations and sabotage had destroyed attempts by the Saigon Government to maintain provincial administration. Government officials were surviving in many areas only because of arrangements they had made with the local Viet Cong cadre. Others slept in government compounds at night in fear of assassination if they remained in their villages.[10]

Of primary concern to General Westmoreland was the military manifestation of the Viet Cong. Due north of the airbase in Bien Hoa Province was the Viet Cong sanctuary known as War Zone D. The ARVN had stopped operating in the area because of heavy losses sustained in pitched battles with Main Force units of the Viet Cong 9th Division. This division was made up of the 271st and 272nd Regiments and was the first regular division to be fielded by the Viet Cong. In December 1963 a mobile battalion from this division had destroyed an elite ARVN unit, the 'Black Tiger' (or Panther) Battalion. Earlier that year divisional units had overrun a number of 'strategic' hamlets in the Ben Cat district and the whole area had been declared a 'liberated zone'.[11] Rather than a 'Peaceful Frontier', War Zone D was Bien Hoa Province's frontier of violence.

In late 1964 the commander of the 9th Division was directed to move his regiments south from War Zone D, take on supplies and weapons in Phuoc Tuy Province, and attack the Catholic village of Binh Gia 70 kilometres south east of Saigon. In a four-day battle, the South Vietnamese 33rd Ranger Battalion and the 4th Marine battalion were ambushed and decimated. The Division withdrew intact having achieved an important psychological victory and giving notice that the campaign for control of South Vietnam was about to enter its final phase—the conventional military offensive.

In June 1965 it was the turn of the 173rd to oppose the 9th Division in its home territory. Man for man, the Brigade would be outnumbered by experienced jungle fighters who would use their intimate knowledge of War Zone D to advantage. However, the Brigade would not be outgunned or outmanoeuvred. Offsetting the numbers and cunning of the Viet Cong would be the Brigade's firepower and airmobility.

Before dawn on 28 June, the Brigade mounted up in 'cattle trucks' and moved to the Bien Hoa tarmac which became known as the 'Snake Pit'. A sign at Snake Pit read: 'Welcome to the Snakepit-base heliport of the

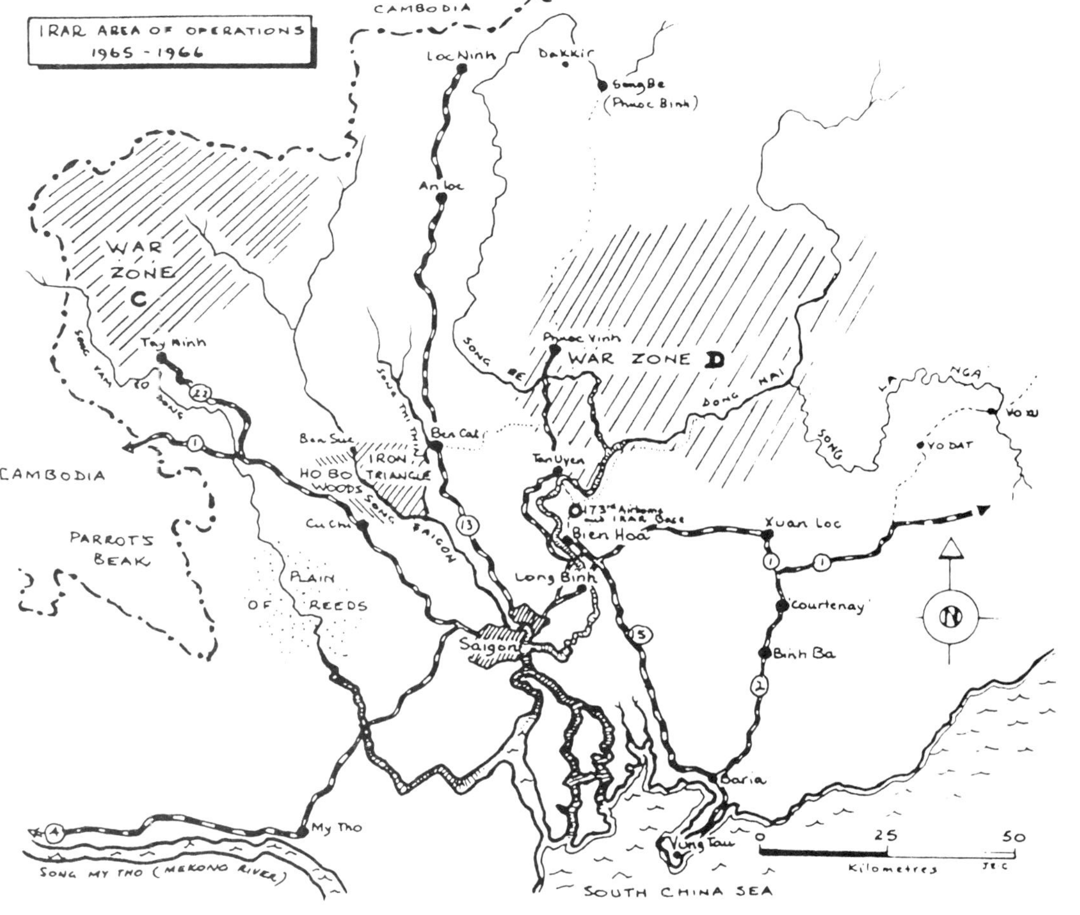
IRAR AREA OF OPERATIONS
1965 - 1966
CAMBODIA
Loc Ninh
Dakkir
Song Be
(Phuoc Binh)
WAR ZONE C
An Loc
WAR ZONE D
Phuoc Vinh
SONG BE
SONG
NGA
LA
VO DU
VO DAT
DONG NAI
SONG SAI GON
SONG THI THINH
Tay Ninh
SONG VAM CO DONG
13
11
Ben Suc
Ben Cat
IRON TRIANGLE
HO BO WOODS
Tan Uyen
CAMBODIA
1
Cu Chi
173rd Airborne and IRAR Base
Bien Hoa
Xuan Loc
1
1
Courtenay
PARROT'S BEAK
PLAIN
OF REEDS
Long Binh
Saigon
15
Binh Ba
2
N
My Tho
Baria
4
Vung Tau
SONG MY THO (MEKONG RIVER)
SOUTH CHINA SEA
0
25
50
Kilometres
JEC

"Rattlers". Company A of the 501st Aviation Battalion is part of the 1st Armoured Division at Fort Hood Texas. Here in Vietnam we fight proudly as part of the 145th Aviation Battalion. As we say in Texas, "Y'all come back now".' A coiled rattlesnake was painted on the nose of their aircraft.[12]

As the first lights of dawn speared over the eastern horizon, the hammer of helicopter rotor blades started. Soldiers were lined up ready to board. Fifteen kilometres to the north west, the first airstrikes were hitting landing zones.

Second Lieutenant Clive Williams wrote:

The Yanks have a fantastic number of choppers. It's nothing to see 140 go past in a straggling line. They're all jet choppers and very fast . . . The chopper crew consists of two gunners and two pilots. Each flight has a different name, this morning we had the Esquires— top hats and canes painted on their noses. They don't bother with seat belts or doors. Two passengers sit in the doorways with their feet dangling over the side—it's a terrific feeling. There are two types, slicks and hogs. Hogs have six machine guns and 48 rockets, and troop carriers (slicks) have two machine guns.[13]

The 'slicks' lifted into the monsoon rain and low clouds, flying through the gloom with heavy ammunition-laden 'hogs' alongside. The Diggers exchanged grins and thumbs-up signs with each other and various crew members and held onto those nervous mates sitting on the floor with their feet dangling outside. Many whitened knuckles were visible gripping seat straps and frames.[14] One hundred and forty four helicopters were used to support this operation. 'Hogs' flew in the vicinity of each landing zone firing at any movement as the 'slicks' approached. The Battalion's mission was to secure Fire Support Base PHOENIX and protect the US gunners. By late afternoon, the Diggers were in position 5 kilometres from the village of Tan Phu at the site of an abandoned fortified village. The Australian APC Troop commanded by Captain Bob Hill joined them there and were then sent to secure a position nearby. By midnight, Captain Hill and his men were busy engaging Viet Cong patrols probing their perimeter.

Bob Hill was an experienced officer with a practical approach to the command of his troop. He was as equally proficient at changing a damaged track as he was at making quick decisions on operations. He was unassuming, ever optimistic and possessed abundant initiative. Bob Hill was no stranger to infantry, having fought as a soldier with 3 RAR in Korea. After leaving the Regular Army he had served in a number of appointments in the Citizen Military Forces before receiving a Short Service Commission in 1963 and joining the 4/19th Prince of Wales Light Horse Regiment in Melbourne.

Alpha Company 1 RAR lines up at the 'Snake Pit' ready to board for their first foray into War Zone D. The obsolete webbing, Second World War vintage boots and gaiters and heavy personal loads are evident. In the foreground is Staff Sergeant 'Dinky' Dean who had been serving with 1 RAR since its formation in 1948.

OUTLINE ORGANISATION OF
173rd AIRBORNE BRIGADE
(SEPARATE)

This diagram does not show organisation for combat but indicates the integral Brigade resources available to the Commanding General. Additional artillery, aviation, engineer etc resources were provided for specific operational needs.

COMBAT UNITS

1/503rd AIRBORNE BATTALION
2/503rd AIRBORNE BATTALION
1 RAR INFANTRY BATTALION *
PWUH APC TROOP *
E/17 CAVALRY COMPANY
D/16 ARMOUR (APCs)

operational control
command

Commander, Australian Force, Vietnam

* Under command of CO 1 RAR but placed under operational control of functional units as shown. All '*' units were part of '1 RAR GROUP'.

** under operational control of 3/319 Artillery Battalion (through CG 173rd Airborne Brigade) but remained under command NZFVN in Saigon.

BRIGADE HEADQUARTERS
Commanding General, his Deputy and
STAFFS   S1 • PERSONNEL
         S2 • INTELLIGENCE
         S3 • OPERATIONS
         S4 • SUPPLY
         S5 • CIVIL AFFAIRS
· and a 'HEADQUARTERS COMPANY to provide administration.

COMBAT SUPPORT UNITS

3/319 ARTILLERY BATTALION
3 x BATTERIES M2A2 105mm Field Guns (18)
105 BATTERY RAA (6 x 105mm towed L5) *
161 BATTERY RNZA (4 x 105mm pack/howitzers L5) **

A/82nd AVIATION COMPANY
(UH1 B/D HELICOPTERS)
161 RECONNAISSANCE FLIGHT *

173 ENGINEER COMPANY
3rd ENGINEER TROOP *

COMBAT SERVICE SUPPORT UNITS

SUPPORT BATTALION, INCLUDING
MEDICAL COMPANY
TRANSPORTATION COMPANY
MAINTENANCE COMPANY
SPECIALIST SIGNALS PLATOONS
LIAISON PLATOONS FOR
 - ARVN and US AIR FORCE
MILITARY INTELLIGENCE, INCLUDING
 RADIO RESEARCH UNIT
 PHOTOGRAPHIC INTERPRETATION
AUSTRALIAN LOGISTIC SUPPORT
 COMPANY *
PSYWAR DETACHMENT
CHEMICAL DETACHMENT

Captain Bob Hill on the right, commander of 1 Armoured Personnel Troop, Prince of Wales Light Horse Regiment, with Major John Essex-Clark, Officer Commanding Support Company 1 RAR, in the back of an APC. Hill was awarded the Military Cross for his bravery and leadership in 1965–1966.

Hill's first challenge on arrival in Vietnam had been when he and his troop had been marooned in the Saigon docks area. 'We couldn't drive through Saigon because our vehicle tracks would have torn up the streets', he had told reporters at the time. 'We managed to get some trucks which ran a shuttle service from the docks to the Bien Hoa side of the city. Then we drove under our own steam the 15 miles [24 kilometres] to the Base.'[15] He now faced a sleepless night commanding his men under fire.

As Hill approached one of his forward sentry positions, he heard a series of scuffling noises. He moved forward and called out quietly but firmly to a figure he assumed was his sentry to stop making a noise. The recipient of this caution was a Viet Cong soldier who engaged Hill at point blank range, sending a round grazing across his stomach. Ignoring the wound, Hill rushed forward and, after striking the Viet Cong several times, was set upon by another enemy soldier. Hill fought off the two enemy soldiers and put them to flight.

After making sure the enemy had left the area, Hill reported to the Regimental Aid Post for treatment of his wound. After treatment, Hill rejoined his troop and continued to direct his men's fire against the enemy patrols. Despite being wounded again in the early hours of the morning by an exploding grenade, Hill moved among his men and directed their efforts after a second trip to the Regimental Aid Post. His steadiness and personal courage that night was an inspiration. For this action and his outstanding professional conduct during the tour, Captain Bob Hill was awarded the Military Cross.[16]

After a day's uneventful patrolling near PHOENIX, the Battalion redeployed to an area near Xom Dom hamlet about 5 kilometres east of Ben Cat. The Viet Cong observed this movement and waited until nightfall before moving a number of mortars within range. The initial rounds from these mortars landed in the Battalion position about 2 a.m. Unfortunately, the Alpha Company headquarters area took five rounds in a 10 metre circle wounding Major John Healy, his Mobile Fire Controller, Corporal John Kennedy, and a signaller, Private Kevin Gray. The 'dust off' (aero-medical evacuation) occurred by night and was a credit to the US Army helicopter pilots who demonstrated their skill and courage by landing despite the risk of being hit by mortar fire. Healy and Kennedy were able to return to duty several days later. Gray was evacuated to Malaysia in July.[17]

On 30 June, the company patrols continued around PHOENIX. The monotony of the day was broken by an incident at the Delta company orders group where Second Lieutenant Craig Leggett fiddled with the trigger of his Owen Machine Carbine and shot himself in the foot.[18] Fortunately, the solid leather TS boot on issue at the time protected the young officer's foot from serious injury and he resumed duty for the next operation (this was one advantage of a boot which was proving to be totally unsuitable for the wet conditions of Vietnam).

Later that day, the Battalion mounted trucks and moved to Bien Hoa escorted by the Australian APCs. It was clear that a significant number of Viet Cong units had bases in the area but had refused to give battle. The first major foray had been successful but not contested. War Zone D had been re-entered for the first time in twelve months. Most importantly, the Brigade had taken two ARVN airborne battalions into War Zone D. With added confidence, Williamson began planning a more ambitious, larger scale operation for the first week in July.

On return to Bien Hoa, the cycle of digging, administrative duties, picket duties and patrolling started again. 'We have been on many ambush patrols so far but we have not shot anyone yet', wrote 19-year-old Private Billy Nalder to his family. 'The ambush patrols go out in the afternoon and stay out all night. We only wear shirts and trousers and carry ammo and grenades and it rains heavily every night. We end up coming back next morning wet as hell.'[19] Billy Nalder's letter did not reach

"Sorry, fellers, I copped a couple of punctures coming through Cambodia . . ."

Cartoon by Paul Rigby portraying the debacle over the mail service to the 1 RAR Group.

his family until well after his death from a sniper's bullet on the next operation.

Many members of the Battalion were angry at the persistent and unexplained delays in the mail arriving from, and being posted to, Australia.[20] Wives, who knew the Battalion had started their first operations, were anxious when mail did not arrive. Visits by well-intentioned Army Family Liaison officers, trying to explain to wives that the mail was delayed, caused more anxiety. Wives thought that the arrival of these uniformed individuals on their doorsteps confirmed their worst fears about the welfare of their husbands. There were other consequences of the mail delays:

> The strange thing about the mail foul up was that after about two months mail from Australia started arriving in country [in Vietnam]. But it took 4 or 5 months before mail to Australia started getting through. I wonder how many marriages foundered because of the utter lack of feeling on the part of both HQ AAFV [Headquarters Australian Army Force Vietnam] and the Australian Government.[21]

It was disgraceful indeed that the Diggers of the 1 RAR Group were not better supported. It was also the first time Australian troops on active service had been forced to pay full postage on mail, and full postage was also demanded of their loved ones. Australian servicemen had been serving in South Vietnam since 1962. It was an indictment of the superior headquarters in Vietnam and Canberra that an efficient, cheap postage system was not established by 1965. The resident Australian war correspondents served the Battalion well by raising the issue of delayed mail in the print and electronic media in Australia. Several pointed cartoons appeared in Australian newspapers. On 30 June an Army spokesman at Army Headquarters stated categorically that there was no delay in the mail and that eighteen bags of mail sent from Sydney on 1 June and 27 June had arrived in Saigon by 28 June. Not one bag was waiting for the Diggers on their return from their first operation in War Zone D on 29 June.[22]

One can only wonder about what happened to all the logistic instructions on such things as postage, canteen supplies, amenities and the like prepared by Army Headquarters at least as far back as World War II. Supporting soldiers overseas was not a new phenomenon requiring new procedures and instructions. However, new instructions were written and new procedures introduced.[23] Sadly, it was not until 1 RAR left Vietnam, and battalions made up of National Servicemen arrived, that a cheap postage rate was introduced.

Another source of irritation for the Diggers was the allowance they were being paid for service in Vietnam. Australian soldiers serving in Papua New Guinea were receiving 90 cents a day and those in Malaysia $1.55 a day. A soldier in 1 RAR received 75 cents a day. Platoon commanders in Malaysia received $1.75 a day and their counterparts in Vietnam received $1 a day. The Paratroopers received several times these allowances. 'Do you know the Yanks get four different kinds of allowances', one Digger told reporters at the time. 'They get Zone Allowance and Combat Allowance and they tell me that if a bloke digs a hole, he gets Foxhole Allowance.'[24] It would be many months before Australian allowances were increased but the Diggers never achieved parity with their fellow US infantrymen in the Brigade.

Tight control was exercised over leave privileges because of the threat to the airbase from Viet Cong saboteurs. Thirty two soldiers were allowed on daily leave to Saigon. One officer or warrant officer, one sergeant and two soldiers were allowed to visit the Bien Hoa Airbase clubs each night. The comedy highlight of each day was the return of the 32 lucky recipients of daily leave to Saigon. 'Fellows literally poured themselves out of the trucks and staggered back to the company lines.'[25]

One Digger's return from one of these trips became an incident worth relating.[26] 'Butch' Williamson was holding a debriefing on the previous operation in a tent at Brigade headquarters which was located near where trucks dropped off US and Australian soldiers who had been on leave. One Australian soldier, in a thoroughly intoxicated condition, slipped away from the vehicle made available to take 1 RAR soldiers back to the Battalion position, staggered to the entrance of the tent and stated loudly,

'What the hell is going on here?' Williamson looked knowingly over to Major John Essex-Clark and said, 'One of yours, John, I think.' Essex-Clark stood up, turned and glared at the soldier who gasped, 'Christ, the Big E!' The soldier then made his escape and ran past several US military policemen who were closing in on him.

The story did not end there. The soldier sprinted into the signposted minefield adjacent to the headquarters and, when he realised no-one was following, turned and started to yell out obscenities at the military police-men. By this time, all those following were lying down and shouting that he was in a minefield. The soldier did not believe this and began to dance around, laughing uproariously.

Meanwhile, Regimental Sergeant Major (RSM) 'Macca' Mckay had been called and arrived with two of his regimental policemen. He moved to the edge of the minefield with his pace stick under his arm and shouted in his best parade ground voice, 'Get out of that bloody minefield, soldier,' and in a quiet but firm voice added 'Slowly, lad.' By this time, a safe path was being cleared to the soldier by two military policemen prodding the ground in front of them with bayonets. Rather sheepishly he walked down the path and reported to Mackay. The sequel to this incident was that the minefield was checked and it was found that all the mines had been lifted by the Viet Cong—probably long before the 173rd had arrived.

The situation in Vietnam was worsening daily as the 173rd prepared for their next operation. The cities of Da Lat, Phan Thiet, Nha Trang, Quang Ngai and Da Nang had been cut off from road and rail resupply by Viet Cong formations.[27] The North Vietnamese 325th Infantry Division had moved into the Central Highlands threatening Da Nang Airbase, and foreshadowing an attempt to cut South Vietnam in half. The Saigon Government was requesting a Berlin-like airlift to stop the beleaguered cities from being starved into submission. Time was running out for South Vietnam. It would be several weeks before the US 1st Air Cavalry Division would be ready to deploy to An Khe in the Highlands to counter the North Vietnamese presence. Other US formations and 15 000 South Koreans were also weeks away. The 173rd in the south and the US Marines in the north had the mission of conducting spoiling operations until these forces arrived.

On 1 July the Marines at Da Nang Airbase received their first taste of the cunning and determination of the Viet Cong when a special operations company and a mortar company infiltrated the airbase. Under the cover of mortar and small arms fire, a thirteen-man demolition team dug under the perimeter fence and destroyed six jet aircraft worth millions of dollars. This successful raid had ominous implications for the security of the Bien Hoa Airbase.

Westmoreland's concept of operations for the 173rd in June and July 1965 was to conduct combined operations with ARVN units to keep Viet Cong units off balance until the US ground forces could build up and wrest the military initiative away from the Viet Cong. Eventually, he hoped to see US forces only having to act as reserves for successful operations by the ARVN. He and Admiral Sharp were very mindful of the fate of the French Groupement Mobile 100 eleven years earlier. 'I'm sure you realise,' Sharp reminded Westmoreland, 'that there would be grave political implications if sizeable US forces were committed for the first time and suffer a defeat.'[28]

Williamson was no doubt made aware of Westmoreland's and Sharp's concerns about avoiding any form of military setback as he planned for the Brigade's next foray into War Zone D. However, he was probably equally conscious of the need to provide his commanders with a substantial victory. His concept of operations was based on the tactics of the hammer and anvil. He planned to position his US and Australian battalions north of the suspected location of the VC A-11 Infantry Regiment and have them sweep south. The ARVN 48th Regiment was to be positioned further south on the banks of the Dong Nai River. Hopefully, the enemy commander would withdraw in the face of the three-battalion sweep and his units would be decimated by the waiting 48th Regiment.[29] This concept depended for its success on achieving tactical surprise. Events were to show that it would be the Paratroopers and Diggers who would be surprised in a number of sudden engagements and several would fall to the sniper's bullet.

Mid-morning on 6 July dust and grit stung the faces of the Diggers and Paratroopers, and strong blasts of hot air washed over them as they waited in lines at the Snake Pit for the thumbs-up sign to board. They jogged forward under their heavy packs. Twenty-seven kilometres to the north several square kilometres of jungle were being flattened by bombs dropped from B52 bombers which had flown from the island of Guam. The silent delivery and terrifying detonation shock of these bombs were intended to disorient and demoralise the Viet Cong. Once again landing zones were being cleared by the bombs and strafing of fighter ground attack aircraft before the arrival of the helicopters.

The 580 men of 1 RAR were inserted unopposed and the companies moved east and west to get in line for the southern drive. They hacked through thick secondary jungle and skirted impassable clumps of bamboo—ideal country for ambushers and snipers. Movement was slow but they and the Paratroopers were in position by night fall. The ARVN 48th Regiment waited expectantly north of the banks of the Dong Nai River. The giant 'partridge drive' was to begin in the morning: it remained to be seen if the Viet Cong felt like being driven.

A group of Paratroopers from 1/503rd Airborne Battalion move through a B 52 bomb crater in War Zone D. In the centre with camera case over his shoulder and camera around his neck is journalist Horst Fass, winner of a Pulitzer Prize for his reporting of the Vietnam War.

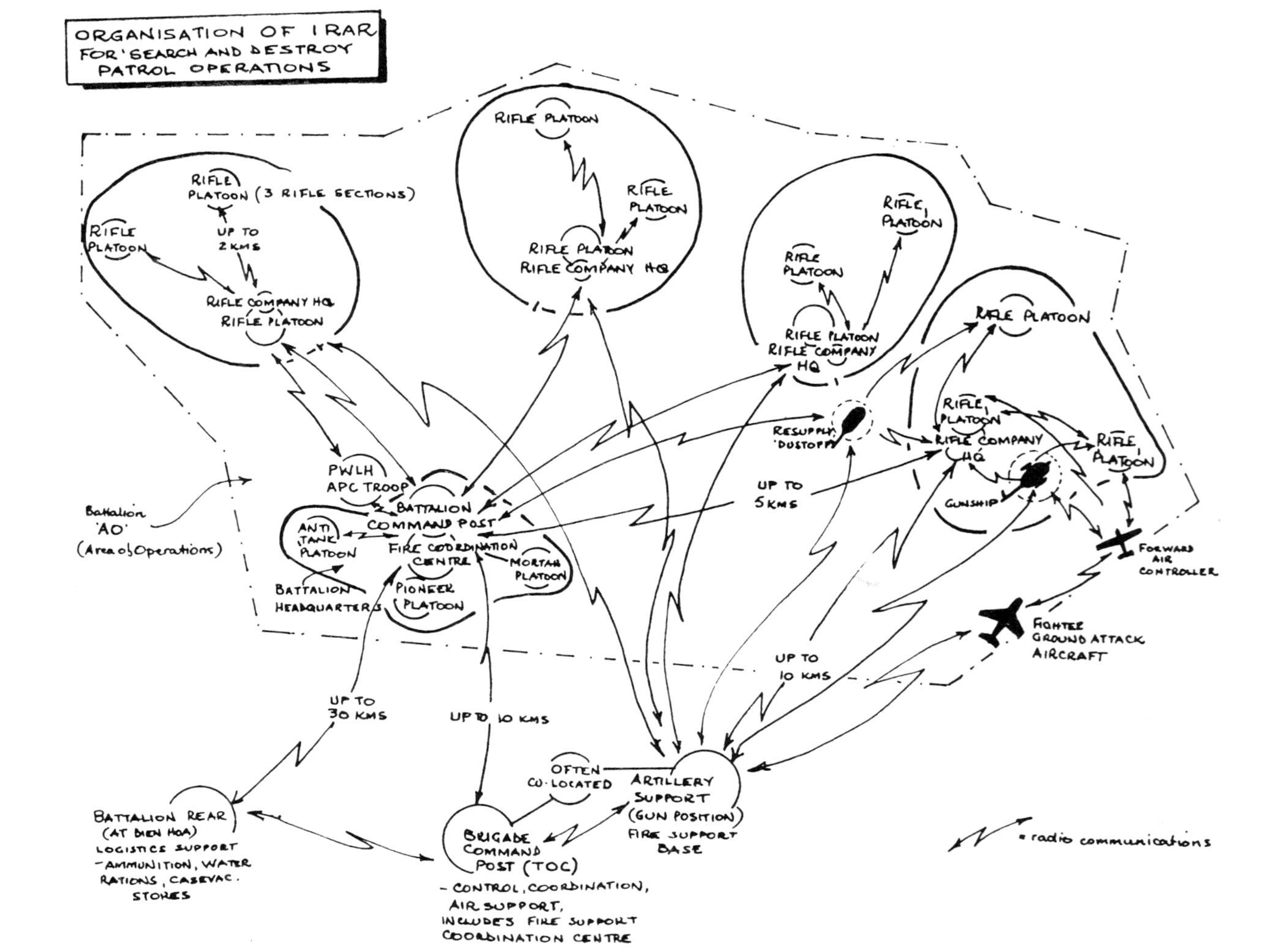

ORGANISATION OF 1 RAR
FOR 'SEARCH AND DESTROY'
PATROL OPERATIONS

RIFLE PLATOON (3 RIFLE SECTIONS)
RIFLE PLATOON
UP TO 2 KMS
RIFLE COMPANY HQ
RIFLE PLATOON
RIFLE PLATOON
RIFLE PLATOON
RIFLE PLATOON
RIFLE COMPANY HQ
RIFLE PLATOON
RIFLE PLATOON
RIFLE PLATOON
RIFLE COMPANY HQ
RIFLE PLATOON
RIFLE PLATOON
RIFLE PLATOON
RIFLE COMPANY HQ
RIFLE PLATOON
RESUPPLY 'DUSTOFF'
UP TO 5 KMS
GUNSHIP
FORWARD AIR CONTROLLER
FIGHTER GROUND ATTACK AIRCRAFT
PWLH APC TROOP
BATTALION COMMAND POST
ANTI TANK PLATOON
FIRE COORDINATION CENTRE
MORTAR PLATOON
PIONEER PLATOON
BATTALION HEADQUARTERS
Battalion 'AO' (Area of Operations)
UP TO 30 KMS
UP TO 10 KMS
UP TO 10 KMS
OFTEN CO-LOCATED
ARTILLERY SUPPORT (GUN POSITION) FIRE SUPPORT BASE
BATTALION REAR (AT BIEN HOA) LOGISTICS SUPPORT - AMMUNITION, WATER RATIONS, CASEVAC. STORES
BRIGADE COMMAND POST (TOC)
- CONTROL, COORDINATION, AIR SUPPORT, INCLUDES FIRE SUPPORT COORDINATION CENTRE
= radio communications

The Paratroopers lined up next morning in two battalion-sized hunting parties. All companies with their platoons forward were along a broad and, as far as the terrain allowed, continuous front. A Paratrooper looking right and left would have seen long lines of men eagerly awaiting the order to advance.[30] The Diggers lined up in platoon-sized hunting parties separated by several hundred metres ready to operate within their own designated patrolling areas. Each platoon had orders to comb its area carefully before moving on to its next designated area. A Digger looking right and left would have seen only members of his section. (A section is equivalent to a 7-10 man US squad.)

Viet Cong commanders had a good idea where the Paratroopers were and had dug in several ambush positions in anticipation of the US commanders using tracks and roads in the area. At the same time they did not know exactly where the Australians were because they were dispersed and did not use tracks unless it was absolutely necessary.

One US company commander recalled:

> I had difficulty locating flanking Australian units when I had been told to link up with them so there would be no accidental clashes and our advance could be co-ordinated. I remember heading out in their direction on the first day and meeting a few riflemen, one of whom stated, while pointing, that his company headquarters was 'Just over there'. I sighted a few other riflemen along the way but must have gone about three hundred yards [275 metres] before I found company headquarters. Now that's an outfit that likes being dispersed.[31]

Poor weather prevented the program of airstrikes which had been planned to precede the Brigade's advance. However, artillery batteries 'softened up' suspected enemy locations as the infantrymen stepped off. The first substantial contact with the Viet Cong was made by Company B of the 2/503rd, known throughout the Brigade as the 'Bulls'. Their tactics typified their nickname. On being fired on by a well-dug-in Viet Cong company the Bulls charged and, after an hour-long fire fight, overran the fortifications for a loss of five killed and eight wounded.[32] The Paratroopers had proved to be too determined, producing too much firepower at close quarters for the Viet Cong who had the tactical initiative taken from them, and were forced to abandon prepared fortifications.

Soon after the Company B contact, Company C also struck a well-dug-in force of Viet Cong. Once again 'up-the-guts' tactics were employed successfully and the enemy were routed from their fortifications. There had been two companies of enemy each dressed in khaki uniforms and deep blue scarves. The opposition was coming from the VC Main Force Phu Loi Battalion. They had set up a number of fortified positions astride the main advance routes. Significantly, the Viet Cong had withdrawn in

The Paratroopers charged into Viet Cong ambushes and shot their way out in July 1965. They were prepared to pay the price in casualties to kill large numbers of the enemy.

good order but had suffered heavy casualties. Many bodies and wounded enemy soldiers had been evacuated during the withdrawal. The US company commanders were confident that many more Viet Cong had been killed and wounded. There was an understandable optimism about how many had been killed and wounded as platoon commanders extolled the courage of their men in their first major fire fight with the Viet Cong.

As B and C Companies exulted in victory, Company A advanced into a carefully sited 'L' shaped ambush. Once again there were enemy wearing blue scarves, dressed in khaki. The commander of the Phu Loi Battalion was about to have his revenge. Also deployed was a company of Main Force Regulars dressed in greens, webbing and steel helmets. Seconds after the ambush was sprung with a murderous weight of fire, Lieutenant Bouldin exhorted his men to get on their feet and charge the enemy. They did this and ten men were cut down immediately; 'up-the-guts' tactics were expensive in ambushes. What this company may have lacked in tactical adroitness they made up for in courage. Once again the Viet Cong could not withstand the firepower and aggression generated by the Paratroopers at close quarters. The Americans literally shot their way out of the ambush and inflicted heavy casualties. However, six Paratroopers lay dead and 31 had been wounded; a quarter of the company were casualties.

The Diggers had a quiet day. The Viet Cong appeared to have ignored them in favour of laying in wait for the Paratroopers. The next morning Second Lieutenant Jim Bourke's platoon patrolled back onto a small camp they had discovered the day before which had shown signs of recent occupation. As a machine gun in Bourke's platoon opened fire, Private Ken Dalton shouted to Alan Ramsay, a journalist who was accompanying Delta Company, 'That's our blokes getting into them. I hope they got the bastards. All the company is after now is a good kill.'[33] Dalton had expressed succinctly the psychology of the Diggers on patrol that day. Success for infantrymen was, and still is, measured finally in terms of a good 'kill'.

Three Viet Cong soldiers had walked up a track while the platoon was taking a ten-minute break. They were observed by machine gunner, Private Bruno Jaudzemis, who killed one instantly at a range of 15 metres; another was wounded and the third crawled forward and dragged his wounded companion away.[34] Five weeks after arrival in Vietnam, Bourke's platoon had recorded the first 'kill' for the Battalion. This small scale success was to be typical of many actions fought by the Australians against the Viet Cong for the next twelve months. Most contacts with the enemy were accidental and characterised by brief but intense exchanges of fire. The initiative would go to the commander who could react first. Often the actions of the section commanders and their men in the first few seconds decided the outcome of the fire fight. Success was dependent on who saw who first, and who was first to engage with accurate fire.

One such contact was fought by Second Lieutenant Peter Sibree's platoon later the same day. Sibree had celebrated his twenty-first birthday just before the Battalion's deployment to Vietnam. He was younger than most men in his platoon but was supported by experienced NCOs. These NCOs carried on the traditions of their previous Platoon Sergeant, Kevin Wheatley, known around the Royal Australian Regiment as 'The Dasher'. He had told the platoon, 'Someday you will have to do it real hard and real dirty.'[35] Accordingly, the platoon trained hard and did not wash in the field. Their nickname was 'The Scungees' which alluded to their filthy, smelly condition after periods in the field. Later that year, Wheatley, as a member of the AATTV, was to 'do it real hard', sacrificing his life trying to save a wounded comrade—an action which was recognised with the award of the Victoria Cross (posthumously).

On HMAS *Sydney* the platoon had been 'adopted' by a journalist named Pat Burgess. Burgess had persuaded his employers at the Sydney *Sun-Herald* to allow him to report the war through the experiences of 32 men in one infantry platoon. Sibree's company commander, Major Ian McFarlane, had reservations about a platoon having a journalist accompany them on operations. He was concerned that this might be dangerous

ORGANISATION OF A RIFLE COMPANY ON OPERATIONS
at just under full strength

RIFLE PLATOON

RIFLE SECTION
Section Commander · Corporal · SLR
Scouts
Rifleman · M16
Rifleman · M16
Rifle Group
Rifleman · M203
Rifleman · SLR

Gun Group
Section 2IC · Lance Corporal · SLR
GPMG No.1 · M60
GPMG No.2 · SLR

Voice Communication

RIFLE SECTION (similar to above)

RIFLE SECTION (similar to above)

PLATOON HEADQUARTERS
PLATOON COMMANDER · LT/2LT · M16
SIGNALLER · M16 · PRC 25
ORDERLY · SLR
PLATOON SERGEANT · SLR
STRETCHER BEARER · HP 35

Voice Communication

radio communication

RIFLE PLATOON
Similar to Left

RIFLE PLATOON
Similar to Left

radio communication

Company Commander · Major · M16
Company Signaller · M16 · PRC 25
Rear Link Signaller · M16 · PRC 25
Company Sergeant Major · SLR
Interpreter · M16
Orderly · SLR
Medical Orderly · HP 35

COMPANY HEADQUARTERS

Forward Observer · Artillery Lt · M16
Signaller · M16 · PRC 25

Mortar Fire Controller · Sergeant · M16 · PRC 25

Support Section
Section Commander · Corporal · SLR
Rifleman · M16 · M72
Rifleman · M16 · M72
Rifleman · SLR

radio communication

separation of many kilometres

Artillery Gun or Mortar positions

FIRE CO-ORDINATION CENTRE

BATTALION COMMAND POST

radio communication

IN BASE (BIEN HOA OR FIRE SUPPORT BASE)
Company Second-in-Command (Captain) · SLR
Company Quartermaster Sergeant · SLR
Administrative Clerk · Cpl · SLR
Cooks · Sergeant and four cooks · SLRs
Driver · (with Transport Platoon) · SLR
Storeman · SLR

KEY
SLR · Selfloading Rifle · 7·62mm 20 rd magazine
M16 · 5·56mm Carbine/Rifle · 20 rd magazine · replaced Owen Machine Carbine
M60 · General Purpose Machine Gun · 7·62mm · Belt Fed
GL · M203 40mm Grenade Launcher · breech-loaded
M72 · Light Anti-tank/'Anti-bunker' rocket Launcher
HP · 35 · Browning 9mm Automatic Pistol
PRC 25 · Short range backpack radio transmitter/receiver
→ Radio communication
--→ Voice communication
Rifle company fighting strength would vary greatly even during combat operations, this is explained in the text.

for the platoon which depended on camouflage and concealment to find and surprise the Viet Cong, and for Burgess who was not trained to operate as a soldier in the field. His fears were partly allayed when Burgess participated in all of Sibree's platoon's training and became proficient in the use of personal weapons and first aid. Soon Burgess' skills in first aid were to be fully tested.

On the afternoon of 7 July Sibree's men were patrolling in a single line though thick jungle. A small overgrown track was the only means of penetrating the clumps of bamboo, vines and dense foliage. 'We moved out a little wary and maybe just a little off guard. The Viet Cong crept in close before opening up,' one eyewitness told journalist Don Peterson later. 'Munday got his real quick but he sat down and kept slamming magazines into his Owen Gun and firing back at them.' Lance Corporal David Munday, Second-in-Command of Corporal Terry Loftus' section, was a quiet but determined NCO who platoon members often sought for advice on personal as well as military matters. He was now seriously wounded and fighting for his life.

' . . . one leg is all but severed and an arm lies spouting and slack at his side' was Burgess' description of Munday after he was hit. 'Then he is up again on one knee cocking his weapon by holding the stock between his thighs. One handed he fires . . . ' Munday called out to his men as he fired, 'They're over here! They're over here!' His voice attracted the attention of the Viet Cong who had begun bringing down fire on the platoon. As a small group rushed forward to finish Munday off, one soldier had his head severed by a withering burst of machine gun fire from Private Trevor Adams and three others fell wounded. Munday sagged forward and lost consciousness.

Private Errol Weatherall, one of Munday's riflemen, had also been caught in the first burst of fire. '. . . a single round has broken his jaw, cut through his throat, passed through his shoulder and out the back of his pack. Weatherall is fully conscious. He is moaning, his legs contract and shoot out in spasms, from the pain.' Burgess crawled over to Weatherall, took his head on his shoulder and lay with him trying to stop the bleeding.

Loftus' section had been the last in the line of march. A contact to the front of a patrolling platoon would usually enable a platoon commander who is positioned forward to gain quick information on the enemy's location and manoeuvre his men forward and to a flank to engage the enemy. Sibree's had been attacked in the rear. The initial confusion gave way to the battle drills of a well-trained platoon. Loftus directed his men's fire and the Viet Cong were held back. Sibree gathered up the other section and attempted to get around to the flank of the enemy. This was impossible due to the thick undergrowth. He decided to conduct a frontal

Sergeant Kevin Wheatley on the left with Korean War cap pictured with Lance Corporal David Munday in the centre and Private Stan Wade on the right, all of B Company 1 RAR in Papua New Guinea in July 1964. Wheatley received the Victoria Cross (posthumously) trying to save the life of a comrade in November 1965. Munday had a leg amputated after it was shattered by a Viet Cong bullet in July of the same year.

attack. He knew the lives of Munday and Weatherall hung in the balance.

By this time Loftus had dragged the headless body of the Viet Cong killed by Adams and thrown it in front of Burgess and Weatherall as protection from the incoming fire. Loftus was a big man, 108 kilograms (17 stone) and an ex-merchant seaman—he had lifted the body like a rag doll, dragged it and flung it down in one continuous motion. Burgess, who had already used several shell dressings to staunch the gush of Weatherall's blood, pulled the deep blue scarf of the Phu Loi Battalion from the Viet Cong's waist and applied it to Weatherall's neck.

All around there was yelling, firing and cursing as Sibree's men tore through the undergrowth and attacked headlong into the Viet Cong who broke and fled, leaving three wounded. There were also a number of

From left to right: *Private Jock Bennett, Corporal Terry Loftus, Second Lieutenant Peter Sibree, Corporal Merv Kirby (holding gun) and Private Dave Haines. Sibree had just turned 21 years when his leadership was tested in combat in July 1965.*

blood trails indicating that others had been hit. Aggressiveness at close quarters had paid off, but not without an element of good luck. Sitting around after the attack, Privates Ross Mangano, Tony Brennan and John Priestly counted several bullet holes in their webbing. Priestly had most to be thankful for as he inspected the remnants of his ammunition pouch. A bullet had hit it, drilled a hole through two magazines full of bullets and set several of them off. He had only suffered superficial powder burns.

The evacuation of Munday and Weatherall exposed a serious weakness in the medical policy at the time. Platoon medics were not permitted to carry morphine. Therefore, these two men waited for aero-medical evacuation in agony. Each could only be administered Panadol tablets for the pain. Compounding the problem was the ineffectiveness of the platoon radios which did not have enough range. Fortunately, very professional radio relay procedures by the Battalion's signallers offset this inadequacy and there was no significant delay.

Pat Burgess flew out with Munday and Weatherall. 'The alloy floor of the chopper is slippery as ice,' wrote Burgess later.

Now you [I] know why the side gunner stares straight ahead. From the floor it isn't his first dustoff by a long way. He's probably been doing it all afternoon, with the Airborne. The floor of the chopper is slippery not only with blood but with shit and a yellow substance and on the seats are thick slicks of new blood, some of it dark, some of it brilliant red.

Munday and Weatherall were evacuated to Terendak in Malaysia the next day where British surgeons were able to save Dave Munday's arm. His left leg had to be amputated the night before. Later he was awarded the Military Medal for his courage in continuing to return fire and direct the fire of others after sustaining such serious wounds. He and Weatherall were to serve in the Army for another twenty years. Weatherall returned to Vietnam with 8 RAR and was Mentioned-in-Despatches for bravery displayed on 21 December 1969.

The actions of Pat Burgess not only did credit to him but to his profession as a journalist. He took the personal risks involved to tell the public what it was like on operations. He produced eyewitness narratives and not the sanitised accounts typical of military after action reports and press releases. Burgess formed close bonds with the men of Sibree's platoon as he told their story and was a friend to the Battalion.

There were other journalists who would stereotype US and Australian infantrymen as destructive killers, and take only ghoulish interest in the suffering they endured on operations. Two of Burgess' Australian colleagues were banned from the Australian camp for periods of time because of their unethical behaviour. One of them had ordered his cameraman to continue photographing the aftermath of the grenade accident in June long after the pictures would have been useful for publication. The efforts to gain close up shots of seriously wounded soldiers after being told to leave them alone was considered to be indecent and unnecessary. Captain Ron Ducie had to eventually rip the camera out of one photographer's hands and throw it in the mud to stop him taking close up shots of Private Billy Carroll's corpse.[36]

Since the start of the operation, snipers had been harassing each company. Late on the first day they hit their marks. Private Doug Hardman was wounded in the face by a bullet which caused a compound fracture of his jaw. Because of the risk of his tongue rolling back down his throat and choking him, Hardman had to remain in the sitting position cupping his hand under his chin to hold his jaw in place and leaning forward at the same time, allowing his tongue to remain forward.

Two days later, Private Billy Nalder of Jim Bourke's Platoon, a nineteen year old from Fairfield, Sydney, died after being shot through the chest by a sniper. His wounds were compounded because the sniper had used a dum-dum bullet which disintegrated on impact.[37] He was the Battalion's first battle fatality. The Viet Cong had evened the score with Bourke. Though they wanted to, Nalder's family could not afford to have his body flown back to Australia for burial. Once again Sydney businessman Mr Ron Wiggins donated the money, and Nalder was buried at Rookwood Cemetery, Sydney. Two thousand people attended the funeral at St Andrew's Cathedral.[38]

After a final day's uneventful patrolling, the Battalion was extracted by helicopter to Bien Hoa. The Brigade claimed over 56 Viet Cong had been killed by actual body count and 150 more were presumed dead. A further 200 were assumed to have been wounded. The Paratroopers had suffered ten killed and 36 wounded.[39] They had paid a bigger price than the Australians, but their methods had resulted in a bigger 'kill'.

The death of Private Nalder and the wounding of Lance Corporal Munday and Privates Weatherall and Hardman intensified the Battalion's desire to get back into the jungle and inflict casualties on the enemy. 'Just drop us in the jungle for a couple of months and let us live with them', one NCO told reporters. 'This is what we are trained for and it's better than marching around for a few days at a time, getting picked off one by one.'[40]

On 10 July, the Minister for the Army, Dr James Forbes, visited the Battalion. Lieutenant Colonel 'Lou' Brumfield drew the Minister's attention to the inadequacy of the clothing, footwear and equipment on issue to the Battalion. He ripped a shirt, already tattered from the operation, into pieces in front of the Minister to illustrate his point. The Australian war correspondents reported this incident and there was extensive publicity in Australia. In addition, Brumfield told the Minister of the delays in mail which were affecting the morale of his soldiers and their families.[41] Quite unfairly Brumfield was reprimanded for his actions and many felt his subsequent career suffered because of it. The truth of the matter was that Brumfield had made his representations to the Minister in private but reporters had found out later what had been done.[42]

During operations, the clothing of the soldiers had been reduced to rags by the thorny, dense jungle and constant saturation. The aging World War II TS boots with heavy metal studs by 1965 were not suitable for tropical conditions. Their prolonged storage resulted in them falling apart after a few days patrolling in the wet conditions. The Minister, who had served as an officer during World War II, promised to rectify these problems. A fitting comment on this situation was made later by Sergeant John Dean, 'No words will ever be able to describe how Lou Brumfield fought for his boys. I am sure that outspokenness marked him out as a trouble maker and affected his later career. He was a first class CO and we loved him.'[43]

One thing Brumfield was not able to get for his boys in those first weeks was beer. Since the arrival of the Brigade in Vietnam, 'Butch' Williamson had directed that there was to be no alcohol consumed in the Brigade area. He stated that, 'Beer and bullets don't mix.' This had been true on 4 June 1965 when a US Signals Sergeant shot an enlisted man in the legs after an argument: both were drunk.[44] Of equal concern was the security of the airbase. Williamson was not going to allow alcohol in the area until he was satisfied that there would be no surprise attacks, and the enemy were cleared out of the approaches to the Brigade position.[45]

The Diggers had dubbed the period where no alcohol was permitted as 'The Prohibition' after the Prohibition era in the US in the 1920s. Like the real Prohibition period, 'The Prohibition' at Bien Hoa was character-ised by illegal shipments of alcohol. The other commodity which was bought in bulk was ice purchased from Bien Hoa Airbase service clubs. 'There was not a fire trench in the Battalion that wasn't at least partly converted into a private 'esky' [an 'esky' is a portable container of ice used to keep drinks cool]. None of us usually went without our beer.'[46]

Several illegal shipments of beer were intercepted. One such inter-ception involved Second Lieutenant Jim Bourke. Bourke was a mischiev-ous, rough diamond who frequently got into trouble with his superiors because of his high-spirited, non-regimental behaviour. However, on operations he was one of the best combat platoon commanders in the Battalion. One evening he staggered out of the Bien Hoa Airbase's Officer's Club. His inebriated condition was not an offence because he was on leave, but the cases of beer he bought for his men and now sat on breached the conditions of 'The Prohibition'. In a typically assertive manner, Bourke stopped the first US jeep that was passing by and de-manded to be taken to Delta Company 1 RAR. He climbed in and struck up a rambling conversation with a silver-haired US officer in the back seat. Instead of dropping Bourke at Delta Company, the jeep pulled up at Battalion Headquarters, the driver honked the horn, and, when Captain Ron Ducie had been summoned, Bourke was handed over to him. The silver-haired US officer was 'Butch' Williamson. Bourke was not to taste beer for a month as the Battalion's Duty Officer.[47]

Williamson recalled later:

The no-beer rule hit the Aussies particularly hard, but they
complied without complaint. Somewhile later the Minister of
War of Australia [sic] came up to visit his forces. We had a long
conversation in which he repeated several times that they were
satisfied with my being their commander. [However] he told me that

they would like to have their beer. I showed the Minister a memo that I had written that morning stating that it was safe enough in the rear base camp to now have beer. I then informed the Minister that I would delay putting out the memo for three days so he could go back and inform his troops that he may have been successful in convincing me that they should have their beer.[48]

During the period 9 July–7 August 1965, the Battalion conducted patrolling operations in their area of responsibility and that of the 2/503rd, who were absent on a search and destroy operation in Phuoc Tuy Province. For five days the Paratroopers, with infantry from the newly arrived 18 Brigade of the US 1st Infantry Division, wreaked havoc with the major supply/staging areas of the Viet Cong. On 29 July there had been a massive bombing raid by B52s. The Viet Cong commanders in Phuoc Tuy Province had their first taste of US firepower and the aggression of the infantrymen from the Division known as the 'Big Red One'.

The requirement for continued concentration and a maintenance of high standards of soldiering was reinforced during local patrolling. On 12 July, Private Graham Haupt was seriously wounded in both legs from a booby trap during a Tactical Area of Responsibility (TAOR) patrol. Two days later Privates Ron Riley and Bill Blaikie were wounded in the legs by similar booby traps. All were evacuated to Australia. For Graham Haupt, nineteen years old from Bellinbopinni near Kempsey, New South Wales, there was added joy on his arrival home. His wife Margaret, also nineteen years old, had given birth to a healthy baby boy just six hours before.[49]

On 16 July, the New Zealand Gun Battery arrived with its four 105 millimetre L5 Pack howitzers and came under the operation control of the Brigade. They were in time to support 1 RAR's sweep of sector J of their TAOR on 17 July. Major Don Kenning and his Kiwi Gunners were welcome additions to the 1 RAR Group. The small Italian pack howitzers were easily transportable. Later Kenning and Captain Bob Hill worked out a way to pack one of these guns into an APC. Unfortunately, the trade off for this mobility, lightness and compactness was 1000 metres less range than the heavier and sturdier US 105 millimetre howitzers.

The Kiwi Gun Battery (161st Field Battery, Royal New Zealand Artillery) had been raised originally for service in Borneo to support Malaysia against the Indonesians during President Sukarno's confrontation with the newly formed federation. It consisted of 89 men, a seventeen-man logistics detachment and a pool of thirteen reinforcements.[50] The New Zealand Prime Minister's announcement on 27 May 1965 of the commitment of the Battery to Vietnam had resulted in hurried preparations. Similar to the 1 RAR situation, the Battery was reorganised under a new commander just a few weeks before deployment. Major Don

Brigadier General 'Butch' Williamson on the right greets Bombadier Ron Mackay of the 161 Field Battery RNZA on the arrival of the Kiwis at Bien Hoa Airbase on 16 July 1965. The arrival marked the renewal of the ANZAC tradition and the formation of an ANZUS brigade.

Kenning, who had graduated from Australia's Royal Military College in 1950, took command of the battery on 2 June 1965, just six days after the announcement. He had six weeks to conduct final training and administration before starting operations with the 173rd in Vietnam.

By coincidence Kenning and Brumfield knew each other from days at Duntroon as staff cadets and having served together in the Commonwealth Division in Korea. The Kiwi Gun Battery's parent unit, 16th Field Regiment, had supported 1 RAR in Korea and both the Australians and New Zealanders were conscious of the renewal of ANZAC traditions and friendly rivalries.

Kenning's job was made more difficult because half the men in his battery were not trained gunners but volunteers from other corps in the New Zealand Army. The New Zealand Army's small Artillery corps was unable to meet the requirement to provide a fully manned gun battery to Vietnam as well as meet commitments to train its Territorial Army gunners and maintain other operational capabilities.

The Battery trained hard in the snow-covered hills near the School of Artillery at Waiouru. Their enthusiasm and spartan regime was typical of the preparation of Kiwi contingents about to represent their country overseas. Ignoring the change from sub-zero temperatures at Waiouru to the hot humid conditions of Bien Hoa, Don Kenning insisted on joining the Australians for the Battalion's operation in Sector J just 24 hours after the Battery's arrival.

On 9 July there was a critique of the last operation into War Zone D. Significant differences had emerged in the US and Australian methods of operation. Williamson and his US battalion commanders were satisfied with the progress that had been made:

> The toll we extracted from the enemy on this operation was fantastic. We killed fifty-six Viet Cong by body count and at least 150 more by estimation. Twenty-eight POWs were taken. Probably over 200 more were wounded. We destroyed well over 300 buildings, 100 tons of rice, numerous domestic animals and recovered literally a ton of documents plus thirty weapons and four radios. In short we literally tore up one of the Viet Cong's best battalion sized organizations and seriously damaged a staging area. Intelligence indicates that there was another battalion in the area that probably accounts for seeing so many companies in motion. It is quite possible that we did more damage than we estimate.[51]

On the other hand, Major John Essex-Clark expressed reservations about the Brigade's dependence on helicopters, 'partridge drive' tactics, use of tracks and ignorance about how to deal with tunnel complexes.

Essex-Clark was a big, bluff Rugby forward with dark eyebrows and a black moustache. Williamson described him later as, 'a tall, raw-boned individual who was one of the roughest, toughest men I have ever known. Everyone respected him and enjoyed his ability to tell stories.'[52] Essex-Clark had joined the Australian Regular Army in 1964 as a Captain having just completed the British Army's Staff College at Camberly. Although educated in Australia he had been a soldier and an officer in the Rhodesian Army and had seen operational service in the Congo (now Angola), Malawi, Zambia and in Malaya with the 17th Gurkha Division. 1 RAR was Essex-Clark's first Australian unit, and he had been promoted quickly and appointed as the Officer Commanding Support Company. He brought to the Battalion a wealth of experience in detailed operational planning. Brumfield used him as an operations officer responsible for the day-to-day running of 1 RAR's Command Post. In effect, John Essex-Clark was the Battalion's 'battle major'. While Brumfield had to orchestrate all aspects of the Battalion's operations, maintain contact with US and Australian higher headquarters, and plan for future battalion operations, Essex-Clark supervised the on-going operations of the Battalion, and became identified by the Americans as 1 RAR's S3 which corresponded to their own nomenclature for operations officer. In his characteristic forthright manner, John Essex-Clark addressed Williamson and the assembled senior officers of the Brigade at the critique:

> We found that resupply is too frequent, and the amount of choppers around give the enemy a regular picture of your position. Now this is unfortunate, but there must be some way of getting around it. We feel perhaps the answer is to carry more rations, and smaller loads. We have some new ideas for the carrying of water. We can also use streams where there are streams . . . While we are sweeping through, I think we are losing a bit of our kill factor, and we can get more if we stand there and wait them out . . . Another point, whenever we've been caught by him, we have been moving on tracks, this is the only time he's caught us. When we are moving through the scrub he has never caught us and we can pick him up, because he uses the scrub himself . . . I would like someone to make an assessment to what extent we lose the initiative by the excessive use of helicopters. By the use of them, the enemy can determine where you are and what strength you're in . . . Solving the tunnel problem is a must. We find that the Viet Cong move back into their camp areas as we move out. We attacked this village three times and three times we went back into the same village, and two times the VC had moved back. It is likely that the VC are moving, hiding and redeploying through the tunnels. CS gas may be the answer [CS gas is more commonly known as tear gas]. We tried smoking them out with green leaves and everything we had, but we must use something more objectionable.[53]

The debates on the tactics to be used against the Viet Cong were to continue for the next twelve months. Williamson had developed a very personal one-man style of leadership within the Brigade and was to find the confidence and frankness of Brumfield and Essex-Clark disconcerting and something that would not have been exercised by his US subordinates. However, he was satisfied with their performance and chose to respect their operating methods. Indeed, he acknowledged that the Australians employed better patrolling techniques, and had already sent some of his officers to learn them. Despite this acknowledgment, Williamson recalled later:

> The Aussies taught us a lot about small unit operations and we taught them quite a bit about co-ordination during large operations. Our job in those days was not to pussy-foot around the jungle hoping to bump into the Viet Cong. Our job was to get in there and bring him to battle—to keep him off balance, shown the ARVN what to do and clear areas for the build-up of other American units.[54]

Lieutenant Colonel George Dexter, Commanding Officer of the 2/503rd, recalled:

I can remember the Australians chattering away on the Brigade communications net about everything they saw and were doing. They were obviously combing their area meticulously noting and reporting on everything. This may have been alright for Malaya but was too detailed for Vietnam. I remember being angry at the time because A Company had walked into an ambush and suffered quite a few casualties, and I could not get onto the Brigade Headquarters because of the constant stream of Australian reports.[55]

The critique of the operation did not change the operating methods of the Americans or the Australians. Indeed, Williamson recommended the technique of reconnaissance by fire be employed more often. This involved units pouring fire into areas that we assessed as suspicious so the Viet Cong could be 'flushed out'. He was also mindful of keeping casualties at an acceptable level.

Slowly the austerity of the Bien Hoa defensive area began to be overcome with the planting of banana trees and palms. Rumours of leave to Hong Kong and Bangkok raised morale. Daily life was set to the background of artillery firing, hammering of helicopter rotor blades overhead, the comings and goings of the sinister black U2 spy planes, screeching of fighter aircraft and the frequent sightings of Viet Cong patrols on the northern banks of the Dong Nai River. All this did not stop the nightly screening of films. The films were well attended, viewed in the open air, and everyone brought their own seats. The only difficulty was that Bien Hoa Airbase operated 24 hours a day and aircraft maintenance was done at night. Many soldiers learned to lip read through the noisy interruptions to sound tracks during film screenings.

Journalist Graeme Connolly:

Life here is an amalgam—an altar set upon the bonnet of a jeep— towering black smoke from a napalm bomb strike on the Viet Cong not far away—brown bodies always carrying a loaded rifle even to meals—a dusty, pitted 'main street'—that's the way of life in the Australian camp at this sprawling powerful airbase . . . The sound of aircraft engines never stops and rarely an hour is undisturbed by American or New Zealand howitzers opening up on targets deep inside Viet Cong territory. At night, artillery screams overhead into the blackness.[56]

The short-term results of Dr Forbes' visit were to take the form of the arrival of a plane load of Australian gum and wattle trees, and the long overdue eighteen bags of mail. Australian newspapers were now only three to four days old. Twenty soldiers returned to Australia suffering from malaria and tropical skin diseases. News was also received that Dr Forbes had called for tenders from Australian manufacturers for the production of new calf-length General Purpose (GP) boots and new combat uniforms.

On 7 August the Brigade conducted another foray into War Zone D. The tactics of hammer and anvil were repeated: the Paratroopers and Diggers were to be used to push Viet Cong units south towards the 43rd ARVN Regiment. The area selected was in the vicinity of the operation conducted during the period 6–9 July 1965.[57]

This time US and Australian APCs and a Landing Craft Tank (LCT) were used to ferry the Battalion across the Dong Nai River. As the platoons were crammed into the LCT, which was like a rectangular floating biscuit box, several soldiers were reminded of the loading of sheep into cattle trucks. Soon there was the melodic sound of 'Baa-Baaaa' as the soldiers shuffled forward into the confined space. This caused some anxiety among the Vietnamese crew and an ARVN liaison officer. The consternation changed to positive alarm when the NCOs entered into the spirit of things and began yapping and barking like sheep dogs. The yelping and mournful bleating had all but the Australians thoroughly confused.[58]

Lou Brumfield had his own amusing incident that day. He had decided to travel in a US command and control APC during the deployment. The US vehicle, with its petrol engine, did not have the water-crossing capabilities of the Australian diesel-powered APCs. His decision to use this vehicle for the operation did not pay off. He was seen with a wry smile miming the actions of a man fishing off a boat as his vehicle slowly twirled its way downstream, caught by the current and out of control. He eventually rejoined the Battalion in an Australian APC.[59]

Once again Peter Sibree's platoon was first to make contact. While the platoon was deployed in a harbour, a machine gun picket, Private Jeff Porter, noticed three people approaching. He carried out the challenging procedure and the three Vietnamese, two men and a woman, stopped, obviously startled. One man quickly took a grenade from his clothing and threw it at Porter. The other opened fire with a concealed automatic weapon. Just before Porter rolled away to avoid the grenade, he squeezed off a burst from his machine gun, which killed two of the Viet Cong soldiers. He received shrapnel wounds up his left side, but they were minor and he was able to return to duty some days later.[60] Because one of the soldiers killed was a woman, Porter's actions were vilified in some sections of the Australian media. Both the Australian people and the Diggers of 1 RAR were slowly coming to terms with the realities of guerilla war in Vietnam.

On 8 August, all companies discovered large company and battalion-sized Viet Cong camps. Once again the Viet Cong had been able to evacuate their installations. Little surprise had been achieved because of the preparatory bombardment of landing zones for the Paratroopers airmobile assaults and the ferrying of the Australians across the river.

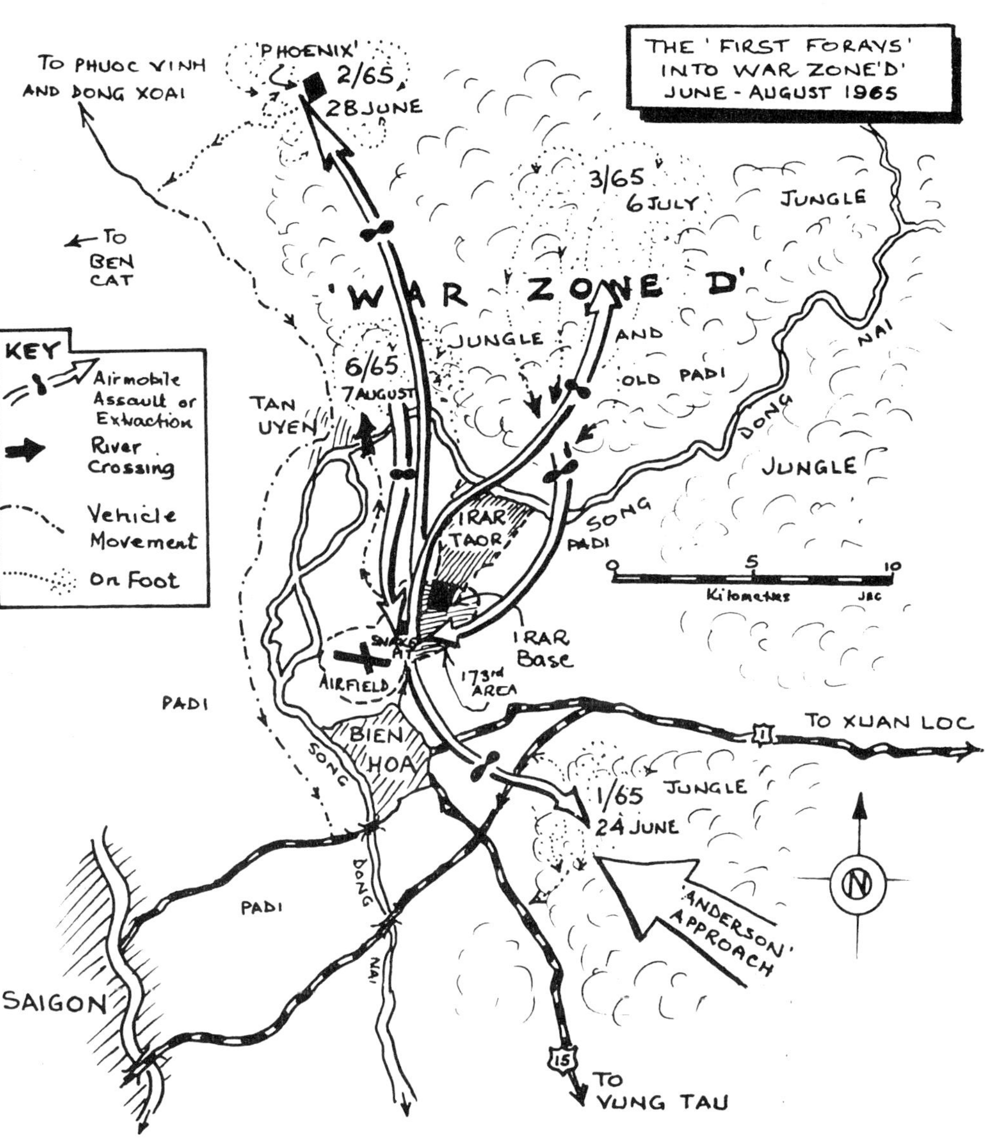

The 'First Forays' into War Zone D, June–August 1965

These were short, spoiling operations to cause maximum casualties to the Viet Cong and to destroy their base camps. After clearing Anderson's Approach to the south-east of Bien Hoa 24–26 June, the Brigade swept through areas of War Zone D 28–30 June, 6–9 July and 7–10 August 1965.

Despite this early warning, there was little doubt that the Viet Cong had prior knowledge of the operation.[61]

Quick decisive action by Australian platoon commanders and their section commanders continued to pay dividends. Second Lieutenant Graham Bolitho's platoon followed up quickly on a sniper attack and wounded two Viet Cong. The next day bold action by the same platoon resulted in a further three Viet Cong wounded. A forward scout, Private Bob Bailey, brought down all three with his Owen Machine Carbine but he was lucky to be alive. Even at close range the Owen did not have the velocity to kill instantly. For his action in successfully engaging the Viet Cong group at close range, Bailey was Mentioned-in-Despatches.[62]

On 9 August, Second Lieutenant Norm Brown's platoon was contacted by a squad of Viet Cong. This time the exchange of fire favoured the Viet Cong, who broke away unscathed leaving Corporal Graham Ferguson wounded in the head and his forward scout, Private L. A. Bakker, clutching a serious wound to his stomach. Frantic cutting of a landing zone by the other platoons of the company saved the lives of these men. Second Lieutenant Clive Williams wrote: 'My platoon carried them [Ferguson and Bakker] out to an LZ because they [Brown's platoon] were pretty shaken up, it's a hell of a shock when your friends get wounded. The funny thing was that they were travelling the same route as me five minutes behind me, maybe the VC heard my platoon and waited for them.'[63]

During the extraction of the Battalion by helicopter from the area the next day, all units left without incident except Second Lieutenant Bill Hindson's platoon. Hindson and his platoon headquarters watched in disbelief as the last helicopters departed without them. They were to spend some lonely minutes cursing their fate, before a gunship, sent to get them by their company commander, arrived to move them back to Bien Hoa. As the gunship circled, they were engaged by a squad of Viet Cong. As enemy rounds thudded into the tree trunks around them, Hindson and his men gratefully scrambled towards the helicopter, and lifted off. This was a 'hot' extraction.[64]

Once again the Brigade had penetrated into War Zone D and dominated an area for several days. Many Viet Cong camps and supply dumps had been destroyed. However no significant casualties had been inflicted. The enemy had decided to avoid contact. They had a new respect for the Paratroopers' aggression and firepower at close quarters.

During this last operation it had been announced that the 173rd had gone from temporary duty status to Permanent Change of Station. 'We must have over-sold ourselves. Our 60 days was extended to 90, then to 120 and then to a Permanent Change of Station' recalled Williamson. Back in Okinawa the families of the men of the 173rd were given seven days to decide on a location in the US they wished to be removed to. Mrs Margaret Williamson was a tower of strength during this period as she and a committee of wives assisted military authorities and the wives of the Paratroopers to move. Sixty days later all the families were clear of Okinawa. 'The US Army did a wonderful job of taking care of our families as they were evacuated back to the United States.'[65] However, there was despondency among families who had seen their husbands and fathers deployed for temporary duty to defend an airbase and now, without seeing them again, and after casualties had begun to increase from the conduct of offensive operations, were leaving for the US to wait out the months ahead.

On 11 August, 1 RAR was left behind with the Kiwi Gunners while the remainder of the Brigade was rushed to the Pleiku/Kontum area of the Central Highlands. A Viet Cong division had assembled in the area and a regiment was besieging a major US Special Forces camp at Duc Co. The siege was broken, and for 28 days the Brigade supported the withdrawal of badly mauled ARVN units and secured the area for the arrival of the US 1st Air Cavalry Division.[66] This counter-stroke by General Westmoreland had averted the long feared Viet Cong strategic coup of cutting South Vietnam in two by occupying the Central provinces. Like the typical sequence of events in a Hollywood western movie, the Paratroopers held out until the cavalry arrived.

In the early hours of 26 August, the Viet Cong mortared the Bien Hoa Airbase through the western sector of the perimeter. This sector was the responsibility of ARVN. The Australians looked on helplessly as 49 aircraft were destroyed or severely damaged 3 kilometres from their positions. Two Viet Cong regiments had been identified only 15 kilometres from the airbase and were probably responsible for the raid.[67] This attack resulted in a further increase in the tempo of patrolling. Already overextended by having to patrol the vacated US sectors, Australian patrols were required to sweep sectors which had hitherto been ARVN responsibilities. While 1 RAR were the custodians of the Bien Hoa Airbase, it was not mortared and Viet Cong activity was reduced to an unprecedented low.

In military terms, 173rd and 1 RAR had achieved much in the first three months after deployment. The Viet Cong had not penetrated their defensive areas. Patrolling had ensured that enemy mortars and artillery could not be deployed within their area of responsibility close enough to cause damage. Three successful forays had been conducted into War Zone D. These had been combined operations with the ARVN and must have done much to raise the latter's morale and take the initiative from the Viet Cong. The 173rd had been used three times to check Viet Cong initiatives in other areas of Vietnam. As Westmoreland's tactical 'fire brigade', the

Sky Soldiers had acted as a reserve for the Battle of Dong Xoai, destroyed supply areas in Phuoc Tuy Province and prevented the capture of the Central Highlands by the Viet Cong before the arrival of the 1st Air Cavalry Division.

However the Australians had failed to protect themselves against a traditional 'foe'. 'We [1 RAR] "borrowed" from the Americans and thought we were clever. When the Kiwis arrived they "borrowed" from us. There is no doubt that the thickest wire entanglement in Bien Hoa was between us and the 161st Battery after they arrived.'[68]

4 The Iron Triangle

The operations in the Iron Triangle were the first attempts by the Allies to destroy this Viet Cong stronghold. For the Paratroopers, Diggers and Kiwis of the 173rd the Iron Triangle would be remembered for death and mutilation from mines and booby traps, and the unreliability of their South Vietnamese allies.

The Iron Triangle had been described as 'a dagger pointed at Saigon'.[1] The northern side of the 'triangle' was an imaginary line between the towns of Ben Suc and Ben Cat. The western and eastern sides were the Saigon and Thi Tinh Rivers respectively. The southern junction of these two rivers was the apex, and the imaginary tip of the 'dagger' pointed down Route 14 to the heart of Saigon 30 kilometres further south. The area was a natural bastion made up of thick secondary jungle criss-crossed by tracks and overgrown unsurfaced roads. Along the Thi Tinh River were areas of impassable swamp.

The Iron Triangle had been given its name in 1963 by Associated Press journalist Peter Arnett, who noticed a similarity between the concentration of enemy in this area and the Communist Iron Triangle of the Korean War.[2] The area was the home of the VC 9th Division's 272nd Infantry Regiment, and was also believed to contain large supply, maintenance and medical facilities as well as the higher co-ordinating headquarters for Viet Cong operations in the Saigon area. Supporting the 272nd were several hundred Local Force guerillas based in the villages and hamlets of the area.[3]

The strategic significance of the Iron Triangle and the neighbouring Cu Chi and Ben Cat districts, which included the infamous Ho Bo Woods, was obvious. These areas straddled the main land and river routes into Saigon:

> During the war these [routes] were the supply routes from Cambodia, where the Ho Chi Minh Trail from North Vietnam ended . . .the Cu Chi District covered the only sizeable territory in South

Vietnam where troops and vehicles can move easily, even in the monsoon . . .The significance of this was not lost upon any of the warring parties and nations that engulfed Vietnam in conflict for 30 years, and the area was to be dotted with the military bases and headquarters of them all.[4]

For Westmoreland the Iron Triangle and its neighbouring districts had to be dominated if he was to ensure the security of Saigon. His plan was to ring the city with military bases from which operations would be launched to push Main Force Viet Cong formations further and further away from the South Vietnamese capital.[5] Eventually, the US 1st Infantry Division was to be located astride Routes 13 and 14 north of the Iron Triangle in bases at Tri Tam and Lai Khe, and the US 25th Infantry Division (Tropic Lightning) was located south west of the Iron Triangle astride Route 1 at Cu Chi.

On 14 September the 173rd was ordered to 'find, fix and destroy VC forces, supplies and equipment' in areas north and north west of the town of Ben Cat to disrupt plans for a concentration of Viet Cong formations.[6] This was to be a sustained effort to open Route 13 and prepare the way for the arrival of a brigade of the 1st Infantry Division. Later, on 8th October the 173rd would be ordered into the Iron Triangle itself to conduct search and destroy operations. This was also intended to keep the Viet Cong 'off balance' so the other brigades of the 'Big Red One' would have time to establish themselves without Viet Cong interference.[7]

The operations came as no surprise to the Viet Cong. Messengers had cycled throughout the area telling civilians that the Americans were coming and to refuse to be removed from their homes. Both US and South Vietnamese security had been loose.[8] Viet Cong units either moved from the operational areas or descended into the labyrinth of tunnels underneath the Iron Triangle and Ben Cat areas, and waited for the opportunity to strike. Throughout the areas small groups of guerillas laid mines and booby traps, and cleaned their sniper rifles.

Williamson deployed the Brigade into the Ben Cat area on 14 September by airmobile assault and road convoy. The move by road resulted in the first two fatalities for the Kiwi Gun Battery. A light truck towing a trailer full of artillery ammunition was blown up by a command-detonated mine which had been positioned under the road. Command detonation meant that the mine was connected to a cable which ran for several hundred metres allowing the Viet Cong to explode the mine using the cable from a distance. Sergeant Al Don and Bombadier 'Jock' White died from their wounds but two others had a miraculous escape. Lance Bombadier Ron Edwards and Mr Chris Turver, a New Zealand Press Association journalist, who were sitting on the boxes of ammunition in the trailer, sustained only minor injuries when they were thrown from the

Cartoon by Paul Rigby depicting the insecurity of US operational plans.

trailer by the force of the explosion. Fortunately none of the artillery ammunition exploded as a result of the mine detonation.[9]

1 RAR's mission was to secure a fire support base near LZ BUSTER. On arrival, Brumfield deployed each company to an assigned area and patrols were sent out soon after to clear the surrounding areas out to the range of Viet Cong mortars. The other Paratroopers shook out into large battalion-sized hunting parties and started to sweep their assigned areas. On the first day there was no contact with the enemy, just glimpses of individual guerillas and small groups withdrawing at long distances.

The next day the approach of Second Lieutenant John MacNamara's platoon towards a group of Viet Cong resting in a bomb crater was masked by a thunderstorm. The platoon's forward scout Private Graham Clarke took aim with his newly issued M16 rifle on automatic and fired a long burst from the hip which killed one Viet Cong instantly and wounded another. Clarke was now in the awkward position of having to reload his rifle while watching the seriously wounded Viet Cong soldier raise his MAS-29 bolt-action rifle and take aim. Behind him several other Viet Cong, who had been startled into retreat by Clarke's burst of fire, also raised their weapons and took aim.

As Clarke reached for a magazine, and the Viet Cong curled their fingers around the triggers of their weapons, two hollow 'chuung' sounds of a M79 grenade launcher were heard in rapid succession and two explosions near the Viet Cong caused them to continue their flight. The wounded Viet Cong fired but missed. He died a few moments later still trying to re-cock his rifle to have another shot at Clarke. The timely use of the grenade launcher by Private Geoff Williams had saved Clarke's life.

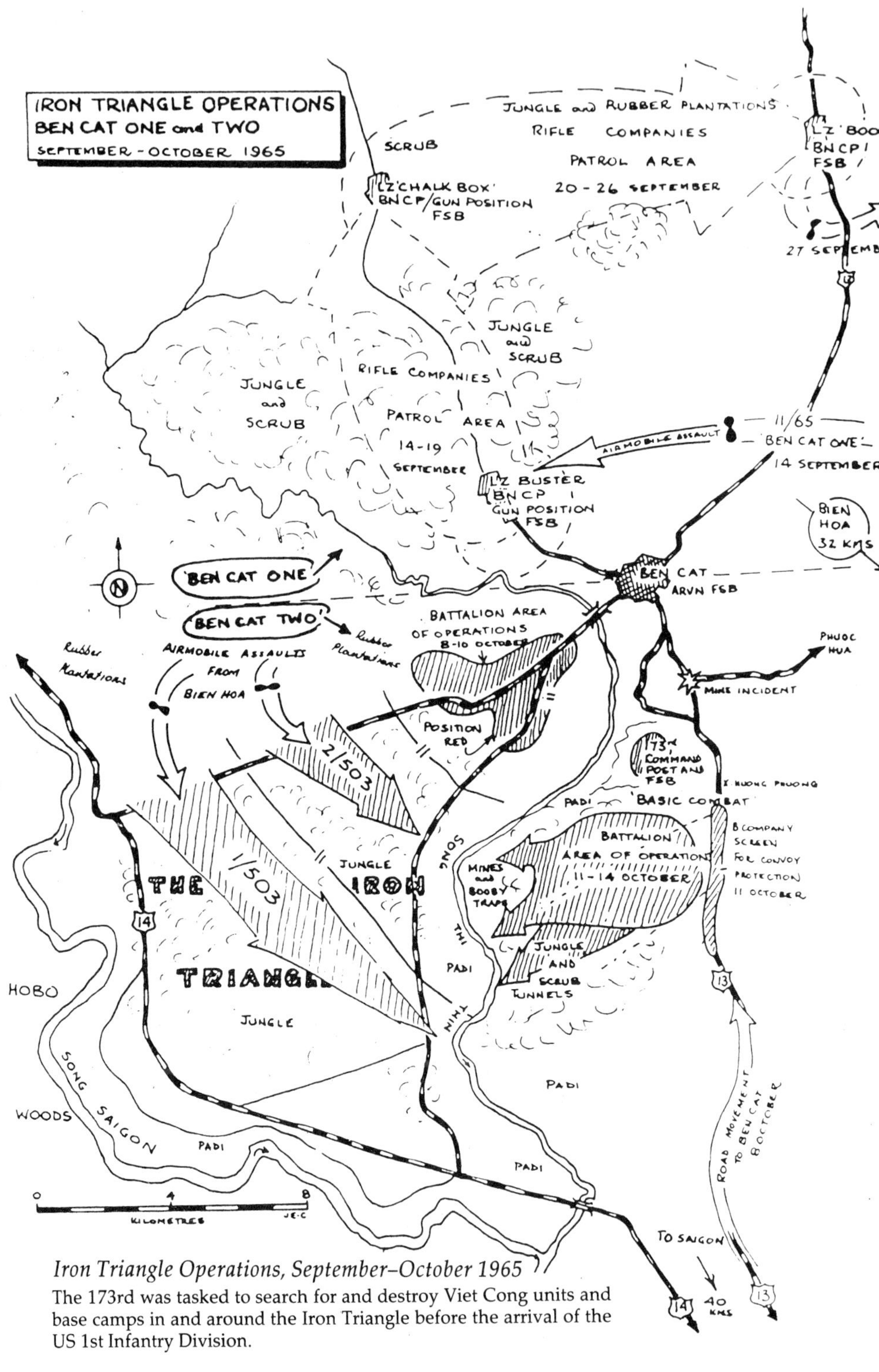

Iron Triangle Operations, September–October 1965
The 173rd was tasked to search for and destroy Viet Cong units and
base camps in and around the Iron Triangle before the arrival of the
US 1st Infantry Division.

Once again speed of reaction had decided this brief contest in favour of the Australians. For his actions that day, Williams was nicknamed 'Wack Wack' Williams by his section commander Corporal Brian Collett as a reminder of those two life-saving shots.[10]

The next day another young officer from Major Brian Harper's company received slight wounds having shot himself while receiving orders. Second Lieutenant Steve Lind was squatted under a hutchie out of the rain and as the butt of the weapon hit the ground, a round went off and gave him a painful flesh wound across the chest and under the arm. After this second incident, it became the standard procedure at the beginning of Delta Company orders for Harper to mockingly instruct Company Sergeant Major Ron Pincott: 'CSM—Disarm the platoon commanders!'[11]

For the next few days there were brief exchanges of fire between Australian patrols and the Viet Cong. The sweeps by the Paratroopers and Diggers were successful in destroying many Viet Cong camps and discovering caches of rice, military stores and equipment. However, the Viet Cong would not be brought to battle, refusing to be found, fixed and destroyed. 'It's frustrating trying to work on being offensive', a Paratrooper was quoted as saying at the time. 'The VC are past masters at not being fixed. They won't fight unless it is on their terms.'[12]

Company C of 1/503rd had found a Viet Cong communications school and destroyed several buildings and captured communications equipment. The haul included 62 brand new, Russian-made sniper rifles and 36 radio sets.[13]

The Commanding Officer of the 1/503rd, Lieutenant Colonel John Tyler, related:

> Shortly thereafter, they [Company C] were executing a stream crossing where the water was actually over the people's heads. They were actually using ropes and anything else they could use to get across. Right smack in the middle of this stream crossing Company C was hit and, as you might expect, some of these young tigers with two or three captured PRC 10 Sets [American-issue portable radios] strapped to their backs said, 'To hell with this jazz and into the creek the PRC 10's went.' The next morning they went back to the same area and low and behold in the same buildings which had been partially destroyed the day before, here were the missing communications equipment [the equipment jettisoned by the Paratroopers] all back upon the shelf, neatly cleaned and everything stacked up and ready for business again.[14]

Tyler did not talk of the results of Company C being fired on while crossing a deep stream. Unlike Lieutenant Colonel George Dexter of 2/503rd who described the strengths and weaknesses of the 2/503rd's conduct of each operation, Tyler summarised his attitude thus: 'I'm not

Lieutenant Colonel John Tyler, Commanding Officer of the 1/503rd Airborne Battalion, standing on the veranda of his quarters that were built for him by his men. Tyler was an aggressive commander who epitomised the motto 'Airborne—All the Way'.

about to tell you the things we did poorly, you can find that out from someone else, you won't find it out from me.'[15]

The Paratroopers had been taking a number of casualties from mines and booby traps since the start of the operation. The 2/503rd had fifteen troopers wounded seriously by booby traps by 20 September, and two killed and one wounded in exchanges of fire with the elusive Viet Cong.[16] The Brigade had not been subjected to so many booby traps before. There was little that could be done to counter these demoralising devices at the time except to avoid the wires which triggered them off.

The Australians' next battle fatality came when 25-year-old Corporal Frank Smith from Ouyen in Victoria was hit in the chest by a sniper on 21 September. 'I called for the dust-off [ambulance helicopter] straight away but it must have been on another job because it took 45 minutes', wrote Second Lieutenant Clive Williams after the operation. 'My Corporal died 32 minutes after he was hit. What a hell of a place to die, just a scrubby old bit of jungle.'[17] Standing in another scrubby old bit of jungle a few kilometres away watching for the enemy was Corporal Len Smith, Frank Smith's older brother, who would survive the remaining months of the tour. The death toll of brothers in 1 RAR had started—three to be killed and three to survive.

Peter Sibree's platoon was to see the deep blue scarf of the Phu Loi Battalion again on 20 September, but under less costly circumstances. A political commissar of that Viet Cong unit scurried down a track right into the midst of Sibree's men who had stopped for a meal. He was not shot because he was not armed. He had probably been using tunnels to move around and had come to the surface believing it to be safe to do so. The savagery of the war caught up with the commissar later when he committed suicide during interrogation by ARVN intelligence personnel at Bien Hoa.[18]

On 22 September Major Ian McFarlane's B Company discovered the vacated headquarters of the VC 272nd Main Force Regiment near Bau Bang village. After being pinned down by snipers and enemy machine gunners firing .50 and .30 Calibre weapons, Second Lieutenant Bill Hindson's platoon assaulted through the area suffering only one casualty, and causing none to the enemy who withdrew in good order. The reinforced-concrete bunkers were deserted and the underground complex of tunnels had been cleaned out. In the area were the remnants of the burnt-out APCs of an ARVN battalion that had sustained heavy casualties assaulting this headquarters area when it had been defended. In early 1966 elements from the 1st Infantry Division would be ambushed at Bau Bang and more APCs destroyed by Recoiless rifles and mines. Bill Hindson's men had assaulted on the right day at the right time—when the VC 272nd Regiment was not at home.

The unlucky casualty had been 20-year-old Private Ray Fraser from Broken Bay near Woy Woy in New South Wales. 'I didn't see the sniper', he told reporters. 'When I was shot I just lay down and sprayed the trees with my rifle. The rest of the boys opened up to protect me while I ran down the road. The leg was going crackle, crackle, snap, snap on the way.' Fraser had run 50 metres with a compound fracture of his leg below the knee.[19]

Corporal Lex McAulay wrote on 24 September:

> Our life is reduced to the bare essentials—Will it rain? What's the area like for today? When is the next resupply? What time am I on picket? The outside world just ceases to exist. The planes that fly over don't belong to us, BHQ [Battalion Headquarters] is a voice at the end of the radio. Viets fall into two categories—those carrying weapons and those not. The first type we shoot on sight—the second type . . . there's not much we can do about. The world, its affairs just doesn't worry us. We haven't got a clue what is going on. India and Pakistan? USA and USSR? Communist China and everyone? Not a word. The country is so beautiful, but there are always signs of war—destroyed houses and villages, bullet holes in everything, and there is hardly a building that has not been damaged or destroyed. The poor bloody Viets are trying to build a

decent country but the VC are destroying any progress as fast as they can. Bloody politics.[20]

As if to say farewell, the Viet Cong mortared the Battalion position on the last night of the operation causing loss of sleep but no casualties. Early on 27 September the Brigade began its return to Bien Hoa Airbase.[21]

Despite the absence of substantial contact with the enemy, the Brigade was satisfied with its efforts during two weeks of trudging around in almost endless rain and evil smelling thin grey mud. There had been widespread destruction of Viet Cong camps, installations and supplies. The mission to disrupt the Viet Cong's plans for a concentration of troops had been achieved. 'It may take a few months but if we keep hunting the Viet Cong by destroying his supplies, he will eventually be driven to hit back at us. That's what we are waiting for', Brumfield had told reporters in July.[22]

While the 173rd conducted their operations near Ben Cat without substantial contact with the enemy, the Viet Cong Main Force regiments were on the offensive elsewhere. On 25 September a brigade of the 101st Airborne Division repulsed a VC divisional attack north east of the new base of the 1st Air Cavalry Division at An Khe. Regimental attacks had occurred at the Phu Cu Pass 480 kilometres north of Saigon and in four separate areas 40 kilometres north west of the capital. The Viet Cong were attempting to further weaken the ARVN and disrupt the arrival of the 1st Air Cavalry Division.[23] Despite *New York Times'* Editor James Reston's assessment that the big Viet Cong units were dispersing and had decided to return to a long war of harassment, the trends showed that enemy units were consolidating and the North Vietnamese were preparing for a show-down in the Central Highlands with the 1st Air Cavalry Division.[24]

In the debrief which followed the first of the Ben Cat operations, the disruption caused to civilians by military operations concerned the senior officers in the Brigade. Lieutenant Colonel George Dexter stated after the operations:

> We did not expect to find the large numbers of civilians in this area, but there they were. Those people were dominated by the VC as there is no government up there at all and they have little choice but to co-operate with the VC. We came in for a few days, we injured and hurt some of them and took civic action, and went out there, and we tried to treat them, and passed out some goodies and so forth, but there is no doubt that as soon as we walked out, the VC moved back and continued to dominate them. This brings up the question—Why do we run an operation when we don't have a government to come in behind us? That is the question on the minds of all the troops.[25]

Williamson emphasised:

One word of caution. We do not burn villages. That is a terminology I would like never to hear again. We destroy VC camps that we find out in the jungle. These are where we know enemy soldiers live. We do not burn villages. Psychologically that is a very poor term, as far as we are concerned it runs counter to what we are trying to do with the local people. If it is an established village, leave it to the ARVN to make the decision whether it is to be destroyed or maintained.[26]

The role of the 7th ARVN Regiment which accompanied the Brigade on this operation was not clear. They had been assigned simple tasks of road clearance and checkpoint security but were not asked to conduct search and destroy operations. They did not constitute a restoration of South Vietnamese Government control in the Ben Cat area. Further, they did not provide permanent security for the people because they came and left with the Brigade. One would suppose that they were there to learn from the conduct of operations by the Brigade and eventually emulate the success of the Paratroopers and Diggers in sweeping through areas dominated by the Viet Cong. As the next operation into the Iron Triangle was to show, the 7th ARVN Regiment may well have had a more sinister role to play when on operations with the 173rd.

On 5 October the remainder of the US 1st Infantry Division landed at Vung Tau in Phuoc Tuy Province. Eleven thousand fully equipped infantrymen came ashore. As these men waited for their vehicles and stores to be offloaded, the 173rd's mission was to prepare the way for them in the Ben Cat area.

On 8 October the Brigade began the second phase of the Iron Triangle operations to clear the Ben Cat area and Route 13. This time the Paratroopers and the Diggers were to sweep into the Iron Triangle itself from the Thi Tinh River in the east to the Saigon River in the west. In so doing, Route 13 would be opened. The 2/503rd was then to seize the Lai Khe area. With Route 13 and Lai Khe in US hands, the 3rd Brigade of the 1st Infantry Division would move by road to set up an operational base for the Division at Lai Khe.[27]

At first light on 8 October, 1 RAR mounted in APCs, and with the US Gun Battalion towing their guns, set out for POSITION RED on the northern apex of the Iron Triangle, near Ben Cat, along Route 13 escorted by the Brigade's Armoured Company and Cavalry Troop. The Paratroopers were to follow and conduct airmobile assaults into LZ RED and LZ BLUE. By nightfall the Brigade's three battalions were to be lined up along the eastern boundary of the Triangle with 1 RAR in the north, 2/503rd in the centre and 1/503rd in the south.

Riding in the back of a US APC was Sergeant Alan Lightfoot, the Platoon Sergeant of Lieutenant John MacNamara's 8 Platoon in Charlie Company. In early September the previous commander, Second Lieutenant Bill Kaine, had transferred to support company. Lightfoot was known throughout the Battalion as a tough and aggressive character who played in the front row of the 1 RAR Rugby team.[28] He was a hard but fair NCO who maintained tight discipline over his men. However, his commitment to his men and his aggressive nature had caused him to punch his original Delta Company platoon commander after arrival at Bien Hoa. To strike an officer while on operational service was a court martial offence.[29]

Brumfield had had the dilemma of whether to 'throw the book' at Lightfoot which would result in discontent and lower morale within the Battalion, or separate Lightfoot from the command of this young officer and consider the matter closed. The latter course was taken and Lightfoot had been demoted to Corporal, moved to Charlie Company, and then re-promoted to Sergeant later.[30]

Lightfoot and MacNamara had co-operated with each other and their platoon had performed well in several brief skirmishes with small groups of Viet Cong. MacNamara was a handsome, dark-haired 21 year old from Hammondville in Sydney who had taken command of 8 Platoon soon after arrival at Bien Hoa. The grenade accident in June had shaken the morale of Charlie Company. It was some weeks after that incident before Major Jim Tattam would allow his men to carry M26 Grenades on operations again. On previous operations they had not been as successful as other companies in killing Viet Cong. Consequently, they had become known in the Battalion as 'The Hard Luck Charlies'. In the Iron Triangle luck was to desert them again.

As the long line of vehicles snaked their way along Route 13, Lightfoot's APC broke down, the driver pulled it over to the side, and the convoy moved on. Another APC dropped out to tow the stricken vehicle. Private Graham Schuts, a 19 year old from Rocky Gully in Western Australia, was perched near Lightfoot on top of the vehicle with his close mate Private Bill Jackson. They watched the surrounding trees for any sign of movement as their APC was linked to the other, and both vehicles gathered speed.

Suddenly there was a deafening explosion and Schuts and Jackson sensed themselves moving powerlessly through the air. 'I was thrown 30 to 40 yards [27 to 37 metres] from the vehicle and landed in three feet [90 centimetres] of paddy water', Schuts recalled later. 'The water and mud broke the fall. I remember lying there stunned—afraid to move because I felt instinctively that I must have busted something. As I became more alert, I realised that I was inhaling water and mud, and drowning. I rolled face up in great pain.'[31] Remarkably, Schuts was only bruised and the pain did not last for long—he was winded. His comrades were not so lucky.

A command-detonated mine had blown the engine clean out of the front of the APC, killing its US driver instantly, flipping it over, and trapping eight men inside. As gasoline dripped ominously from the ruptured fuel tank, Lightfoot, still in the overturned vehicle, called out to see if anyone else was alive: there was blood everywhere over a tangle of bodies, equipment and weapons. He was bleeding profusely from a head wound. Corporal 'Jock' McKillop lay unconscious, also bleeding from the head. Private Bobby Morton regained consciousness and began to moan: he had a compound fracture of the ankle. Slowly and painfully Lightfoot crawled out through the gaping hole where the engine had been and staggered down the road to get help which arrived a few minutes later.[32]

The US driver was the only fatality in this incident. Bill Jackson had also landed in a paddy field with shrapnel wounds to the chest. Another piece of shrapnel which would have killed him was embedded in the stock of his rifle. He had been carrying the weapon in the ready position across his chest.[33] Of the others, Privates Jeff Williams and Billy Allan had shrapnel wounds, and Lance Corporal Allan Nelson, Privates Allan Wilson and John Kerr were severely bruised. A short time after being pulled from the wreckage all involved went into deep shock, and to varying degrees none ever fully recovered from this incident.[34] One man had to be evacuated to Australia in a psychotic condition despite psychiatric treatment and the support and reassurance of the other victims.[35] There were now thirteen men left in John MacNamara's platoon.

As the Battalion moved west from Ben Cat, across the river and up the slope, against the clear blue sky could be seen fluttering bravely the yellow and red flag of the isolated Regional Forces' defence post. The South Vietnamese soldiers and their families lived there, able to observe the area, to see Ben Cat, but knew they could not count on help from there if they were attacked at night. These soldiers and their families were the unsung heroes of the war. At anytime, if the Viet Cong wanted to eliminate them, for whatever reason, the outpost could be obliterated. This beleaguered outpost was there before the Battalion arrived and would be there after it left—waiting.[36]

There were mixed reports on the attitude of the peasants to the return of the Brigade. 'The people are happy to see us', wrote Corporal Lex McAulay. 'We have received gifts of bread and bananas and cold drinks. The vendors of fruit and drinks did a roaring trade as the infantry waited atop the APCs, and bombs from the B52s raked back and forth across the jungle horizon.'[37] The Brigade's Civic Action officer reported:

> Villages along Highway 13 were hostile, and fire on helicopters came from them throughout the operation. Artillery and air was used against them and stopped 95% of the fire . . . In outlying areas of Ben Cat district it is considered unsafe for soldiers to purchase food and beverages. Reports received indicated some vendors might

be selling contaminated goods to the American troops in order to reduce the efficiency of the Brigade.[38]

That afternoon Major John Healy's and Major Brian Harper's companies took up the advance into the Iron Triangle. The forward platoons were soon engaged by 60 millimetre mortars, machine gun and rifle fire.[39] Despite the volume of fire, casualties were light. Lieutenant Bill Giles of Delta Company recalled a lucky escape after Private Graham Constable had been wounded by a grenade:

> As Platoon Headquarters was passing the prone Constable, the VC threw another grenade. Corporal Fred Morrison yelled 'Grenade!', and I will recall to my dying day watching that black ball arc across the sky. It all seemed to happen in slow motion. I recall thinking the ground is hard and clear, the shrapnel will spread and there is no cover. Therefore, my best bet is to lie down with my head away from the point of impact and to present the soles of my boots, which had steel inserts to the threat. Happily no one was injured. I have read since that in times of sudden danger, the brain is able to speed up the thought process such that things around you appear to move at half pace. It was certainly the case that day.[40]

As the Viet Cong withdrew behind volleys of machine gun and rifle fire in front of the Australians, the 1/503rd met solid opposition and lost seven killed and 24 wounded. However they caused heavy casualties to the enemy and pushed forward. Twenty-five Viet Cong bodies were counted and many more Viet Cong had been wounded.[41] The Paratroopers had swept forward on a broad front. Lieutenant Colonel George Dexter had all his companies forward and at least two of the three platoons in each company were also forward. Because of the thickness of the foliage, Dexter's battalion front was made up of fifteen parallel platoon and squad-sized columns. The Australians had fanned out and dispersed into company patrolling areas.[42]

That night all companies of the Battalion were probed by small groups of Viet Cong and subjected to grenade attacks.

Corporal Lex McAulay wrote:

> A rather interesting night while standing to [a time when Australian units hold their weapons ready, and listen and observe for enemy activity], three plus VC came tippy-toeing along. 7 Platoon MG [machine gun manned by Private Bill Hall] waited until they got close then chopped them. The first ten rounds chopped two, the next lot got one running away, and they put 200 rounds into the bloke. About an hour later their big brothers came back and threw grenades at us. So we had 50% stand to all night. After sweeping around this morning, we have 3 VC killed, 7 grenades and 1 US carbine (and a watch). No documents etc. One, the wounded one who died, was selling pineapples yesterday. Hope he had time to

spend his profits. So the old C Company now has 5 kills. They're coming good at last.[43]

While the Battalion was enduring this harassment, Major John Essex-Clark and the Intelligence Officer Captain Alan Thompson made a disturbing discovery. The attached US Radio Research Unit (RRU) had been monitoring Viet Cong and ARVN radio frequencies in the area and had deduced that Viet Cong operations against the Brigade were being co-ordinated by the 7th ARVN Regiment.[44] The RRU was a Corps level unit which, because major US formations had not arrived in the country yet, were attached to the battalions of the 173rd to gain experience. Radio interception or signals intelligence was, and still is, one of the most secret means of gathering information on the enemy. At the time, no-one spoke of the capabilities of these detachments. Members of the RRU were Americans trained as Vietnamese, Chinese or Russian linguists, used to find enemy radio frequencies, listen in, break codes if necessary, and deduce intelligence which would be useful in anticipating the enemy's intentions and assisting the planning of operations.

Brumfield had directed Essex-Clark to work closely with Thompson to make best use of the information provided by the RRU commander who had been nicknamed 'The Chicken Hawk' by RSM McKay after a character in the 'Fog Horn Leg Horn' series of cartoons because of the excited, eager way he acted and spoke. Thompson would receive the information from the RRU commander and, if it could be exploited, he passed it on to Essex-Clark in the Command Post.

In earlier operations Essex-Clark and Thompson had used information from the RRU to shell concentrations of enemy. One technique was to deduce enemy locations when the Viet Cong radio operators described the terrain around them. These descriptions, accumulated as clues, were plotted eventually on the map, and then the location was shelled speculatively. On several occasions the resultant excited chatter on the radio indicated that the shells had found their mark. On one occasion the operators moved to a location where they stated that a printing press had been destroyed. This location was plotted onto a map easily because an Australian patrol had given that location in an incident report when they had destroyed the printing press earlier. The position was shelled, the Viet Cong radio operator was silenced, and the headquarters and unit he was travelling with probably took casualties: the enemy command station called frantically for several minutes before giving up.

On the night of 8 October the RRU commander reported to Thompson that the radio nets of the 7th ARVN Regiment had stopped transmitting for 15 minutes, and then the same operators had come onto the air using different frequencies, callsigns and codewords. Further, the operators were talking about operations against the Australians and Americans. The

Viet Cong probing the perimeters of the rifle companies were probably being directed by radio operators who were ARVN by day and Viet Cong by night. This cast doubts on the loyalty of the commanders of the 7th ARVN Regiment.

Williamson was informed and it was likely that he told Westmoreland. 1 RAR Headquarters was moved 300 metres because of this new threat. In the early hours of the morning, the old position was subjected to small arms and mortar fire. In due course a reply was received from Williamson that action would be taken on the information, but for the time being, the Australians were to regard the 7th Regiment as allies, and the information from the RRU was to be kept secret. In short, the 7th ARVN Regiment was to be regarded as an ally by day and, if any of their soldiers reappeared at night as Viet Cong, they could be killed.

This ambiguous order did not please Essex-Clark at all. He ensured that the Battalion's patrol plan protected the flank shared with the 7th ARVN Regiment and stepped up the shelling of suspected enemy locations when they were deduced from RRU reports. Later the next day Lieutenant Colonel Tu, the Commanding Officer of 7th ARVN Regiment, complained bitterly that his headquarters had been shelled by the Australians. Essex-Clark denied these accusations and resolved to continue to bring fire to bear everytime he could substantiate that he was reacting to intercepts of Viet Cong radio nets.

As the next day dawned, most of the Australians expected stiff resistance from the Viet Cong to their advance through the Iron Triangle. This resistance was not forthcoming. However, the ever-present Viet Cong scouts seized on every opportunity to pick off the Diggers singly. Private Ron Field died instantly from a well-aimed shot fired at close range while on sentry duty.[45] Another sentry, Private Peter Riddett, was wounded in the back and buttocks by grenade fragments while turning to warn his platoon about enemy movement to his front.[46] The day passed with only brief glimpses of small groups of Viet Cong withdrawing in face of the patrolling companies.

On 9 October Lance Bombardier Ron Edwards, a Kiwi Gunner, was nicknamed 'Lucky Nine Lives' Edwards. On 14 September he had a miraculous escape when the truck towing the ammunition had been blown up and he had been thrown free. Several days later he received minor shrapnel wounds from a grenade thrown into a Viet Cong hut which bounced back after hitting the side of the hut entrance. On 9 October he was crouched on the front of a vehicle taking photographs of US engineers felling trees which were in the way of the trajectory of the rounds fired by the Kiwi guns. A piece of wood, thrown from one of the trees during its demolition, broke Edward's jaw. He remained with the Battery until 25 July 1966 when he was seriously injured in a vehicle accident. 'Lucky Nine Lives' Edwards returned to New Zealand after this accident and did not test his luck again.[47]

On 10 October there was still only light contact with the enemy. Second Lieutenant Clive Williams' platoon ambushed and killed one well-armed Main Force soldier and wounded another. Both had new Russian-made AK47 rifles.[48] Privates Peter Fagerlund and Ron Styles from Major Jim Tattam's company were wounded in the legs by booby traps. The device which wounded them was an improvised tin-can-type grenade connected to a trip-wire mechanism which had been stretched across a jungle track.[49]

On 11 October Major John Healy's company had the task of clearing an area in the vicinity of POSITION RED called BASIC COMBAT. He was directed to contact Lieutenant Colonel Tu who was to brief him on the new area. Healy brought Corporal Lex McAulay with him to act as interpreter. McAulay recalled later:

> 'We dismounted near the ARVN fort (high dirt bunds surrounding the camp) and the ARVN CO and his US adviser came to meet us.
>
> As interpreter I was not needed—the Viet spoke perfect English—I believe he was a graduate of several US schools and courses. I heard everything said and followed on my map what he said to Major Healy. He (the ARVN CO) indicated an area well out from his camp or fort and said in a proud and assured way it was secure, patrolled and controlled by his troops—'There is nothing there.' We shook out, moved, and the explosions began.[50]

Second Lieutenant Rick Culpitt initiated the first booby trap and suffered slight shrapnel wounds to the left foot.[51] He was lucky. Behind him others were not as fortunate.

Corporal Lex McAulay wrote of the incident:

> Someone yelled out 'Contact Front' and as normal we began to close up. I was alongside a Kiwi Arty bloke, Howard Dalton, Int [Intelligence] bloke, the ARVN policeman, and on the other side was an A Company cook. The first three turned off to go through a small gap in a line of branches. I kept going. Up the side. Loud bang and cries from the Kiwi, Howie and ARVN. Another booby trap. They got it in the legs, groin, stomach and chest. The Kiwi set it off. The other two, being bunched up, got it also.
>
> Can I explain the bloody feelings I experienced—we thought we'd bumped the VC and they were in the bushes; there were blokes on the other side of the bush—I couldn't fire or grenade, and I hoped they wouldn't either. Then the ARVN came running back and collapsed; I thought he was OK, then Howard came rolling back out of the bushes down into the creek, crying out—and I still did not know if there were VC or not. To run over and help would mean getting hit too, and the best way to help the wounded is to get rid of

> the VC first, then help them. It's no good trying to help under fire.
> Then everyone realized it was a booby trap. All happened in about
> two seconds. I dumped my gear and went to help Howie.
>
> Howie was in a pretty bad way—bleeding like no-one's business.
> [Warrant Officer] Jack Currie [CSM Support Company] started
> helping the ARVN. I went to Howie . . . Both Howie and the Kiwi
> had legs shattered, Howie went into shock. They [Dalton, the Kiwi
> Gunner, the ARVN policeman and Private Kevin Redford who was
> also wounded by the booby trap] were choppered out about 1830
> [6.30 p.m.]. Howie went straight to Saigon. He had turned an ugly
> shade of grey and I thought I would not be seeing him again. This
> morning I found out that he was OK. [After the incident I] put up a
> miserable hutchie, everything soaking, dug a shell scrape, ate some
> biscuits and cheese and tried to sleep. Couldn't for quite a while.
> Turned out the cook on the other side of me had been hit, but his
> gear took the force and all he had was broken skin, not even a drop
> of blood.[52]

At the US hospital the doctors had wanted to amputate Dalton's legs
but he was alert enough to protest and insist he would take the risks of
treatment and possible infection. He was treated, told that he would not
walk again, and probably not be able to father children because of wounds
to his groin. Twenty-three-year-old Dalton was too tough for such a
pessimistic prognosis. He became fully fit, served in Vietnam for a second
time, got married and fathered three children.[53]

Further south of POSITION RED, 'The Bulls' of the 2/503rd met the
Viet Cong once again head on in an ambush. The leading platoon commander had gone forward to find out from his point squad leader what he
had seen.

> He had no sooner arrived at the squad's position than numerous
> claymore mines, set off by the enemy, detonated simultaneously
> and raked the open area with flying metal. Booby-trapped 81mm
> mortar rounds exploded and heavy small arms fire poured into the
> platoon from the jungle wall. The first enemy blast killed five men,
> including the platoon sergeant and the platoon's aid man; eleven
> others were wounded including the platoon leader. The bodies of
> the wounded and dead lay completely isolated in the killing zone,
> making it virtual suicide for any one to attempt to help those still
> alive.
>
> The enemy continued to fire at the bodies in the road while the
> remaining men of 1st Squad—in a heroic gesture—stood up,
> opened fire and assaulted the enemy positions. But less than 30
> metres from the road, enemy soldiers in bunkers and trenches
> returned the fire, supported by compatriots in the numerous trees
> which bordered the road. The 1st Squad went to the ground but
> kept up its fire . . . The fighting was at extremely close quarters and
> even though friendly armed helicopters were in the air overhead

'DUST OFF!' Aero-medical evacuation saved many lives but was an all-too-frequent occurrence as the Paratroopers lived up to their motto of 'All the Way'.

and the platoon was within range of friendly artillery, the close distances prohibited the calling in of the available supporting fires.[54]

Private First Class James Wright was in the thick of this fighting:

> They were in the trees and they opened up with a .50 Cal machine gun which pinned us down. I was scared real bad. After we got organized, we could see that they had two .50 Cal and two .30 Cal guns on us. We killed some of them in the trees and then my platoon started after the gun bunkers. But they were on a hill and the firepower was too much for us. Four of our guys got it right there. The rest of us stalled. So then we regrouped and made another stab to get on line. About then I saw where one of the .30 Cals was positioned and I decided to rush it. I kept low and tried to make a small target but they zeroed in on me. Next thing I know they hit me in the face with two slugs. But I didn't black out. I knew what was going on. And the machine gun was still firing up there. So I kept moving towards it—threw a grenade and knocked it out. Our guys told me later that I killed five people.

Wright had lost two pints of blood, an undetermined number of teeth, some of his jaw bone and part of a lip. 'I ain't so bad off', he said later. 'We lost a dozen men back there and I'm alive and anyway they say plastic surgery ain't too bad now.'[55]

Eventually, the enemy withdrew when the Paratroopers were able to concentrate their fire and outflank the ambush position. Seventeen Viet

Cong bodies were found in the bunkers and trenches, with the likelihood of many more dead and wounded having been evacuated during the fire fight. Company B had lost eight men killed and 24 wounded.[56] True to their creed, the Sky Soldiers had not taken a backward step and, despite being outnumbered and exposed to the full weight of enemy fire, had driven the Viet Cong out of their prepared fortifications.

On 12 October booby traps continued to cause casualties among the Diggers. Similar to Major John Healy's A Company the day before, Major Ian McFarlane's B Company was tasked to clear the approaches to the new Battalion Headquarters position. The area had been the responsibility of the 7th ARVN Regiment. It was now Second Lieutenant Peter Sibree's platoon's turn to take casualties. Soon after setting out to clear the main track leading to the new Australian location, Privates John Thatcher and Jim Watts suffered multiple shrapnel wounds from a booby trap.[57] The point section was rotated and the Australians pushed on.

The lead scout of the forward section was Private Ross Mangano, a small, skinny, lively soldier with a ready, cheeky smile. He had been the lead scout for the past four months and had had a few close calls. Behind him strode Corporal Terry Loftus, a giant of a man who played front row in the Battalion's Rugby team. Loftus weighed 108 kilograms (17 stone) and Mangano 51 kilograms (8 stone). These two were close friends, and their contrasting physiques made Loftus look like a father following his young son. In the next few seconds Loftus' heroic concern for Mangano would give substance to this analogy. The booby trap blew them both off their feet. Mangano lay in a critical condition with one leg reduced to pulp and the other torn up by shrapnel. Despite his own leg wounds, Loftus crawled in agony to Mangano and administered life-saving first aid.[58]

Because of the proximity of Battalion Headquarters, an APC fitted out as an ambulance with Captain Peter Haslau and two medical assistants aboard arrived quickly. With them was Chaplain Gerry Cudmore who held Mangano's head in his hands during the agonising journey to the Headquarters landing zone for 'Dust Off'. As they travelled over the rough terrain, Loftus talked to Mangano reassuring him that things would be all right. Cudmore allowed his own anger at the mutilation of this young, friendly soldier to get the better of him. He told Mangano, 'Don't worry, Rossy, we'll get those bastards who did this to you. The Battalion will make the bastards pay.' Gerry Cudmore was to remember Mangano's reply for the rest of his life, 'Father, you should not be saying that. You are a priest.'[59]

McFarlane's men were very much in the mood to kill Viet Cong after these booby trap incidents. Second Lieutenant Bill Hindson's platoon had been sent north to follow up the blood trails of two Viet Cong who had been dragged off by their comrades from an earlier exchange of fire. As the point section advanced into a Viet Cong camp, a platoon of Viet Cong was sighted resting in the shade of several trees. Lance Corporal Sinclair, the forward section commander, and his forward scout, Private 'Blue' Waring, opened fire at close range and the Viet Cong scrambled for their weapons. Two enemy officers lay dead and several of their soldiers were seriously wounded.[60]

Surprised, the Viet Cong started to break and run. Several more were wounded by Sinclair's men. However, supporting enemy automatic fire forced Sinclair's men to take cover permitting the enemy to make a clean break. There were several heavy blood trails leading from the area. These blood trails were followed up without success. It is likely that the enemy disappeared down well-camouflaged tunnel entrances. Private Waring's personal courage and aggression in this action was acknowledged with the award of the Military Medal.[61]

While returning to the company position, Hindson's platoon contacted an enemy squad. The initial exchange of fire favoured the Viet Cong as forward scout Private R. K. MacLean fell with wounds to his stomach. Despite a quick platoon sweep, the Viet Cong withdrew unscathed. Ian McFarlane's company had sustained more casualties that day than on any other day of the year they were to spend in Vietnam. Initially, when Loftus and Mangano had been wounded, the booby traps had demoralised his men, but these feelings had been replaced with a fierce aggression. McFarlane was to change his tactics the next day to ensure his men did not fall victim to booby traps again.

Ian McFarlane was an aggressive officer who smoked a pipe and carried a shotgun as his personal weapon. By nature he was a lone wolf—very independent, self-confident and assertive with professional cunning to match the Viet Cong at their own game. He had trained his men using his own distinctive methods learned when he was in the Special Air Service and, like him, his men were fiercely independent, confident and kept to themselves. Pat Burgess had described McFarlane as 'a Duntroon stiff' when he first arrived in Bravo Company. He was partly right. McFarlane had an aloof, intense and serious leadership style. However, this intensity reflected a commitment to very high professional standards. He was hard on himself and his men. He had little time for those who, in his opinion, did not measure up. He would argue forcefully with Brumfield and Essex-Clark to ensure he was allowed to do things his way and his men always got a fair deal. Brumfield was to comment later, 'His value to me was that he loved his soldiers but would lead them wherever I sent him. McFarlane would drive his men and lead them harder than the others. B Company's efforts during the second operation in the Iron Triangle have never been fully recognized.'[62]

John Healy's A Company was the last to take casualties that day. The

'The Scungees'. From left to right: *Privates Trevor Adams, Ray Earea, Gunnas Ramma, Bob Cross, Dave Haines, and Boris O'Brien, Corporal Terry Loftus and Private Ross Mangano. Loftus and Mangano were blown up by the same booby trap. Loftus gave life-saving first aid but nothing was able to save Ross Mangano from losing one of his legs.*

now familiar explosion brought instinctive cries of 'Contact!', but Diggers now knew what the explosion meant. Lance Corporal Thomas 'Jock' Ross lay on the side of a track clutching his chest. Near him lay Private 'Blue' Unwin. The booby trap which had caused these gaping wounds was a 60 millimetre mortar shell encased in metal piping. Within the piping, nuts, bolts and ball bearings had been packed tightly to ensure maximum shrapnel effect. The Alpha Company medic, Private Les Tait, could do nothing for Ross who died of his wounds. Unwin was evacuated and survived.[63] Back in Australia Corporal Ross' fiancee, 21-year-old Beverly Lane, had recently made the last payment on a block of land she and Jock were buying before their marriage which had been planned for April 1966.[64]

An hour later Corporal Ray Seipel triggered off another booby trap wounding himself, Corporal Trevor Hagan and Private Charlie Marktelow. Marktelow was seriously wounded, and was evacuated eventually to Butterworth Airbase in Malaysia with other booby trap victims. Seipel and Hagan returned to duty several days later.[65] All rifle

Major Ian McFarlane on the right, Officer Commanding B Company, with his Company Second-in-Command, Captain Peter Arnison (holding a Viet Cong printing press). McFarlane had the answer for avoiding booby traps in the Iron Triangle. He bombarded the route ahead of his men with an artillery and mortar barrage.

companies in the Battalion had taken casualties from booby traps on 12 October. No-one who saw the shocking wounds suffered by these men ever forgot them.

That night morale was low. Brumfield had anticipated the feelings of his men and had ordered Major Peter Sharp to provide each man in the Battalion with a can of ice-cold beer. To Sharp's credit, this was done at short notice with the men of Administration Company going to extraordinary lengths to obtain the ice and containers to satisfy their Commanding Officer's request.[66] As they drank their beer, Corporal Lex McAulay was to comment in a letter the next day, 'The Yanks put on their usual show—blatting away, flares, artillery, until about 10 p.m. It was like Christmas or Cracker Night.'[67]

On 13 October the emotions throughout the Battalion were high:

> End of the op[eration] tomorrow. Thank God. We came off second best in casualties. Spent yesterday afternoon walking around the Battalion talking to people. Constant stream of casevacs [casualty evacuations]. Companies who were out to the North and West came in savage and blood thirsty—losing blokes to rotten booby traps, never coming to grips with the VC, who were constantly sniping. B Company dropped a bloke at 300 yards [274 metres] with an M60, through the head, and killed two VC carrying a BAR and .30 Calibre MG, coming in to shoot us up last night. A Coy caught two women

Lieutenant John MacNamara sitting on the edge of a fighting trench at 1 RAR's defensive position at Bien Hoa. Behind him is Charlie Company Headquarters. MacNamara was the unluckiest platoon commander in the Iron Triangle. He and eleven others were wounded by mines or booby traps.

> seen talking to 4 VC. The women and a disgusted, snarling A Coy (1 dead and 4 wounded) came in at last light.

Talking about one of his friends who had witnessed a booby trap incident, McAulay commented, 'Yesterday changed him a bit. There aren't many juveniles here now.'[68]

The Battalion's mission for the day was to move to the banks of the Thi Tinh River and cover the extraction of the 2/503rd by helicopter. Four helicopters had been shot down already over the area the Australians had to secure.[69] The Diggers knew there would be booby traps between them and the objective. However, they were keen to avenge those who had been killed and wounded by the booby traps. Any VC who dares confront this mob will be torn limb from limb', wrote McAulay. 'I said before that 1 RAR was not aggressive enough yet. Now they are.'[70]

'This morning I came back to C Company. Not much talking or anything. Everyone is serious. I don't think I was the only one with a dry mouth and butterflies,' recalled McAulay as the Battalion shook out and platoons went forward.[71] The first booby trap wounded forward scout Private Ron Brown in the groin and right shoulder. Near him lay his section commander Corporal Dave Jenkinson. They were both evacuated and survived. Major Jim Tattam pushed Lieutenant John MacNamara's remaining thirteen men from 8 Platoon through to take up the lead.

MacNamara recalled later:

We moved out of the harbour where most of the Battalion had stayed overnight. We passed through A Company—my platoon was in the lead. CSM A Company [Warrant Officer Jack Cramp] called 'Be careful—watch out for the mines and booby traps.' We pushed into deep scrub and crossed an over-grown path. An explosion and I have dim memories of a stretcher, an APC, a helicopter (and the cool air), another stretcher, the MASH at Bien Hoa and nothing for 24 hours. My war was over. 8 Platoon, strength nine, almost ceased to exist. . .the main blast was taken by myself and my signaller— from the rear. Our packs, water bottles and bum packs absorbed most of it, hitting us in the legs and arms. If we had left our big packs in the position it would have been a different story. An infantryman's best friend can sometimes be his webbing![72]

McAulay wrote later that morning:

We had not gone more than 100 yards [90 metres] when four of 8 Platoon got it. Two sections had gone over the booby trap when someone set it off. The Platoon commander, his sig and two scouts in the last section. And they were spread out. That's the worst of these bloody things. They can be anywhere and many people can miss them. Every step forward, back or to the sides is an effort and a decision. C Company already lost two this morning [Jenkinson and Brown]. So up until now they have lost 19. The OC [Jim Tattam] refused to use the track, came back and split what was left of 8 Platoon among the other platoons (they had 14 cas) and began to go around the men.[73]

Major Jim Tattam was a courteous, methodical officer known in the Battalion as 'Gentleman Jim'. He liked to gamble and his company used to run casino nights. He had worked hard to build the confidence of his soldiers after the grenade accident in June. He knew the odds were now stacked against his men. He did not want to gamble any more with their lives against the booby traps.

He told his men to stay where they were, and, taking his signaller, strode in the direction of Battalion Headquarters. He met Brumfield near the rear of his company. He told his Commanding Officer that any further advance would be playing into the hands of the Viet Cong who were causing casualties without any loss.[74] Brumfield changed the order of march and pushed John Healy's and Ian McFarlane's companies through on different routes to the western banks of the Thi Tinh River.

McFarlane had learnt from his experiences the day before and the fate of Jim Tattam's men that morning. He pre-planned and fired a rolling barrage of artillery and mortar fire ahead of his men.[75] This use of fire-power was expensive but probably saved lives. Further down the track they were using as an axis, McFarlane's men found some Viet Cong bodies near the camp where Hindson's men had engaged the Viet Cong platoon the day before. On them were ARVN enlistment papers.[76] It was likely they were members of the 7th ARVN Regiment who had been operating part-time as Viet Cong. Evidence was also gathered that many of the booby traps and mines in the area were of ARVN origin and had been set by these 'part-time' Viet Cong.[77]

McAulay wrote:

> Feeling is high against the useless ARVN. There is a Regiment [7th ARVN Regiment] 2000 yards [1800 metres] from here and they don't go out on ops. Sit around talking, drinking, making merry and the bloody young kids from Aussie and NZ (and US) have to go out into ARVN's sector, and get blown up. . .They [the Diggers] want to go down and round up the ARVN and herd them out here at gun point. The bastards! A lot of young Diggers have grown up a lot in the last 48 hours. I think I have too.
>
> . . .we moved out, as usual, in the hottest part of the day walking past the valiant ARVN sitting there drinking and swinging in hammocks. They [the ARVN soldiers] must have known, for not one came to scrounge cigarettes. C Company were pretty savage. As we were moving to the Bde HQ, the US 2/503 went out. We were itching to come across some opposition. But no VC farewell.[78]

The Viet Cong had planned to attack the Battalion the night before. Fortunately their radio transmissions had been intercepted by the RRU unit. The subsequent artillery bombardment of their forming up places, which had been deduced and plotted on the map, caused casualties and forced them to abandon their plans.[79] Ten bodies were found in the area later and there were numerous other blood trails.[80] One wonders how well the Viet Cong would have done in combat against the Diggers of 1 RAR who would have been forewarned and were in the mood to avenge their mates who had been killed and maimed by the booby traps.

In military terms, the Brigade had succeeded in its mission. The Viet Cong had been kept at bay while the 'Big Red One' settled into its new home. There had been many friendly verbal exchanges between the Diggers and the US infantrymen from the 1st Division as they rode up Route 13 in long convoys. The 173rd had awarded itself 106 Viet Cong killed, four wounded and 115 captured. However only five rifles, 200 rounds of ammunition and four hand grenades had been retrieved.[81] Brigade records noted that 90 per cent of the Brigade's casualties of nineteen killed and 110 wounded had come from mines and booby traps.[82] Williamson reported, 'Mines, booby traps, shells and claymores are low manpower intensive but effective defences.' On a more optimistic note he wrote, 'We can go, and stay anywhere and anytime in Vietnam where we choose. Further, the longer we stay, the firmer becomes the allegiances of the civilians to the government forces.'[83]

Corporal Lex McAulay, one of the two Vietnamese linguists serving with 1 RAR, sitting on the edge of his fire trench in the Iron Triangle. His letters to his wife during his time with 1 RAR give an insight into the soldier's view of the fighting in Vietnam.

Brigadier David Jackson, the senior Australian officer in Vietnam, was even more optimistic at the time. 'A situation has now been created in which the Ben Cat area and the Iron Triangle can be fully restored to Vietnamese Government control. In both of these operations, the Australians again proved they are well-trained, well-equipped, determined and tenacious.'[84]

McAulay wrote sadly:

> Back in the old Bien Hoa. Came back in the first lift at 0800 hrs. Had a shower, a shave, a haircut, 2 cans of coke. Now the reaction is setting in. Low spirits, don't care, it's an effort to do anything. Must soak the socks I wore, scrub my J Boots (stink!), clean the Armalite and .38 Smith and Wesson and grenades. We [1 RAR] had 2 dead and 36 wounded. 1 [dead] and 19 [wounded] in booby trap area. C Coy alone lost 19. God that area was bad. We should have stayed there and fought the VC to a stand still, but using our Australian tactics. God I feel down. It's the usual winding down feeling.[85]

Postscript

On 27 November 1965 the 7th ARVN Regiment was reported to have been wiped out in a battle with Viet Cong units in the Michelin Plantation north of the Iron Triangle. It was rumoured that the Regiment's US advisers had been killed and many soldiers had defected.[86]

On 8 January 1967, after discovering that the Iron Triangle was still operating as a major Viet Cong base and contained the headquarters which directed operations against the Saigon area, the US 1st and 25th Infantry Divisions reinforced with ARVN units re-entered the Iron Triangle for the largest scale search and destroy operation of the war to date.

The 6000 citizens of Ben Suc were evacuated and the town razed to the ground in a preliminary operation by the 1st/26th Battalion (the Blue Spaders) commanded by future US Secretary of State, Lieutenant Colonel Alexander Haig.[87]

The tactics of the hammer and anvil were used on an enormous scale. West of the Saigon River was General Weyand's 25th Division (Tropic Lightning) with the 196th Light Infantry Brigade. To the east along the line of the Thi Tinh River was General Dupuy's 1st Division and the 173rd. Because of the individual reinforcement system employed by the US Armed Forces, few members of the 173rd would have been to the Iron Triangle in October 1965. The Big Red One was the hammer and Tropic Lightning was the anvil.[88]

The differences between October 1965 and January 1967 were the attention paid to physically clearing the jungle and destroying tunnel systems. Bulldozers, Rome plows and tank dozers flattened large areas of jungle and created 80-metre-wide tracks through the jungle criss-crossing the entire area. The mission was to make the Iron Triangle unusable as a Viet Cong sanctuary. Tunnels were entered by specially trained soldiers known as 'tunnel rats' and demolished. Once again the Viet Cong defended through the setting of booby traps and mines. Seventy-two Americans were killed and 337 wounded. Viet Cong losses were calculated as 720 killed and 280 captured.[89] Because all civilians had been evacuated from the area, and villages and hamlets razed, the Iron Triangle was declared a Free Fire Zone. Once again, after causing heavy casualties, and destroying installations, tunnels and tonnes of weapons, equipment and food, the Americans left the Iron Triangle to the Viet Cong. Two weeks after this massive effort, large numbers of Viet Cong had returned to the Iron Triangle.[90] A year later it was the spring board for the Viet Cong–North Vietnamese operations against Saigon of the 1968 Tet Offensive.

5 The bloody hump

The commander of the Viet Cong 9th Division decided that the time had come for a test of strength with the 173rd. He deployed one of his crack regiments. Williamson's Operation HUMP took place at the six-month point of the 173rd's tour of duty and this test of strength with the Viet Cong proved bloody for both sides.

In line with Westmoreland's plan to use the 173rd to keep the Viet Cong off balance and conduct search and destroy operations in the enemy's home bases, an operation was planned to begin on 5 November 1965 near the junction of the Be and Dong Nai Rivers, 20 kilometres north east of the Bien Hoa Airbase. The communications and resupply routes between War Zones C and D met the Ho Chi Minh Trail in this area which had become a major staging point for Main Force formations and the flow of arms and supplies to the units based around Saigon and in the Mekong Delta. The area was also reported to contain hospitals and supply dumps.[1]

The start date of the operation marked the halfway point in the twelve-month tour of most of the members of the 173rd who had arrived in Vietnam on 5 May 1965. Williamson titled the operation HUMP to acknowledge this halfway point.[2] 'Reaching the Hump' was a term symbolising the completion of the hardest part of a journey and passing the halfway mark. This halfway point of the Brigade's tour of duty was to be a bloody one for the Paratroopers and the Diggers, and the next six months were to be harder than the first.

The operation proved to be a chronological and tactical turning point. Unlike previous operations where the Viet Cong had withdrawn in face of the aggression and firepower of the Brigade, the commander of the Viet Cong 9th Division had deployed one of his most experienced regiments, supported by Local Force battalions, for a test of strength.[3] With probable forewarning of the operation, the 271st Regiment waited for the Brigade, eager for a big 'kill'.

Since the completion of the operations near the Iron Triangle and another operation in War Zone D during the period 23 – 26 October, there were signs of stress among the Diggers. For example, the thoughts of Second Lieutenant Clive Williams at the time were:

This battalion I'm afraid is going rapidly downhill due to lack of leave and too many operations. At the moment we are spending two weeks out and one week in. The ops are always hard with much fighting, all with no tangible results. The Yanks are losing a lot of troops here. The official rate of kills is 5:1 in favour of us. Our Battalion's is about 3:1, but the other units in the Brigade have been taking heavy casualties. One has had all the officers in one company and a whole platoon killed. They withdrew through us, and they were a hell of a mess. There is no doubt that we are winning, but is it worth the cost? I sometimes wonder.[4]

McAulay wrote:

At present I am going through a stage that I think is pretty common. People who've been here less than 6 months or more than 18 have got it. Don't like Viets, don't like talking to them, don't like Vietnam. I have no patience with these bloody people who are caught in our TAOR. Other signs are short temper, my spelling is falling off, I shake when artillery fires, the smallest things irritate me and I feel like crying over the stupidest things. The blokes in the rifle companies are much worse. A C Coy fellow went to pieces two days ago—the mortars firing was the last straw. They have been at it 5 months without a break—out in the TAOR since June, come back in, go out on an op, 2 hours after we're back, there is someone out in the TAOR again. The fact that there are no kills in the TAOR does not lessen the strain. About 30 people went home a few days ago. So far we must have lost 100 people, who were unfit for the tropics. This is our Army's farsighted policy of siting our Army camps near Adelaide, Sydney and Melbourne, and doing S.E. Asian type ops in freezing weather and sometimes snow.[5]

In October an unnamed operation had been conducted in appalling heat. 'Usual Aust[ralian] Army—we hung around camp until 0930, rode up here and began walking across open paddy and low scrub in the heat of the day. Sweat streaming off us. When we Queenslanders start feeling sick from the heat, then I think it is hot enough . . . God it was hot. I really felt sick—even with salt.'[6] The tension had been high because of many short, sharp exchanges of fire with small groups of Viet Cong.

Some contacts met with success. 'Apparently we got a swag of VC in a C Coy contact', wrote McAulay on 2 November.

Bernie Le Seuer, CPL in 9 Pl, [Platoon] saw the VC and deployed his men in an immediate ambush, with MG in position to enfilade the VC. [To site a weapon in 'enfilade' means to enable it to fire into the flank of the enemy.] Bernie himself put a full magazine into a VC at

20 yards [18 metres], aiming from the shoulder. All they could hear from the killing ground were screams and cries. Found great pools of blood everywhere. The body they got was not the one Bernie shot. If he could run with a mag (20 rds) of Armalite in him, good on him.[7]

Le Seuer was to receive the Military Medal for this action. He had not only executed a successful ambush of a larger enemy force but also had exposed himself to enemy fire several times to engage the enemy and direct the fire of others.[8]

Other contacts had their humorous moments:

All that firing yesterday was 9 Pl [Platoon] C Coy, who saw ½ dozen people in greens [clothes] and floppy hats, who waved them on. The platoon waved back and moved up. Bang! The VC were trying to lure them into an ambush. Great amounts of ammo expended and no cas[ualties] on either side. First thing this morning, C Coy up and trailed them, caught them, killed 1 and wounded 3. Captured one weapon.[9]

This operation had served as a final shakedown for the newly arrived Australian Gun Battery. Late in September Australia's military contribution to the Second Indochina War had been increased with the provision of a field artillery battery, a troop of engineers, a light helicopter reconnaissance troop, a signals detachment and logistics personnel. All were placed under the operational control of the 173rd. Williamson commented at the time that the title of the 173rd should have changed from '173rd Airborne Brigade (Separate)' to '173rd Airborne Brigade (Accumulated)'.[10]

The deployment of 105 Field Battery, Royal Australian Artillery, to Vietnam had many parallels to that of 1 RAR. At short notice the Battery Commander, Major Peter Tedder, had been called in by his Commanding Officer, Lieutenant Colonel John Stevenson, and told that his battery had been selected to serve in Vietnam in about four weeks' time.

Tedder recalled later:

We didn't have time for training. There was just too much paperwork and administration to do to ensure the soldiers and equipment were ready. . .The rush of impending departure meant receiving innumerable shots in the arm or bum, having our teeth drilled, being totally re-equipped, painting everything green and making sure all the wives and loved ones were reconciled to the fact that we were not going to be around much longer.[11]

There was a high and sudden turnover of personnel, some for medical reasons but many more because Stevenson gave Tedder the best men in 4th Field Regiment. 'The battery I had been leading since January was not the battery I took to Vietnam', Tedder went on. 'John Stevenson and I had to cull the Battery of all those that, for some reason or other, could not be reasonably expected to serve overseas. I was forever grateful that John gave me a first-rate staff.'

Another appreciated legacy Stevenson left the Battery was an intense period of training in air mobility in the Battery's last field exercise at Casino in New South Wales. Stevenson must have known of the likelihood of deployment before Tedder and he emphasised quick deployment by air. Admittedly this training was not at the same level as the subsequent airmobile operations in Vietnam, but the Battery became experienced in separating and assembling their 105 millimetre L5 Howitzers into air-packages, as the B series Hueys could not lift the complete gun.

During these frantic weeks, the Gunners were not told their exact departure date but were given warning times. Operation TANTON was Top Secret and the date of embarkation was kept from everyone. As it turned out, the warning orders for three weeks' notice to move (codeword 'Tanton Yellow') and 24 hours' notice to move ('Tanton Red') were given through operational channels, but the date of embarkation was given out by a prostitute. She informed an acquaintance from the Battery that on a particular night she had serviced a sailor from HMAS *Sydney* who had demanded special attention because he was going to sail on 14 September for Vietnam—the Battery departed on that day after loading on 10 September.[12]

Like 1 RAR, the actual departure of the Australian Gun Battery was closely controlled, low profile and conducted very early in the morning in great secrecy. 'There is nothing to make you feel like cattle as to take part in a military embarkation', Tedder recalled later. 'My outstanding memory was the almost total silence of the Gunners as it finally sank in that we were off, and the memory of the widening gap between us and the wharf remains vividly in my mind to this day.'

Major Peter Tedder was an aloof and formal Duntroon officer with an intense dedication to excellence in gunnery. His manner contrasted markedly with the story-telling, gregarious Major Don Kenning of the Kiwi Gun Battery. However, the common denominator for both officers was their success in providing quick and accurate artillery support for 1 RAR. Brumfield had the problem of having two senior artillery advisers. To avoid conflict between the two Battery Commanders or confusion as to whose advice was final, he made the rule that on operations he would only take the advice of one gunner—usually Kenning, who was more senior.

The arrival of the Australian Gun Battery lowered the morale of the Kiwi Gunners. Some Battery members felt that 1 RAR would prefer the six-gun Australian Battery to their own four-gun battery which had to use its spare fifth gun to increase its firepower. Fortunately, Brumfield did not discard the close relationship he had developed with Don Kenning and the Kiwis were kept on in support of 1 RAR for several more months. Kenning made representations to his government for his Battery to be brought up to a full strength of six guns. The New Zealand Government, ever mindful of cost, did not reinforce the Battery until early in 1966 when it became clear that the Australian Government would not accept the Kiwi Gun Battery in support of the incoming 1st Australian Task Force until it was made up to its full complement of six guns.

Further sources of low morale in the Battery was the low pay received by the 19-year-old gunners and the policy that married members of the Battery would serve nine months in Vietnam and single members eighteen months. Also the L5 guns were becoming unserviceable at an unexpectedly fast rate due to the climate and dust wearing out important parts. Kenning had to order improvised procedures with charge bags, the care of sights and securing of sight mountings. This did not prevent the Battery celebrating Guy Fawkes Night by firing coloured smoke, illumination and white phosporous rounds into the sky above War Zone D. Some US units, ignorant of the significance of Guy Fawkes Night, asked Brigade Headquarters what was going on to be told that the Kiwis were celebrating some 'Guy' called 'Fox'.[13]

When the Australian Gunners arrived at Bien Hoa on 28 September, they were surprised to find themselves allocated to an area on the western perimeter of the Brigade's defensive position between the US Cavalry Troop and the 2/503rd. Australian tactical doctrine was that gun batteries were always sited in depth, with infantry units forward of them for protection. The Gunners' reaction to this unaccustomed exposure to the 'front line' was to surround themselves with an elaborate wire barrier—a double-triple stack of concertina barbed wire with a cattle fence and apron of wire on both sides, 82 metres long and 7 metres wide. This edifice was constructed under the supervision of the only man in the Battery who had any real experience in defences of this type, Warrant Officer 'Jesse' James, a veteran of the Korean War. The barrier was regarded with some amazement by the Paratroopers. One US officer was heard to remark how odd it was to allow the inmates of a Prisoner of War camp to carry weapons.[14]

Soon after arrival, the Battery's officers were welcomed formally by their counterparts in the 3/319th Artillery Battalion's Mess Tent. The operations officer welcomed the Australians and added, 'We're mighty pleased to have you Australians join us. We didn't know you were coming —if we had, we would have brought our cricket racquets with us.' There was a good laugh all round. However, this effort to seek common ground characterised the relationship between the US and Australian Gunners. The Australian Gun Battery quickly became a part of the Brigade's already substantial inventory of firepower.

Tedder recalled later:

Second Lieutenant Clive Williams (right) during orders with two of his section commanders, Corporals John Pearce (left) and Chris Webster. Williams' platoon saw action throughout 1965–1966 and killed more Viet Cong than any other platoon in 1 RAR. However, he saw several of his men killed and over half of them wounded in combat.

The amount of firepower available to the 173rd Airborne Brigade was truely awesome. It reflected a scale of military values and technology which Australian soldiers never had the opportunity to see or even imagine in times of peace. This firepower was illustrated in the operation in the Iron Triangle. . .I can recall standing with the Battalion Headquarters just outside the village of Ben Cat and observing the insertion of the American battalions. Behind me was a battery of 8 inch [203 mm] guns. Somewhere close by batteries of 105 mm guns were thumping away. To the north were the 107 mm [Self Propelled] mortars. Above us were successive layers of aircraft. From the bottom and across the low skyline you could see the little gnat-like figures of the Iroquois helicopters proceeding in clumps to and fro as they delivered the assaulting infantrymen. Immediately above the low skyline you could see this lone, little, silver 'Bird dog' aircraft where Forward Air Controllers indicated targets for a brace of ground attack aircraft laying down CBU (Cluster Bomb Units), napalm and the occasional stick of bombs, and way, way up in the sky were the B52s. What a sight! I realized there and then that this was no small war.[15]

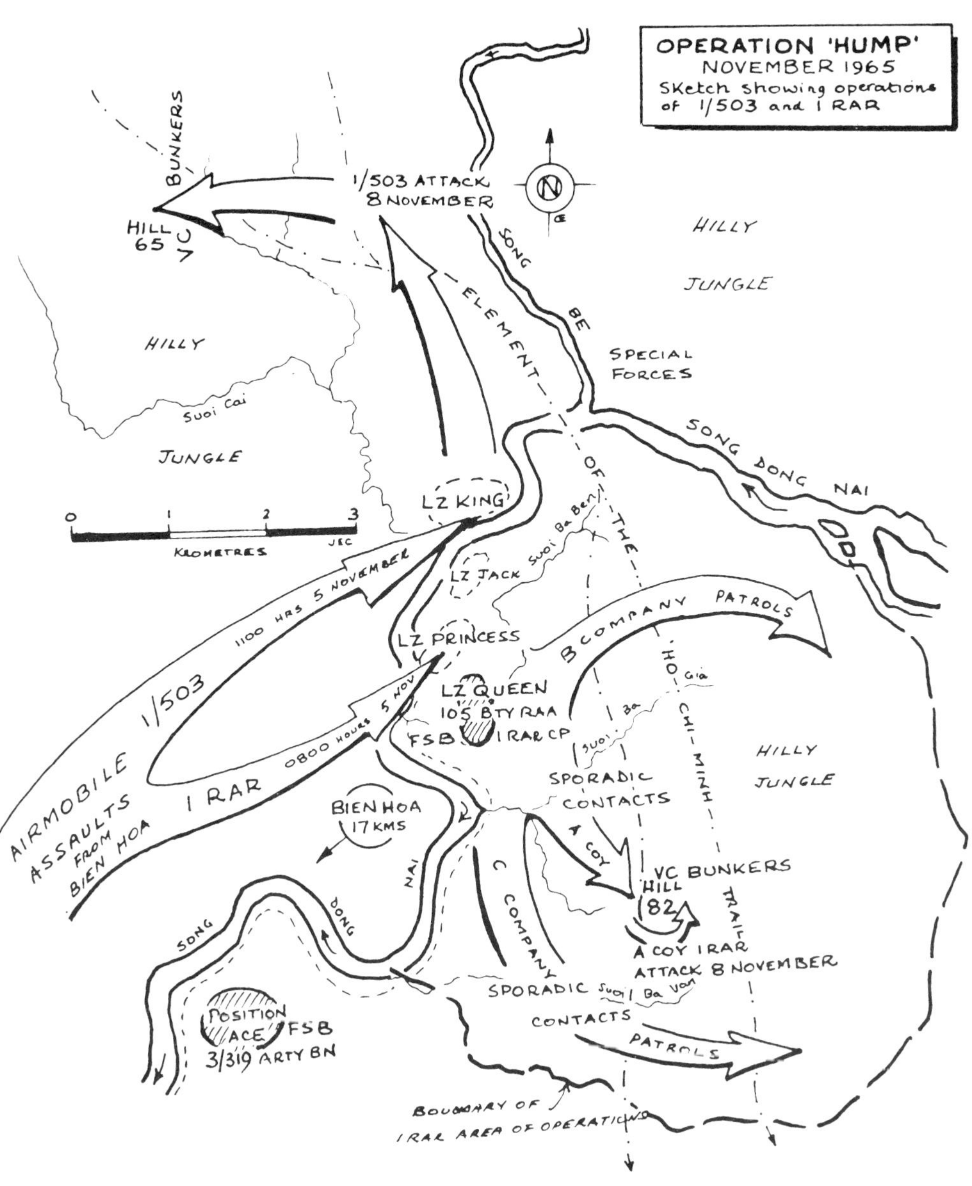

Operation HUMP—November 1965

On 5 November 1/503rd and 1RAR assaulted into a Viet Cong supply/staging area cloaked in thick jungle. On 8 November the Paratroopers found and assaulted a Viet Cong bunker system but were in turn attacked by a Viet Cong regiment. They survived, killing over 700 enemy with small arms, artillery and mortar fire. On the same day the Diggers assaulted a bunker system but were denied the chance to mount a battalion attack so one 1RAR could assist in the evacuation of over 200 American casualties.

Tedder was correct in his assessment of the scale and intensity of the war in October/November 1965. Time was running out for the North Vietnamese and the Viet Cong. The summer monsoon was nearly over. The central provinces of South Vietnam had not been captured, the US had begun a massive buildup of ground forces and morale in the ARVN was rising. Subsequent events were to show that higher North Vietnamese and Viet Cong commanders had decided to attack US formations already deployed in order to gain victories which might have sufficient political impact on the US public for them to regain the strategic initiative and still force the military and political collapse of South Vietnam. The semi-conventional war of the preceding ten months was now to become a conventional showdown between the North Vietnamese and the US 1st Air Cavalry Division in the Highlands, and the Viet Cong and the US 1st Infantry Division and the 173rd near Saigon.

On 19 October a siege started which was to set the scene for a set-piece battle between the regiments of the North Vietnamese 325th Division and the US 1st Air Cavalry Division. The isolated Civilian Irregular Defense Group Special Forces camp at Plei Me, 45 kilometres south west of Pleiku, was surrounded by the 32nd and 33rd North Vietnamese Regiments. Though having the strength to overrun the camp, the North Vietnamese waited to ambush relief forces. Initially, a battalion from the US Cavalry Division had been deployed from An Khe to Pleiku to allow a relief column of South Vietnamese to set out for Plei Me. However, after the inevitable ambush of this column, Major General Harry W. O. Kinnard, Commander of the US 1st Air Cavalry Division, requested and received permission from Westmoreland to assist the ambushed column. The Cavalrymen did this successfully, counting 120 North Vietnamese corpses on the battlefield. The relief column arrived at Plei Me to find that the North Vietnamese had disengaged.[16]

After establishing that the two North Vietnamese regiments had regrouped a short distance away in the Ia Drang Valley, Kinnard requested that his Cavalrymen be tasked to destroy them. On 27 October Westmoreland ordered Kinnard to find, fix and destroy the forces that had threatened Plei Me. Like the 173rd, the 1st Air Cavalry had been raised in 1963 as the 11th Air Assault Division to give the US Army more flexible, lighter scaled, mobile and hard-hitting military formations. As the Paratroopers and Diggers prepared for their test of strength with the Viet Cong 271st Regiment in the valley of the Song Be and the Song Dong Nai, the Cavalrymen, which included the lineal descendant's of General George Custer's 7th Cavalry, prepared for what was to be their test of strength with the North Vietnamese 325th Division in the Ia Drang Valley.

Williamson was not warned that he could enounter a Viet Cong regiment on his next operation. He left 2/503rd defending Bien Hoa

Airbase and only deployed 1/503rd and 1 RAR for Operation HUMP which began as planned on the morning of 5 November. The operation started with a close call for the Australians. Despite a lengthy preparation of LZ Queen before the arrival of Delta Company, now under the command of Captain Peter Rothwell, Viet Cong forces began engaging the helicopter gunships swooping over the landing zone which were providing last minute close fire support. Rothwell had seconds to decide whether to go into LZ Queen and risk being hit, or redirect the helicopters carrying his men to the alternate LZ PRINCESS which had not been 'softened up', and take a risk of there being no Viet Cong there. 'My greatest fear at the time was having a "slick" hit with my blokes in it, either crashing or burning', recalled Rothwell later. 'It would have been a bastard of a way to go.'[17]

Captain Peter Rothwell was one of a group of combat-hardened veterans who gave 'backbone' to the Royal Australian Regiment in the 1960s. After joining the Regular Army in 1952, he had served as a soldier and junior NCO in Korea. He was commissioned in 1961 after two operational tours of Malaya during the Malayan Emergency. 1 RAR was his 'home battalion' and infantry soldiering had been the focus of his life during his fifteen years in the Regiment. He was a swarthy, rugged-looking individual whose looks matched his pugnacious, blunt character.

Rothwell requested his helicopters be redirected into LZ PRINCESS. 'We were supposed to be on the LZ [LZ QUEEN] by 0800 hrs', wrote McAulay later that day.

> There was a delay—2 VC battalions were seen on the southern ridge which D Coy was to occupy. A nice mess they would have made of D Coy had they landed [at LZ QUEEN]. So the ridge was worked over and we used an alternative LZ. The assault took a circular course, flying at about 150 feet [46 metres]. Very exhilarating, contour flying. I was sitting on the outside. We raced low over towns, villages, farmers, trees, ARVN outposts, bridges etc. Then coming into the LZ someone opened up and everyone was firing. I saw a couple of smoke puffs but whether they were VC or Huey grenades exploding, I don't know. Very exciting. I thought the landing was opposed—MGs chattering away—great long bursts. As they settled to land, I put a mag[azine] on my Armalite and thought 'Surely they are not going to land us here!' But they were. Touched down and jumped out, ran to cover and cocked the rifle. No opposition—Thank God.[18]

Rothwell's men arrived safely and swept back to LZ QUEEN, securing it for the remainder of the Battalion. Major John Healy's A Company followed them into LZ PRINCESS. By mid-morning the Battalion and the Australian Gun Battery were in position at LZ QUEEN. Meanwhile, 1/503rd had assaulted into LZ KING a few kilometres north of the

'Sheets of interlocking thirty and fifty calibre fire rained down on us with deadly accuracy. The noise was deafening, but we could hear the piercing screams of young men whose bodies lay punctured and shattered all around us', Major James Hutchens wrote later. On Operation Hump the Viet Cong decided to stand and fight. The Paratroopers of 1/503rd became involved in savage close quarter combat.

Australians, on the other side of the Dong Nai River. Further south, the US Gun Battalion with the New Zealand Gun Battery had deployed into LZ ACE.

Healy's company patrolled east; McFarlane's to the north along the Song Be to the village of Xom Xoai where they and the Australian Sappers began destroying tunnels and fortifications; Tattam's and Rothwell's patrolled south.[19] Once again Brumfield had given each company its area of operations and dispersed them in opposite directions. The 1/503rd also sent out patrols from company bases over a wide area looking for concentrations of Viet Cong, and deployed two Long Range Patrols which found enemy groups and called in air strikes against them.[20] This was the first time the Paratroopers used dispersed patrolling in favour of battalion-sized sweeping manoeuvres.

For the first two days the Paratroopers and Diggers slogged through the heat of the day in wet, leech-infested areas of swamp and then dense primary jungle with a high canopy. Healy's A Company had had several contacts. A Viet Cong scout following the company had been shot, but Privates Andy McIvor and Greg Woodward had been shot while on sentry. Both survived but McIvor had to be evacuated to Australia.[21] A further two Viet Cong scouts had been killed and one wounded by Lieutenant Ian Guild's platoon. Documents recovered from one of the scouts contained plans for attacks on ARVN outposts near Bien Hoa Airbase. Before he died of his wounds the same soldier had told Corporal Ivan Welsh, the other of the Battalion's two Vietnamese linguists, that a Main Force Viet Cong Regiment was in the area and planned to kill as many Americans and Australians as possible.[22]

By nightfall on 7 November there were signs that the Paratroopers had patrolled to within 2000 metres of a major Viet Cong bunker system sited on two spur lines in dense jungle under a high thick canopy. Healy's company, now several kilometres away from the other companies of the Battalion, had patrolled into a network of tracks and roads packed hard from frequent use. One well-used dirt road led to Hill 82 and it was planned to follow it the next day. Healy's men spent the night astride part of the infamous Ho Chi Minh Trail.

After two days patrolling in the heat, wet, mud and leeches, the Paratroopers and Diggers were tired and dirty. On the morning of 7 November, McAulay wrote:

> The main items for the day were leeches, heat, thick bamboo bush.
> The bloody leeches. Back in Aust[ralia] they never bothered me.
> Over here we all get them. The little beasties cluster in 6s and 8s,
> busily sucking, attacking in packs. Matches, salt, mosquito repellent.
> We've done in [killed] hundreds but they still come. What do the
> bastards feed on when we aren't here. . .My socks and canvas boots

are soaked and stiff with blood, as are the lower parts of my trouser legs. My boots are rotten—they are falling off me. Hope a resupply brings in replacements. My trousers have gone at the knees and I have not shaved. I look pretty scruffy. All my nerves previous to the op are gone.[23]

A Viet Cong document translated later in November stated:

At 0530 on 8th November, we received orders to attack a large force of Americans. . .Our fiery lads were hungrily searching for the few enemy reaction force battalions left. HQ said this time we would clash head on with US combat troops, an entire airborne brigade of the Johnson–MacNamara gang. On learning we were to hit the Americans, we were enthusiastic, as for a long time we had wanted to match our strength with the Americans, to see what 'spirit' they possessed. What made for our stomach's strength (translator's note: courage) and belief in individual strength was the entire unit's resolution to hold the battlefield to the last moment. The political officers exhorted us to remember the compatriots and comrades slaughtered in North and South Vietnam by the Americans. Our wish to come to grips with the Americans rose higher.[24]

The Paratrooper's of 1/503rd also had a keen desire to join battle with the Viet Cong. No flanking manouevres were executed. The Americans moved forward briskly with two companies up and two platoons leading in each company. The third company of the Battalion followed. The fortifications were 30 metres inside a thick tree line and overlooked an open area in between two spurs. The Paratroopers headed into this open area with one company moving up one of the spur lines.[25]

Company C commanded by Captain Henry Tucker was ahead of Company B commanded by Captain Lowell Bittrich and was the first to be engaged by the Viet Cong at close range.

Major James Hutchens wrote later:

We had moved no more than 40 yards [37 metres] into the jungle when the whole earth seemed to erupt furiously before our eyes. Staggered claymore mines exploded all around us. Sheets of interlocking thirty and fifty calibre machine gun fire rained down on us with deadly accuracy. The noise was deafening, but we could hear the piercing screams of young men whose bodies lay punctured and shattered all around us. Only seconds before they had been strong and daring. Now they lay lifeless, forever lost to this world.[26]

Tucker ordered his two forward platoons to outflank the position they were facing. Both platoons ended up in the midst of several machine gun positions. By 9.30 a.m. Tucker's men were surrounded and had already had to repel several Viet Cong assaults. Tucker ordered his platoons to withdraw and they fell back in reasonable order and formed a company position. There were many incidents of heroism as Paratroopers risked their lives to bring back wounded comrades. Specialists Sergeant Lawrence Joel, a medic with Tucker's company, was to receive the Medal of Honour for his actions in administering lifesaving aid to wounded soldiers under enemy fire. Despite being wounded twice in the leg, Joel continued his work for nearly 24 hours.[27]

Meanwhile, Tyler had given orders to Bittrich to fight through and assist Tucker's men. Bittrich did this, and consolidated on Tucker's right flank, only to find that his company was now also being enveloped. Tyler then committed Captain Walter Daniels' men from Company A.[28]

The translated Viet Cong document recounted these events:

We calmly let them come to within 20 metres before opening fire, to be sure of a hit. This group of 'rice flower dandies' decided that they were not brave enough to close with the Liberation Forces positions. We had not encountered an entirely American unit before, though we had put scores of American advisers to flight. 7 Section commander looked at me and said, 'They are as big and as slow moving as buffalo. They crawl along with their behinds stuck up in the air, taking routes that make them good targets, and always move on old tracks.' Each time they came in groups of 7 or 8 against we three. They were crying and yelling wildly, and at first this was strange on the ears. . .After we listened carefully and heard them crawling around, yelling and bellowing like cattle, we all couldn't help smiling. You can see their feeble spirit—how can this red-faced scoundrel Johnson stand against us?[29]

Tyler had co-ordinated a heavy barrage of artillery and numerous airstrikes behind the enemy positions and Bittrich and Tucker began to walk this curtain of fire into their positions. However, there was no relief from hand-to-hand combat as wave after wave of Viet Cong soldiers began to assault the US positions. The Paratroopers could not pull back and use the artillery effectively. They were now committed to savage close-quarter combat.

The Viet Cong document went on:

Suddenly the call to attack roared out! Our Number One Company received orders to advance. We leapt onto the parapet. When they saw our gleaming bayonets lifted in their direction, the Americans scattered and ran, but whatever they did, they could not escape our hate-filled bayonets.[30]

This report did not tell the true story of who was not able to avoid the thrust of bayonets. The Paratroopers lived up to their motto of 'All the Way' and literally cut their Viet Cong opponents to pieces in ferocious bayonet fighting and point blank shooting. Captain Daniels' men had become incensed at the Viet Cong machine gunners who had kept hitting American bodies with rounds in a ghoulish game—turning them over and over with the impact of the rounds.[31] Company A fought through to their comrades and joined them in repelling assault after assault supported by withering machine gun fire from well-sited bunkers.

The air and artillery strikes began to take effect by noon and the tempo of the battle slowed after three hours of intense combat. However, assaults occurred occasionally until later afternoon. The Paratroopers stood firm and the Viet Cong regimental commander was unable to reinforce his assault forces successfully through the artillery barrage and air strikes which had isolated the battle area. To their detriment, the Viet Cong unit commanders had stuck rigidly to their superior's plan and depleted their forces in futile attacks. By the late afternoon, the Viet Cong regiment was a spent force, dragging away as many dead and wounded as possible. They withdrew from the battlefield under the full weight of the US, Australian and New Zealand artillery and mortars. The Paratroopers, amidst their own dead and wounded, were too exhausted to pursue them. Despite having been put on alert to be deployed to the battle area, 2/503rd remained at Bien Hoa.[32] A pursuit was not ordered. However, artillery and airstrikes continued to harass the remnants of the Viet Cong Regiment. Documents discovered later confirmed that battalions which had taken this severe mauling came from the VC 271st Regiment. One of the battalions, the 501st, was to reappear on the battlefield against the 173rd in March 1966. By that time, 90 per cent of its strength was made up of North Vietnamese reinforcements.[33]

Meanwhile, on the same day, Major John Healy's men were about to receive their first baptism of fire from a Viet Cong force fighting from a bunker system. Earlier that morning he had continued his patrol east, astride a well-used road heading up a long, low spur line which culminated in Hill 82. By the afternoon they were in contact with several pairs of Viet Cong soldiers. Two were shot and killed by Privates Tom Baxter and Geoff Cave of Second Lieutenant Rick Culpitt's platoon which for this operation was commanded by the Platoon Sergeant, Sergeant Gordon Peterson. Both Viet Cong were dressed in khaki uniforms, new webbing and carried new Russian-made AK47 assault rifles.[34]

Another of these well-dressed and equipped enemy soldiers was killed while following the company. This soldier's death brought the 'kills' for Second Lieutenant Clive Williams' platoon up to seven, making them the most successful platoon in the Battalion. Williams was a lanky 20 year old who wore thick black-rimmed glasses. His quietly spoken, studious manner contrasted with many of his fellow subalterns. Indeed, Williams was not even in the Infantry Corps. He had graduated from the Officer Cadet School to Intelligence Corps and was completing two years regimental service in 1 RAR before starting a career as an Intelligence Officer. Thus, he was not typical of his contemporaries in the Battalion,

Captain Bruce Murphy, Forward Observer 161 Field Battery, RNZA. Murphy won a Military Cross on Hill 82 during Operation HUMP saving two of A Company's platoons from Viet Cong machine guns using close artillery support.

and, by now, had been through enough adversity to have matured well beyond his 20 years. Williams had watched some of his Diggers die and receive serious wounds. He had watched them kill and wound enemy soldiers. This last 'kill' had had a grisly aftermath. A round had detonated a grenade attached to the Viet Cong's web belt and blown him apart. Williams viewed the mangled corpse dispassionately but with some professional satisfaction.[35]

Two more similarly dressed and equipped Viet Cong were killed an hour later by Second Lieutenant Bob Loftus' platoon. The quiet patrolling techniques of the Australians were paying off. Both soldiers appeared to have been on sentry and had not heard or seen the Diggers approach until it was too late.[36] Healy directed Sergeant Gordon Peterson's platoon to take up the lead. The road now took a turn before going up onto Hill 82. Lance Corporal 'Tiny' Parker took a bearing with his compass to the top of the hill and signalled to his scout, Private Ted Townsend, to move in that direction.

The lower slopes of the hill had been cleared and there were several clusters of wooden benches signifying a training area close to a camp. Townsend and Parker emerged from the jungle into the cleared area.

Private Geoff Cave told reporters later:

> I was the third man in the lead section and was carrying the machine gun. We were probing thick jungle and were coming up to a ridge. The two blokes in front of me [Townsend and Parker] were in a clear patch and I was just going into it when the Viet Cong opened up. They were using at least four machine guns from a distance of 20 to 30 yards [18 to 27 metres] from in front and both sides. The other two guys were hit. I returned fire, but I think my machine gun was hit because it stopped. I scrambled up to Townsend and started firing at the enemy using his rifle. He and I started to crawl back. I took a hit in the head but kept crawling.[37]

Townsend and Cave were able to crawl back safely to the remainder of the platoon in the tree line. The second section had moved up at the sound of firing and its commander Corporal Danny Hayes fell with a wound to his arm and his scout, Private Tom Baxter, also fell with wounds to the arm and lower back. The remainder of the platoon had closed up and were now exchanging fire with Viet Cong positioned in bunkers. Sergeant Gordon Peterson and the acting Platoon Sergeant, Corporal Trevor Hagan, quickly ordered those not pinned down by enemy fire into a hasty defensive position. First aid was being administered frantically to Townsend, Cave, Hayes and Baxter. The Diggers of 1 Platoon were unable to manoeuvre because of the crossfire of machine guns sited to each flank and on the crest of the hill.

The pressure was now on John Healy. He had crawled forward and was in time to stop Hagan leading what would have been a suicidal assault to take out the bunker that faced them and recover Parker who had been firing his rifle but had been silent for a few minutes. Healy was known affectionately by his fellow officers as 'Tubby' due to his stocky build, and humorous and easy-going manner. However, he was also known for displaying remarkable coolness in the most demanding circumstances and great personal toughness.[38] He needed both these qualities now. Healy had already served in Vietnam for 12 months in 1962–63 with the Australian Army Training Team—Vietnam. This experience now stood him in good stead. He was one of the few in the Battalion who had seen Viet Cong bunkers before and knew of the dangers in attacking them head-on.

Healy had assessed that the bunker system his men faced was too extensive for his company to take alone. His plan was to extract Peterson's men using fire support from another platoon and artillery; the other platoon would have to assault from a flank to take out the bunker directly threatening Peterson's men. He ordered Peterson to keep his men where they were and return fire until he could relieve the pressure so they could withdraw safely with their casualties. If possible he hoped the pause in enemy fire would be long enough for members of the platoon to recover Parker as well.[39]

Healy ordered Williams to move his platoon up to the left of the bunker firing on Peterson's men, and take it out from that flank. Williams' soldiers moved quickly and reached a position 300 metres from the bunker. They shook out into an extended line and assaulted. The line of men had only travelled 50 metres when they were engaged by machine gun fire from other bunkers. As Private Peter Gillson was climbing over a great entangled mass of roots between two trees, the Viet Cong shot him. He fell over and two Viet Cong ran over to take his M60 machine gun. He was still conscious and at point blank range lifted the heavy gun and riddled them with bullets.[40]

Williams now attempted to work his men forward using fire and movement within sections. Groups of men covered the rush forward of other groups but the fire was too heavy. The assault stalled and stopped. A machine gun had opened fire from the left rear of the platoon and several khaki-clad soldiers had been seen moving in that area. Williams' platoon was being outflanked.[41]

While Williams reported his situation to Healy by radio, his Platoon Sergeant, Col Fawcett, crawled forward to where Gillson lay wedged in the buttress roots of a large tree. Fawcett could see bullet holes where rounds had exited through the back of Gillson's pack. He got close enough to take Gillson's pulse: there was none. Every attempt Fawcett made to recover Gillson's body was met with prolonged bursts of machine gun fire. Gillson was being hit again and again. With tears of anger and frustration in his eyes, Fawcett gave up his heroic efforts and crawled back to the remainder of the platoon. He was to return twice more to try to get Gillson's body back but each time the firing was too intense.[42] For his bravery and persistence under fire, Fawcett was awarded the Military Medal.

By now, artillery support had begun to take effect. The Company's New Zealand Forward Observer, Captain Bruce Murphy, had positioned himself among Peterson's men and adjusted the fire of three available artillery batteries. Other batteries were still in support of the 1/503rd in its battle with the 271st Regiment. The locations of these batteries and the crest of Hill 82 meant that Murphy had to bring fire in unobserved, relying on the sound of the rounds falling on the other side of the hill. One error and those rounds could come crashing down on Healy's men. Exposing himself several times to enemy fire to ensure the rounds were falling where they were intended, Murphy slowly adjusted the fire to where

Healy wanted it. Both officers had come to a very good understanding during their five months together. In fact, Healy would often have Murphy supervise the positioning of the company after a day's patrolling while he prepared orders and carried out other duties.[43]

With darkness approaching, Healy knew that he did not have much time to extract his platoons from the bunker system. Murphy signalled to him that an open-ended square of artillery fire had been adjusted and was now ready for sustained firing. The accurate Kiwi guns were adjusted to fall as close as possible to protect the Australians. Lieutenant Ian Guild's men were positioned to cover the withdrawal of the other two platoons. Carrying their casualties, Williams' and Peterson's soldiers broke contact. Groups of men covered the movement of their comrades carrying the wounded. This fire and movement was successful as there were no further losses. Murphy's artillery fire had worked and given the Australians the time to withdraw. Unfortunately nothing could be done to recover the bodies of 'Tiny' Parker and Peter Gillson.

Corporal Trevor Hagan recalled later:

> My feelings were that not only had we let our mates down by
> leaving Tiny and young Gillson, but as we moved away, the looks
> on everyone's face was one of, 'Let's go and kill the bastards'. I don't
> think there was one man who didn't want to attack and I pity the
> opposition if we had gone in. To this day I wonder if we could have
> taken the position. I am sure the Company would have got to the
> top of Hill 82, but I am equally sure I and a lot more would not be
> here today making comments.[44]

The Viet Cong followed Healy's men and there were several intense exchanges of fire as night fell. At least two enemy soldiers were killed and several others had been hit. Healy spent the night wondering if the enemy knew their location and was preparing for an attack; he had no difficulty keeping his men alert.

The night of 8 November was one spent in great pain for the American and Australian wounded. 'There was not a murmur of complaint among the miserable dug-in troops', wrote Major Jim Hutchens of 1/503rd later. 'Not a groan was heard throughout the long night. It is amazing what the human mind and body can endure when they must. Men with torn, mangled bodies lay quietly as the pounding rain splashed mud on their bloody hands and faces. Patiently they waited for the dawn of a new day.'[45] The 1/503rd spent all night cutting a landing zone in the thick jungle with chainsaws dropped to them by brave helicopter pilots. Frequently, the sound of these saws was drowned out by the noise of small arms and artillery fire as the Paratroopers engaged groups of Viet Cong returning to the area to retrieve their dead and wounded.[46]

Early next morning, Major John Essex-Clark was airborne in a UHIB flown by Lieutenant Duane Ingram from the Brigade's helicopter company, who was later to serve in Australia as an Exchange Officer at the Staff College at Queenscliff. The priorities were to drop in a resupply of ammunition and smoke grenades, get the casualties out and assess whether reinforcements could be landed to enhance the company's security. One of the penalties of dispersed patrolling was that other companies were not close enough to assist Healy's men to extract from the bunker system nor reinforce them now to counter enemy attack. He asked Ingram to swoop 60 metres over Healy's position so he could drop the ammunition and grenades. As luck would have it, the boxes landed on a tree stump, burst open and disgorged their contents ready for immediate issue. Essex-Clark was quite proud of his first attempt at aerial resupply and radioed down to Healy, 'I even opened them for you, Tubby.'[47]

The next priority was to get the casualties out. All available helicopters were being used to evacuate the seriously wounded Paratroopers from the 1/503rd, on the northern side of the Dong Nai. There was also a requirement for the helicopters to have a winch. Two Vietnamese National Air Force (VNAF) casualty evacuation Sikorsky helicopters with winches were deployed but even after one pilot had a gun pointed at his head by a US NCO, refused to go low enough to evacuate casualties because of the threat of Viet Cong small arms fire.[48] Eventually a courageous US Air Force pilot, flying a Kaman H-43B search and rescue 'Huskie' helicopter, 'hugged' the tree tops and winched the casualties out.[49]

The problems of evacuating casualties from the 1/503rd were complicated by the thick vegetation and the numbers involved. The Paratroopers had suffered 49 killed and over 100 wounded. During the night they had cut a 75 metre deep and 25 metre diameter 'helicopter funnel' through the thick jungle and its canopy. Williamson decided to stage the casualties through an area to be secured by the Australians at LZ PRINCESS. A US Graves Registration Team was flown in to identify and properly register the remains and personal belongings.

McAulay wrote:

> Had a busy rather unpleasant 3 hours. D Coy secured an LZ as a staging post for US and Aust[ralian] casualties. Unloading dead and wounded off one chopper and into another . . . The US 1/503rd had 49 dead and lots wounded—called down artillery on themselves again. The VC are having a lash back this time. The Yanks we were loading had been killed about two days ago. They were pretty ripe. I felt like being sick a few times, but only because of the smell. We were loading them off stretchers, the Yank team was identifying them, if possible, then putting them into big green plastic bags. They showed us what to do. All military gear—weapons, grenades, etc— was piled up and only personal items such as cameras and radios

24 - 11 - 65.

37 Bidda St
Fairfield NSW

Dear Mr Williams,
I have just received a letter from you in which you said how sorry you all were about my husband. I really appreciate you writing to me and I'd like to thank you for your kindness in writing also I would like to thank you personally for risking your life to try and bring the lads back.
I am praying for each and every one of you because only a soldier's wife knows exactly what you are going through over there.
I am really proud to be called a soldier's wife, even though it's heart breaking at times, but I suppose we all must expect these things and when it does happen we

must be as brave as our men were.

But in a way I am very lucky because I have a son which Pete never seen he is only 4 months old but he'll never know just how much strength he has given me to go on, I only hope that his son will grow up to be as fine a man as Pete was.

Well I must close now but before I do I would like to thank you again for trying to bring back Pete.

May God bless you all and give you all a safe return.

mrs P. R. Gillson

P.S. excuse my wording in this letter but I just don't feel up to writing just yet

Letter from Mrs Peter Gillson to her late husband's platoon commander, Second Lieutenant Clive Williams, in November 1965. Her few words epitomise the pain and the courage of young war widows.

(transistor radios) went with the body. Only the Yanks would take radios to the bush with them. The US organization came to the fore—at the end there was a line of Hueys like a cab rank. As the casualties were brought in, the lead Huey would move forward, pick up its 6 bodies and away. How many all up, I do not know.[50]

Those who assisted the Graves Registration Team that day never forgot the sights of the grey bodies of the young Paratroopers, the blood-soaked webbing, the big green plastic bags and the stench of death. Captain Peter Rothwell commanded Delta Company at LZ PRINCESS that day and later wrote a poem of the experience:[51]

Secure the ground call it princess
ready a nest
for the hovering bird
a lull in the fighting
spread the word

Two bundles are thrown
to the sodden earth
each shroud
a poncho
caked with blood and dirt
from the ground
where they lay and fought
till the reaper
reached out

Are they ours
or theirs
Friend or Foe?
look
Afro hair
a negroid face
not ours
not theirs
but them

Does the reaper
choose
black
white
or
grey?

All is still
each noisily sweats
except for the two
who do not draw a breath

A sound
then a roar
a second green bird
comes to rest
on the sodden princess

A bundle of bags drop
the undertakers alight
a joke
a grin
here we are
let the play begin

This is the age of the package deal
we have zip-ups
custom made
seven by four
Man oh man
it's a clean clean war

A giant bird lands
its tail flops down
tumbling
stiff bundles of dead
onto the ground
the lap of a weeping princess

The curtain rises
let the play begin
to the audience
a circle green*
who sit
and watch
not the actors
with their puppets still
but for the reaper
look!
be careful
he may score a kill
a metal tag
it spells a name
labelled from the womb
en route to the tomb?

Strings are pulled
puppets dance
pockets shake open
treasures drop
a letter
a biscuit
a forgotten flip-can top

*The sentries securing the fringes of the landing zone.

An I is dotted
a T is crossed
are there two N's in unknown?
No tag
No head
Oh joy for the day
when head transplants will be
an act in the play

The finale is near
costumes are changed
each puppet shrouded
with a new coat of
green waterproof twill
with a zip and label
that spells out
'why kill?'
The puppets are loaded
the curtain comes down
applause?
encore?
who cares?
The sleeping princess
a cross on a map
a paddy field bare
nobody knows
except those who were there

Meanwhile, Brumfield demanded the right to return to Hill 82 to destroy the bunker system and recover the bodies of Parker and Gillson. He and Essex-Clark had worked out a plan of attack. Emotions among the Diggers were running high. Professional pride was at stake. The Australian code of infantry soldiering demanded that bodies were not left to the enemy and that, having found an enemy who was prepared to put up a fight, the challenge should be taken up. Williamson pointed out that the priority was evacuation of casualties and consideration would be given to the whole Brigade returning to the area later.[52]

Late in the afternoon the feelings of defeat were increased when the helicopter extraction of the Battalion became disorganised from the Diggers' point of view:

The heli extraction was a shambles. The companies were on the sides of the LZ, organized into slicks. The choppers were coming in 3s, landing anywhere. The organization collapsed. I came back on the third lot of 3. Back here they were landing everywhere—among the tents, on the road, near the Arty, at Bde HQ, near the US battalions—everywhere.[53]

Actually the decision to return to the Battalion area was made to save time because light was fading. The turn around time was shortened by flying direct to the Battalion area.

Back at Bien Hoa, Brumfield and Essex-Clark continued to propose attack plans to Williamson for a return to Hill 82. On 11 November a full written military appreciation and verbal briefing was presented to Williamson and Brigadier David Jackson who had been called upon to assist in representing the Battalion's case.[54] The plan was for Tattam's and Rothwell's companies to seal off Hill 82 so no Viet Cong could escape, and for Healy's and McFarlane's companies to conduct the assault. A reserve made up of Major Peter Sharp's cooks, drivers and clerks, and Major John Essex-Clark's Anti-Tank and Assault Pioneer Platoons, was to be ready for rapid deployment if required. The whole Battalion was to participate in the recovery of Parker's and Gillson's bodies and take the hill that had been too strongly defended for one company to capture alone.[55] Williamson changed his mind and the operational planning for returning to Hill 82 was stopped. The Diggers were bitter, but clear thinking had prevailed over emotion and pride. A return to Hill 82 may have brought the Australians the victory they yearned for, but it may have been costly. This reality was understood by some.

McAulay wrote:

> I was glad to be going back to see if we could get the bastards, but not glad at the thought of advancing through that bloody thick mass into pre-sited dug-in machine guns. There is a difference between moving along and meeting a group of VC and getting stuck into them, and going into an area and going up a hill knowing there are VC dug in with pre-sited MGs waiting. I feel free in saying that everyone is afraid—me also, as I will be with a rifle company all the time.[56]

For Williamson, the battle of Operation HUMP marked a turning point for the tactics of the Brigade. He was very proud of his Paratroopers: 'The enemy killed came to 403 by body count. This was the largest kill, by the smallest unit, in the shortest time in the war in Vietnam to date.'[57]

However, in his critique of the operation, he emphasised again and again the requirement to minimise casualties by using the firepower available: 'We must find a way to use the firepower at our disposal. The ground commander must, during contact, be obsessed with finding ways to employ artillery and air fire to assist his forces . . .We must use bombs and bullets instead of bodies.'[58]

The Viet Cong's substantial body count was later increased to about 700 when captured Viet Cong documents revealed the losses caused by artillery and airstrikes.[59]

However the rate of US casualties had to be reduced if the 173rd was to continue to achieve its mission. This type of attrition had raised concern in the US. On 14 November journalist James Reston wrote:

> There is a quiet uneasiness in the United States about the war in Vietnam—far more widespread than noisy demonstrations—and the Government's information policy is doing very little to relieve it. The fear is that Americans are being sucked into a larger war under conditions and tactics highly favourable to the enemy.[60]

During November 1965 the operations of the 173rd were to be overshadowed by the battles between the North Vietnamese and the US Cavalrymen in the Ia Drang Valley. There were several similarities between the battle fought by the Paratroopers on 8 November and the battalion-sized battles fought by the Cavalrymen. Typically, the Americans would encounter enemy forces equal to, or outnumbering, them and attack immediately. Most of the time the enemy initiated contact on their own terms, at a place and time of their own choosing, and remained in contact for as long as they deemed necessary. US units in contact would be reinforced as rapidly as possible in a manner known informally as 'piling on'. Concurrently, every effort would be made to engage the enemy with artillery and airstrikes. Using these tactics, the Paratroopers and Cavalrymen were able to snatch the tactical initiative from the enemy time and time again. A US Army study at the time reported that 46 per cent of all battles at this time began as enemy ambushes, and in 88 per cent of the fighting, the enemy initiated contact.[61]

The battles at LZ X-RAY and LZ ALBANY were examples of the Cavalrymen 'piling on' and turning initial tactical disadvantage into victory-by-body-count.[62] At LZ X-RAY a company of 1st Battalion, 7th Cavalry Regiment ran into the North Vietnamese 33rd and 66th Regiments. While the company attacked and then held off the North Vietnamese, killing 75 and losing eight men with about 40 wounded, hundreds of their comrades were flown in to assist them and a phalanx of artillery and air strikes was brought to bear. After a three-day battle, the Cavalrymen counted 834 enemy bodies and estimated that hundreds more would have been killed and wounded by artillery and airstrikes. US casualty figures were 79 killed and 121 wounded. Soon after the fighting around LZ X-RAY had stopped, one of the cavalry battalions which had participated in the fighting was ambushed by a North Vietnamese battalion while moving to LZ ALBANY for extraction. Despite suffering 150 killed and over 250 wounded, and having one company wiped out and another panic, the US battalion offset their losses by killing many more enemy in close combat and by artillery and airstrike.

The Paratroopers and Cavalrymen had very favourable killing ratios. In military terms the mission of 'find, fix and destroy the enemy' was being achieved when the Viet Cong decided to fight. The Australians had the same mission during operation HUMP and previous operations. Why were they not more successful in killing Viet Cong? Several factors explain the low casualties taken by the Australians and caused to the enemy. Firstly, the Australians' dispersed, stealthy patrolling techniques, highly disciplined operational procedures and frequent movement meant that Viet Cong commanders were not able to determine the locations of the Australians for long enough to mount sizeable attacks. Conversely, the vague Intelligence available on the Viet Cong and the Viet Cong's forewarning of US operational plans did not enable the Australians to use their stealth to locate and surprise their opponents. Furthermore, the operations were too short for the Australians to deduce patterns of enemy movement and overcome the disadvantage of surprise lost through deployment by helicopter. The Viet Cong could not be fixed in large numbers and engaged on Australian terms at this stage of the war. Hill 82 was the first opportunity for a set-piece battle but Healy's company was not strong enough to capture the hill alone.

Brumfield and his company commanders were trained not to allow the enemy to dictate the terms of battle. Australian commanders were taught to fight using surprise, deception, manoeuvre and firepower, and to achieve results without sustaining heavy losses among their own men.[63] Since World War II the Australian Army had been small; comprised of only three regular infantry battalions. An army this size could not afford heavy casualties. However this attitude did not diminish the aggression of the commanders and their Diggers when the time was right. For Major John Healy the time and conditions were not right on Hill 82. He assessed correctly that he would have squandered the lives of his men had he ordered a company assault into the bunker system. After it was realised that the Viet Cong would stand and fight, Brumfield and his commanders eagerly sought the opportunity to attack when they had assembled the combat power to do so.

Brumfield's attack plan for Hill 82 was an example of how an Australian commander would manoeuvre to ensure he dictated the terms of battle. Companies were to deploy into blocking positions as quietly as possible by night to cut off the enemy's escape routes. Before an attack at first light, Hill 82 was to be subjected to intense artillery fire and airstrikes to cover the assaulting companies for as long as possible before they closed with the enemy in their fortifications. The artillery and airstrikes would neutralise the Viet Cong long enough for the assaulting companies to be among them. A reserve of one company had been constituted to react swiftly to exploit any situation that would arise during the attack or afterwards. This force would most likely be used to maintain the momentum of the attack and pursue withdrawing enemy forces, who would be tired and slowed down by having to drag away dead and wounded.[64]

Australian commanders were just not prepared to pay the price the US commanders were for success in causing enemy casualties. The prospects of tactical success were examined before commitment of troops to an assault. Many times this carefulness may have lost opportunities to cause enemy casualties. However, lost opportunities were deemed better than lost men. The Australians had the patience to wait for another opportunity. Unfortunately they were on short operations designed to obtain quick results. US commanders took the risks required and drew the Viet Cong to them for battle. The Australians remained elusive, patiently waiting for their chance to join battle on their terms and not those of the Viet Cong. An Australian attack on Hill 82 would have been an interesting contest.

1 RAR was like a close-knit tribal group within the larger tribe of Australian infantrymen. Every death within the group was felt deeply. The losses of Parker's and Gillson's bodies were especially felt because of a loss of 'tribal face'. There was a strong ethos of mateship within the Royal Australian Regiment and 1 RAR's position as an Australian battalion in a US brigade had served to bond the Diggers more closely together than if they were serving with an Australian force. This bonding had increased as the months went by and the scale and intensity of operations increased. On 14 November news of the death near Danang of one of the Battalion's most respected and colourful characters caused strong reaction within the ranks of young and older soldiers alike.

For the Diggers of 1 RAR the death of Warrant Officer Kevin 'Dasher' Wheatley increased their anger at the perceived cowardice of the ARVN and the denial by their US brigade commander of the opportunity to assault to Hill 82 and take revenge for Parker and Gillson. Wheatley was a very popular character in the Regiment. He epitomised the rugged individualism which the Diggers liked to associate with the Australian infantryman. 'He was a rough, wild man and a good soldier', Staff Sergeant Doug Fyfe told reporters at the time. 'He never changed but always had a smile when things went wrong. You could fill a book with "Dasher" stories.'[65] 'I bet he took a few with him', another soldier said:

> It wouldn't have been any mistake he made that got him killed. You expect anyone else to get killed but not 'Dasher'. Battalions would come and go, but 'Dasher' went on forever. He was a legend in the Regiment for his beastie acts [games played while intoxicated]. Eveyone in the Battalions knew 'Dasher' Wheatley.[66]

Wheatley and fellow Australian adviser Warrant Officer Ron Swanton had been deserted in the field by their South Vietnamese unit during a contact with the Viet Cong. Swanton was wounded and

Wheatley refused to leave him. After carrying Swanton for some distance, Wheatley realised that he could not outrun the following Viet Cong. He lay by Swanton's body and threw two grenades at the enemy before they closed in on them, killing them both. For his bravery Wheatley was awarded the Victoria Cross.[67] A later post-mortem by Major Michael Naughton, the senior Australian medical officer in Saigon, revealed that Swanton was dead from a single wound before Wheatley had begun to carry him from the battlefield. Wheatley's heroism demonstrated the Australian ethos of never leaving your mates behind—dead or alive.

McAulay wrote:

> A new feeling (older) has been apparent around here, since the last op, and news of Dasher's end reached us. I can't describe it—it's a mixture of stiffening the sinews and summoning up the blood but also as far as I can make out, a determination to dig deeper, quicker, and to move through the J[ungle] more skilfully, to carry a bayonet (I always do)—in short, better soldiers.[68]

The death of Private Peter Gillson had deeply affected the men of John Healy's company. He was a well-liked soldier who had only been married a few months before embarkation for Vietnam. Most of his platoon had attended the wedding. His platoon commander, Second Lieutenant Clive Williams, wrote to Peter Gillson's wife to console her on the loss of her husband and tell her what happened. She replied:[69]

> Dear Mr Williams,
> I have just received a letter from you in which you said how sorry you all were about my husband. I really appreciate you writing to me and I'd like to thank you for your kindness in writing. Also I would like to thank you personally for risking your life to try and bring Peter back.
> I am praying for each and every one of you because only a soldier's wife knows exactly what you are going through over there. I am really proud to be called a soldier's wife, even though it is heart breaking at times, but I suppose we all must expect these things and when it does happen we must be as brave as our men were—but in a way I am very lucky because I have a son which Peter never saw. He is only four months old but he'll never know just how much strength he has given me to go on, I only hope that his son will grow up to be as fine a man as Peter was.
> Well I must close now but before I do I would like to thank you for trying to bring Peter back. May God bless you all and give you all a safe return.
>
> Signed
>
> Mrs P.E. Gillson
>
> PS. Excuse my wording in this letter but I just don't feel up to writing just yet.

Postscript

For the battle on 8 November 1965 with the Viet Cong's 271st Main Force Regiment, the 1/503rd Airborne Battalion was awarded the US Presidential Unit Citation. The area in which they and the Diggers had fought continued as a junction of major Viet Cong supply routes for the remainder of the Second Indochinese War.

6 The false harvest

The 173rd was deployed to capture a large 'rice bowl' area in the La Nga Valley and deny the harvest to the Viet Cong. In terms of protecting the rice crop and the people from the Viet Cong, Operation NEW LIFE was to be a false harvest.

After Operation HUMP the Diggers were unsettled and moody. The insularity of each rifle company became more pronounced because of their different experiences during the past months. Major John Healy's men were coming to terms with their experiences on Hill 82 and the denial of the opportunity to return there; Captain Peter Rothwell's men could not have quickly forgotten their first-hand experience of mass casualties. The corpses of their US comrades would have been stark reminders of their own mortality and the risks of meeting the Viet Cong on their terms.

Morale was weakened further by the news that Lieutenant Colonel Brumfield was to return to Australia within weeks. An old spinal injury caused by playing Rugby Union football as a cadet at the Royal Military College, Duntroon, was creating severe medical problems. Despite treatment by Doctor Stirling Mutz, a US orthopaedic surgeon at 3rd Field Hospital in Saigon, Brumfield was in intense pain which could not be relieved without treatment in Australia.[1] His condition had worsened to the point where he was so stiff that he had to be helped to sit up and get out of bed in the mornings.[2]

Relations between those who went on operations and those who did not appeared to have deteriorated significantly by this time. McAulay wrote:

> Our pals the base bludgers. The CO [Brumfield] is in trouble with Brigadier Jackson. The Logistic Support Company (may Allah curse them) have all sorts of stuff but won't part with it. They refused our request for 6 radios—so Lou went down and demanded 6 personally. Now all the base bludgers are screaming about the

"

uncouth Infantry. We only have 11 vehicles and one ambulance on the road. There is a 'normal' wait of 7 days before they'll look at the vehicle. They have 6 new ambulances—won't give us one. The New Zealand Arty FO [Forward Observer] for D Coy went to get some timber and plywood. 'Go to Bien Hoa and buy it', says an LSC warrior, barefacedly sawing kangaroos and boomerangs out of ply, for their own beautification and profit. They and all the Saigon commandos are all wearing the new Aussie jungle boot. I had to walk for 2–3 days in rotten old J-boots. Our pals the base bludgers. They should have been out there loading up two to three-day-old corpses.

They ought to drag all those people out of their snug little corners and replace them with older rifle-company people. There are section commanders and SGTs of 35–40 years old, tramping around the bush, and these other rats are sitting back there, first preference at all the things to make life more pleasant, going on leave all the time, dealing on the black market (officers too I might add) and resisting any attempt to get them outside the wire. Our pals the base bludgers.[3]

The officers also came in for their share of criticism. McAulay went on:

Yesterday had an example of officer's pig headedness. We haven't got a flag pole because the mast would be a good aiming point for the VC outside. Now things are safer and the other units have them, our officers want one. Our Battalion sign is the biggest in the area so we are going to have the tallest flagpole in a 'T' shape. The RSM tried to tell them that the cross bar would make it too heavy and it would buckle. 'Nonsense RSM. Get the truck up here.' So they pulled it up. They got it to the vertical position, then before the eyes of the know-it-all wheels [officers] gracefully folded at the knees and waist and drooped, drooped and drooped to the ground. 'Well RSM, get it pulled down and moved over there. I'm going to the Mess now, we'll continue in the morning.[4]

The whole incident had been observed by a growing crowd of on-lookers who had erupted in laughter as the flag pole crumpled to the ground.

Heavy drinking while off duty had been the norm for several months and not unusual for soldiers of any nationality experiencing the stresses of combat and frequent operations. However, it seemed as if the daily routine and relative safety of the defensive position at Bien Hoa was no longer as restful as before, and was producing its own type of tension. Possibly the Diggers had become too used to the constant pump of adrenalin on operations and the resultant concentration on the immediate environment. At Bien Hoa there was time to think of other things. Heavy 'binge' drinking now typified social behaviour among some members of

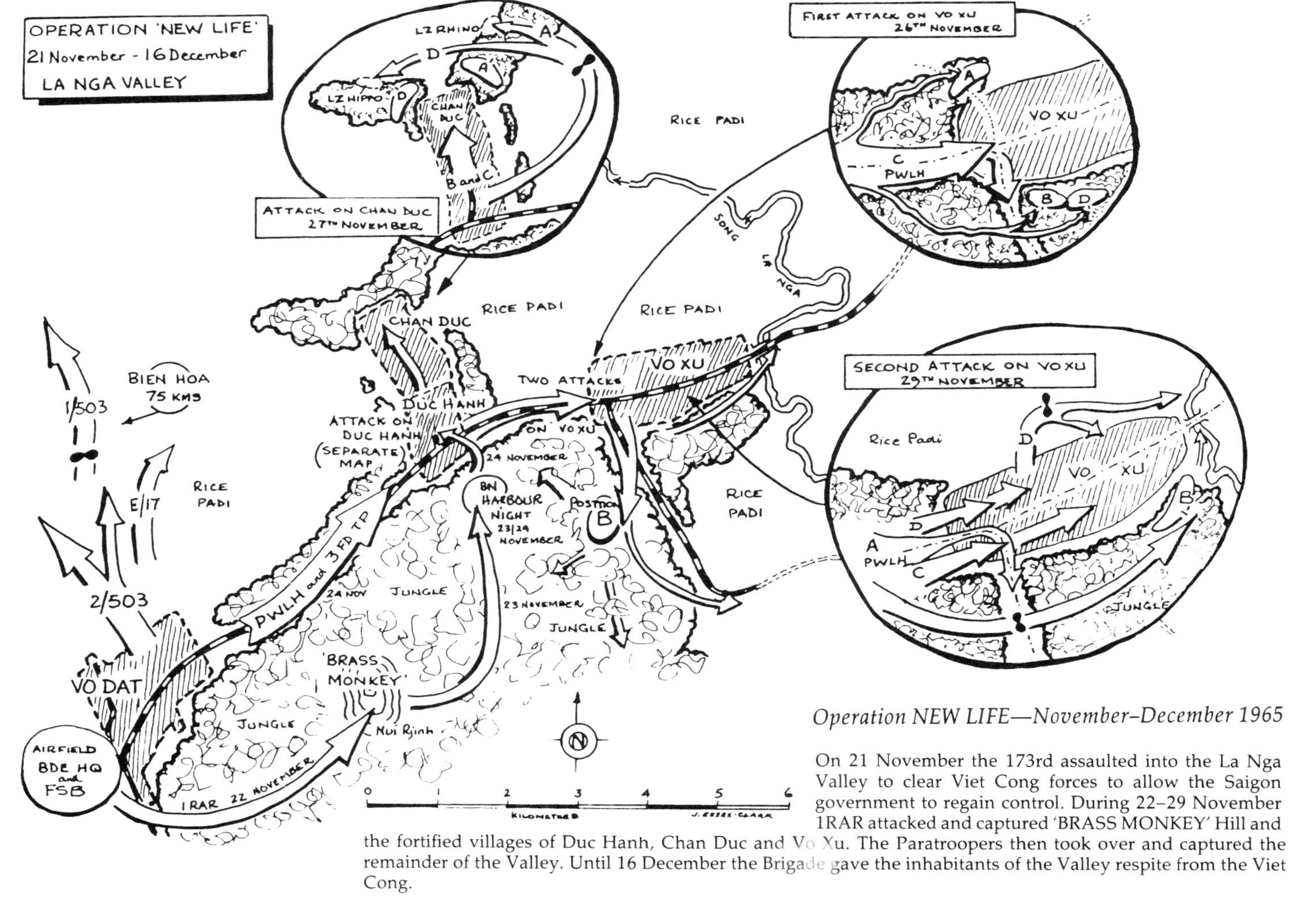

Operation NEW LIFE—November–December 1965

On 21 November the 173rd assaulted into the La Nga Valley to clear Viet Cong forces to allow the Saigon government to regain control. During 22–29 November 1RAR attacked and captured 'BRASS MONKEY' Hill and the fortified villages of Duc Hanh, Chan Duc and Vo Xu. The Paratroopers then took over and captured the remainder of the Valley. Until 16 December the Brigade gave the inhabitants of the Valley respite from the Viet Cong.

Aerial photograph of the La Nga Valley looking west to east along the road from Vo Dat to Vo Xu.

the rifle companies. Rather than drinking to relax and settle down between operations, this type of drinking was often characterised by rowdy hyperactive behaviour and games of physical risk followed by coma-like sleep. 'There is nothing else to do when you are off duty. A lot of blokes have things they want to forget. We need to get back into it again.'[5] Several days later orders were received for an operation of a scale, duration and type not conducted before.

Since May the Brigade's operations had been focused on Viet Cong home-base areas in an effort to cause as many casualties as possible and destroy enemy installations and supplies. They were conducted away from inhabited areas and concentrated on bringing Main Force units to battle. The Brigade was now ordered to conduct a sustained operation in a densely populated area in conjunction with the ARVN 10th Division to protect the imminent rice crop from capture by the Viet Cong.[6]

The Brigade's mission for the initial phase of the operation was to establish an air-head at Vo Dat Airfield in Binh Tuy Province and from there breakout to capture the La Nga Valley, reputed to be the fifth largest rice-producing area in South Vietnam. The valley formed a 'bowl' of flat low-lying terrain. In 1957 the area was one large swamp. The Saigon Government settled North Vietnamese refugees in the area and, after years of hard work, the swamp had been transformed into productive paddy fields. Surrounding the 'bowl' were extensive thickly forested mountain ranges. On the slopes leading to these ranges was some secondary growth, mostly long grass. Because it was the dry season, the rich red soil of the area now took the form of fine, powdered dust. For the North Queenslanders among the Australians the terrain was very much like that found in sugar cane-growing areas.

Since November 1964 the La Nga Valley had been under the military and political control of the Viet Cong. For the North Vietnamese who had fled to South Vietnam to escape Communist control, this situation was depressing. Most were Roman Catholics who had worked hard to create a livelihood from the inhospitable land given to them by the corrupt Saigon Government, which joined the Viet Cong in heavily taxing their produce. These problems were compounded by political divisions and rivalries in the valley between the newly settled, enterprising northerners and the more complacent, easy-going southerners. This was exemplified in the differences between the villages of Vo Dat which was Catholic and anti-Communist, and Vo Xu, which was Buddhist and either neutral or sympathetic to the Viet Cong.

The 173rd, with two attached infantry battalions from the US 1st Infantry Division, had the dual missions of capturing the valley and remaining in the area to provide security. The long-term aim was to restore the area to the control of the Saigon Government. After the

Brigade had cleared the area, the newly raised ARVN 10th Division (later re-titled 18th Division) was to provide for the security of the population with the assistance of locally recruited Popular Forces. The name Operation NEW LIFE was selected to symbolise the intended benefits of the operation for the people of the La Nga Valley.[7]

Within the 173rd there was always a yearning for a return to the airborne tactics for which the formation had been trained. Dear to the hearts of the Paratroopers was the chance to earn a combat jump star for their parachute wings like their forefathers who had jumped into Nadzab in Papua New Guinea and conducted the famous parachute assault onto the fortress of Corrigedor in the Philippines. To earn this star, and start the operation in a spectacular manner which would impress the people of the La Nga Valley and attract favourable publicity for the Brigade, 'Butch' Williamson planned a Brigade parachute assault. 1 RAR was to travel to the area by road and secure the drop zone.

Unfortunately the Paratroopers were not to have the chance to earn their combat stars. Over a week before the operation was due to start, local vendors in Bien Hoa began to sell combat stars to the Paratroopers in anticipation of their jump. This was an obvious demonstration of the forewarning that was available to friend and foe alike of the operational planning of the Brigade. To counter this breach of security, the date for the start of the operation was moved forward by four days.[8]

The move forward of the dates caught the Australians by surprise. After ten days of relative inactivity since Operation HUMP, the Battalion had just over 24 hours' notice to move. This was a rushed start for Major Mal Lander who was now temporarily in command. The Brigade operation order was signed at 10 p.m. on 19 November. The orders were delivered by Williamson at 7 a.m. the next morning to the battalion commanders. Lander delivered his orders to his company commanders two hours later, and at 6 a.m. the next morning the first flights of helicopters were taking off from the Snake Pit.[9]

After a 40-minute flight, the helicopters carrying the Diggers circled over the La Nga Valley while the last airstrikes were completed on the approaches to the Vo Dat Airfield. Once again the Viet Cong were to be left in no doubt about the arrival of the Brigade. Lieutenant Colonel George Dexter's 2/503rd assaulted first, followed by the Australians, and then Lieutenant Colonel John Tyler's 1/503rd. The open, flat terrain afforded good observation of the area around the landing zones. This degree of observation combined with air superiority ensured that the airmobile assaults were not opposed.

The only obscuration was the clouds of red dust thrown up by the landing and taking off of helicopters. 'You jumped out and the bloody dust is in your eyes, mouth, ears, nose, back of the neck, down your collar—everywhere.'[10] After the infantry battalions had landed and secured the airfield, dozens of C130 Hercules transport aircraft began flying in supplies to sustain the Brigade for the next 21 days. The night was spent in a large Brigade defensive position. The only casualty for the day had been Private Ray Gillson of Delta Company who dislocated his knee jumping from a helicopter. This injury spared the brother of the late Peter Gillson the risks of operations, and he completed his tour of Vietnam in Administration Company as a steward in the Officers' Mess.

On the morning of 22 November the breakout into the La Nga Valley began. Objectives around the Brigade's perimeter erupted with artillery and airstrikes. The Paratroopers and Diggers assaulted behind this barrage. Ian McFarlane's B Company was assault company for a battalion attack on a feature known as BRASS MONKEY. This feature was a prominent, lone, steep hill which overlooked most of the valley. Since the brigade's arrival it had been pounded by artillery and airstrikes. The assault line soon broke up into groups of soldiers clambering up the steep slopes in stifling heat. BRASS MONKEY was deserted. All of the other battalion assaults that morning were not opposed. The Viet Cong had withdrawn further up the valley and were waiting to see what the Brigade would do next.

The next day the Australians secured a section of road for the arrival of vehicle convoys carrying the attached infantry battalions from the 1st Infantry Division. The weather was hot and there was no shelter from the sun. The crump of artillery and the crack of mortar rounds, intermingled with the howl of fighter ground attack aircraft, could be heard in every direction. The capture of the La Nga Valley was going to be carried out as a conventional war operation; Williamson was going to decide the battle using bullets and bombs, not bodies. Opposing 1 RAR were two companies of Main Force Viet Cong probably from the 5th Division's 274th Regiment supported by two companies of Local Force guerillas from the villages in the area. However, the 274th Regiment was known to operate in the La Nga Valley and was estimated to be able to concentrate its battalions for a deliberate attack in 48 hours. Williamson gave Lander the mission of clearing a series of fortified villages and hamlets astride interprovincial Route 3 which ran north–south across the valley. Once this route was secure, the ARVN 10th Division was to move through to the eastern part of the province to start operations. The first of the villages astride the route was the village of Duc Hanh, 1800 metres north of BRASS MONKEY.[11]

In the early 1960s, the village complex of Duc Hanh-Chan Duc had been a part of the failed Strategic Hamlet Program and still had its fortifications in place. The village was surrounded by a deep, but now overgrown, dry moat and a thick barbed wire fence. Within the village

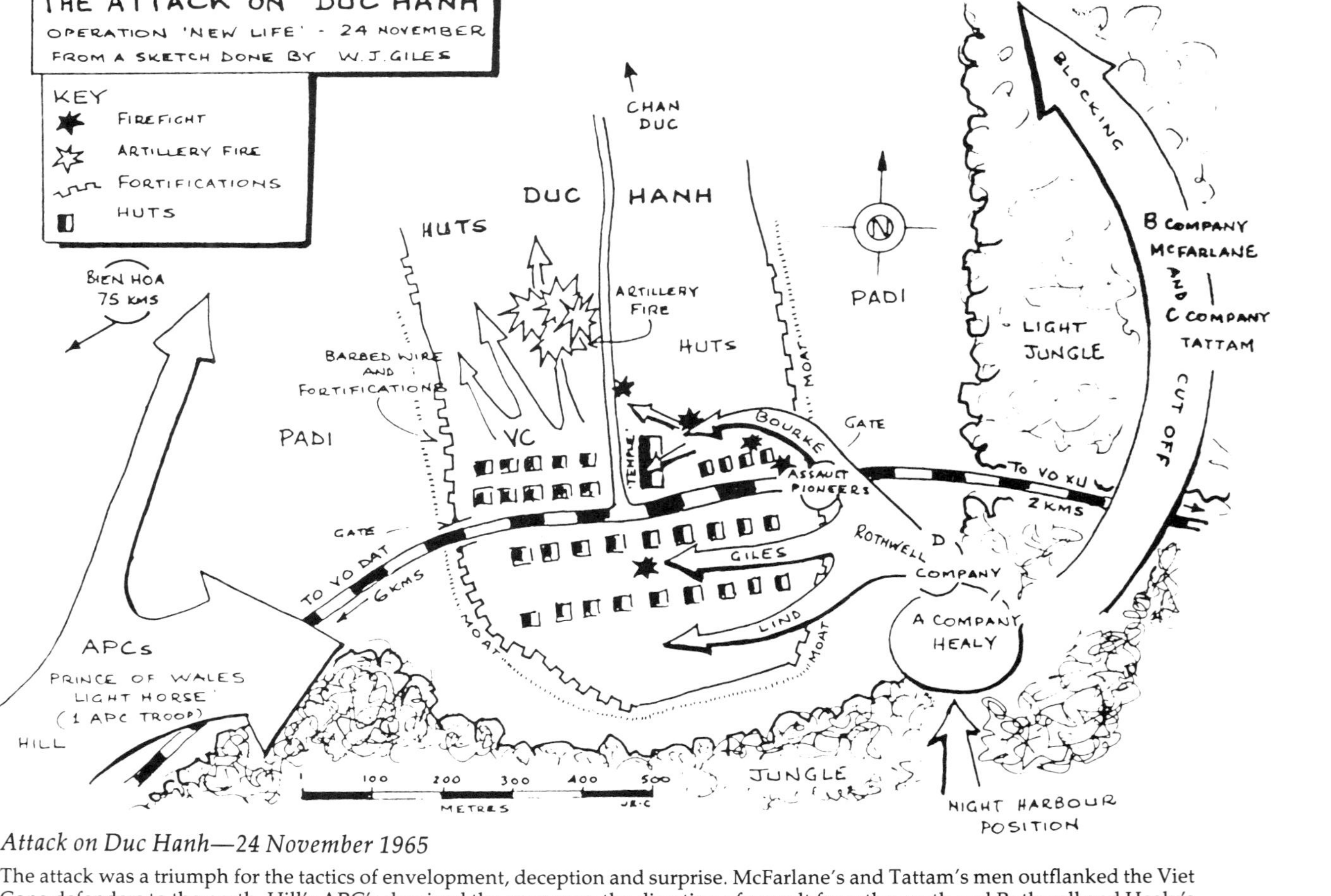

Attack on Duc Hanh—24 November 1965

The attack was a triumph for the tactics of envelopment, deception and surprise. McFarlane's and Tattam's men outflanked the Viet Cong defenders to the north. Hill's APC's deceived the enemy on the direction of assault from the south and Rothwell and Healy's men attacked from the east. The Viet Cong suffered heavy casualties and the Australians none.

there was a series of trench systems which radiated from the centre. The road entry and exit points were sealed by stout timber-framed gates which were covered with barbed wire. It was expected that the moat area would be seeded with antipersonnel mines and booby traps.[12]

In May 1965, the village had been assaulted by a South Vietnamese Regional Force company which had failed to penetrate the moat and the booby-trapped outer perimeter. The attackers had withdrawn under a hail of automatic fire from the village. Of a population of about 1500, most were North Vietnamese Roman Catholics; however, some Buddhist villagers were expected to have relatives among the Viet Cong Local Force companies.

Major Mal Lander developed a simple but deceptive plan for the attack on Duc Hanh in consultation with Major John Essex-Clark.[13] The village was to be assaulted by two companies at dawn after the other two rifle companies had moved around the western side of the village by foot to cut-off positions to the north. The noisy movement by helicopter to the north was intended to deceive the defenders in the village about the direction of assault. It was expected the enemy would occupy trenches facing in that direction while the real assault came in from the south east. There was to be no artillery or mortar bombardment of the village before the attack, due to the likelihood of causing civilian casualties, and to give the Viet Cong the freedom to redeploy to face the expected assault from the north west. Four artillery targets had been planned and registered silently to support the attack, if and when such support was needed against an enemy position.

Captain Peter Rothwell's D Company was tasked to lead the assault into the village. His men were to be followed by Major John Healy's A Company. Rothwell had been able to study air photographs of the village area and conduct an aerial reconnaissance. When he and his platoon commanders, Lieutenant Bill Giles and Second Lieutenants Jim Bourke and Steve Lind, flew over the area, the village appeared to be deserted. The population of 1500 and their Viet Cong defenders were all either indoors or underground in domestic air-raid shelters or an extensive bunker and tunnel system.

Rothwell had been assigned the Assault Pioneer Platoon to assist him to breach the obstacles of the moat and the barbed wire entanglements. He tasked Bourke's platoon to move in with the Assault Pioneers and protect them while a route was cleared for Giles' and Lind's platoons. After moving through the cleared route, Giles was to deploy his men north of the road which entered the village from the south east, while Lind was to deploy his men south of the road. Together these platoons were to assault the village and Bourke's platoon was to follow, in depth. Further

D Company 1 RAR officers. Major Brian Harper (left), Captain Peter Rothwell, Lieutenant Bill Giles and Second Lieutenant Jim Bourke (right). Rothwell commanded the company for Operations HUMP and NEW LIFE and led the attack on Duc Hanh. Jim Bourke's platoon assaulted Duc Hanh and inflicted heavy casualties on the Viet Cong.

back, Healy's company was also to assault along the same axis, with two platoons leading to give depth to the attack.

Reveille for the Battalion was 3 a.m. The Diggers were given a hot brew of tea or coffee before they moved out. There was no talking, no noise and no lights. Occasionally there was a muted call for men to form up and be ready to fall in according to the order of march.

The movement of Major Ian McFarlane's B and Major Jim Tattam's C Companies to the north east of the village to act as block and cut-off forces had been conducted without incident, while Rothwell's and Healy's men had moved silently and quickly without being detected. Bourke's men now moved forward with the Assault Pioneers, commanded by Sergeant Col Evans, to clear a route through the wire, mines and booby traps. This task had just been completed when Corporal Ron Smith's section was engaged by rifle fire from a hut on the edge of the village. Bourke called out to Smith, 'Get that machine gun working, Corporal Smith.' His platoon sergeant, Sergeant Jim 'Shagger' Carnes, called out, 'Let's go get 'em, boss.' Without waiting for an answer, Carnes opened fire. 'I can still see the old lout,' Bourke wrote in his diary later. '—feet apart, hunched over but standing in the open, firing his SLR [rifle] (which fires fully automatic) from the hip, poised ready to attack.' Bourke called back, 'Right, let's have a look, old fellow. Cover us Smithy!' Bourke and Carnes then ran towards the hut.[14] Firing then started from other locations across their front. Seeing their platoon commander and platoon sergeant leading an assault and hearing the area to their front erupt in small arms fire, Bourke's men 'summoned up the blood' and charged. Two Viet Cong were killed in this initial assault by machine gun fire.

The platoon was now engaged in a running fight with about 30 Viet Cong who had been firing from trenches, but having been outflanked, were trying to withdraw. Bourke was in the thick of the action exhorting his men and leading groups of soldiers into the flanks of the enemy position. Carnes' rifle, modified to fire on full automatic and take 30-round magazines, was heard in action well forward of the skirmish line. Carnes had nicknamed his rifle 'The Big Iron'; he and 'Big Iron' were hard at work showing the way.

Meanwhile, Rothwell had issued further orders by radio to adjust his plan of attack. Bourke's platoon had become the northern assault platoon in place of Giles' platoon and was quickly drawing away from the rest of the company. Rothwell ordered Giles to assault forward to catch up with Bourke and become the southern assault platoon. Rothwell expected Giles and Bourke to co-ordinate their assaults and give each other mutual fire support when required. Lind was also ordered to deploy south and assault alongside Giles' left flank to ensure a wide frontage through the village so no Australians could be cut-off or outflanked by enemy that had been overlooked. By this time, Major John Healy had joined Rothwell to find out first hand what was going on and how changing events would affect his company.

The three platoons were now assaulting east to west, along three lines of huts. Bourke's platoon still retained the initiative because of the momentum their quick initial assault had created; Giles was meeting light opposition from soldiers firing hurriedly and withdrawing; Lind was making good progress without having encountered any enemy.

Bourke's skirmish line was now about to reach an open area of about 100 metres between the last in a line of huts and a small, corrugated-iron Catholic Church. The Viet Cong had withdrawn across this clearing and would have had good cover and fields of fire to engage Bourke's men if they assaulted across the open area.

Giles recalled later:

> I was level with Bourke by the time he could observe the open area between his men and the temple [the Catholic Church]. I moved to a point where I could observe the temple and along the North–South road behind the temple. I called Jim on the radio and discussed two fairly obvious options. I would provide fire support from my side of

the road for his assault from the East and also fire down the road behind the temple to cut-off withdrawing enemy, or he could provide fire support for an assault by my platoon from the south at right angles to his axis. My main concern would have been a very exposed left flank open to threat from VC known to be west of my position. However my assault frontage was narrow and I could have used a section of Assault Pioneers to secure my flank. The advantage for Bourke's platoon was that they would not have to move over 100 metres of open ground in a frontal assault.[15]

Bourke ignored the options presented to him by Giles and continued exhorting his men on in pursuit of the enemy. He had the Viet Cong on the run, and was not going to pause and give them a chance to escape. This had been a very quick discussion and decision by two platoon commanders in the heat of battle. There was no time to call Rothwell forward to assess the situation personally and decide on a course of action. To Rothwell's credit, he monitored Giles' and Bourke's conversations and left it to his two young officers on the spot to make the right decision.[16]

Despite the risks of a frontal assault without fire support against an enemy who by now knew what was going on, Bourke ordered his men into the open area, continuing the assault. The Diggers rushed forward without hesitation, firing from the hip, from the shoulder, calling for machine gun fire, encouraging each other and firing again. A group of about fourteen to twenty Viet Cong fired on Bourke's men, but quickly broke and ran. Three Viet Cong were killed and several others wounded. As they withdrew several more fell as Bourke's men engaged them with accurate fire.

A few seconds later the right flank of the platoon was engaged by a .30 calibre machine gun from the north. This group of about six Viet Cong was soon pinned down by machine gun fire, but then one Australian machine gun malfunctioned and stopped. The Viet Cong machine gunner seized this opportunity to fire at his Australian opponent who was going through his immediate drills for getting the gun to work again. 'Out went SGT Carnes, rifle blazing while the gunner carried out an immediate action on the gun', wrote Bourke in his diary later. 'It worked . . . We put Shagger in for a medal, an MM immediate award [Military Medal]. Good man, Shagger, but almost as big a rat as me, I'm afraid.'[17]

As Bourke reached the church he had his signaller radio for artillery to neutralise the machine gun position that had engaged his platoon from the north. He remembered that an artillery target had been registered silently in that area. After a quick adjustment of fire, he ordered the Kiwi Gun Battery to fire for effect and the enemy position erupted as the shells found their mark.

Rothwell decided that now was the time to halt the assault for ammunition resupply and regrouping. Bourke's men were exhausted and running low on ammunition. Lind's men were ordered to continue their sweep until they could keep the rest of the village under observation. The Viet Cong had withdrawn to the north and west but had been able to evade the companies positioned there to cut them off. They probably used the tunnel system in the area to escape.

Bourke's men recovered seven bodies and about fifteen more Viet Cong had been wounded but not captured and a further seven Viet Cong had surrendered. Bourke's timely use of artillery on the enemy's withdrawal routes accounted for eight more bodies and several trails of blood. Despite the premature execution of the assault by Bourke's platoon, and the resultant change of plans, Rothwell's men had been able to capture Duc Hanh without any casualties to themselves and only one civilian had been killed.

The success of the Australian tactics became even more obvious later. On the north-western approach to the village, a newly dug and carefully camouflaged horseshoe-shaped ambush position, capable of being occupied by 80 to 100 soldiers, was discovered. Had Lander ordered an assault along this obvious approach route, there would have been heavy casualties. The village chief of Duc Hanh revealed later that day:

> The Liberation Armed Forces [Viet Cong] moved us out of our homes last night to the nearby hamlet of Chinh Duc. They said that when the Australian mercenaries drove through the main gates in their motor vehicles [APCs], they would catch them in ambush and annihilate them.[18]

One civilian had been killed during the attack. Giles wrote later:

> We had been receiving fire from both sides of the east-west road, I suppose in an attempt to prevent us out flanking the VC in the temple. As a result we were careful to ensure that each hut we passed was clear before we turned our backs on it. The civilians we had encountered were the usual mix of women, very old men and very young children—no young men. As we approached one particular hut, one of my men called out that there was a 'funk' hole in front of me and that he had seen a young man armed with what appeared to be a pistol peering out of it. The hole was covered with thick planks and was about 10 feet by 10 feet [3 metres by 3 metres] and six feet [1.8 metres] deep. There was no way to neutralize it by small arms fire, so an M26 grenade was dropped through an opening. When the sound of the explosion had died, I could hear children crying. When we lifted the lid, we found a woman and three youngsters. Apart from some minor cuts, none of them were injured though they were all in a state of shock. Lying on the floor was a man's body—the father. He had caught the grenade and laid down on top of it. He was not armed. This was the most tragic event that occurred to me during my tour of South Vietnam and yet was the greatest act of love and devotion I have ever witnessed.[19]

Corporal Lex McAulay went in with Bourke's platoon, and was called for by Giles, who wanted the population out of their homes and moved to a gathering area while the area was secured. With all the firing and presence of foreign soldiers, they were reluctant to come out of their shelters. After some patient talking by McAulay in Vietnamese, one group clambered out of their shelter just as a burst of machine gun fire thumped into the wall of the hut next to them. Like startled rabbits, they dived back into their underground shelter and the whole process of coaxing them out began again.

In another shelter McAulay was able to convince all but one very old man to come up to the surface. The old man, who looked to be over 80 years old with a long, white wispy goatee, remained at the bottom of the steps. His family would not leave him there, and one girl about seven years old was very upset and could not be persuaded to leave her grand-father. Giles noticed that the girl wore a Catholic religious medal on a necklace. He reached into his pocket where he kept a set of rosary beads for luck on operations. The girl's face lit up with recognition and she told the old man that the foreign soldiers were Catholics. He came up the steps and grasped Giles' hand in a surprisingly strong grip, and refused to let go until McAulay was able to assure him he was a Catholic too, and led the old man away. For McAulay's consideration in remaining with the old man, who could only move slowly and enduring his steel-like grip, he was fired on by a sniper several times from a distance of 300 metres all the way to company headquarters.[20]

Having captured the southern section of the village, the Battalion harboured there and were joined by the Kiwi Gunners, the Australian APC Troopers and Sappers. Healy's and McFarlane's companies occupied an area south of the village of Vo Xu in preparation for a battalion advance next day to clear the section of road between Vo Dat and Duc Hanh. The 2/503rd was operating south of Vo Dat and were responsible for clearing out from the airfield to the southern boundry of the village.

The performance of the Kiwi Gun Battery had been particularly good during the attack on Duc Hanh. 'They're the best damn gunners in the world', Private John Smith told reporters at the time. 'They pull their guns to pieces, move them through the bush in APCs, and from the time the carrier stops, they get their first shots away in two minutes. They are dead accurate too.'[21]

Later Major Jim Tattam set up his headquarters in the Catholic Church. One of his platoon commanders had 'captured' a Buddhist flag in a neighbouring hamlet and decided to fly it from a flag pole near the church. Corporal Lex McAulay told Tattam that the flag was causing some resentment among the Catholic villagers and the Buddhist villagers nearby wanted it back. The platoon commander, Second Lieutenant

Kevin Lunny, who had replaced the ill-fated John MacNamara, was told to take the flag down and return it to its owners. This incident was an example of the care the Australians took to maintain the rights of the Vietnamese villagers. At no time during their tour did they have the right to enter houses, or arrest South Vietnamese citizens without being accompanied by an official from the South Vietnamese Government. South Vietnamese policemen accompanied the rifle companies on operations and affected liaison with local village authorities. Dwellings could not be entered without permission except in declared operational areas such as War Zone D, or if it was considered not doing so would endanger the lives of the soldiers.[22]

On that day three South Vietnamese officials were flown in to assert the authority of the Saigon Government. One was to be the new village chief and the others his two deputies. There was no provision made for them by their government: no accommodation, food, money, vehicle, weapons or radio. They were terrified, fearing for their lives. Seeing their plight, Tattam decided to host them for the period his company was in the village, provided food and allocated an area for them to sleep.[23]

During the aftermath of the Duc Hanh attack Major Ian McFarlane's B Company took 'possession' of a surrendered Viet Cong soldier.[24] McFarlane wrote later:

> It seemed liked a good idea to keep him as he could throw light on the locations and habits of his former colleagues. After some discussion he became resigned to joining us (he was worried about being recaptured by the VC) and so I gave him back his rifle plus one round and Sergeant Nien, my South Vietnamese interpreter, found him a spare set of small-sized, Australian-pattern greens. From then until Christmas he became part of the team. He wrote me the following note when we finally sent him home as a Christmas gesture:

> 'Since the day I left the VC ranks to return to the
> nation
> Good fortune led me to meet you [the Major] a kind
> person, a person
> who knows the wish for peace of each soldier
> And person living in society
> I do not sing prayers but I clearly understand all
> the [Australian]
> people have a boundless heart, to know and love the
> [Vietnamese] people,
> This I believe.
> Australia lives in happy peace and whose fault is it
> that they send
> their Army to help all the Vietnamese people destroy
> Communism.

Without pity, I never wasted time, to go and take my
place in and
eat with, the Australians.
And you [Major] who always looked after me as if I
were one of your soldiers.
Finally, I wish you good health, and all the
Australian soldiers health so as to destroy the
Communists more than ever.
Nien—I remember you, and thank you, Greetings and
Good health.
I shall always regard you as a member of my family in
this society.
Regards to the CSM, Jim, Ivan, John, Medic
Thank you, sir,
Hung
I write like this because I can't speak Australian.'

At 1 a.m. on 26 November, the Battalion was subjected to several
probing attacks. The perimeter held firm and there were no Australian
casualties. Viet Cong casualties were unknown, but several blood trails
were discovered by the clearing patrols at first light.

At first light that morning, Major Jim Tattam's C Company, mounted
in the Australian APCs, captured the road junction on the eastern edge of
Vo Xu. Healy's A Company moved by foot into a cutoff and fire support
position north west of the village. McFarlane and Rothwell had moved to
a position south of the village during the night to provide cutoff, to
deceive the enemy about the direction of assault and to give flanking fire
support. During these movements, which involved sweeping through a
number of small hamlets, the only action was when a lone mortar round
impacted near Battalion headquarters. The true origin of this 'mortar
round' has now come to light.[25]

During a sweep through the hamlet of Duc Hoa, a section commanded by Corporal Ron West had shaken out into extended line formation. As the line of men passed a pen containing a water buffalo, the
buffalo panicked, broke out of its pen and charged. All stepped back to let
the buffalo through except the last man, Private 'Rollo' Weitzman. As the
buffalo rammed into him, Weitzman hit the terrified animal across the
head with a loaded and cocked M79 grenade launcher. The whole section
heard the familiar hollow-sounding 'chuung' as the grenade was propelled into the air, in a high trajectory. No-one moved. After what seemed
like minutes, but could only have been seconds, they heard an explosion
to the west, in the vicinity of Battalion Headquarters. West rushed to check
Weitzman and found him to be uninjured. West and his men said nothing
and continued the sweep. Each man must have wondered whether there
had been any casualties; the tension among the soldiers was extremely

high. The penalty for an unauthorised discharge of a weapon was severe enough; what would happen to Weitzman if someone had been killed?

It was not long before the news was received that Battalion headquarters had been mortared but no casualties had been taken. This information broke the tension, and Ron West and his men broke into hysterical laughter. 'Rollo' Weitzman's confrontation with the buffalo was kept as a closely guarded secret among West's section for the remainder of the tour. However, this did not prevent many a laugh being had at Weitzman's expense when a section mate would ram into him in a bull-like manner at unexpected moments during beer drinking sessions for the amusement of the others.

That afternoon the Battalion prepared for another attack at first light the next day. This time the mission was to capture the village of Chan Duc immediately north of and contiguous with Duc Hanh. Healy's A Company had the task of capturing LZ HIPPO and Tattam's men were to assault and capture LZ RHINO, north west and north east of the village. At the same time McFarlane's B Company was to assault into the village itself. Chan Duc was a Catholic village which had been infiltrated and controlled by the Viet Cong for some time but, unlike Duc Hanh, was not fortified and there was easy access.[26]

The attack was not launched as planned because of some confusion about the route which would be used by elements of the ARVN 10 Division. At the last minute, McFarlane's men were given the task of picketing the southern route to Vo Xu for the passage of these elements. The South Vietnamese passed through without incident and the Battalion harboured for the night in the southern section of Duc Hanh.[27]

At this point of the operation, the advance by the Brigade up the La Nga Valley had gone well. The 2/503rd had increased the Brigade's area of control out from the airfield to the southern boundary of the village of Vo Dat. 1 RAR had captured the southern portion of the village of Duc Hanh and the road north from Vo Dat to Duc Hanh was secure.

At first light on 27 November, the attack planned for 26 November went ahead as Tattam's and McFarlane's companies assaulted to capture Chan Duc. Healy's and Rothwell's companies had been positioned by helicopter to cut-off positions in the north east and north west respectively. Under a shroud of thick fog, the assault into the village gained momentum. Rolling behind McFarlane's and Tattam's companies were the Australian APCs. These vehicles were used as mobile detention cells for Viet Cong suspects. During the 2-kilometre assault there was no opposition and 110 suspects were loaded into the APCs and moved to a central collection point manned by Second Lieutenant Bill Kaine's Anti Tank Platoon.[28]

That night the Battalion went into a defensive position. On 28

Major Mal Lander, Second-in-Command of 1 RAR, on the left with Major Paul Lipscombe, Officer Commanding 161 Reconnaissance Flight. Lander commanded 1 RAR during Operation NEW LIFE until the new Commanding Officer, Lieutenant Colonel Alex Preece, arrived. By that time he had planned and executed four battalion attacks.

November, companies conducted local patrolling and the Battalion consolidated its position while suspects were screened and intelligence information was gathered. To the east lay the fortified Viet Cong village of Vo Xu, and unlike Vo Dat which was Catholic, this village was considered to have been a Viet Cong stronghold for some years. Air photographs revealed that the village was criss-crossed with over 16 kilometres of trenches which interconnected a large complex of bunkers.[29]

That day Brumfield flew into Duc Hanh and toured the Battalion area saying farewell to his officers, NCOs and soldiers. It was a very sad moment for the Diggers as this very popular and well-respected officer made his last rounds of the unit he had virtually raised after its reorganisation and taken to war. He was accompanied by Brigadier David Jackson.

It was an especially poignant moment as he shook hands with his friend from Duntroon days, Major Don Kenning. As often occurs, such moments are interrupted by well-intended humour. The US pilot who flew the helicopter, used for psychological warfare, delivered the message through loud speakers as he flew over the battery position. In his best attempt at a British accent he said, 'I say, Colonel old chum, now that you have had a spot of tea with the Kiwis, how about you come over to say goodbye to us Yanks.'[30] Brumfield had lunch with Williamson that day and gave him a boomerang. In return, Williamson gave Brumfield a plaque with a US Infantryman's Combat Badge on it and the inscription, 'To the combat infantrymen of First Battalion, The Royal Australian Regiment, proven professionals.'[31]

Back at Duc Hanh, Major Mal Lander developed the plan for a battalion advance back into the fortified village of Vo Xu. This time he decided to vary the tactics employed for the D Company attack on Duc Hanh on 24 November. Deception was to be achieved by first deploying McFarlane's B Company by helicopter to a blocking position south west between Vo Xu and the Song La Nga. Then Rothwell's and Tattam's companies attacked the village in a line from the east: Rothwell north and Tattam south. Healy's A Company was in reserve mounted in APCs moved between Rothwell's and Tattam's companies with much noise and swept through the south eastern section of the village along the road and remained in reserve.[32]

Tattam's men assaulted in a thick blanket of ground fog. Unfortunately, an over-zealous soldier threw a canister of CS gas too close to the line of assaulting troops. The intention was to use these canisters to flush out defenders from their tunnels and bunkers. The soldier had been carrying the grenade ready to throw when ordered by his section commander, had seen some movement, and thrown it prematurely and inaccurately.[33]

Despite the uncomfortable sting of the CS gas, Tattam's men made good progress and did not encounter armed opposition. The villagers came out of bunker positions crying and wailing as the Australians strode in. Soon Tattam was joined by Rothwell's platoons and each company spread out on either side of the main road through the village. All of this was done to the pitiful sounds of crying and screaming and much over-acting as the CS gas affected the villagers. 'I can still see the old grandma striding through the gas, tears streaming, abusing the Australians for such nonsense', recalled McAulay later. 'Behind her was a waiting crowd of old men, women and kids following their "strong" leader.'[34]

The attack on Vo Xu was unopposed from within the village, but there was occasional inaccurate sniper fire from nearby jungle. All military-aged males were bundled into the APCs, which again served as mobile detention cells. After six hours of painstaking searching, screening and detaining suspects, Vo Xu was secure. The Battalion was orderd to return to Duc Hanh. Vo Xu was then attacked by an ARVN battalion supported by the US Cavalry Troop. The Australians were disgusted at this unnecessary and politically motivated show of force.[35]

On the same day, the northern approaches to Vo Xu were cleared by

Corporal Ken Forden (left) and Private John Jarrett (right), Anti-Tank Platoon 1 RAR, tying up Viet Cong Prisoners of War after the attack on Vo Xu. In the centre is an ARVN interpreter.

Rothwell's company using 'eagle flight' tactics. These tactics involved swarms of helicopters flying low across the ground with door gunners blazing away at any sign of movement. Thirty-nine Viet Cong suspects were cut off during these operations and, later, twenty were identified as members of the Local Force Viet Cong battalion. In all, 126 suspects were detained and many found to be Viet Cong.[36]

The other companies had secured a bridge over the La Nga River. The location was scenic and gave the Diggers an opportunity for swimming and washing themselves and their uniforms. Unfortunately this idyllic situation was spoiled because the area swarmed with snakes. No-one was going to share their sleeping space with these unwelcome reptiles. The villagers and Viet Cong alike must have been mystified by the sound of rhythmic thumping on the ground each night as the Diggers methodically pounded their sleeping areas with the backs of their entrenching shovels.[37]

Information had begun to flow a few days earlier on the identity and loctions of Viet Cong personnel. The strong show of force by the US, Australian and South Vietnamese troops had convinced villagers that the Viet Cong would never regain control of the area. Many relatives took advantage of a surrender program, offering the South Vietnamese govern-

Lieutenant Colonel Alex Preece. Preece faced the challenge of asserting command over the 1 RAR Group after they had been on operations for six months and had lost a popular commanding officer.

ment authorities sons, uncles, brothers, fathers and husbands for amnesty.[38]

Until early afternoon, McFarlane's men had no contact with the enemy. Second Lieutenant Bill Hindson's platoon had just finished having lunch when they were engaged by a platoon of Viet Cong from the eastern bank of the La Nga River. As luck would have it, Hindson's men became caught in a cross-fire from enemy and their comrades in the village engaging the same enemy. The Viet Cong platoon engaged the Australians in the village and maintained steady fire on Hindson's men.

The company mobile fire controller, Corporal Ken Phipps, quickly called for fire to suppress the enemy. Luck had really run out for Bravo Company, when the first fire mission fell 1500 metres short and landed among Second Lieutenants Graham Bolitho's and Rick Culpitt's men. Remarkably there were no casualties. There had been a problem with gridding Bravo Company's position relative to the mortar base plate location. After 30 minutes of exchanging fire, the Viet Cong were dispersed by mortar and artillery fire, and helicopters equipped with MAD (Mortar Air Delivery). They left four Viet Cong dead and several blood trails. The only Australian casualty during this engagement was Corporal Reg Hillier of 4 Platoon, shot in the chest while directing the fire of his section at the enemy. He died in the medical helicopter on its way to Bien Hoa and was awarded a posthumous Mentioned-in-Despatches for this and previous actions.[39]

After the capture of Vo Xu, the Battalion spent the next two days conducting an extensive patrol program to secure the surrounding area. Several very large rice caches were discovered and the contents backloaded or destroyed. The area of control expanded to 3000 metres around the village. The Australian Sappers spent much of their time performing road repair and trench-filling tasks.

A few days earlier Williamson had held his normal daily conference. Each of the unit and sub-unit commanders briefed the Brigade Commander on their activities. The US Engineer liaison officer reported that 20 000 gallons (100 000 litres) of water had been pumped from the Brigade water point in the last 24 hours but his unit had suffered one sapper killed and two wounded from sniper fire, bringing the total casualties at the water point to four killed and twelve wounded.

Williamson enquired why the engineers were suffering these casualties which were higher than any of the infantry battalions. With disarming clarity, the engineer officer replied that the Viet Cong were shooting them. Williamson then asked to have the location of the water point shown to him on the map. Noting it was some distance from Brigade Headquarters and other unit locations, Williamson then asked pointedly why it was so far away. The engineer in an equally blunt manner replied, 'Well, that's where the water is, Sir.' Suitable security arrangements were made for the water point for the remainder of the operation.[40]

At midnight on 3 December 1965, Lieutenant Colonel Alex Preece assumed command of 1 RAR from Major Mal Lander. After graduating from the Royal Military College, Duntroon, in 1946, Preece had joined 1 RAR's direct ancestor, 65th Battalion, during the occupation of Japan. He returned from Japan as Adjutant of the newly formed First Battalion of the Australian Regiment as it was then (before approval was given for the new regiment to be called the 'Royal' Australian Regiment). He had seen operational service in Korea in 1951–52 with 3 RAR.

In March 1965 Preece had been posted as Commander of the Australian Army Training Team—Vietnam. He was also the Deputy Commander, Australian Army Force—Vietnam. In this latter capacity, and having not been allocated any staff, he had been responsible for the disembarkation of 1 RAR from HMAS *Sydney* in June.[41]

Alex Preece was silver-haired, tough-minded and hard-driving. He now had the problem of taking control of an infantry battalion and a number of attached sub-units who had fought together for almost six months and had lost prematurely a popular Commanding Officer. One of Preece's first orders was to direct the resumption of daily shaving. The bearded warriors of 1 RAR now became clean-shaven, and the company commanders had to blacken their boots before attending orders at Bat-

From left to right: *Major John Healy, Officer Commanding A Company; Major John Hooper, Second-in-Command 1 RAR from November 1965; Major Don Kenning, Battery Commander 161 Field Battery, RNZA; and Lieutenant Colonel Alex Preece.*

talion Headquarters. There was no doubt that a new commander had taken over.[42]

Soon after Preece's arrival, Major Mal Lander left the Battalion. He had been selected to attend the Australian Staff College, Queenscliff, and was required to commence studies in January 1966. Lander left with mixed feelings. He had proven to be a capable Second-in-Command and a sound battalion commander on operations. To become just another student at Staff College must have been a letdown. After Preece arrived, Lander returned to Bien Hoa and made preparations to hand-over to his replacement.

On 4 December 1 RAR's new Second-in-Command arrived. Brumfield had asked for Major John Hooper to replace Lander having known him for some years and having grown to respect his abilities. They were not to serve together in Vietnam but met at Tan Son Nhut Airport as Brumfield departed wearing a neck brace and Hooper arrived with an agonising toothache caused by a molar which had split the evening before in Manila on a piece of chicken which Hooper recalled later must have been killed with a club.[43]

Hooper settled in quickly at Bien Hoa after treatment by dentist Captain Peter Naughton, and several days of being shown the ropes by Lander. He was a graduate of Duntroon, who had seen action with 3 RAR in Korea as a reinforcement platoon commander. He had served with 1

RAR in Australia and Malaya as Adjutant, and as a company commander. After attending the Australian Staff College, he had replaced Brumfield as the Tactics Instructor at the Royal Military College in 1964 when Brumfield joined 1 RAR. Hooper seemed destined to join battalions on operations as a reinforcement officer. He was to complete six months with 1 RAR before joining 6 RAR as the Second-in-Command when that battalion arrived in Vietnam in June 1966.

Hooper proved to be an ideal Second-in-Command. He was a quietly spoken, unflappable officer whose steady temperament and patience combined with Preece's irascible personality to produce a balanced command climate for the Battalion. Hooper was always able to anticipate the Battalion's supply needs and, therefore, respond promptly to Preece's operational demands. This was not an easy task given the intricacies of the dual US and Australian supply systems and the increasing tempo of operations which were being conducted at short notice in scattered and distant locations.

During the period 21–30 November, 1 RAR had conducted four deliberate battalion attacks. The attack plans had been characterised by deception, stealth, surprise and restraint in the use of artillery and air firepower. These tactics were very different from the tactics of the other two battalions of the 173rd. While 1 RAR consolidated its position and area of control over the southern part of the La Nga Valley, Lieutenant Colonel George E. Dexter's 2/503rd Battalion was given the mission of capturing the northern part of the valley.

On 1 December, 2/503rd began the first phase of its assault on the village of Thanh Duc, 7 kilometres north of 1 RAR's position at Vo Xu. An armoured wedge of 22 APCs assaulted into Thanh Duc behind a rolling artillery barrage and supported by several airstrikes. Commenting on this heavy reliance on firepower, two Americans who were there wrote:

> The use of air and artillery preparation had presented a complicating
> factor in the operation, for there was always the chance that
> innocent civilians, mixed in with enemy soldiers, would be injured:
> but, fortunately, through the professional competence of the
> forward air controllers and the artillery forward observers, the
> civilians in the village were unharmed—only the enemy, who
> offered resistance by manning defensive positions, were brought
> under the supporting fires.[44]

It was clear that Brigadier General Williamson's policy of 'bombs and bullets, not bodies' was being followed.

The next phase of the operation began on 2 December with the use of a mass of concentrated firepower. Areas of 1000 square metres were selected in the hills overlooking the northern area of the valley on the criteria that it was likely that enemy units were located inside them. Under

Dexter's direction, the artillery liaison and air liaison officers co-ordinated the resources of the Brigade to be able to saturate each 1000 square metre area at will. At the same time, Dexter ensured that his Battalion's 81 millimetre and 4.2 inch mortars were able to also concentrate their fire into these areas when required.

When the fire plan was executed, an area within the selected grid square was covered in one instant by several sorties of fighter ground attack aircraft followed by hundreds of rounds of artillery and mortar fire. These massive concentrations of fire were delivered randomly into the selected areas. The results were sketchy, but captured Viet Cong soldiers and the occasional deserter later described the terror caused by the selective use of concentrated firepower.

The 2/503rd achieved its mission by integrating firepower with patrolling. After an area was saturated with air, artillery and mortar fire, patrols would be flown in rapidly to assess results and engage any enemy that may have survived or moved into the area to investigate. The Paratroopers were pleased with the results of these tactics. They took few casualties and there were definite signs that the enemy had suffered heavy losses in the hills. There was one report of 40 soldiers from one Viet Cong company being killed in one combined air and artillery strike.[45]

The contrasts in tactics between 1 RAR and 2/503rd are obvious. The Americans enjoyed the orchestration of firepower, vehicles, aircraft and men. It was an exciting staff function to have these resources to manoeuvre. Equally, the Americans felt that the display of mobility and firepower would have a deep psychological impact on the Viet Cong. Not only would the enemy be kept off balance, but also he was not likely to contemplate concentrating his forces for operations because of the risk of being discovered and destroyed by forces deployed in helicopters and supported by vast quantities of air and artillery fire support.

Australian tactics were still influenced by the Malayan experience. Deception and surprise were the means used by the Australians to gain the advantage over the enemy, not a reliance on air and artillery fire support. However, Major Ian McFarlane probably summed up the Australian view at the time when he wrote:

> When the enemy became increasingly better equipped and we were finding him in greater strength and better organized, our attitudes to firepower changed. I believe that the other company commanders shared my conviction that our best interests were served, when we found the enemy, by hitting him with the hardest weaponry available, with due regard to the civilian population, and then using the foot soldier to mop up. We did not believe in the Audie-Murphy concept of hand-to-hand heroism practised by some American units.[46]

On 6 December there had been an example of what McFarlane had written about. Near the Michelin Plantation north of Ben Cat a battalion of the 1st Infantry Division had been credited with killing 200 Viet Cong and wounding many others after what the Commanding Officer had called a 'meeting engagement'. US casualties were described as moderate.[47] Second Lieutenant Clive Williams wrote to his family about this engagement a few days later:

> ... The US 1st Inf[antry] Div[ision] have just returned to Ben Cat. The VC ambushed a battalion of theirs at Ben Cat killing 60 and wounding 140. This was only about a mile from where my Corporal [Frank Smith] was killed a while back. You never read about an American mistake, in this case it was described as 'a US battalion came to grips with the enemy killing 200 and suffering moderate casualties'. Actually they only recovered 10 weapons so you can see it was a very one-sided affair. This annoys me because our battalion has only ever claimed when we have been able to produce a body.[48]

First-hand reports confirmed Williams' assessment. 'Some Americans were killed after fighting to their last bullet and using their rifles as clubs ... Men assaulted the enemy positions knowing they would die. More died trying to save wounded buddies. There were too many acts of heroism to say that one man was a hero.'[49] 'We got our tails kicked', Lieutenant Donald Noble was reported to have said at the time. 'Evidently the Viet Cong had this planned for a couple of days. They had freshly-dug bunkers camouflaged with escape tunnels—good defensive positions. We lost better than 50% of our company.'[50] Some battalion officers denied that they had been ambushed but admitted that they had looked for a fight and had 'piled on'.[51]

There is no denying that the infantrymen of the Big Red One had fought bravely and, during close quarter combat and through the use of artillery and airstrikes, had probably killed enough enemy to claim victory-by-body-count. However the Viet Cong had once again selected the time and place for battle and caused heavy casualties. Thus, Williamson's policy of 'bullets and bombs, not bodies' and the Australian's policy of 'hit with the hardest weaponry', then mop up with foot soldiers to defeat a well-equipped enemy with the tactical initiative, made good sense.

On 15 December, a warning order was received for an operation in the area of Xuan Loc in Long Khanh Province. There had been reports of the movement of battalion-sized Viet Cong forces in the area. The Battalion moved from Vo Xu and occupied a defensive position on the edge of the Vo Dat airfield. Unfortunately, Operation NEW LIFE drew to a close with the death of Corporal 'Jock' Fotheringham, the acting Platoon Sergeant of the Assault Pioneer Platoon. He suffered multiple shrapnel wounds while using a locally made Viet Cong grenade to detonate other grenades he was throwing down a disused well—it had an instantaneous fuse.[52] 'Later that day he was to return to Bien Hoa and from there back to Australia', recalled RSM McKay later. 'His wife was to have a baby by caesarean section and her doctor felt that he should be there. Poor Jock never made it.'[53]

This had been the Battalion's longest operation. It started briskly with airmobile and armoured assaults into the villages of Chanh Duc, Duc Hanh, Vo Dat and Vo Xu in the first week. For the next two weeks, the Brigade had dominated the area with firepower, eagle flights and foot patrols. Just over 250 local force Viet Cong had been captured. Sixty-one had been killed and 143 wounded. Twenty huge caches had been discovered which could have fed two Viet Cong regimental-sized groups for a year.[54] The price paid was two Australians killed and two wounded. For this operation casualties among the Paratroopers were comparable to the Australians—six killed and nineteen wounded.[55]

Most significantly, political control of the area had returned to the South Vietnamese Government; the sustained nature of the operation had paid off. The Viet Cong political infrastructure had been torn up through a series of desertions and captures. The Brigade was probably well satisfied that an area had been cleaned out and the Viet Cong military and political organisation destroyed.

Despite infrequent contact with the Viet Cong and the low casualties, many Australians were feeling the strain of prolonged exposure to danger. One NCO recalled:

> By this time people were starting to become worn out, especially those who had done every operation . . . I was worn down to the extent that at night I would curl up and bite my thumb knuckle to stop crying out when the guns fired. I broke the nights up into small sections, the way one does with a 9-mile run (ie, up to that tree, up to that corner, etc) and hung on up to the next burst of fire, then to the next and so on. I would promise myself constantly that I would go to the medic. I never did. I kept this routine up right through the bad time, came out at the other end after a few weeks and never had a bad time again. War became 'home' for me.[56]

Postscript

During Operation NEW LIFE, many members of the Viet Cong political cadre had been identified by village informers and captured. The villagers had co-operated with the Americans and the Australians in destroying Viet Cong control of their lives. They had demonstrated that they wanted a 'new life', or at least to be left alone to pursue their livelihoods.

When the 173rd left, the villages of Vo Xu, Vo Dat, Duc Hanh and Thanh Duc were occupied by ARVN units and restored to the political control of the South Vietnamese Government. On 28 February 1966, the 274th Regiment of the Viet Cong 5th Division attacked and overran the La Nga Valley. As an example to the inhabitants, the village of Vo Xu was razed to the ground and 3500 people were left homeless.[57]

It was also found during Operation NEW LIFE that the La Nga Valley was no longer the fifth largest rice-producing area in South Vietnam. The war had taken its toll and the farmers had been unable to even feed themselves and their families in face of lower yields and the confiscations of their produce by the Viet Cong. Despite the discovery of several large Viet Cong rice caches, thousands of tonnes of rice had to be transported into the La Nga Valley to feed its inhabitants.[58] For the campaign to protect the people of the La Nga Valley from domination by the Viet Cong and deny the enemy the surplus of the rice crop, Operation NEW LIFE had been a false harvest—the South Vietnamese Government was incapable of taking control after US and Australian units had cleared the area of Main Force Viet Cong units. This was the refrain for the remainder of the Vietnam War.

7 The river battles

In late December 1965 and early January 1966, 1 3RAR deployed for operations near the Nai and Oriental Rivers. The Paratroopers fought pitched battles with the Viet Cong and the Diggers had only fleeting contact with their opponents. Why was this so? Part of the answer can be found in the differences between two men: Major Ian McFarlane and Captain Les Brownlee.

On 17 December the Brigade was rushed to the Xuan Loc area after Intelligence reports that Viet Cong battalions were assembling south west of the Courtenay Plantation to attack three large towns in Phuoc Tuy Province over the Christmas and New Year period. The 173rd was to be joined by the 3rd Brigade of the Big Red One for a sweep down the banks of the Nai and Suoi Ca Rivers which were the probable locations of Viet Cong staging areas, transit camps and supply dumps.[1]

The only incident during the insertion of the Australians was the forced landing, due to mechanical failure, of the CH47 Chinook helicopter carrying Lieutenant Colonel Alex Preece and his battalion headquarters staff. The helicopter was repaired quickly under the watchful eyes of gunship pilots who ensured the Viet Cong did not attack this stricken aircraft and its occupants. When the Chinook took off, Second Lieutenant Jock Irvine, the Assistant Quartermaster, and two of his staff were left behind. Irvine responded to his predicament by throwing the entire headquarters supply of smoke grenades he was carrying. The resultant multicoloured smoke cloud attracted allied aircraft from several kilometres away, and he and his men were picked up promptly.[2]

The tactics of hammer and anvil were repeated. The 2/503rd swept down the western banks of the Nai River and 1 RAR patrolled forward in platoon groups along the eastern banks. The 1/503rd and the 3rd Brigade extended the line of advance to encompass an area between Highway 15 and Interprovincial Route 2. ARVN forces waited to the south for the Viet Cong to be flushed out. Ahead of the advancing infantrymen, B52s lay a carpet of bombs and other aircraft bombed and strafed suspected Viet Cong locations.

Captain Les Brownlee, Officer Commanding Company B 2/503rd Airborne Battalion. Company B, 'The Bulls', had had three company commanders in five months before Brownlee took over. They were proud of their record of killing more Viet Cong than any other company in the 173rd. In five months the equivalent of every man in the company had been wounded.

Major Ian McFarlane, Officer Commanding B Company 1 RAR. McFarlane did not want to give the Viet Cong any tactical advantage. His company patrolled in silence, waiting for the opportunity to surprise their opponents.

The only contact for the day was the wounding of Private A. P. Ling of Second Lieutenant Graham Bolitho's platoon. Bolitho's men had been sweeping through a village and had captured four military-age male suspects. A single burst of sub-machine gun fire wounded Ling in the stomach and right shoulder. He as evacuated immediately and later was flown back to Australia on Christmas Eve. He spent Christmas in hospital with his family courtesy of an unknown Viet Cong guerilla.

Despite the bombs, rockets and shells that preceded the advance, the Viet Cong were able to concentrate in strength against Company B 'The Bulls' and Company C of the 2/503rd. On the morning of 18 December these companies were surrounded and attacked. The Viet Cong broke contact an hour later. Five Paratroopers, including Lietuenant Joe Yatsko of the Reconnaissance Platoon, were killed and 25 others were wounded. The Paratroopers claimed 62 Viet Cong 'kills' for the engagement. Among the wounded was Captain Lee Wakefield, commander of 'The Bulls'—the third company commander to be severely wounded in command of this company.

Wakefield's replacement was Captain Romie 'Les' Brownlee, an enthusiastic, gregarious 26-year-old from Pampa, Texas. He was proud to have been given command of 'The Bulls' because of their reputation for fighting and beating the Viet Cong at close quarters. In six months, members of the company had been awarded 160 Purple Hearts which signified that the equivalent of every original member had been wounded at least once in battle. By December 1966 about a third of the company had been killed. 'The Bulls' claimed several hundred Viet Cong 'kills' and many more presumed killed and wounded in their numerous engagements.[3]

Brownlee was in no doubt about his company's mission: kill Viet Cong. To this end, his company was to operate as a noisy hunting party. There was little attempt to disguise their position on operations, whether on the move or stationary. On the move, all suspicious areas were engaged by small arms fire, known as 'reconnaissance by fire' and, if required, by artillery and airstrike. Paratroopers talked and smoked, and badges of rank, unit embellishments and other distinctively coloured items of dress and equipment were obvious. Rarely had the company surprised the Viet Cong. More often, the Viet Cong selected the time, place and duration of battle. The Bulls had not lost a battle and had shot their way out of several ambushes.

While stationary for any length of time, 'The Bulls' formed a tight circular defensive position but did not dig individual fighting trenches. It was common for them to join the other companies of the 2/503rd in a battalion position each night after a day's patrolling. In the evenings or the mornings they would fire off a 'basic load' of ammunition to clear any enemy from around their position and to make room for another 'basic load' of fresh ammunition, delivered daily by helicopter, either in the evening or early in the morning. Noisy movement, helicopter resupply and casualty evacuation, and clearance of their perimeters by fire continually updated the Viet Cong on Company B's location.

Representative of Australian methods of operation was the B Company of 1 RAR commanded by 32-year-old, taciturn and intense Major Ian McFarlane. McFarlane's B Company operated in a totally different manner to Brownlee's B Company. He did not allow his Diggers to speak during operations. All communication was by hand signal or whisper. On the move, the company was dispersed into platoon patrols where the only sounds would be the whispers of the signallers sending and receiving messages. Everyone was dressed in the same drab green uniforms with no badges or rank or unit embellishments showing and all shiny objects and surfaces were painted black. Smoking was restricted to 10 minute breaks in patrolling and only after sentries and machine guns had been positioned to observe likely enemy approaches. At night there was complete silence. At first and last light the Diggers would 'stand to' on full alert and patrols would be sent out to clear the areas surrounding the company position. Rarely would the company spend the night in a battalion defensive position. Helicopter resupply was restricted to every few days and the company would always move away quickly from the location of resupply. Quiet movement, frequent changes of location, infrequent resupply and dispersion meant the Viet Cong were never sure of the location of McFarlane's company or the other companies of 1 RAR.

Paramount in McFarlane's mind was to never allow the Viet Cong to gain any tactical advantage. He wanted to find Viet Cong units, manoeuvre his platoons into the best tactical position, co-ordinate as much firepower as possible and then attack. Paramount in Brownlee's mind was to attack the Viet Cong as quickly as possible under the cover of as much firepower as possible. The difference between these two officers was their perceptions of the need for tactical security, manoeuvre and risk-taking. Within the next three months, both McFarlane and Brownlee would be wounded leading their companies in battle and be recommended for bravery awards. However the results of their efforts would be very different.

The last days of this operation passed with only light contact with the Viet Cong. An engagement was fought by Second Lieutenant Rick Culpitt's platoon which resulted in two Viet Cong being killed and several more wounded. The Diggers and Paratroopers were pleased the operation finished before Christmas as there were rumours of a Christmas truce, peace talks and a de-escalation of the war.

On Christmas Eve 1965 President Johnson ordered a pause in the bombing of targets in North Vietnam and declared a truce throughout South Vietnam. These measures were taken to prompt the Government in Hanoi to start negotiations to end the war. Johnson promised that, if there was diplomatic progress, the pause in the bombing would continue and a cease-fire declared.[4]

Johnson's initiatives contributed to an already festive mood among the service personnel of Bien Hoa Airbase. Air and artillery activity were at an unprecedented low. The relative quiet of the airbase suggested there might be some hope of the war scaling down and permitting troops who had already served six months to return home. There were strong rumours that 1 RAR would return to Australia in March 1966.

The parties around the airbase started on Christmas Eve and many did not stop until the dawn of Christmas Day. Many Diggers paused from their festivities to attend midnight Mass said by Father Gerry Cudmore. On Christmas Day Cardinal Spellman from the US said Mass in the open

Left: *Chaplain Gerry Cudmore, Roman Catholic Padre 1 RAR, riding a captured Viet Cong bicycle at Bien Hoa. Cudmore said Mass on the bonnet (hood) of a jeep and comforted the wounded on operations.* Right: *Entertainer Lynne Fletcher at Bien Hoa during Christmas 1965. She was 18 years old when she sang to the soldiers in Vietnam. Many were reminded of their wives, sisters and girlfriends, and a life they had almost forgotten that existed away from the requirement to kill or be killed.*

at the airbase. Early on Christmas morning, the officers, warrant officers and sergeants served the Diggers café royale—rum with a little coffee added to taste. At midday the Messes began serving beer again and traditional roast dinners followed by Christmas pudding were consumed in the tropical heat.

Of special significance was the promise of Australian entertainment on Christmas Day. Bill Watson, an entertainment manager, who had been providing Australian entertainers for the Hilton chain of hotels in Asia for a number of years, led one of the first troupes to Vietnam. In 1965 he had returned from an entertainment tour via Vietnam and discovered that no Australian entertainment was being provided to the Australians serving there. He approached the Australian Government through the Returned Services League and received a curt reply that the government would take no responsibility for the welfare of Australian entertainers who decided to perform in Vietnam. Enclosed were indemnity forms which were to be signed as verification that the entertainers would expect no assistance and compensation from their government should they entertain in Vietnam. Watson persevered and eventually gained sponsorship from the US Overseas organisation which provided a $5-a-day fee, and accommodation, meals and transport courtesy of the US armed forces.[5]

One Australian entertainer Lucky Starr recalled later: 'We did it out of purely emotional reasons—honest emotional reasons. We didn't do it because we wanted to make money there or to further careers. I did it because no one else was there.'[6]

The troupe that entertained the Diggers from an improvised stage on the back of a semitrailer on Christmas Day included Lucky Starr and his band the Rajahs, 18-year-old singer Lyn Fletcher, Hal Wayne and Patsy O'Hara.

An unexpected arrival during the show on Christmas Day was Don Lane, an American-born entertainer, who had been based in Australia for some years. For some weeks previously he had been canvassing the possibility of entertaining Australian troops in Vietnam. He was furious when he found out that a troupe was going to entertain them on Christmas Day. He flew into Saigon on Christmas Day and went immediately by helicopter to Bien Hoa Airbase, arriving in the middle of a song being sung by Lucky Starr. The rotors of Lane's helicopter sent dust swirling over the entertainers and the audience. After initial anger at the interruption to his song, Lucky Starr had the crowd of Diggers applaud Lane and invited him to finish the song with him.[7]

Bill Watson's troupe had entertained at the Australian Gun Battery and Tommy Hanlon, another American-born entertainer based in Australia, put on a show in the rear of the 1 RAR position. In his troupe were Ian Turpie, Buddy England, Pat Carroll and Yvonne Barrett. They were

Regimental Sergeant Major Don 'Macka' McKay on the right, pictured with Warrant Officer Jack Currie who succeeded him as RSM after McKay returned to Australia in December 1966. McKay always preferred to carry an Owen Machine Carbine. This was the weapon he had used in 1943 as a 19-year-old corporal to kill Japanese on the Kokoda Trail in Papua New Guinea. For his valour in that campaign he was awarded the Military Medal.

overwhelmed by the enthusiastic reception. The Diggers had an insatiable desire for anything that reminded them of home. Christmas cards and presents from loved ones, school children and fellow Australians partly renewed their faith that they were not forgotten. Don Lane recalled: ''Of all the Diggers I talked to, they said the same thing to me, just tell the people back in Australia not to forget about us because we get the feeling that many do not care that we are here and many have forgotten that we are here.'[8]

Lucky Starr became a particular friend of the Battalion, having been the first to entertain them in October. He was remembered by many Diggers for setting up his band on a truck near the wire entanglements of the 1 RAR defensive position and singing songs to the weary patrols returning from the Tactical Area of Responsibility.

However, the most consistent source of comfort to the Diggers returning from patrols was Brigadier Aubrey Hall of the Salvation Army, providing hot and cold drinks, biscuits and chewing gum. Hall was in his early 60s, being easily the oldest member of the 1 RAR Group in Vietnam. His tireless efforts did great credit to him as a man in the service of God and to the Salvation Army who had sent him. Many letters from the Diggers to their loved ones were written on stationery bearing the Salvation Army Red Shield provided free by Aubrey Hall. Other organistions that provided timely amenities and commodities for the Diggers were the Red Cross and the Returned Services League.

On Christmas Day Brigadier David Jackson was one of the many visitors to the Battalion. He issued the following message to the Australians serving in South Vietnam:

> During Christmas and New Year our thoughts very naturally turn even more to those at home who are near and dear to us. We can only pray that our efforts here will help the Vietnamese people to win their long struggle for the same human rights enjoyed by those loved ones. How long it takes depends on our efforts, the efforts of those with whom we fight, and the speed with which the Communists realise that they are not going to impose their will on the South Vietnamese people. I am deeply proud of your soldierly achievements and of your determination, courage and cheerfulness in face of the very considerable challenges you have had to face. Australia can be very proud that you have done everything that has been asked of you and more, and done it well . . . The Force has received an enormous volume of Christmas mail and parcels and heart-warming messages.[9]

The Battalion had lost about 10 per cent of its strength in six months. Since June, 112 men had been replaced with fellow regulars, mostly from 2 RAR. The Army had decided not to reinforce 1 RAR with conscripts. This was a wise decision because the Diggers of 1 RAR were very conscious of their professional, volunteer status. About half the replacements were made because of battle casualties and the rest because of injury and sickness.[10] Second Lieutenant Peter Sibree left the Battalion in December suffering from scrub typhus echoing the feeling of many of his fellow platoon commanders: 'I've had fellows in my platoon hit and I did not like it. When it's the Viet Cong it's not too bad because you've got something to go for. When it's booby traps, there isn't anything to fight back against.'[11]

Having lost the Commanding Officer, Lou Brumfield, and Second-in-Command, Mal Lander in December, the Battalion was further saddened to lose the Regimental Sergeant Major, Macca McKay. He had not been fully fit on embarkation but nothing would prevent him from joining his

Officers of 1 RAR January 1966. (Front row left to right) *Major B.J. Harper, Major I.D. McFarlane, Major J.A. Hooper, Lieutenant Colonel A.V. Preece, Major J.B. Healy, Major I.S. Fisher, Major J.J. Tattam, Major J. Essex-Clark, Captain R.A. Ducie.* (Second row left to right) *Second Lieutenant W.E. Kaine, Captain M.C. Peck, Captain M.J. Carroll, Captain T.J. Buckley, Captain P.M. Arnison, Chaplain G.A. Cudmore, Second Lieutenant H.E.N. Martens.* (Third row left to right) *Second Lieutenant R.J. Davis, Second Lieutenant G.E. Bolitho, Second Lieutenant W.F. Hindson, Lieutenant I.M. Guild, Second Lieutenant C.O.G. Williams, Second Lieutenant E.J. Culpitt.* (Back row left to right) *Second Lieutenant H.L. Gauvin, Second Lieutenant O.S. Lind, Lieutenant W.J. Giles, Second Lieutenant R.D. Loftus, Lieutenant G.J. Porter, Second Lieutenant C.J. MacIntyre, Second Lieutenant N.E. Brown.*

battalion at war. The stress of the past six months had led to a further deterioration in his health. McKay had a unique flair for exercising firm control while maintaining a rich sense of humour. He and his closest friend, Warrant Officer Jack Currie, often kept social gatherings alive with their antics. Elsewhere, they were the masters of the practical joke and the spontaneous playlet. He had a fierce pride in the traditions of the Australian infantry, insisting that every member of the Battalion maintain the reputation earned in previous wars. Most appropriately, Jack Currie was appointed to his position until a replacement arrived.

On 27 December the truce ceased and the artillery and aircraft of the airbase roared to life again. A patrol from the 2/503rd was ambushed in their Tactical Area of Responsibility by Viet Cong using .50 calibre and .30 calibre machine guns, killing four and wounding six—a sudden reminder to the Brigade that the killing was about to start again.[12]

Westmoreland planned to consolidate the gains made in 1965 by conducting further spoiling attacks against major concentrations of Viet

Cong troops and key installations. Although he felt that his US forces had progressed from being 'fire brigades' and would spend more time maintaining population security, the emphasis continued to be on short-term search and destroy operations. Around the Saigon area the US 1st Infantry Division, reinforced by the 173rd Airborne Brigade, was to keep the pressure on the Viet Cong's 9th and 5th Divisions, who were receiving hundreds of North Vietnamese reinforcements each week.[13]

On 28 December Williamson issued orders for Operation MARAUDER to be conducted along the Oriental River in the Boa Trai area of Hau Nghia Province. The quarry for this search and destroy operation was the Viet Cong 506th Local Force Battalion.[14] It was the first by an Allied formation into the Mekong Delta area known as the Plain of Reeds, a flat swampy area interlaced with canals and natural waterways servicing extensive rice paddies.

The operation started on New Year's Day: there had been little celebration the night before. The new year was ushered in with the familiar trip to the Snake Pit in 'cattle trucks' amidst the din of helicopter engines and the roar of fighter ground attack aircraft overhead. The Diggers had a wet and uncomfortable start to the operation when they were inserted into waist deep, inundated swamp, 1000 metres away from the intended landing zones. This error saved them from being fired on by Viet Cong who were positioned to cover the landing areas. The 1/503rd assaulted into their landing zones and were fired on by 50–60 Viet Cong. Two hours later the Paratroopers forced the Viet Cong to withdraw. They had suffered five wounded with Viet Cong casualties unknown.[15] Once again the Viet Cong had forewarning of the Brigade's operational plans.

1 RAR and the 1/503rd were positioned astride the Oriental River—the Paratroopers to the west and the Diggers to the east. The next day the 2/503rd flew in east of the river, south of 1 RAR's area. The Viet Cong were waiting and twelve helicopters were hit by ground fire. The larger CH47 Chinook helicopters which could carry 30 combat-laden soldiers attracted most of the enemy fire. The Paratroopers had leapt from their helicopters firing their weapons and charging fortified positions that had been constructed on the periphery of their landing zones. The Viet Cong had begun to counter airmobile assault tactics by surviving the artillery missions and airstrikes preceding the arrival of the helicopters, and anticipating where the Brigade would land.

Captain Les Brownlee's Company B had led the assault through knee- to waist-deep water and were now involved in a fire fight with two reinforced companies from the Viet Cong 267 Main Force Regiment positioned in a series of bunkers built into rice paddy bunds. His company was soon joined by Company A and Company C. A stalemate ensued with both sides pouring thousands of rounds into each other's positions.

The Paratroopers of 2/503rd moving through waist-deep water after airmobile assaults into the Plain of Reeds on Operation MARAUDER.

Two more helicopters were hit by ground fire with every man in one crew wounded. After three hours, 'The Bulls' had suffered seven killed and fifteen wounded. Four Paratroopers, including a platoon commander, had been killed and six wounded when a bomb had been released prematurely from a US fighter ground attack aircraft.

The Commanding Officer of the 2/503rd, Lieutenant Colonel George Dexter, was faced with the prospect of the battle continuing as a fire fight until nightfall and the Viet Cong withdrawing under the cover of darkness. He decided on a deliberate attack under the cover of artillery and airstrikes, supported by the Brigade's six M56 90 millimetre Self Propelled Anti Tank guns commanded by Captain John 'Moose' Dunlop.

At 4 p.m. after the Viet Cong positions had been pounded once more by artillery and airstrikes, Dexter's three companies rose along one broad front and charged. Despite not being able to find the flanks of the Viet Cong positions, the Paratroopers forced the Viet Cong to withdraw and the killing started. Each company had been given a battery of field artillery in direct support. Once over the enemy bunkers, Brownlee and his fellow company commanders co-ordinated small arms and artillery fire onto the withdrawing Viet Cong who were caught in the open paddy fields. Ninety-eight Viet Cong bodies were counted the next day. In all, the Paratroopers had killed 114 Viet Cong by actual body count and captured six wounded. Many Viet Cong weapons were lost in the soft grey mud of the flooded paddy fields. In the assault, three more Paratroopers had been killed and about 30 wounded. By 11 a.m. the next day overall casualties to the Brigade were ten killed and 61 wounded. For his bravery in this day-long engagement, Captain Les Brownlee was recommended for the Silver Star.

On the same day the Diggers had little contact with the Viet Cong. Small groups had tried to infiltrate into the Australian area but had been driven off by accurate small arms fire. Second Lieutenant Kevin Lunny's platoon had killed two and wounded two others after co-ordinating fire from the Australian APCs protecting Battalion headquarters.[16] This brought some satisfaction to the Diggers of this platoon: half were veterans of Lieutenant John MacNamara's old platoon that had taken heavy casualties in the Iron Triangle and the other half were reinforcements who now considered themselves to have been 'blooded'.

One infiltrator, nicknamed 'H and I Charlie' because of his personal efforts to pin down the entire Battalion headquarters and an US gun battery, caused anxiety for some hours. A fire support base had been set up on a large piece of high ground amidst the flooded area where the Australians had been landed. A lone Viet Cong soldier kept popping up from the surrounding waters and spraying the area with rounds from a Thompson sub-machine gun. This brave individual kept this up for some time—popping up, firing, disappearing and reappearing in a different place. Eventually, one of Captain Bob Hill's vehicle commanders received permission to float his APC out from the high ground and wait for 'H and I Charlie'. This paid off as the Viet Cong soldier popped up from the water and was killed by a long burst of .30 calibre machine gun fire.[17]

Early on 3 January two rounds from the New Zealand Gun Battery fell among Company C of the 2/503rd, killing three Paratroopers and wounding seven more. After the data was checked on the guns and found to be correct, Major Don Kenning concluded that the two erratic rounds from the eight-round mission had malfunctioned because of 'damp powder, cold tube or climatic conditions'.[18]

Later that morning a platoon from Delta Company mounted in Australian APCs travelled at speed across a number of inundated paddies and small streams. Most of the streams were fast flowing and shallow. Because of the risk of getting bogged, the drivers were intent on maintaining maximum speed until there was firmer ground. One APC hit a stream which looked much like the others but, instead of a few centimetres of fast running water, was a canal 3 metres deep. The vehicle sank rapidly into the slowly churning black water.

Lance Corporal Denis Shergold surfaced with five others including the vehicle's driver and commander. He did a quick roll call of the men in his section and realised that three had not surfaced from the submerged

APC. After discarding his webbing, he dived into the murky water, felt his way into the open hatch, grabbed one unconscious Digger and then another. Hugging them to him, he pushed off and reached the surface. Though exhausted, he dived again for the other soldier and pulled him out from inside the APC. All of those recovered by Shergold survived.[19]

The other APCs had stopped, driven to the scene of the accident and seven had become bogged. They could not be extracted before nightfall so Second Lieutenant Rick Culpitt's platoon was tasked to guard the vehicles overnight. These men spent a very uncomfortable night, some sleeping in, and on top of, vehicles and others on improvised platforms made of jerry cans of water. The next morning Captains Peter Rothwell and Bob Hill devised a plan to link unbogged APCs and pull out those that were bogged. There was a need, however, for an initial jerk to free the bogged APCs from the glutinous mud. A US warrant officer agreed to use his CH47 Chinook helicopter to provide this initial momentum.

Rothwell sat next to the pilot as the Chinook took up the strain on the steel cable that linked it to the first APC. Rothwell asked the pilot what would happen if the cable broke. The pilot turned to him with a wide grin and said, 'If that cable snaps, brother, this bird is going to turn itself on its arse and we will burn, man, burn!' The Chinook was a success as an aerial tow truck and all the APCs were recovered.[20]

Near last light on 4 January, Major Ian McFarlane's B Company had found a position for the night near a hamlet about five kilometres from the other companies of the Battalion. As the company approached this position, Corporal Bob Evans reported that he and his scout had heard voices on the other side of a canal that was between the company and the hamlet, and had seen two soldiers wearing steel helmets.[21]

McFarlane was concerned since only Main Force Viet Cong soldiers or North Vietnamese regulars wore steel helmets.

> I suspected a major force of NVA [North Vietnamese Army]. Last light was not the time to start action against dug in North Vietnamese regulars, particularly since we were far from back-up support and in difficult terrain. I harboured the company up between the two canals and prepared to attack the next morning.

As an additional precaution, McFarlane had Corporal Evans lay an ambush on the bank of the canal in case a force of steel-helmeted enemy soldiers left the hamlet and attempted to cross the canal near where the remainder of the company were positioned.

McFarlane's attack plan was to pull back in the morning and hit the hamlet with artillery and airstrikes. Second Lieutenant Graham Bolitho's platoon would then assault into the hamlet covered by the two other platoons who would remain on the canal bank. Bolitho's men were to use wooden planks to cross the canal.

After an hour's delay getting air clearance for the artillery to fire, the company Forward Observer from the Australian Gun Battery, Captain Ken Bade, brought several missions onto the hamlet, concluding with incendiary white phosphorous rounds. The hamlet which was already ablaze was then hit with napalm, Cluster Bomb Units and 20 millimetre cannon from Skyraider aircraft. Minutes after the last strafing run, Bolitho's men assaulted into the ruined hamlet in time to see nine unarmed military-aged males running into the dense sugarcane fields south east of the village.

Afterwards ten women and a number of children were discovered in the bunkers in the hamlet area. The only casualty was an old man who had been hit by shrapnel. He was evacuated later by helicopter to hospital. Though reluctant to talk, the women eventually admitted that about twenty Main Force Viet Cong had spent the night in the hamlet and had fled as soon as the airstrikes had finished. The escaping, unarmed males were probably the women's husbands and relatives.

McFarlane's attack on this hamlet typified many of the dilemmas involving tactical security, manoeuvre, risk-taking and civilians in target areas that faced commanders in the Vietnam War. McFarlane's first thoughts on discovering enemy in the hamlet were to assess the risk involved in attacking immediately despite the fading light, the canal obstacle and the probability of there being a force of Main Force regulars in bunkers in the hamlet.

He decided to forego the opportunity presented at last light and wait until the morning when he would have been able to develop a plan, give orders to his platoon commanders, have them pass orders onto the Diggers and co-ordinate fire support for the attack. He had thought of manoeuvring his platoons around the hamlet to cut off escape routes but decided instead that he wanted the attack to be preceded by airstrikes which precluded such manoeuvre because of the safety distances required between the exploding bombs and the nearest troops.

The other factor which might have influenced his use of firepower was the probability of civilians living in the hamlet. As far as he was concerned, the occupation of the hamlet by the Viet Cong classified it as a military target and allowed him to use as much firepower as was operationally necessary. His first loyalty was to the survival of his men who took the risks of war, not to Vietnamese civilians who were unlucky enough to be in the wrong place at the wrong time. Moreover, he knew that the hamlet, like all the others in the area, had bunkers in which civilians could shelter.

McFarlane had decided to maintain his tactical security at all times and conduct an attack which would ensure his men had the optimum advantage over the enemy before being committed to the assault. In so doing, he lost the element of surprise and a platoon of Main Force Viet Cong escaped to fight another day.

In contrast, Captain Les Brownlee's Paratroopers would have most likely fired immediately on sighting the two steel-helmeted soldiers and charged into the hamlet with weapons blazing. However, it is equally likely that the noisy approach of the Paratroopers would have warned the Viet Cong who may have fled after trying to pick off one or two Americans, or without even firing a shot.

By 6 January the Brigade had captured 326 Viet Cong suspects, killed numerous domestic animals and destroyed a number of Viet Cong camps in which weapons, supplies and documents had been found. Hamlets were destroyed if aircraft received ground fire from them. The peasants of the Plain of Reeds were paying dearly for the Viet Cong presence in their area; just over 500 had been made homeless.[22]

On 6 January the 506th Local Force Battalion hit back at the 2/503rd. Two companies, supported by 82 millimetre mortars, attacked the Paratroopers from two directions just before last light and withdrew having only wounded two Americans and leaving two of their own dead. It was a futile gesture by the local Viet Cong Commander.

The operation concluded on 7 January and was deemed to be successful. The Brigade claimed 131 Viet Cong killed and 43 wounded and captured. Of the several hundred military-aged males rounded up in the hamlets of the area, 61 had been identified by ARVN interrogators as Viet Cong. Despite the numbers of Viet Cong killed, only thirteen rifles, two machine guns, one grenade launcher and five sub-machine guns had been captured. The price paid for this success had been fifteen Paratroopers killed and 82 wounded.[23] The Diggers had killed three Viet Cong, wounded four and captured two rifles without taking any casualties.[24]

On 7 January preparations were made in great secrecy for an operation into the Ho Bo Woods near the Iron Triangle. Rather than return to Bien Hoa Airbase, Major General Dupuy, Commander of the Big Red One, sought tactical surprise by redeploying the 173rd within 24 hours of the completion of Operation MARAUDER against one of the most highly prized installations in South Vietnam: the Viet Cong Headquarters of the 4th Military Region which co-ordinated all political and military operations in the Saigon area and surrounding provinces.

8 The Ho Bo Woods

Operation CRIMP caught the Viet Cong by surprise. The ARVN were not informed of this operation.[1] The aim was to capture the Ho Bo Woods area and destroy the Special Sector Headquarters and the extensive tunnel system. The fighting was fierce and the casualties high.

The Ho Bo Woods was a heavily defended Viet Cong sanctuary four kilometres west of the Iron Triangle. The Saigon River ran north to south along the eastern edge of the area which was a mixture of abandoned rubber plantations, village gardens, cleared areas and clumps of secondary jungle. The ARVN had not conducted operations in the area for three years and Westmoreland and Dupuy suspected that in the intervening period the Viet Cong had built the Saigon–Cholon–Gia Dinh Special Sector Headquarters which controlled all the military and political operations in the Saigon area.[2]

Dupuy gave two of his infantry brigades, reinforced by the 173rd, the mission of destroying this headquarters. He deployed his third brigade to Bien Hoa Airbase to take up the 173rd's responsibilites for perimeter defence. The operation was called CRIMP to symbolise how Dupuy planned to squeeze the Viet Cong between his brigades. The concept was to block escape routes to the north and south of the Ho Bo Woods and sweep through the area with the 173rd and the 3rd Infantry Brigade. Williamson in turn devised a similar concept with 1 RAR blocking in the north of the Brigade's area of operations while the Paratroopers assaulted likely locations for the Viet Cong Headquarters to the west and south west—he intended the Special Sector Headquarters to be destroyed by his Sky Soldiers.

On the afternoon of 7 January Major John Essex-Clark flew low and fast in a helicopter over the assault landing zone proposed by the Brigade staff for 1 RAR's use on the operation. This was his standard practice before operations to confirm the locations and suitability of landing zones.

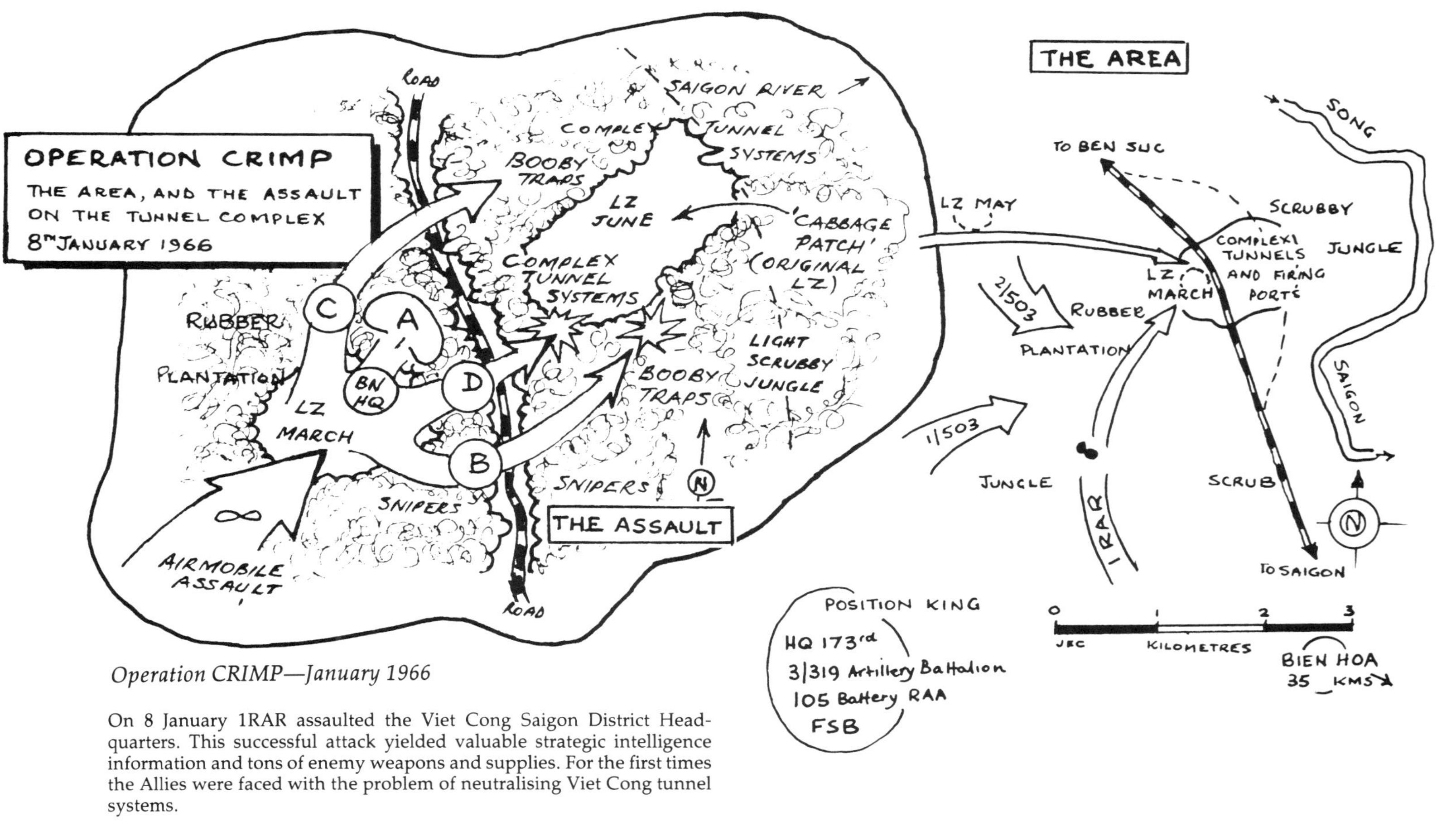

Operation CRIMP—January 1966

On 8 January 1RAR assaulted the Viet Cong Saigon District Head-quarters. This successful attack yielded valuable strategic intelligence information and tons of enemy weapons and supplies. For the first times the Allies were faced with the problem of neutralising Viet Cong tunnel systems.

He often took photographs for use in briefing the company commanders. As he flew over LZ JUNE he noticed that there were no leaves under the trees surrounding the area where the helicopters would set down the next day. He thought the leaves were probably covered with soil from recently constructed enemy fortifications. On his return to the Brigade assembly area in the Plain of Reeds, he spoke with Preece and was directed to raise the matter with the Brigade staff. Heated argument followed as the staff were reluctant to change their plans at the last moment. Essex-Clark had his way only after Williamson himself became involved in the discussions. The landing zone was changed from LZ JUNE to LZ MARCH.[3]

The written orders for Operation CRIMP were deliberately delayed so they would not reach ARVN III Corps Headquarters until the assault helicopters were in the air. Despite this effort to achieve tactical surprise, the Radio Research Unit detected and monitored a radio transmission to the Saigon–Cholon–Gia Dinh Special Sector Headquarters as the first helicopters were leaving on the morning of 8 January warning the Viet Cong that the Paratroopers and Diggers were inbound.[4]

Major Ian McFarlane's B Company led the Australian airmobile assault into LZ MARCH. The first flight of helicopters was not opposed and McFarlane ordered his men to push out and clear an area of rubber trees to make room for the incoming companies. As the second flight of helicopters approached, two gunships swooped in and began strafing those Diggers from the first flight who had pushed out. Bullets impacted only centimetres from some soldiers. The gunships were warned off after frantic radio calls, and the hurried throwing of smoke grenades and display of marker panels.[5]

During their assaults, the Paratroopers suffered light casualties from ground fire and several helicopters were hit. The 1/503rd assaulted out of their landing zone killing several Viet Cong who had been firing at them and their helicopters from well-camouflaged spider holes on the edge of the landing zone.[6]

The Australian companies were consolidating in areas around the landing zone under increasing enemy sniper fire when artillery shells started to fall and 'walk' towards Battalion headquarters. Chaos ensued as everyone looked for somewhere to protect themselves. McAulay wrote:

> Sluggo, Blue Talbot and I squeezed into ONE shellscrape [narrow one-man rectangular hole dug by Australians for protection]. Talk about scared. Many people had no shellscrape because we had not been there very long and had to run back where we were—ran around like chickens with their heads cut off. The Arty just kept coming across the landing zone.[7]

Lieutenant Colonel John Warr, Commanding Officer of 5 RAR, was visiting the Battalion and had decided to accompany the Battalion headquarters into the Ho Bo Woods dressed in an officer's peak cap, light-weight polyester summer dress shirt and trousers, black walking shoes, and carrying a brief case. Major John Essex-Clark recalled vividly the sight of Warr, with brief case still in hand, diving into a shellscrape at the same time as Essex-Clark's orderly, Private Mick Lourigan.[8]

Private Carey McQuillan recalled:

> The first salvo hit a line of rubber trees in a ball of flame with disintegrating metal and wood. The line of trees was no more than 200 metres from where I stood. I remember thinking, 'What the bloody hell was that?' My answer arrived very shortly after when the next salvo impacted 20–30 metres closer, amid yells of 'Take cover!' These salvos then proceeded to walk right over and through us. I recall during this the words of an instructor at the Infantry Centre when I was a bit idle digging a weapon pit, 'One of these days, lad, you will dig a bloody hole with your hands faster than that! Get working! He would have been proud of me—deep and fast, by hand![9]

The steady approach of shells was stopped by an irate Essex-Clark about 100 metres from unprotected troops lying on the ground. He had rushed to the Fire Control Centre and delivered a strongly worded message to the US Gunners by radio. Later in the afternoon, a further nine rounds were to impact about 150 metres from the Battalion Command Post. This time Essex-Clark visited the US battery commander responsible in person to express his disappointment at his battery's shooting.

The Australians consolidated around LZ MARCH until the Para-troopers completed their airmobile assaults. At midday Preece ordered the move to the village area located on the banks of the Saigon River. The Diggers advanced cautiously because of reports of enemy fortifications between them and the village. They were also advancing towards LZ JUNE which had been the proposed landing zone for the operation. Because of the possibility of enemy-occupied fortifications, Preece ordered his US Forward Air Controller, Major Hank Snow, to saturate the area ahead of the Diggers with bombs and rockets. The Australians stepped off with the sounds of the explosions of bombs and rockets still ringing in their ears. Preece had taken all the tactical precautions possible but had not counted on the ingenuity of his opponents who waited unharmed below ground ready to strike.

'My platoon was hit, and properly hit soon after we crossed the road', recalled Second Lieutenant Jim Bourke.[10] Bourke's men had been leading their company towards LZ JUNE. As he approached the cleared area of the landing zone, he observed Battalion headquarters personnel led by Captain Mick Carroll laying out the future site for Battalion headquarters in light timber to the west and the lead elements of McFarlane's B

Company moving in the jungle to the north. Assuming that the area had been cleared, Bourke decided to have his men save time by cutting across the clearing to avoid elements of Healy's A Company that had stopped to search fortifications in their area to the south east. He planned to cut into the jungle further north.

'There was a washout in front of us, where the water had gouged out the track like a creek bed. That's where we had our first casualties', recalled Bourke. As the leading sections moved into the open and through the tree line from the south-west corner of the clearing, they were engaged by a Viet Cong soldier firing a Thompson sub-machine gun from the north-east corner of the clearing. Bourke's men rushed forward and sought cover in the depression caused by the sunken road. Unknown to them, they had deployed into the Viet Cong commander's 'killing ground'. A mound of earth like an island dominated the washed-out gully areas where the Diggers took cover. The mound had been hollowed out and small firing slits constructed so soldiers could crawl through a connecting tunnel undetected and fire at troops crossing the clearing without being seen.

The opening burst of automatic fire from the mound scythed through Corporal Ron Smith's section. Private Eddy Grills was hit in the hand and right leg, and a bullet broke Private Grinter's jaw. 'Smith, poor bugger, took two bullets through the eye. One came out his forehead and the other came out further up. I coud see his brains exposed, but he was still moving a little so I knew he wasn't dead yet', Bourke recalled. As Smith's forward scout, Private Barry Delaney, turned to assist Smith he was 'laced up' the front with three bullets at point blank range by a Viet Cong soldier firing from a 6-centimetre-wide slit in the mound just above ground level.

Bourke recalled:

> I yelled out to the rest of the boys to give me some cover and went forward to try and bring Delaney and Smith back. But when I got to Delaney some bastard got me from a slit in the washout. There was a tunnel behind it and firing slits all along. I dropped Delaney, and he was alright because he was below the level of the slits. My face was a bit of a mess though. The bullet had gone in through the cheek, broken my jaw and taken out a handful of teeth. I remembered noticing how blue the sky was and hearing birds singing, while I looked at my blood dripping on the sand. Shit! I'm dying, I thought. Then I decided 'I'm not', and told myself to take cover.[11]

Up until this time none of Bourke's men had been able to determine exactly where the fire was coming from and had not returned fire. Bourke screamed in agony for a few moments as the pain set in. With immense effort he settled himself down and, although badly shaken and in pain, he

MACJOO

Serial No 1097

1 3 FEB 1966

Mr. Stanley Clark
10 Langdon Avenue
Campbelltown, New South Wales

Dear Mr. Clark:

I am deeply distressed to learn of the death of your son, Private Christopher Clark, 1st Royal Australian Regiment. I always have a feeling of close personal loss when informed of the death of anyone who has died while serving their country here in Vietnam. I know that it must be especially difficult for you because of the fact your son was serving so far from home and family.

Please accept the deepest sympathy and heartfelt condolences of all personnel of the United States Military Assistance Command, which I hope will be of some consolation at this time of personal sorrow and bereavement. You may rest assured that all of us will continue to do our utmost to bring eventual victory so that your son's sacrifice will not have been in vain.

Sincerely,

W. C. WESTMORELAND
General, United States Army
Commanding

Private Chris Clark (left), a 20-year-old medic, was shot and killed while giving first aid to another medic who had been wounded giving first aid under fire. His family received a telegram of condolence from the Australian Government (below) and letters personally signed by Prime Minister of South Vietnam, Air Vice Marshal Nguyen Cao Ky (right) and General William Westmoreland (below left), Commander of the US Military Assistance Command – Vietnam. He was buried at Terendak Barracks, Malaysia, and his headstone reads, 'No greater love hath any man than this that he lay down his life for a friend.'

Chủ-Tịch

Uỷ-Ban Hành-Pháp Trung-Uong

SAIGON.

Kính gởi

Mr. Stanley Clark
10 Langhon Avenue
Camp Belltown NSW.

Dear Mr. Stanley Clark,

      I learn with great distress of the death of your son, Private Christopher Clark, Royal Australian Armed Forces in Vietnam. He has died a hero to defend this country against Communist aggression at a moment when the war enters the decisive phase.

      On behalf of the Government and the people of Vietnam, I should like to pay heartfelt tribute to your son, for his selfless sacrifice.

      For the noble ideal of preserving freedom for Vietnam and happiness for mankind Private Christopher Clark left his beloved country and family to join the Vietnamese people in the struggle against a common enemy who seeks to destroy peace and liberty. His name will go down in the History of Vietnam together with those of other soldiers from allied countries, who have made the supreme sacrifice for the independence of Vietnam and that of the Free World.

      You may rest assured that your son, has not died in vain since the Vietnamese people are determined to fight to the last man to crush the Communist expansionist danger.

      Please accept the deepest sympathy and sincere gratitude of the people of Vietnam and myself.

Air Vice Marshal NGUYEN CAO KY
Prime Minister.

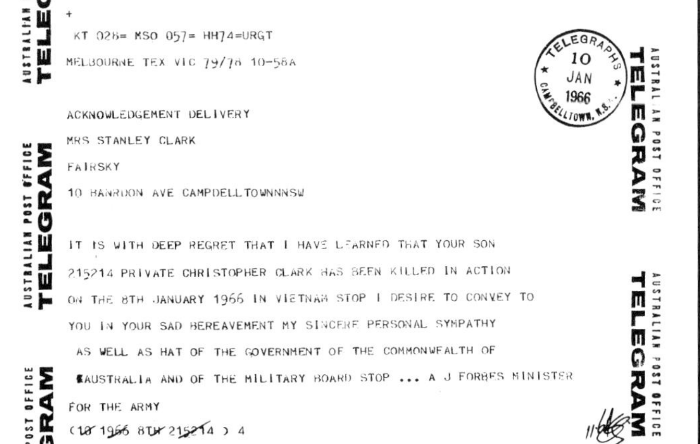

continued to direct his men. Holding his jaw, he whispered to his rear section commander, Corporal Jim Ehlers, to assault through the treeline to the west, take out a machine gun position and bring fire to bear on the mound area. 'My jaw started to fall out of place. Then a medic raced in and tied it up. We were both covered in blood—mine!' At the same time Bourke was injected with morphine, temporarily relieving the pain of his wound.

Ehlers' section spread out in the tree line to the west and assaulted. Their movement attracted fire from trenches behind the mound and Ehlers fell after a bullet had drilled a hole through his mouth and nose. His Diggers went to ground and stayed there firing at the machine gun positions on the other side of the clearing.

About 100 metres to the rear Major Ian Fisher, the new commander of D Company, faced his first test in combat. He tried frantically to find out what was going on by radio without success. He was forward enough to estimate where Bourke's men were fighting but did not have a clear idea of enemy locations. Assessing that the enemy were most likely firing on Bourke from the north, he ordered Lieutenant Bill Giles to take his platoon through the tree line around to the east and see if he could relieve the pressure on Bourke's men. Giles' men did engage the Viet Cong who had initiated the contact with a Thompson sub-machine gun, but were unable to position themselves to relieve Bourke.

The medic who had treated Bourke, Private Merv Wilson, had run forward to treat Delaney while the medic from A Company, Private Chris Clark, bound up Smith's head wounds. Using the same slit that he had used when he shot Delaney, a Viet Cong soldier shot Wilson in the neck as he administered first aid. Wilson fell on Delaney, bleeding profusely. Clark saw Wilson had been hit and, despite the warnings of the soldiers nearby, crawled towards his fallen comrade. As he opened his medical pack to pull out a dressing to staunch the gushes of blood from Wilson's punctured jugular vein, Clark was shot in the back at point blank range and died quicky. Wilson bled to death next to him.

Meanwhile, Bourke was issuing orders to Lance Corporal Jim Pratten, Smith's Second-in-Command, to assault the mound and stop the fire from the slits. Pratten gathered the few unwounded men from Smith's section and charged the mound under the covering fire of a machine gun. Pratten shoved the barrel of his rifle into one slit and kept firing until his magazine was empty. He was rewarded with the sound of a scream and scuffling noises as the Viet Cong made their escape through the connecting tunnel. Pratten and his men then pushed grenades into the slits and took cover. After the explosions there was silence from the mound but the machine gunners positioned in trenches behind the mound continued to fire, pinning Pratten and his men down.

Meanwhile, D Company's Company Sergeant Major, Warrant Officer Ron Pincott, had gathered up the company's support section and advanced from the east towards the sounds of the fire fight. He stopped short of the clearing and decided to attack the machine gun positions firing on Pratten's men from the flank. As Pincott and his group assaulted, the Viet Cong began a hasty withdrawal. They were gone when Pincott's men entered the fortifications behind the mound.

With Pincott's group holding in the north and Giles' platoon holding in the east, the area was secure and the evacuation of casualties began. Some minutes before, Bourke had given command to Sergeant Jim Carnes because he was fainting from loss of blood and the effect of the morphine. 'Sergeant, take command and get the casualties back', he had said as he was led away. He was already agonising over the mauling his platoon had received because of his decision to cut across the clearing. The two medics, Wilson and Clark, were dead. Smith and Delaney were fighting for their lives and four others had been seriously wounded. He wrote in his diary a few days later:

> I was evacuated on the OC's [Fisher's] orders even though I felt OK
> after the morphine. My thoughts: Professionally, I was a fool to
> expose myself to recover Delaney. Tactically, even though it would
> not have affected the outcome, I should have used smoke and
> covering fire to help in his recovery. Morally, I probably did OK.
> The OC thinks so and old Nero [Preece] said the other day, 'Bourke,
> I'm proud of you.' Never thought I'd hear Colonel Preece say that
> after all the trouble I've caused in camp.

After hasty dressings were applied to Corporal Ron Smith's wounds, he was led back to the Company Aid Post. On his way there Major Ian Fisher called out to him, 'Corporal Smith where is your weapon and gear?' Smith replied, 'Back there.' Fisher, not knowing the extent of Smith's wounds, said, 'Well you had better go and get it.' Smith said as he turned to face Fisher, 'If you want the bastard, you go and get it.' Fisher, seeing Smith's wounds, put out his arm and assisted him to the company Aid Post. When Smith arrived, the medical corporal, reaching out to take off Smith's bush hat, said, 'Jesus, Ron, what have they done to you?' Smith held his blood-soaked hat down over his head and said, 'Don't take me hat off, mate, or my brains will fall out.'[12]

Major Mike Naughton, the Australian medical officer at the military hospital in Saigon, recalled his meeting with Smith:

> I had been in the operating theatre for some 17 hours. We had
> received an unusually high number of casualties. I decided to go
> outside the theatre and take a break. I became aware of some rather
> loud yelling and cursing coming from down the hall. I remember
> thinking to myself, 'That is an Australian.' So I went down the hall

to investigate. Near the end of the line of stretcher cases was a large black medic attempting to shave the head of a shockingly injured Digger, preparatory to him going into theatre. The Digger was yelling that when he got out of there he was going to buy the so and so American Army some sharper razor blades. Clearly he was in great pain and the shaving was an agonising process. He was shockingly injured. His right eye had apparently exploded and small pieces of it lay among the area of a gaping wound that was once his eye. The top part of his head, you might as well say, was not there. He was a mess. I remember thinking then, well he will not even get into theatre he has not got too long. Amazingly this same fellow clung to life, and eventually made it into theatre. I operated, cleaning and rebuilding and doing generally what I could for him. I was never able to find out if that fellow survived. He certainly deserved to.[13]

Ron Smith continued to cling to life and 21 years later he and his wife Eunice were introduced to Mike Naughton at a reunion of 1 RAR veterans.

Barry Delaney also survived and, with Jim Bourke, was evacuated to Australia. He received the US Army Commendation Medal for Service for the selfless support he gave to fellow patients in hospital in Saigon. The other casualties returned to duty some weeks later. Eddy Grills survived but his luck ran out in February 1966 when he drowned accidentally while on leave at Vung Tau Beach.

Many were to be surprised later when Jim Bourke's and Chris Clark's actions were not recognised through the award of decorations for valour. Lieutenant Patrick Graves, a US officer from the 101st Airborne Division (the Screaming Eagles), had accompanied Bourke's platoon into the Ho Bo Woods on 8 January and had almost been killed in the opening burst of fire which wounded Smith and Delaney. In 1967 he wrote to the Australian Minister for the Army, the Right Honourable Malcolm Fraser:

In January 1966, I was sent by my unit to observe the operations of the First Battalion of the Royal Australian Regiment in the Republic of Vietnam. The purpose of my visit was to learn from an army more experienced and adept in fighting in jungle terrain. While assigned to this battalion, I was tasked to observe the platoon of Second Lieutenant J. R. Bourke of D company commanded by Major Ian Fisher. I was with the platoon on Operation CRIMP which was conducted west of the infamous Iron Triangle. As the platoon neared a large open field, Second Lieutenant Bourke correctly deployed a squad on either side of the clearing to clear the woods, while one squad fanned out over the open area. As the unit proceeded forward, lead elements in the open came under point blank fire from enemy concealed in a bunker, firing automatic weapons from small slits. Several men were wounded immediately . . . I escaped injury by a matter of a few feet. At this time I observed Bourke dash from his position with the squad in the open area. As he approached one of his wounded men near the enemy position, the enemy fired a burst hitting Bourke in the face. A round entered his mouth and went out the left side of his jaw. Though visibly shaken and in much pain, Bourke continued to command his platoon. He pinpointed the hidden enemy bunker and directed the efforts of his unit in the destruction of the enemy until he was overcome with loss of blood and became too weak to remain erect. It was at this time, and only at this time did he turn over command of his unit to his platoon sergeant. I feel that Second Lieutenant Bourke's selfless action was both courageous and gallant in view of his painful wound. It is a rare experience to witness such outstanding personal bravery and leadership.[14]

Fraser's reply was:

I must thank you for your eye witness account of the actions of this officer [Bourke] . . . and have arranged for it to be noted in his records. All recommendations for gallantry awards are initiated within individual units and eventually considered by the theatre commander, who, with his on-the-spot knowledge of the various operations, selects the most outstanding individual for preferment. There is no doubt that many brave deeds go unrewarded but this must be so if the high standards set for decorations are to be maintained.[15]

During Bourke's action, Preece had ordered McFarlane to by-pass Fisher's company to the east and Tattam to move his company to the west. Soon both companies were fighting through Viet Cong fortifications. The battle area was a nerve-racking shooting gallery. There were snipers and small groups of Viet Cong everywhere—in and behind trees, in bunkers, popping up from spider holes and tunnel entrances at ground level, and scrambling away after firing quick bursts. The area was seeded with numerous booby traps. Diggers noticed the ominous wires and saw the shells and bunches of grenades dangling from trees and clumps of bamboo. The stomachs of the veterans of the Iron Triangle operations tightened in anticipation of the inevitable explosions.

Typically, the Diggers would have fired at any movement in these circumstances. However, complicating the battle was the presence of groups of old men, women and children sheltering in bunkers and breaking cover as the fighting progressed. On several occasions the Viet Cong used the hesitation created by the presence of women and children to withdraw safely. McFarlane exhorted his men to maintain momentum and keep assaulting forward. Individual Viet Cong were being hit and scrambling down tunnel entrances, others lay dead where they fell.

As McFarlane and his headquarters passed a thick clump of bamboo,

Captain Peter Haslau, RMO (left), Major Mike Naughton, RMO (centre) with Private Jim McClelland.

a mortar or artillery shell hanging in a tree was detonated. McFarlane and those around him were blown off their feet. Captain Ken Bade, the company's forward artillery observer, had taken the main blast in his chest and lay mortally wounded. A signaller, Lance Corporal Scottie Alcorn, suffered multiple shrapnel wounds in the lower back. Captain Peter Arnison, McFarlane's Second-in-Command, rushed to assist Bade but it was too late and Bade died while Arnison comforted him in his last moments. Private Mick Burgess went to assist Alcorn and was shot in the chest by a sniper in the clump of bamboo. During the aftermath of the explosion, the clump of bamboo was engaged by rifle and machine gun fire.[16]

Though wounded and temporarily stunned by the explosion, McFarlane refused medical treatment until others more seriously wounded were treated. He ordered Second Lieutenant Graham Bolitho's platoon to move around and avoid the area of the bamboo. Unfortunately this movement did not prevent the death of Private Neil Horne who was shot dead from the same clump of bamboo a little while later.

Major Jim Tattam's men were also firing at fleeing groups of Viet Cong as they advanced towards the village. A booby trap also went off near Tattam's company headquarters group, wounding Tattam and three others. A further three soldiers went into severe shock and had to be evacuated with the wounded. Tattam was lucky not to have lost his right eye when a piece of shrapnel lodged in his forehead. Privates Ray Raines, Steve Mehag and Ken Gudgeon recovered from shrapnel wounds to the upper body and returned to duty with Tattam for the next operation. Captain Mike Le Bars, the company Second-in-Command, took command.[17]

By this time, Preece had ordered his companies to link with each other and form a tight battalion defensive perimeter. He suspected that they were on top of the Special Sector headquarters and the time had come to dig in and see if the Viet Cong would mount a counter-attack. As the Diggers moved into position they were under constant fire from individuals and small groups of Viet Cong. One sniper poked his rifle out from a firing slit just above ground level, took aim at Private Sloan of McFarlane's company, but was discovered. Grenades were pushed into the slits near him but the results were unknown. In another incident Corporal Snowy Wright's section opened fire on a group of Viet Cong, killing two and wounding several others. All of these random contacts increased the tension among the Diggers. The Viet Cong appeared to be able to pop up and disappear from anywhere in the area. The presence of civilians added to the pressure. Preece was concerned that the situation would not only lead to civilian casualties but also casualties among the Diggers as they became tired and fired at any movement without distinguishing whether the movement was caused by friend or foe.[18]

As night fell there was a long burst of machine gun fire from C Company's area. Private Ray Payne had positioned his machine gun on the corner of a deep zig-zag trench. He had been warned by Lance Corporal Garry Bland that a patrol had gone out to clear the area in front of the platoon and would be returning through Payne's gun position. A few minutes later, Sapper Keith Mills, an attached Australian engineer, alerted Payne to movement along the trench. Because of the depth of the trench, all Payne could see was a line of green bush hats bobbing along. He prepared to challenge the returning patrol. Instead of a section of Australians, a squad of Viet Cong soldiers turned the corner of the trench. The first soldier was centimetres away from the machine gun muzzle before Payne overcame his shock and fired. The Viet Cong's upper body exploded from the impact of the machine gun rounds. Several others in the squad fell wounded and were pulled away by their comrades under the cover of a hasty volley.[19]

1 RAR was on a human ant hill. From below ground the Diggers could hear constant scuffling noises, digging sounds and Vietnamese voices. After they had finished digging their fighting trenches, these sounds appeared to be even closer. Every now and again a Viet Cong would come to the surface and crawl away. The Diggers would hear the noises but were under strict orders not to fire unless an enemy was positively identified. Any undisciplined fire could have resulted in casualties to other Australians. Above ground were the pathetic sounds of

Some of the defenders of the Ho Bo Woods before burial.

hundreds of women and children crying, probably lamenting the fate of their husbands, fathers and sons who were trapped in the tunnels below the Battalion.

In the early hours of the morning, there were many short exchanges of fire as small groups of Viet Cong began to return to the area. The Diggers would not use machine guns for fear of giving their positions away and threw grenades forward of the perimeter. Most did not sleep that night; straining to hear movement to the front, worried that any movement from behind could be a Viet Cong surfacing from a tunnel entrance and all the time hearing noises from below.

The next day was spent discovering the extent of the Viet Cong headquarters complex. There were three levels of tunnels connecting concrete-reinforced and earthen chambers filled with documents, weapons, equipment and supplies. Lance Corporal Ned MacAuliffe discovered a deep well while digging a latrine which concealed hundreds of documents and photographs. Among these were lists of the names of members of military units and political cadres in the Saigon area. There were detailed maps of US installations in the Saigon area and the names and addresses of many US diplomatic and military personnel. This information could only have been gained from South Vietnamese sources.[20] MacAuliffe's main interests, however, were several Russian and National

Liberation Front flags which he confiscated for the adornment of his company's recreation tent back in Bien Hoa.

Aircraft in the area were receiving ground fire continuously. One NCO recalled:

> The constant low level helicopter traffic across the area encouraged many eager VC to get in some target practice. One in particular, to the south-east, was persistent and accurate. He even shot at Westmoreland as he flew over the area. Rather than use a ground force unit to get him, it was decided to use air bombardment. Two A-1 Sky Raiders arrived, one with bombs and one with napalm. The napalm carrier flew in low circles, the other began a series of climbs and dives, finally releasing a 250 pound [113 kilogram] bomb. The Diggers gathered to watch. The VC could not see either plane while they were low, but each time the bombing plane climbed, a burst of tracer would flicker up at it. Every bomb and napalm canister was dropped, but still the VC gunner fired. Then the pilots used cannon, flying east to west across our front. Still he fired back. One of the A-1s turned towards us, and the wings flickered. Diggers scattered as the 20 mm shells cracked through the tree tops. As the A-1s flew away, the VC gunner fired one long, defiant burst after them.[21]

The Australian Sappers from 3 Field Engineer Troop led by Captain Alex MacGregor led the search into the tunnel system. This was the first time they or the Allies had attempted to explore and destroy a complete tunnel complex systematically. MacGregor improvised a number of techniques which were to become standard practice for subsequent tunnel searches. The tunnels were first flushed out with smoke and CS gas using US-made Mighty Mite air compressors. This would reveal further tunnel entrances and air vents, and hopefully force the Viet Cong to surface or at least move away from the immediate area to be searched. Then a Sapper would be sent down a tunnel entrance wearing a gas mask, carrying a pistol and a flashlight, to find documents, weapons and equipment. This was cramped, laborious and dangerous work. MacGregor soon discovered that the tunnel complex was so extensive that it would take weeks for his men to search them and hundreds of tonnes of explosives to ensure their complete destruction.

The discovery of the Special Sector headquarters was a major tactical victory for Westmoreland. Major General McChristian, the US Pacific Area Command Chief of Staff—Intelligence, visited the Battalion and was amazed at the value of the numerous documents, weapons and equipment. Eventually over 7000 documents and 100 weapons were captured with thousands of rounds of small arms and mortar ammunition. Tonnes of foodstuffs, medical supplies and other military equipment completed the haul.[22]

While 1 RAR continued to explore the tunnel complexes of the

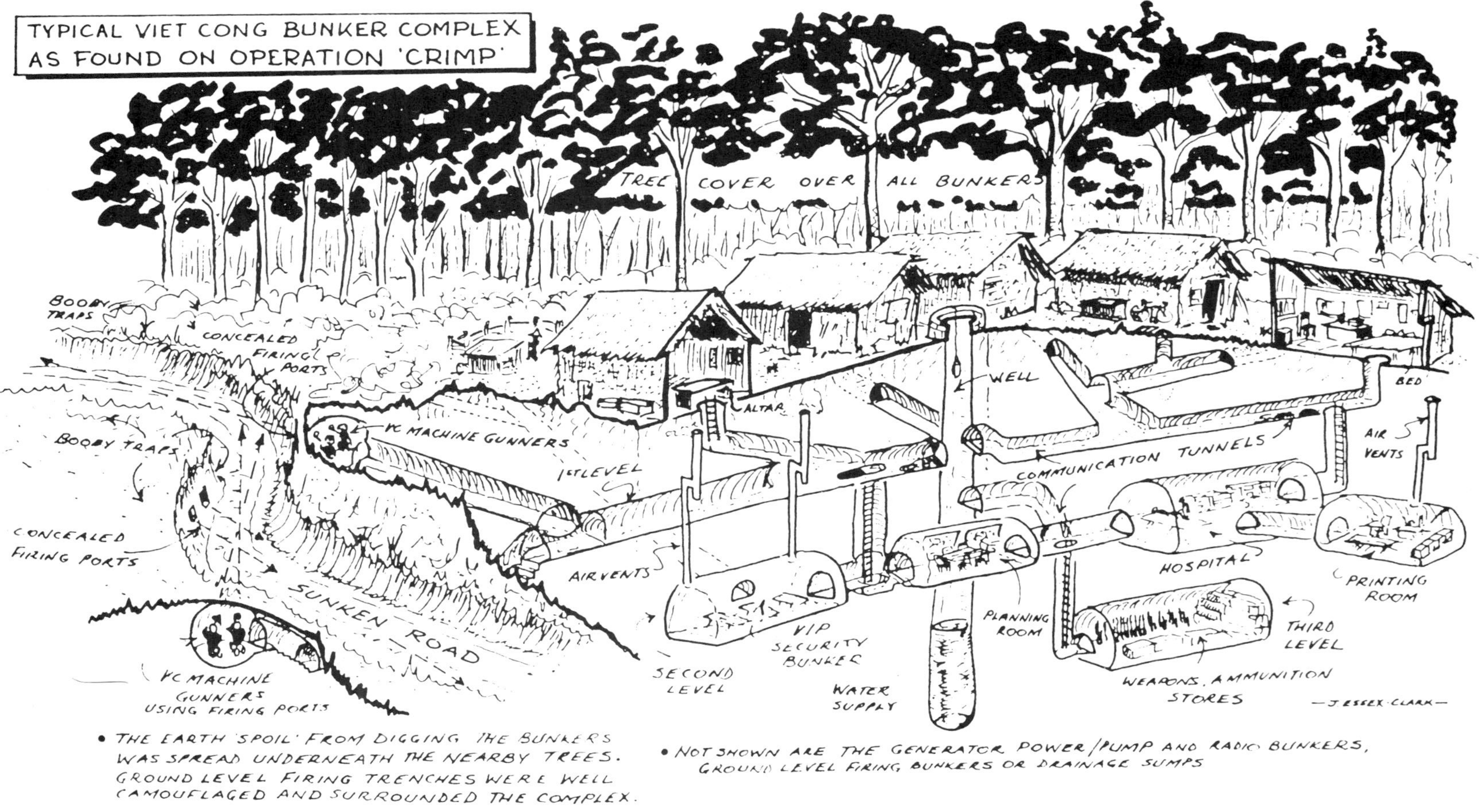

TYPICAL VIET CONG BUNKER COMPLEX AS FOUND ON OPERATION 'CRIMP'
TREE COVER OVER ALL BUNKERS
BOOBY TRAPS
CONCEALED FIRING PORTS
WELL
BED
AIR VENTS
ALTAR
VC MACHINE GUNNERS
1ST LEVEL
COMMUNICATION TUNNELS
BOOBY TRAPS
CONCEALED FIRING PORTS
AIRVENTS
HOSPITAL
PRINTING ROOM
SUNKEN ROAD
VIP SECURITY BUNKER
PLANNING ROOM
THIRD LEVEL
SECOND LEVEL
WATER SUPPLY
WEAPONS, AMMUNITION STORES
VC MACHINE GUNNERS USING FIRING PORTS
—JESSEX-CLARK—
• THE EARTH 'SPOIL' FROM DIGGING THE BUNKERS WAS SPREAD UNDERNEATH THE NEARBY TREES. GROUND LEVEL FIRING TRENCHES WERE WELL CAMOUFLAGED AND SURROUNDED THE COMPLEX.
• NOT SHOWN ARE THE GENERATOR POWER/PUMP AND RADIO BUNKERS, GROUND LEVEL FIRING BUNKERS OR DRAINAGE SUMPS

Unknown soldier lifting off the top to a tunnel entrance during Operation CRIMP. The tunnels were dug to three levels and ran for over 17 kilometres.

Special Sector Headquarters, the Paratroopers swept their areas in search of Viet Cong, who were waiting in well-camouflaged ambush positions. The 1/503rd took heavy casualties in one battle with a dug-in platoon of Main Force Viet Cong on 11 January. Williamson's aide d'camp, Lieutenant Anthony Hartle, wrote in his diary;

> The character of this operation was quite different from any of the others that the Brigade has been on. We were fighting at a relative disadvantage, both in the Delta and, particularly, in the Ho Bo Woods region, with the enemy concealed and in highly defensible positions, knowing the terrain and fighting with determination.[23]

Complicating the Paratroopers' problems with the Viet Cong were several incidents of US artillery and airstrikes falling in their positions. Some artillery and mortar fire was received from neighbouring battalions of the 1st Infantry Division while the misplaced airstrikes resulted from poor target identification by aircraft.[24]

The Paratroopers were also finding tunnel complexes and elaborate fortifications. The task of exploring and destroying them was well beyond the capabilities of the Brigade. There were several incidents of soldiers being badly affected by CS gas or lack of oxygen while searching tunnels. In one incident, Corporal Bob Bowtell, an Australian engineer, was asphyxiated after his gas mask was torn off as he fell from one tunnel level to the next. It took two and a half hours to recover his body. Private Jim Daly was Mentioned-in-Despatches for his efforts to rescue Bowtell before he died.[25]

After two days on top of the tunnel system with the constant harassment of snipers and the dangerous job of searching tunnels, the Diggers were becoming tired and tense. On the night of 10 January a newly arrived reinforcement was shot by his section commander. This young soldier was so terrified that he had begun to crawl from his sentry position to wake the next sentry. Hearing this movement and observing the form of a crawling man, his section commander called out, 'Halt! Who goes there?' When there was no reply, he shot the reinforcement at point blank range through the arm and shoulder. Those in the vicinity never forgot the sounds of this young man calling for God to save him as Captain Peter Haslau treated his wounds. Haslau told him to quiet down or the Viet Cong would hear and fire on them. Eventually, the soldier lay mute with desperate eyes on those around him. He died on the helicopter carrying him to Bien Hoa having completed two days on operations.[26]

1 RAR had been receiving a steady stream of reinforcements since December to make up for losses due to death, wounding or sickness. These soldiers came from other battalions in the Royal Australian Regiment. Some were not seen as the best soldiers from those battalions and none had gone through pre-embarkation training as far as members of 1 RAR knew. This situation led to more incidents which resulted in casualties. On 10 January one reinforcement, Private 'Bo' Petersen, was killed by Viet Cong snipers while moving outside the perimeter without his weapon.[27]

In the early hours of 12 January, another reinforcement arrived at his sentry post quivering with fear and told the soldier on sentry that he had just stepped over a Viet Cong soldier lying on the company perimeter path a few metres away. The sentry, who assumed the reinforcement was seeing things or had stepped over a member of the company sleeping, said sarcastically, 'Why didn't you shoot him, you silly bastard?' Hearing this, the reinforcement, now manning the machine gun, swung the gun around and fired a burst into a prone figure on the perimeter path before the sentry could stop him. Machine gun bullets thudded into the trees and tents in the company area. The sentry knocked the reinforcement over with a blow to the side of the head. A few metres away Private Eddy Pinoli lay seriously wounded in the chest and left arm. In his sleep he had rolled onto the perimeter path. It was a credit to the bravery of the US helicopter pilots and the communication skills of an Australian signaller, Corporal Bruce Davies, that Pinoli was evacuated in time for the doctors to save his life on the operating table just over an hour later in Saigon.[28]

By 13 January over 17 kilometres of tunnels had been mapped out in the 1 RAR area. Sappers had taken telephone lines down with them and, by measuring the length of line and recording the changes in direction with a compass, they were able to determine the routes of many tunnels underground. There was much work to do and even though the operation had been extended for several days, Williamson was impatient to leave the area when the supply of documents and weapons began to dwindle and enemy contact became infrequent. In contrast, Preece wanted to stay and explore the tunnels further and devise means by which they could be at least sealed off to prevent reoccupation by the Viet Cong. Preece's attitude was to consolidate on gains made and deliver a permanent blow to the Viet Cong's prosecution of the war. Williamson's attitude was to leave the area in search of other opportunities to fight Viet Cong Main Force units and keep them off balance in the III Corps area.[29]

The last hours of the operation were spent maintaining a protective patrolling program, setting charges in the tunnels and backloading captured weapons, documents and equipment. There were several fire fights as patrols ran into small groups of Viet Cong scouts. Second Lieutenant Steve Lind's platoon moved forward to the sound of a woman crying only to be fired on by several automatic weapons which wounded Lance Corporal Jock McDonnell and Private Tom White.[30]

Snipers continued to take their toll of the Diggers. Lance Corporal Ron Coxon was standing among a group from D Company waiting for helicopters to arrive to take them out of the area. Several shots rang out and he was hit in the temple and died instantly. Two other Diggers were wounded—one only losing a piece of his ear. Coxon had been a storeman in the company a few months before and had been evacuated to Malaysia, suffering from malaria. Given the choice of returning to D Company in Vietnam or another battalion in Australia, Coxon had requested to return to his old company. On arrival a few days before, he found that his job as storeman had been taken. He was appointed as Second-in-Command of a rifle section: CRIMP was his first and last operation in this position.[31]

On 14 January 1 RAR was airlifted to Bien Hoa. The Diggers felt satisfied that they had proven themselves in many short, sharp fire fights with the Viet Cong. Because of the rivalry between companies for recorded 'kills', the Battalion headquarters staff had been meticulous in their recording of enemy bodies and probable enemy deaths and wounded. In total the Australians accounted for 25 Viet Cong killed with a further 30 likely. Many more Viet Cong perished under the weight of falling earth as Captain Alex MacGregor's charges and 75 millimetre and 8 inch [203 millimetre] guns firing rounds with delay fuses collapsed parts of the tunnel system.

The Paratroopers lost fifteen killed and 72 wounded and the Diggers eight killed and 30 wounded. The Viet Cong casualties were recorded as 128 killed (confirmed) and 190 killed (probable). Over 500 suspects had been detained and a further 1000 refugees screened. Most buildings in the area had been flattened and livestock killed. One Viet Cong soldier had surrendered.[32] As a final legacy of their work in the area, the Brigade's civil affairs unit had distributed nearly 400 T-shirts to Vietnamese children in the area bearing the motto 'Airborne All The Way'.[33]

Before leaving the area one of the Australian interpreters had asked some villagers whether they knew the nationality of the soldiers who had captured the area and destroyed the tunnel system. After a pause, one of the war-weary peasants replied, 'probably the French'.[34]

Postscript

The Ho Bo Woods was restored as a major Viet Cong transit and supply area a few months after Operation CRIMP in January 1966. The US 1st and 25th Infantry Divisions were to operate in the area several more times subsequently and caused significant destruction to the tunnel complexes on each occasion. The Ho Bo Woods were never occupied permanently and continued as a Viet Cong base for the remainder of the Second Indochinese War.

9 The construction site

The Viet Cong needed a major victory and searched for a 'soft' target. They found the lightly protected headquarters of the US 1st Infantry Brigade near a construction site, and planned to overrun it. They had not counted on the intervention of the Australians who were protecting a US engineer battalion nearby.

During early January 1966 Westmoreland had mounted a widespread offensive against the Viet Cong and North Vietnamese units fighting in South Vietnam as part of President Johnson's diplomatic offensive to force the North Vietnamese into peace negotiations. The US had stopped the air war against North Vietnam but, at the same time, was trying to show that Allied forces were unbeatable on the ground. In the north, Operation MATADOR by the US Cavalrymen and Operation VAN BUREN by US and Korean Marines pushed North Vietnamese formations back into their sanctuaries in Cambodia. In the south, Operations MARAUDER and CRIMP, accompanied by other spoiling operations by the 1st Infantry Division, had kept the 5th and 9th Viet Cong divisions off balance and stopped temporarily large-scale Viet Cong military and political operations in the Saigon area.[1]

After this demonstration of conciliation in the air and determination on the ground, President Johnson ordered Westmoreland to scale down operations and offered the Viet Cong and the North Vietnamese a truce over the Tet (Vietnamese New Year) holiday period. The truce was accepted and there was a new feeling in South Vietnam and around the world that peace negotiations might begin in the near future.

These new expectations of peace coincided with a visit by *Playboy* magazine's Playmate of the Year, Jo Collins, to the 173rd. In November 1965 Lieutenant John Price of Captain Les Brownlee's company had noted *Playboy* magazine's promise that, if anyone signed up for a special Christmas offer of a lifetime subscription, the first issue would be delivered in person by a *Playboy* Playmate. With this promise in mind, he wrote to the Publisher of *Playboy*, Hugh Hefner:

Playmate of 1965, Jo Collins, with Private First Class Manuel Soza, Company B 2/503rd Airborne Battalion, during her visit to present 'The Bulls' with a lifetime subscription to Playboy *magazine in January 1966.*

. . . The loneliness here is a terrible thing—and we long to see a real, living, breathing American girl. Therefore, we have enclosed with this letter a money order for a Lifetime Subscription to *Playboy* magazine for B company. It is our understanding that, with the purchase of a Lifetime Subscription in the U.S., the first issue is personally delivered by a Playmate. It is our most fervent hope that this policy can be extended to include us . . . If it is not important enough . . . to send a Playmate, please just forget about us and we will quietly fade back into the jungle.[2]

The visit was arranged for February 1966 but Price was shot in the arm on 3 January 1966 by a sniper in the Plain of Reeds. *Playboy* magazine and the US Army brought the trip forward before Price was due to leave Vietnam for further surgery on his arm in the US. Jo Collins arrived on 9 January in one of the Brigade's helicopters, specially painted and bearing the *Playboy* bunny logo. Because Browlee was still with his company on Operation CRIMP and Price was in the field hospital at Bien Hoa, the Playmate of the Year was met by two blushing B Company reinforcements carrying a large bunch of red roses, arranged in a whitewashed

Sydney Go-Go dancer, Miss Pat Wordsworth (also known as the Big Pretzel), entertaining the troops at Bien Hoa in January 1966.

skull of a water buffalo to remind Miss Collins that the company she was visiting were known as 'The Bulls'. The visit over the next few days proved to be a public relations success for *Playboy* magazine and the Paratroopers. On 11 January Price received the first issue of the 'Bulls' lifetime subscription, and he and Miss Collins visited many of the wounded in the 3rd Field Hospital in Saigon.

In anticipation of the truce over 20–23 January, troupes of entertainers from the US and Australia began arriving. Once again a festive atmosphere grew among the service personnel of the Bien Hoa Airbase as the level of military activity waned. Famous Australian entertainer, Bobby Limb, led a troupe which included Frank Ward, Gus Merzi and two female performers—vocalist Sammie Woods, and Sydney-based Go-Go dancer Pat Wordsworth who went by the stage name of 'The Big Pretzel'. The Diggers now had their own 'real, living, breathing girls' from back home. Pat Wordsworth's raunchy performances were greeted with howls of appreciation. The Kiwi Gunners on duty in their battery area watched the first of Bobby Limb's shows through binoculars and were delighted with the dancing of 'The Big Pretzel'. During the next show they quietly loaded the Battery's guns and waited for the moment in the show when Miss Wordsworth gyrated her hips slowly towards the finale of a pelvic thrust.

As the pelvic thrust was executed, they fired all the guns. After the initial shock and the sight of the Kiwis falling about in hysterical laughter, the entertainers and the audience also broke up in laughter. This was the only breach of the Tet truce recorded that day as duty staff from all over Bien Hoa Airbase radioed to find out what the Kiwis were firing at.[3]

As a result of his visit to entertain the Australians in Vietnam, Bobby Limb published an open letter to the wives and mothers of those serving there in the *Sunday Telegraph* in Sydney. The afternoon tabloid press in Sydney had been publishing accounts of the plight of the Diggers in Vietnam which ranged from accusing them of atrocities to describing them as being riddled with malaria. He wrote:

> Dear Wives and Mothers: Don't believe all those gloomy reports about your boys over in Vietnam. I've seen those chaps, talked with them, and do you know what upsets them the most?—EXAGGERATED REPORTS IN OUR AFTERNOON PAPERS . . . As for Australian troops 'slitting throats, planting the Australian flag through Viet Cong bodies—this is SHOCKINGLY UNTRUE. The soldiers were staggered by these reports. It is not in their character, or in their training to act this way, and such behaviour would never be tolerated for a moment in the Australian Army. So much for that. You needn't worry—the boys have NOT CHANGED INTO MONSTERS! You know, I'm not a flag-waving, noisy patriotic type, but I was ten feet tall when, as we came into Bien Hoa for the big show there, I saw the Aussie flag waving up ahead. It was hot—incredibly hot—and dusty. Our stage was set up on the back of a truck and I watched 400 soldiers roll up for the show, stripped to the waist, their bronzed bodies glistening with sweat. They had their guns over their shoulders and they were carrying their chairs, sun tanned, healthy fellows. 'Down with malaria, eh?' . . . THEY STILL LOVE YOU—FROM THE BOTTOM OF THEIR HEARTS.[4]

During this period 1 RAR was visited by Brigadier Hall (RL) and Mr Bill Bunting of Australia's Returned Services League (equivalent to the American Legion). The visit was important because it highlighted the flaws of the honours and awards system applying to Australians fighting in Vietnam. On 17 January, an editorial in the *Australian* had this to say:

> The decision to award Australian troops fighting solely at Australia's direction [in Vietnam] with the British General Service Medal was incredible. It represents a hankering after the old associations with the British Empire, a distaste for the Commonwealth of independent nations and a triumph for Colonel Blimp, who still thinks of the Australian Army as a colonial appendage of the British Army.[5]

It was ludicrous indeed that Australia, an independent nation since 1901, should still depend on Britain for its system of honours and awards. The situation was partly rectified later in 1966 when a Vietnam Service

"Working on our ration of one for every 350 men for each six months, I make it .0026 of a Military Medal each . . ."

Cartoon by Paul Rigby depicting the differences between the American and Australian attitude to awarding medals for service in Vietnam.

Medal was introduced. However, the Imperial system of honours and awards continued, with the Queen of England remaining the authority for the award of military decorations to Australians for service in Vietnam.

The expectations of peace were not met in January 1966. President Johnson ordered Admiral Sharp to resume bombing targets in North Vietnam and directed General Westmoreland to go all out to destroy Viet Cong and North Vietnamese military units in South Vietnam. A war of attrition started which was to continue for several more years. January 1966 was the last time there was little bloodshed and battle over the holiday period of Tet.

February 1966 started with 1 RAR conducting an independent operation with sub-units of the Brigade under operational control. Preece was ordered to search for and destroy Viet Cong units and supply dumps in the Phuoc Loc area and was given a US gun battery and the Brigade's Cavalry Troop to supplement the Battalion. He was told by intelligence sources that against him were three Local Force battalions numbering 1200 guerillas and possibly the 271st and 273rd Main Force regiments numbering about 4000 regular troops.[6] This intelligence picture typified the vague but threatening intelligence information that was provided before most operations at the time. 'Very rarely is the intelligence accurate or timely enough to allow planning to be based on information received. Information is nearly always sketchy and unreliable. This means the information on which we act has to be established by patrolling.'[7] This reliance on intelligence from patrolling was to save many lives in a few weeks' time.

By 6 February, the Diggers had found hundreds of tonnes of rice and other food supplies as well as three trucks, stolen from the French-owned Plantation Des Terres Rouges. Most of the rice was still packed in bags bearing the US 'Hands Across the Sea' symbol of foreign aid. The Viet Cong did not appear to have been operating in the area for several weeks (further evidence that they were warned of Allied operations). Small groups had been left in the area, however, to pick off the Diggers and Paratroopers as they destroyed the supply dumps.

On 7 February, Second Lieutenant Jim Bourke's platoon, now under the command of Sergeant Jim Carnes, was ambushed again. Bourke's replacement platoon commander had not fitted in well and his jaw had been broken when a member of the platoon had butt-stroked him a few nights earlier. He was eventually evacuated back to Australia. The young officer had arrived overconfident and keen to assert himself before gaining the respect of the war-hardened Diggers. This incident showed the tribal nature of an infantry platoon and that the leadership of soldiers who have killed and seen comrades killed in combat had to be earned.

Captain Peter Rothwell recalled the seconds before the ambush:

It was early morning and I was travelling next to Fisher [OC D Company]. The company was virtually in an 'arrowhead' formation with one platoon up (Carnes). We were moving through some thick secondary growth and I almost stepped in a pile of hot noggie [Australian nickname for Vietnamese] shit with steam still coming off it. I put my hand up to Fisher in a 'stop' signal and whispered, 'Sir, we are about to be ambushed,' and pointed to the noggie shit that the forward platoon had not seen. As I said the word 'ambush', a burst of fire came from the front and hit young Densley.[8]

The survivors of the Ho Bo Woods ambush were once again pinned down by automatic fire and Private John Densley lay screaming with gunshot wounds to the stomach. His liver was punctured and bleeding profusely. Fortunately help was on the way.

Lieutenant Bill Giles recalled:

About 20 minutes before Jim Carnes' contact, my platoon had been sent off on a sweep to the left of the main body. When 12 Platoon was hit on the edge of the camp, I was at that time inside it but about 100 metres to the left flank of Jim Carnes. When I heard the firing, I took a [compass] bearing and deployed the platoon in assault formation in anticipation. I informed Ian Fisher and waited. He gave me the go ahead within seconds and we attacked left to right across Jim Carnes' front while he provided fire support. The VC must have been very impressed with the speed with which we outflanked them.[9]

There were no further casualties to either side during this action. Nineteen-year-old John Densley was pale, cold and sweaty, telling those around him, 'I've had it, mates.' Captain Peter Haslau assured him that he would be all right while compressing his wound and administering plasma in generous quantities. Densley responded well initially but had several serious relapses in hospital and was critically ill for some weeks. Following a recommendation from Haslau, Brigadier David Jackson approved the visit by Densley's mother to assist in his recovery.

Dr Mike Naughton recalled:

> Mrs Densley was a delightful, simple old dear who had spent all of her life in one area of Australia, only to be plucked out at very short notice to find herself in hot, humid, smelly, nasty Saigon with a son whose life was in the balance. She coped with it admirably: the soldiers from Saigon chipped in and bought her some suitable clothing (members of the AATTV organised this I think). She helped her son and other wounded soldiers in the intensive care unit, devoting much of her time to a black American soldier who had lost both his legs.[10]

Densley survived his ordeal and no doubt his mother had a few stories to tell her friends at morning tea parties back in Australia.

On the same day, a booby trap was detonated while Major John Healy's company was backloading rice from a 75-tonne cache. Private Bob Joyce suffered multiple shrapnel wounds to his right leg. Soon after, Healy sent Second Lieutenant Clive Williams' platoon to secure a stretch of road for the passage of the Brigade's Cavalry Troop. Earlier, a claymore mine had been fired, killing two Paratroopers, and there had been several incidents of mines being command detonated as the Troop used the roads in the area. Williams' men moved out with Corporal Ray Seipel's section leading. As Seipel's scout, Private Leonard Battley, reached a clearing before the road, he called Seipel forward to assess how the section could cross the area safely. Suddenly from thick undergrowth across the clearing came a volley of automatic fire. Seipel was shot through the heart and died instantly. Battley fell with a gunshot wound to his left foot. As the remainder of the section reached them, a Viet Cong platoon broke cover from ambush positions. Seipel and Battley had been fired on by Viet Cong soldiers positioned to the rear of an ambush set to cover the road. Later, the Cavalry Troop moved along the road at high speed, probably unaware that an Australian infantryman had lost his life safe-guarding their route.[11]

On 9 February the Battalion moved back by helicopter and vehicles to Bien Hoa. The Viet Cong farewelled the Diggers by firing bursts of automatic fire at the departing helicopters. They had reason to be angry. A major supply dump had been destroyed, their stolen trucks had been returned to their rightful owners, and six of their comrades had been killed and several others wounded.

While the Australians had been away, Brigadier General Paul Smith had replaced Brigadier General Butch Williamson as the Commanding General of the 173rd. Williamson had completed three very busy years raising, training and then leading the 173rd in an unfamiliar and complex Asian war. He was appointed the Deputy Commandant of the US Army's School of Infantry at Fort Benning in Georgia with a special responsibility to pass on his experiences of fighting in Vietnam to the infantrymen who were soon to fight there in increasing numbers. After two years there, he returned to Vietnam in 1969 as the commander of the 25th Infantry Division, Tropic Lightning. On 7 February 1966 he wrote to Preece:

> As I conclude my command of the 173rd Airborne Brigade, I would like to express to you and all your countrymen my sincere appreciation and deep admiration for the manner in which all of you have performed here in Vietnam. I have always had the feeling of confidence and assurance that the Australians would produce the desired end result under all circumstances. This feeling has been confirmed many times. You, your officers and men, have every right to be extremely proud of the contributions you have made toward the security of the Free World. Each time I meet an Australian I will think of your fine organization with many fond memories.[12]

Brigadier General Paul F. Smith had been the deputy Commanding General and the Chief of Staff of the US Army Task Force Alpha, later designated US Army Field Force—Vietnam. He had been called to active duty as a Second Lieutenant in April 1942 and participated in the Normandy, Ardennes–Alsace, Rhineland and Central Europe campaigns with the 507th Parachute Infantry Regiment. In that time he rose from platoon to battalion commander and had been awarded the Silver Star, three Bronze Stars for Valour, the Purple Heart and the Infantryman's Combat Badge.[13]

Smith brought a different style of command to the Brigade. Williamson had been a pugnacious commander with an aggressive, hard-driving manner, tactically adventurous, and confident that his Sky Soldiers were an elite force capable of fighting anywhere and at anytime. Smith had a dry sense of humour and a reserved manner, was elegant and a deep thinker. He was forced to be tactically more cautious and methodical because battlefield resources were becoming limited as the buildup of US military units continued rapidly. Like Williamson, he had complete confidence that his Brigade could fight and win anywhere in Vietnam at anytime.[14]

Typifying Smith's style was the letter he wrote to Preece after Operation ROUNDHOUSE in early February 1966:

Brigadier General Paul Smith. Smith took over command of the 173rd in February 1966.

Dear Colonel Preece: You will notice from Mr Van Dingenen's letter, copy attached herewith, that the Plantation Des Terres Rouges is extremely grateful for your recovery of three of its trucks from the VC. It is my understanding that the 1st RAR [sic], and its attached units, recovered the trucks during Operation ROUNDHOUSE. Accordingly, and since the 173rd Airborne Brigade, as such, was not overtly involved, I consider the gift tendered by Mr Van Dingenen to the 173rd Airborne Brigade Officers' Mess more properly should be directed to the Officers' Mess of the 1st RAR. It is my pleasure, therefore, to forward to the Officers' Mess, 1st RAR, three cases of champagne received this date from Mr Van Dingenen. I trust your Mess will be quite capable of disposing of the gift without further instructions from this headquarters.[15]

After returning from Operation ROUNDHOUSE, the Brigade was visited by US Vice President Hubert Humphrey accompanied by US Ambassador Averell Harriman, General Westmoreland, other dignitaries and a large group of noisy, rude and pushy journalists. Captain Ron Ducie singled out a rather comely female journalist and told her he would save her a seat in the front of the truck carrying the journalists by placing his hat on the seat next to the driver. His gallant gesture came unstuck when a male journalist rushed to the front seat and sat on Ducie's slouch hat. Ducie reached in, grabbed the journalist by the scruff of the neck and threw him to the ground in front of the rest of the entourage. The gaggle of journalists remained quiet and subdued for the remainder of their visit to the Australian battalion.[16]

The Diggers' next mission was to protect the 1st US Engineer Battalion while it constructed a road between Routes 13 and 16, west of Ben Cat on the northern apex of the Iron Triangle. This road was planned to cut across the Viet Cong supply and liaison routes between War Zone C, the Mekong Delta, the Iron Triangle and War Zone D and would link the forward brigades of the 1st Infantry Division.[17] This road-building program was called Operation ROLLING STONE and directly challenged the Viet Cong's ability to deploy and manoeuvre men and supplies for operations in the Saigon area. Westmoreland's circle of US military installations was starting to tighten around the South Vietnamese capital.

The US Sappers were contending with command detonated mines and snipers during the day, and raids by small groups of Viet Cong saboteurs by night, destroying vehicles and plant, and sowing more mines. Bulldozers towing rooters to expose mines and cut booby-trap wires, supported by tankdozers, had to be sent out each day to clear Route 13, which formed the western boundary of the Iron Triangle, and newly constructed sections of road.[18]

1 RAR was detached from the 173rd and put under the operational control of Headquarters 1st Infantry Division until 5 March 1966. General Dupuy had personally selected the Australians because of their expertise in dispersed patrolling. He hoped that the Diggers would be able to dominate the large area in which the engineers had to work and protect them from harassment by Local Force guerillas. This mission suited Preece and Essex-Clark. Together they planned an innovative patrol program to protect the engineer base, the laterite pit, road work parties over a distance of 6000 metres, and engineer reconnaissance parties when they went forward to plan new sections of road and find new deposits of laterite.[19]

About 1000 metres east of the engineer base camp was the Headquarters of the US 1st Infantry Brigade. Battalions of this Brigade were dispersed over a wide area carrying out search and destroy operations, and Civil Affairs and Psychological Warfare programs. Contact with the Viet Cong had been infrequent for some weeks and intelligence information on the locations of Viet Cong Main Force regiments was typically sketchy. The Australian intelligence staff had assessed that a minimum of two Local Force platoons and possibly a Local Force company operated in the area, but warned, 'The VC have the ability to bring a Main Force battalion against any elements with a considerable degree of surprise.'[20]

The Diggers flew in on 19 February and took over from the 2/28th Battalion of The Big Red One's 3rd Infantry Brigade. Preece sent out

Lieutenant Colonel Alex Preece on the right with Major John Essex-Clark delivering of orders for Operation ROLLING STONE. They planned a patrolling programme to run 24 hours a day to prevent the Viet Cong from killing off US engineers as they built a tactically vital road link for the US 1st Infantry Division.

patrols immediately and, as night fell, the Australians 'stood to' and looked ahead for the sight and sounds of the Viet Cong. Behind them they heard the sound of the US Sappers opening their beer cans for their regular evening libations, the start up of radios tuned to the US Armed Forces Radio Station and the laughter of soldiers celebrating the end of another day's work. Preece issued orders that there was to be no 'fraternisation' with the US Sappers which extended not only to turning down their offers of a cold beer but also the offer to cook the Australian rations in their kitchen.

> We have a standing invitation for a few beers as soon as we 'stand down' at night. The Yanks are actually sitting next to us drinking ice-cold, foamy beer, and all we do is take our hats and webbing off to signify 'leisure time'. A couple of minutes after 'stand down', all around the Aussie positions you can hear the hiss and pop of cans opening. What a circus.[21]

Lieutenant Chris Peacock, a 21-year-old Englishman who had graduated from the Australian Army's Officer Cadet School in December 1964, was sent to Colonel Glotzbach's brigade headquarters to the north to act as a liaison officer for the Australians. On arrival he was amazed at the absence of fortifications and physical security. There were a few machine gun posts and a few sentries to keep them manned but there were too few troops to patrol and maintain surveillance of the approaches to the area. Peacock was not the only foreign officer to notice the vulnerability of the brigade headquarters: 30 kilometres away, the commander of the 9th Viet Cong Division had ordered its destruction.[22]

The next day the Diggers patrolled to protect the engineer working groups, reducing the number of sniping, mine and booby-trap incidents, but not stopping the Viet Cong ambushing and sniping at some road parties during the day, and booby trapping the laterite pit and cratering sections of newly made road at night. Preece stepped up the number of night ambushes. On 21 February the level of Viet Cong activity declined significantly. The Australians were now playing the Viet Cong at their own game. Before this, the Viet Cong had been confident that they could move about freely under the cover of darkness. They were now up against soldiers who could also move silently by night.[23]

In an attempt to increase the protection for the US Sappers, Dupuy deployed two platoons of M48 Patton tanks into the area. By day they patrolled with the Australian APC Troop and at night secured the laterite pit where engineer plant and vehicles were located. The Diggers were amused at the titles emblazoned on the tanks such as 'Butt Buster', 'Bad Fox', 'Barbarian', 'Backwoods Bill' and 'Bourbon Baby'.[24] Additional security was provided by armed helicopters, aggressively swooping back and forward at low level, 'sniffing' for Viet Cong.

By 22 February, Preece and Essex-Clark were satisfied that the patrol program was working but were concerned about the type of Viet Cong that were being killed in ambushes and observed moving in the area. Most of the Viet Cong killed had been Local Force personnel which confirmed the intelligence assessment that only Local Force platoons were in the area conducting harassing operations. In the early hours of 23 February three well-equipped soldiers from the 761st Main Force Regiment were killed by machine gunner, Private Bob Currall, and there were several blood trails from the area of the ambush indicating others had been wounded. Three new AK47 rifles and four sets of webbing containing full loads of ammunition, rations and medical supplies were captured. Confirmation that a Viet Cong attack was in its final planning stages came when a North Vietnamese engineer officer was killed in another ambush on the same night.[25]

As dawn broke on 22 February, two half-platoon ambushes from Major Ian McFarlane's B Company engaged two squads of Main Force Viet Cong soldiers. Preece directed Essex-Clark to brief Colonel Glotzbach that a major attack was imminent. Preece then informed Lieutenant Colonel Howard Sargent, the engineer battalion commander, that the Australians were moving to set up a defensive position and he recommended the engineer base camp be relocated to join them. By late afternoon the Battalion and the US Sappers had moved into new defensive positions near a creek. One thousand metres to the east, Colonel Glotzbach had issued orders for Lieutenant Colonel Y. Y. Phillip's 1/26 Infantry Battalion to come in from the field and deploy to defend the Brigade headquarters. Engineer plant dug a continuous trench for 1/26 Battalion in a large triangle surrounding the Brigade headquarters, and the fire support base which had been reinforced by an additional gun battery and a platoon of tanks.

That afternoon, 1 RAR's Intelligence Officer, Captain John Dermody, conducted his normal briefing as part of Preece's daily conference. He alerted the sceptical company commanders to the chance of a major attack. When asked for the basis of his assessment, he pointed to the Main Force reconnaissance elements that had been sighted, the unusual occurrence of a North Vietnamese engineer officer being in the area and other signs. However, no-one could have guessed that, as they debated the veracity of Dermody's assessment, three Main Force battalions had already left assembly areas 25 kilometres to the west and were marching to attack Colonel Glotzbach's Brigade Headquarters.[26]

By 8 p.m. the Viet Cong commanders of J10 Battalion of the 761st Regiment, 707 Battalion of the 763rd Regiment and D800 Independent Battalion had marched their men 25 kilometres in a few hours and were in assembly areas near the village of Ap Bo. Many local women and youths were pressed into service to carry ammunition, equipment and supplies. Small parties began to move forward to familiarise themselves with the area before launching the assault. It was not difficult to locate the US areas which were noisy and giving off light. The Viet Cong Regimental commander had decided to attack on three axes from the east and then send a force around behind the Brigade Headquarters and assault from the west. Thus, the objective would be surrounded and the defenders unable to deploy sufficient troops to every sector of their perimeter. In fire support, he deployed 60 millimetre mortars in between the Engineer Battalion and the Brigade Headquarters and 82 millimetre mortars in the village of Ap Bo.[27]

At about 10 p.m. Major Ian McFarlane's men on the northern sector of the Battalion perimeter noticed mysterious lights 250 metres to their front. Even closer to these lights was a small standing patrol (protection post) led by 23-year-old Private Walter Brunalli. Brunalli and his men were in a 'ring side seat' for a Viet Cong regimental attack by 2000 determined soldiers who had marched 25 hard kilometres to destroy a 'soft' US target. McFarlane requested artillery and mortar fire missions be brought down on the locations of the lights which were increasing in

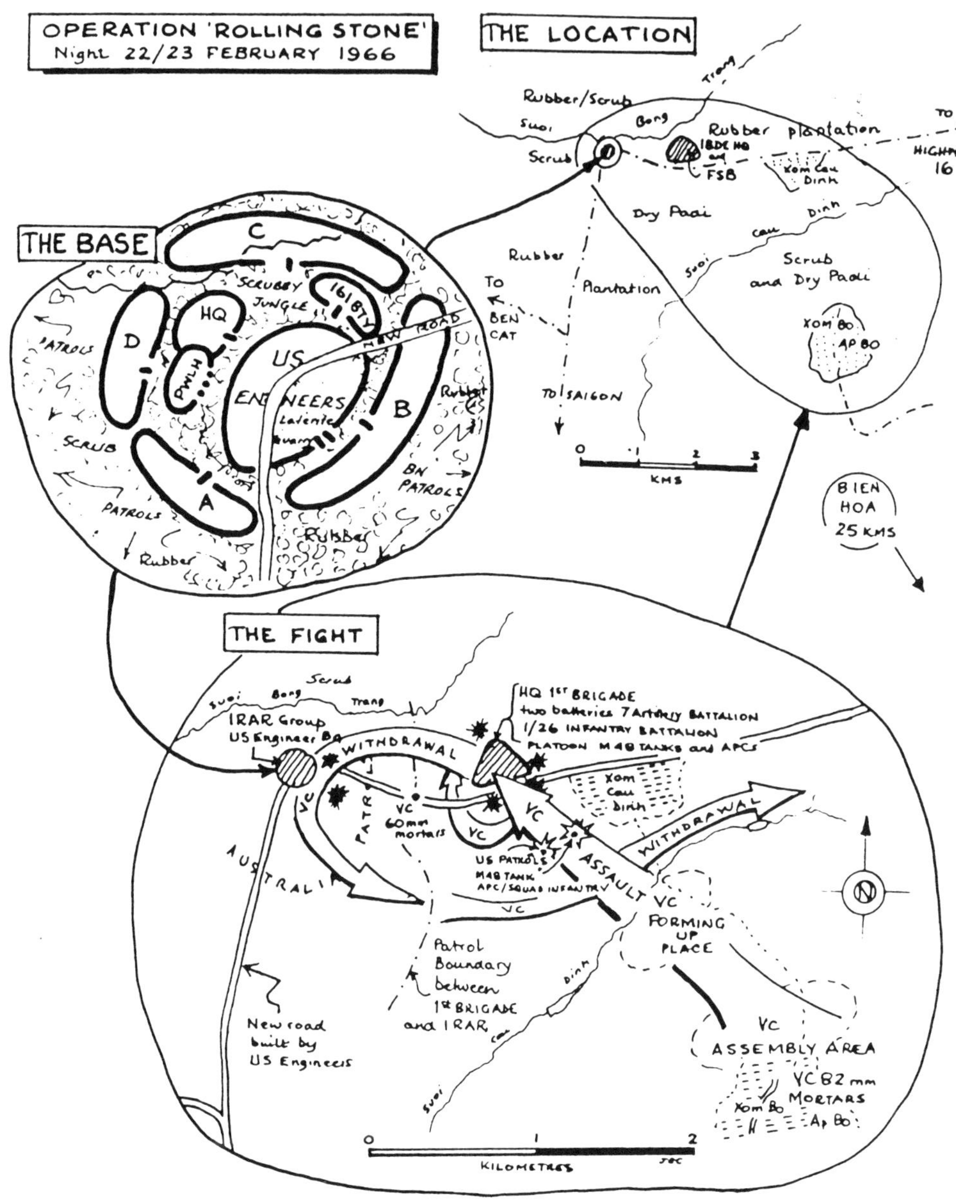

Operation ROLLING STONE—Night 22/23 February 1966

On 22 February 1RAR warned a neighbouring US Brigade Headquarters that a major Viet Cong attack was imminent. Early the next morning the defenders of the Brigade Headquarters, joined by Australians, repulsed a 2000-man Viet Cong attack.

number east of the Brigade Headquarters. He recalled:

> I argued with the BC [Battery Commander] and then with the CO [Preece] for mortar and artillery fire. The CO told me to 'Wait until you see the whites of their eyes'. If fire had have been made available, the attack on the Brigade Headquarters would not have occurred in the strength it did. Reconnaissance the next day showed that the lights were marking Forming Up Places for the attack.[28]

At about midnight there was sporadic firing around the Brigade Headquarters area. Glotzbach waited expectantly for the Viet Cong to attack, holding back his direct and indirect firepower. All day the the units protecting his Headquarters had been stocking up on ammunition. Two tanks had been positioned as mechanical sentries with a squad of infantry on the eastern approaches and were reporting sounds of movement and intermittent flashes of light through the trees: hundreds of Viet Cong were getting into position for the assault.[29] Corporal Lex McAulay described the opening few minutes of the battle:

> At 0225 hrs [2.25 a.m.] the most fantastic outbreak of firing from the tanks, guns, mortars, more tanks, HMGs [Heavy Machine Guns], grenades, LMGs [Light Machine Guns], rifles—the lot—became a waterfall of firing, which died down to one or two guns and then swelled up again. Thousands and thousands of rounds. Many of which were coming in our direction—snapping overhead, cutting leaves and branches, plucking into the dirt, putting holes in hutchies. Great flaming .50 calibre tracers whizzing overhead.[30]

The Viet Cong had opened the assault with a mortar attack on the Brigade Headquarters. Seconds after the Viet Cong mortarmen threw the first rounds down the barrels which resulted in the unmistakable drum roll of 'popping' sounds, Glotzbach unleashed his full inventory of firepower. The Viet Cong commander had not had time to complete a 'last minute' reconnaissance of the Brigade Headquarters. If he had, he would have noticed that his choice for the direction of the assault had sent his men towards the barrels of a company of tanks and a battery of field guns. The US Tankers and Gunners fired round after round of canister shot and splintex into the closely packed ranks of charging Viet Cong. These rounds, like giant shot gun shells, destroyed all human and plant life in front of them. They were supplemented by bank after bank of anti-personnel claymore mines which had their own explosive shot gun effect, sending torrents of ball bearings flying towards the Viet Cong.

Brunalli's patrol was finding their 'ring side seat' uncomfortable. The rounds from the battle were flying overhead and striking all around them. Brunalli was wounded in the arm and just ahead of them they could clearly see and hear hundreds of Viet Cong milling about in some confusion. The position became even more perilous when US aircraft began lighting the battlefield area with flares. At 2.45 a.m., three Viet Cong moved to within 25 metres of Brunalli's position and took up fire positions facing to the north. Brunalli's men fired killing one, and wounding another who was dragged away by the third soldier. Brunalli moved his men after this engagement.[31]

The Viet Cong mortars positioned between the Engineer Battalion and the Brigade Headquarters were engaging both positions and causing much confusion. A US Sapper had been killed and several more wounded by this fire which appeared to be coming from the Brigade Headquarters. Likewise, this fire had caused casualties in the Brigade Headquarters and appeared to be coming from the Engineer Battalion. Many angry words were exchanged between Glotzbach and Preece as each accused the other of firing on their men.

The two tanks positioned forward of the Brigade Headquarters position were being overrun and the crew commanders asked the tanks in the position to fire on them to clear the Viet Cong soldiers who were now clambering all over them. Eventually, both tanks exploded and their crews were lost.

The illumination of the battlefield gave the defenders a distinct advantage over the attackers and enabled the Diggers to join in what was becoming a murderous 'turkey shoot'. At 4 a.m. the Viet Cong began to withdraw from the battle area. To do so they had to run the gauntlet of fire put down by eight field batteries, an 8 inch [203 millimetre] battery and a 175 mm battery: the slaughter continued. Retreating Viet Cong were now filtering into 1 RAR's area. Brunalli's patrol was in an untenable position as groups of Viet Cong in single file began to pass them. One group of fifteen with their rifles carried carelessly were fired on at close range by Brunalli's men and dispersed: they probably had no more fight left in them after being subjected to the awesome US firepower. McFarlane gave Brunalli permission to return to the company position so he could engage the Viet Cong with artillery and mortars. To achieve a clean break, Brunalli ordered his men to fire a volley of shots at a group of ten Viet Cong before turning and running towards the company position. After 30 metres he stopped to listen and heard the sounds of enemy soldiers following them. He deployed his men into a quick ambush and waited. At a range of a few metres, the first of the Viet Cong was shot and Brunalli used the confusion caused among those behind him to make a safe return.[32]

Brunalli's performance was a fine display of professional soldiering. He had not returned to the company position until he was ordered to do so despite the pressure of being close to the enemy. He had controlled the fire of his men, deployed them to suit changing tactical circumstances and caused casualties to the enemy without taking any among his own men. Brunalli was awarded the Military Medal.

More and more groups of disoriented Viet Cong—tired, defeated and carrying their wounded—passed the 1 RAR position. Preece kept up a steady barrage of artillery and mortar fire to the front of the Battalion and Ian McFarlane's men fired relentlessly at the retreating Viet Cong.

> 120 bodies were found. How many were carted off, dead and wounded, we can only guess. It was a well planned attack, up until the Yanks opened fire. Then the devastating wall of fire they put out literally shot the VC assault to shreds. As it was they overran two thirds of the US perimeter.[33]

The US defenders lost eleven killed and 72 wounded. Over 150 Viet Cong bodies were bulldozed into an extended B52 bomb crater. There were countless other pieces of flesh and other human remains, and those rubber trees still standing were covered in red pulp, running with blood and latex. The Australians estimated that another 200 Viet Cong had been wounded.[34] Despite finding 89 bodies and eleven wounded Viet Cong in their vicinity, the '1 RAR War Diary' only credited the Battalion with killing seventeen Viet Cong and capturing seventeen weapons. This was an acknowledgement that the Americans, and the artillery and mortars had caused the majority of the casualties.

McAulay wrote of the aftermath:

> The poor civilians. The VC forced them to carry their ammo and stores and go in with them as porters. So a large number of women and youths were also mown down. The fools who parade around protesting and praising the VC ought to see this. The Yanks bulldozed a huge pit and pushed the VC bodies into it. Individual graves were out of the question.[35]

The villagers of Ap Bo who had also been forced to carry the wounded and dead from the battlefield and were prey to the artillery and mortar fire which was falling in the area.

Essex-Clark recalled:

> I remember hearing this weird noise in the quiet after the firing died down. It was a kind of creaking. Then I realised it was the ox-carts they were using to tow away their casualties. The noise made me think of the tumbrils carting the condemned to the guillotines of the French Revolution.[36]

There was no immediate pursuit of the decimated Viet Cong battalions by tanks or troops mounted in APCs. A combination of the shock of the attack, the exhaustion of the defending troops, the priority for the evacuation of seriously wounded personnel, low stocks of ammunition, the requirement to secure the battlefield, the caution of commanders to pursue a retreating enemy force that might be supported by other units and the absence of a reserve force were factors militating against conducting a pursuit.

Interrogations of Viet Cong prisoners after the battle revealed that they had not been told who, where or when they were going to attack and, after a 25 kilometre forced march, had arrived exhausted. They were not told they would be attacking a position that was defended by tanks and the volume of fire generated from the Brigade Headquarters had killed hundreds of soldiers. Their officers and political cadre had forced them into assault after assault despite the weight of fire.[37]

The Diggers protected the US Sappers for two more days before being replaced by an infantry battalion from the 2nd Brigade of the Big Red One. Lieutenant Colonel Howard Sargent sent the following letter to Australian Army Headquarters in Australia:

> . . . The 1st Battalion's careful planning and intensive exemplary aggressiveness during the operation is worthy of the highest praise. The extraordinary competence of LTCOL Preece was especially noteworthy. The 1st Engineers, US Army, were able to construct 11 miles [18 kilometres] of a vital link in the US 1st Division's main supply route because all harassment by the Viet Cong was quickly and efficiently countered.[38]

The Diggers flew out on 26 February having gained new respect from the Americans for their patrolling methods and ability to gather intelligence. A potential disaster had been turned into an impressive victory. The war in Vietnam was escalating rapidly and the Viet Cong were eager to attack when they assessed their chances of success were high. The ability of the Viet Cong to march 25 kilometres, assemble and execute a regimental-sized night attack was reminiscent of the capabilities of the Viet Minh against the French. At close quarters the Americans had once again proved to be superior to the Viet Cong. However, the key to victory had been timely intelligence and firepower.

10 The showdown

US Army Intelligence found the location of the headquarters of the Viet Cong 7th Military Region. The Paratroopers went in and destroyed it. The Commander of the Viet Cong 9th Division was ordered to destroy a battalion of Paratroopers. He assembled a regiment of crack troops with artillery support for a showdown with the 173rd Airborne Brigade.

February 1966 ended in tragedy for the Paratroopers. On 26 February the 2/503rd deployed at short notice against a target of opportunity due west of the Bien Hoa Airbase where they had operated many times before. A Viet Cong force had been observed in the area and the Paratroopers did not want them to escape. Unknown to them, they were to be the target of opportunity, not the Viet Cong. On the same day, the Diggers arrived back from Operation ROLLING STONE and Major Jim Tattam's C Company became the Bridgade's reserve.

That afternoon a Viet Cong company ambushed Company A of the 2/503rd, inflicting heavy casualties. An airstrike intended to neutralise the Viet Cong position fell among the Paratroopers killing fifteen and wounding over 30 more.[1] In all, Company A had sustained 81 casualties. Brigadier General Smith ordered Tattam's company to mount up in the Australian APCs and they, and the remainder of 1 RAR, were ordered to be ready to deploy to assist the 2/503rd at first light the next day.[2]

The situation for the 2/503rd had been made worse by the loss of their commander, Lieutenant Colonel George Dexter. Dexter had flown in to assess the extent of Company A's casualties. As his helicopter took off, a Viet Cong sniper shot him through the leg and hip. He recalled:

I had the good fortune to be shot while travelling in a helicopter, thus reducing the time it took to get me to the operating table. All I could think of as the pilot flew me to hospital as I gripped my leg tightly to reduce the blood flow, was how my wife and eight kids would handle me not being around anymore. I was losing so much blood I thought it would all be drained out of me before I got to the hospital.[3]

Dexter survived, but his days as a battalion commander were over.

The danger for the Paratroopers was that the Viet Cong would use the dire circumstances Company A found themselves in to mount a quick attack. The afternoon and evening were spent evacuating the dead and wounded. Aircraft hovered over the Paratroopers that night, ready to illuminate the area, and the artillery batteries of Bien Hoa Airbase were alerted to provide support. At first light, Tattam moved out in the APCs to a position closer to the 2/503rd and 1 RAR moved to the tarmac in preparation for airmobile assaults to support the Paratroopers. The Viet Cong had disappeared, refusing to give battle. The Diggers returned to their lines and the Paratroopers flew back to Bien Hoa safely. The Viet Cong were not to refuse battle the next time they met the Paratroopers of the 2/503rd.

On 7 March the Sydney University Australian Labor Party Club announced the establishment of a fund to provide medical supplies to the Viet Cong called 'Medi Cong'. The next day the newly appointed Australian Prime Minister, Harold Holt, announced that 1 RAR was to be relieved in Vietnam in June 1966 by 1st Australian Task Force made up of regular and conscripted troops.[4] Like the US, Australian society was now caught up in its most divisive debates for decades. For the Diggers, Holt's announcement ended months of speculation about when they would be going home. At the same time they wondered about how it was possible that fellow Australians could be providing aid and comfort to the ruthless Viet Cong.

Early in March another political crisis erupted in South Vietnam. Premier Ky had sacked his northern commander Lieutenant General Thi which led to Buddhist and student groups challenging the authority of the Saigon Government in a series of violent protests in Hue and Da Nang. Political turbulence was to continue until late June when ARVN regained control of Da Nang by force. The Saigon Government under Ky and Thieu was fighting for survival against militant Buddhism as well as the Viet Cong.

Further complicating the situation in the northern provinces was the abandonment of the A Shau Valley to the North Vietnamese. An ARVN Special Forces Camp had been attacked by two North Vietnamese regiments and fallen, allowing the A Shau Valley to be developed as an advanced logistics base in South Vietnam. It took two years before the area was restored to South Vietnamese control. Until then Westmoreland did not have the resources to reclaim the A Shau Valley and have enough formations deployed on the Demilitarised Zone to defend against a North Vietnamese invasion.[5]

Against the background of political unrest and a strategic setback in the A Shau Valley, Westmoreland continued to prosecute the war. Intelligence sources had located the headquarters of the Viet Cong's 7th Military Region in War Zone D. This headquarters co-ordinated the political and military operations of the Viet Cong 9th Division and the numerous Local Force units in the provinces around Saigon. Westmoreland ordered Dupuy to destroy it. In turn, Dupuy gave the mission to the new commander of the 173rd. Smith was delighted to start his period of command with this opportunity and began planning for Operation SILVER CITY.

The Diggers were given the task of protecting the Brigade's fire and logistic support base. Operation ROLLING STONE had demonstrated how the Australians could turn patrolling into an aggressive form of defence and also a means of gathering timely intelligence. Lieutenant Colonel George Dexter recalled, with hindsight, the problems his Paratroopers had in fighting the Viet Cong, and that it was the Australians who turned ambushing from being a security patrol into a fighting patrol:

> When we [the Paratroopers] found something, we shot at it. We did not wait, establish the patterns, look for opportunities after out-thinking the local Viet Cong commander. We were just not patient enough — there was too much to do in too little time. We did not use reconnaissance enough. Our ambushes were for security, not to kill. Australians were quiet hunters — patient, thorough, trying to out-think the Viet Cong. I would not have liked to operate at night and know there was a chance of ending up in an Aussie ambush. [6]

Smith had decided to deploy stocks into the area of the operation to sustain the Brigade in the field more efficiently and have additional gun and mortar ammunition on hand. In so doing, he created a lucrative target for the Viet Cong. He gave Preece the task of 'poking out the Viet Cong commander's eyes' by setting up a patrol screen around the fire and logistic support base. The aim was to kill off Viet Cong reconnaissance patrols and dominate the area around the base.

At first light on 9 March, the Diggers took off in 50 'slicks' and headed for LZ BUGS BUNNY, 25 kilometres north of Bien Hoa on the southern banks of the Song Be. The airmobile assaults were not opposed and the area was secured for the arrival of the road convoy and CH47 Chinook helicopters bringing the Brigade's guns, mortars and supplies. Preece was given the Brigade's Cavalry Troop, and Armoured and Engineer companies under operational control. [7]

Preece's first task was to conduct an assault river crossing to the eastern banks of the river. Smith's plan called for the Diggers to secure a crossing point for the Paratroopers so they could advance deep into War Zone D. The Australian river assault was opposed by an increasing number of small groups of Viet Cong firing from the northern and eastern

The Kiwi gunners clean their guns before deployment by helicopter to Operation SILVER CITY.

banks of the river. Gunships swooped in and strafed the Viet Cong but could not prevent an Australian Assault Pioneer, Corporal Les MacDonnell, and a US engineer officer, Lieutenant Gills, from being killed; both were struck in the head by accurate sniper fire.[8]

Major Jim Tattam's C Company assaulted across the river in rubber boats. They took no casualties as they paddled through thick fog hanging over the water. On the other side gunships strafed the banks and neutralised several groups of Viet Cong. By 12.30 p.m. the Diggers were in position, sharing a defensive perimeter with the Brigade's Cavalry Troop and Tank Company. Soon CH47 Chinook helicopters began arriving with guns and ammunition slung below them in cargo nets. At the same time a steady stream of Hueys brought in Brigade Headquarters Company personnel and C123 aircraft delivered weapons, ammunition and stores by LOLEX (low level parachute extraction). Lieutenant Colonel Bruce McDonald, the Commanding Officer of 3 RAR, joined 1 RAR for the first day of the operation. His battalion was fighting in Malaysia against Indonesian raiders. Major John Hooper recalled McDonald staring at the scale and speed of the Brigade's deployment and muttering, 'Unreal, John,

Diggers paddling across the Song Be during Operation SILVER CITY.

absolutely unreal'. By now the Diggers of 1 RAR were used to being a part of the 173rd's intensive, firepower-oriented operations. McDonald was experiencing the amazement they had felt ten months ago.[9]

Later that afternoon the Paratroopers of the 1/503rd flew in and, under the protective guns of the Diggers, crossed the river into the area that the Brigade staff had called AO (Area of Operations) ARIZONA. This proved to be an appropriate name for an area which was to be the scene of a US 'Western-style' shoot out between the 173rd and the Viet Cong 9th Division. The next day the 2/503rd crossed the river into AO ARIZONA. Smith had given them the mission of attacking the Viet Cong head-quarters. The Paratroopers had code-named the location of the head-quarters 'George' after their wounded commander and their orders stated that everyone found in AO ARIZONA was to be regarded as Viet Cong.[10]

By 11 March the Diggers were waging an intensive patrol battle with up to platoon-sized groups of Viet Cong. Most patrol clashes were brief exchanges of fire. Second Lieutenant Bill Hindson's and Graham Bolitho's platoons were in several fire fights during the day, killing and capturing several well-equipped and armed Viet Cong dressed in the khaki uni-forms of the 273rd Main Force Regiment. Second Lieutenant Chris MacIntyre's platoon engaged a patrol at a range of 30 metres in one contact, wounding and capturing two Viet Cong. All these Prisoners-of-War were from the 271st and 273rd Main Force Regiments of the 9th Division. It was also discovered that the D800 Independent Main Force Battalion was in the area. This battalion participated in the attack on the

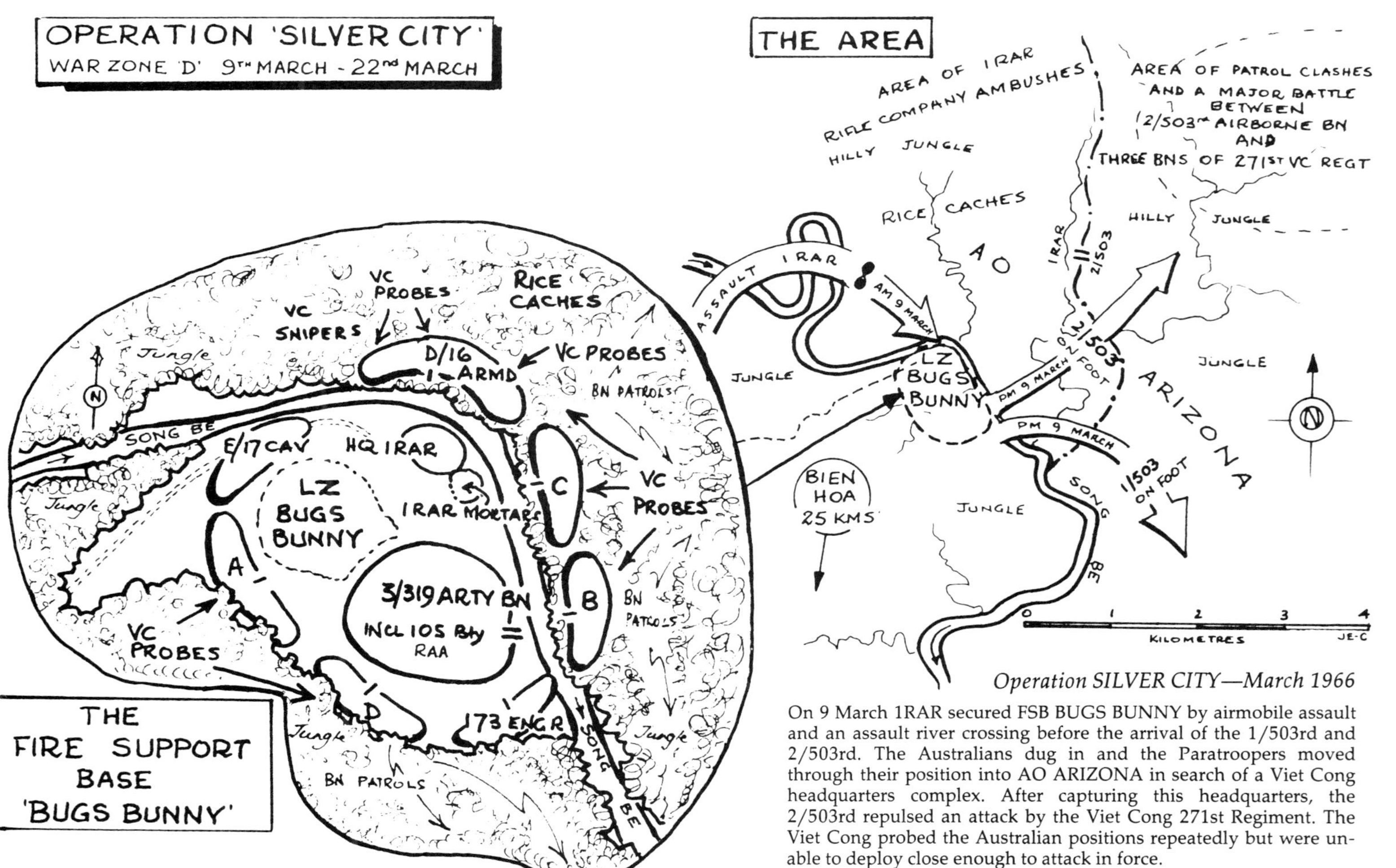

Operation SILVER CITY—March 1966

On 9 March 1RAR secured FSB BUGS BUNNY by airmobile assault and an assault river crossing before the arrival of the 1/503rd and 2/503rd. The Australians dug in and the Paratroopers moved through their position into AO ARIZONA in search of a Viet Cong headquarters complex. After capturing this headquarters, the 2/503rd repulsed an attack by the Viet Cong 271st Regiment. The Viet Cong probed the Australian positions repeatedly but were unable to deploy close enough to attack in force.

headquarters of 1st Infantry Brigade on Operation ROLLING STONE. Preece and Essex-Clark concluded that the commander of the 9th Division was trying to 'sniff out' the fire and logistic support base to assess whether he might attack.[11]

At night the patrol war continued. Small groups of Viet Cong crept in close to the Australian positions trying to identify the locations of machine guns, other heavy weapons and troop dispositions. The Diggers were under strict orders not to fire their machine guns but to throw grenades. The night was punctuated with grenade explosions and the cries of wounded Viet Cong. Once again the Viet Cong displayed a miraculous ability to drag away their dead and wounded. In the morning there were only blood trails left to show where they had been.

On 12 March several mortar rounds fell among a patrol of Diggers from Major Jim Tattam's C Company. Almost all of Corporal Ron West's section were wounded. West and Privates Boyd, Mcleod, and Doorely suffered multiple shrapnel wounds to their legs and torsos. Private Jagers, Tomkison and Willett were treated for minor shrapnel wounds and stayed on duty.[12] These men came from the same platoon that had suffered casualties from the grenade accident in June 1965 and had also fallen victim to booby traps in the Iron Triangle operations. The source of the mortar rounds was never discovered. The platoon commander, Second Lieutenant John Dwyer, may have wondered if their run of bad luck with exploding ammunition would continue: to lose men in combat was tolerable, to lose them to random explosions was demoralising.

On the same day, the Diggers discovered large caches of foodstuffs, mainly rice and fish oil, and medical supplies. It seemed as if the whole of War Zone D was a source of replenishment for the Viet Cong. The Paratroopers had also begun to find ammunition and weapon caches. The widespread use of caches explained why the Viet Cong were more mobile and able to break clean from contacts. They could afford to be lightly armed and equipped because their next meal and ammunition resupply did not need to be carried. The opposite was true for the Diggers who were ordered to patrol for three days without resupply so helicopters would not give away their positions. Mobile Fire Controller, Sergeant John Dean, recalled:

I weighed my kit once. With four water bottles, three days' rations (cut down to the absolute minimum), two spare pairs of socks, toilet gear, sleeping gear, hutchie [small tent], ANPRC 25 [radio] set, spare batteries, SLR [Self Loading Rifle], 100 rounds of ammo, binoculars, compass and maps, it totalled 123 pounds [56 kilograms]. The bulky American 'C' rations did not help. To carry more than three days' rations was an impossibility — we threw out all the extraneous

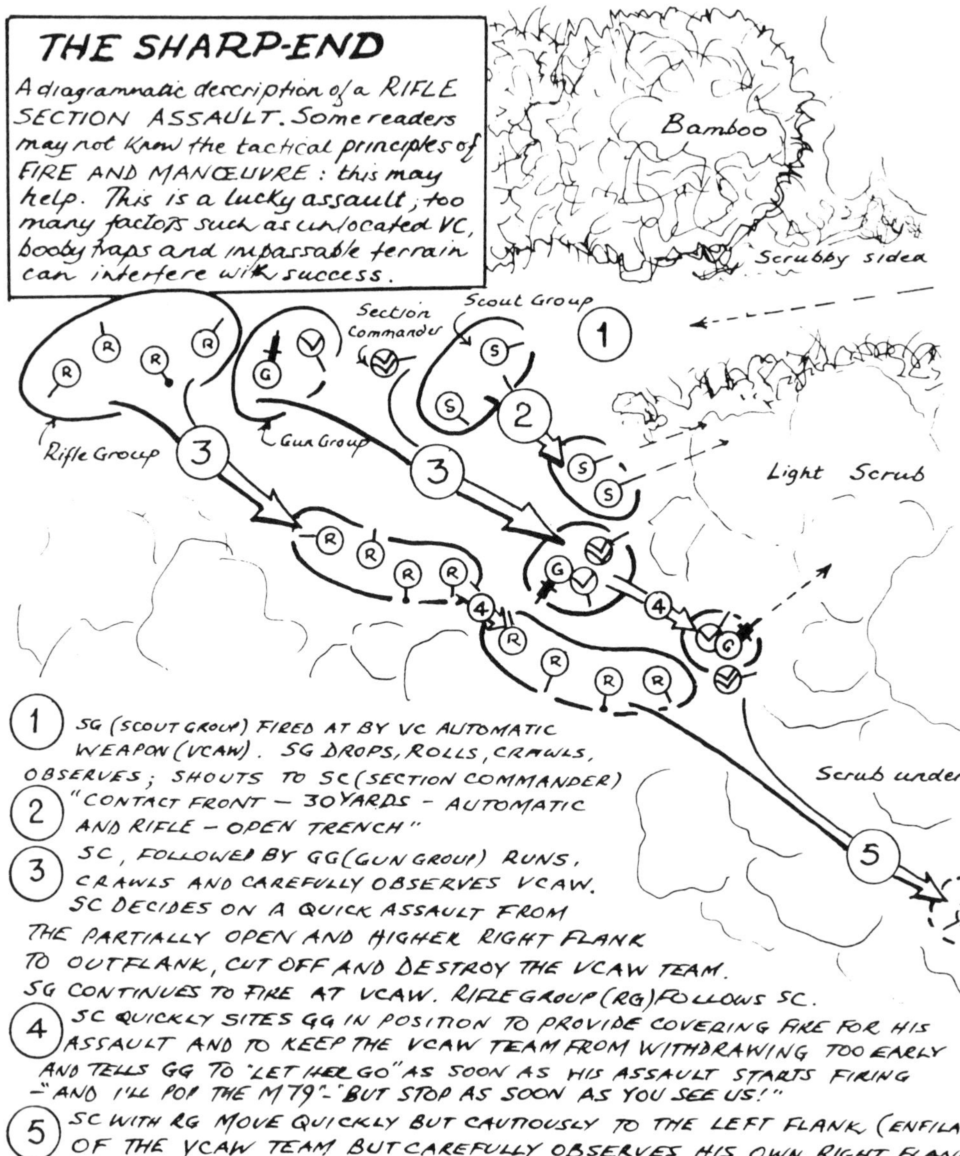

1. SG (SCOUT GROUP) FIRED AT BY VC AUTOMATIC WEAPON (VCAW). SG DROPS, ROLLS, CRAWLS, OBSERVES; SHOUTS TO SC (SECTION COMMANDER)

2. "CONTACT FRONT — 30 YARDS — AUTOMATIC AND RIFLE — OPEN TRENCH"

3. SC, FOLLOWED BY GG (GUN GROUP) RUNS, CRAWLS AND CAREFULLY OBSERVES VCAW. SC DECIDES ON A QUICK ASSAULT FROM THE PARTIALLY OPEN AND HIGHER RIGHT FLANK TO OUTFLANK, CUT OFF AND DESTROY THE VCAW TEAM. SG CONTINUES TO FIRE AT VCAW. RIFLE GROUP (RG) FOLLOWS SC.

4. SC QUICKLY SITES GG IN POSITION TO PROVIDE COVERING FIRE FOR HIS ASSAULT AND TO KEEP THE VCAW TEAM FROM WITHDRAWING TOO EARLY AND TELLS GG TO "LET HER GO" AS SOON AS HIS ASSAULT STARTS FIRING — "AND I'LL POP THE M79" — "BUT STOP AS SOON AS YOU SEE US!"

5. SC WITH RG MOVE QUICKLY BUT CAUTIOUSLY TO THE LEFT FLANK (ENFILADE) OF THE VCAW TEAM BUT CAREFULLY OBSERVES HIS OWN RIGHT FLANK TO ENSURE HE IS NOT 'ENFILADED' BY ANOTHER SUPPORTING VC WEAPON. THE SG AND GG CONTINUE TO FIRE SLOWLY TO COVER THE MOVEMENT OF THEIR SC AND THE RG AND TO PREVENT THE VCAW TEAM 'BUGGING OUT'.

Note : A platoon attack would use similar tactics but it would be slower. A rifle section would provide supporting fire, and another section could protect a flank and provide the platoon reserve should plans fail.

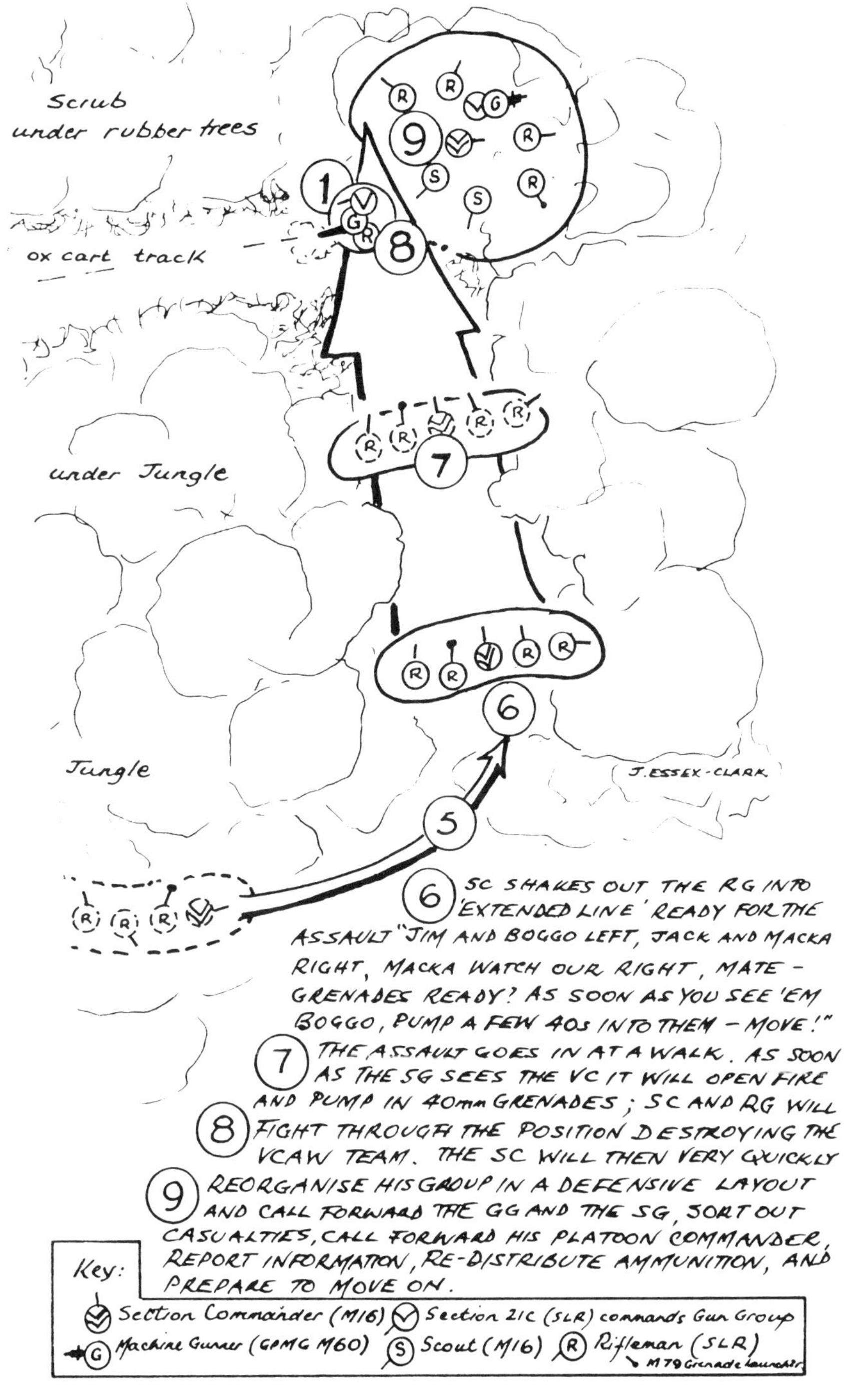

Scrub
under rubber trees
ox cart track
under Jungle
Jungle
J. ESSEX-CLARK
SC SHAKES OUT THE RG INTO 'EXTENDED LINE' READY FOR THE ASSAULT "JIM AND BOGGO LEFT, JACK AND MACKA RIGHT, MACKA WATCH OUR RIGHT, MATE — GRENADES READY? AS SOON AS YOU SEE 'EM BOGGO, PUMP A FEW 40s INTO THEM — MOVE!"
THE ASSAULT GOES IN AT A WALK. AS SOON AS THE SG SEES THE VC IT WILL OPEN FIRE AND PUMP IN 40mm GRENADES; SC AND RG WILL
FIGHT THROUGH THE POSITION DESTROYING THE VCAW TEAM. THE SC WILL THEN VERY QUICKLY
REORGANISE HIS GROUP IN A DEFENSIVE LAYOUT AND CALL FORWARD THE GG AND THE SG, SORT OUT CASUALTIES, CALL FORWARD HIS PLATOON COMMANDER, REPORT INFORMATION, RE-DISTRIBUTE AMMUNITION, AND PREPARE TO MOVE ON.
Key:
Section Commander (M16)   Section 2IC (SLR) commands Gun Group
Machine Gunner (GPMG M60)   Scout (M16)   Rifleman (SLR)
M79 Grenade Launcher

Unknown group of Diggers with Viet Cong Prisoner of War captured during Operation SILVER CITY. Valuable intelligence information was gathered from these prisoners.

material from the ration packs, kept the meat, fruit and cigarettes, filled one of the socks with rice and bought a small bottle of 'hot' sauce from the market before an operation. That would keep you going for six days. There was a cost though — my fighting weight is about 13 stone [83 kilograms]. I returned from Vietnam at just a shade under 11 stone [70 kilograms] and had never felt worse in my life.[13]

Because the Viet Cong were being forced out of the area by Australian patrols by day, they increased their efforts at night. On 13 March platoons of Viet Cong crept up to the perimeter and set up above-ground anti-personnel claymore mines. These mines were detonated and followed by volleys of automatic fire. The Diggers returned fire only with their rifles, threw many grenades into the darkness but took no casualties because they were living in and fighting from well-constructed trenches. Blood trails discovered by clearing patrols in the morning showed that the Viet Cong had paid dearly for their attempts to cause casualties and discover troop dispositions. That day, Australian patrols pushed out further, dis-covering regimental, battalion and company-sized camps. Viet Cong groups left behind to guard these camps were cleared out, and the camps

Lance Corporal Barry Adams, signaller with C Company 1 RAR, photographed before departing on operations. Note the webbing and equipment carried by signallers.

Captain Les Brownlee's period of command came to an end on 13 March 1966 when he was wounded leading his men in combat. After his return to the US he was awarded two Silver Stars for valour.

and their food caches destroyed. In one engagement, Corporal 'Snowy' Wright fired at several withdrawing Viet Cong, killing two and wounding two more. One Viet Cong soldier took over twenty bullets to the legs and body from Wright's M16 rifle before falling to the ground.[14]

The 13 March was Captain Les Brownlee's last day in comand of 'The Bulls'. At 1 p.m. Company B was in a fire fight with a reinforced Viet Cong platoon. Brownlee had gone forward to see what was going on and had noticed a group of Paratroopers was cut off some distance forward of the company. There were casualties among the group and they were in danger of being overrun. Brownlee co-ordinated covering fire and went forward to this group. He took command of the situation, organising the men to return fire and pick up casualties. In a series of short bounds, he and the others that were not wounded carried back the casualties. When Brownlee had handed over the man he was carrying, he realised that a radio set on the fire support frequency had been left behind. Without thinking, he raced back without his rifle to retrieve the radio. Two Para-troopers followed him. Just as he picked up the radio, several Viet Cong rushed towards him and one shot him in the shoulder. The others fired but missed, and then withdrew under the fire of the Paratroopers who had followed.

'The Bulls' had taken three killed and eighteen wounded in this engagement. The Viet Cong were forced to withdraw eventually when Company C positioned themselves on a flank and assaulted.[15] Brownlee lay wounded, waiting for the 'Dust Off' helicopter. He had led his Paratroopers for just under six months and they had achieved all that had been asked of them. Brownlee told reporters soon after he was evacuated to the US:

> They do exactly what you tell them. It never enters your head that they might not be brave enough. As a commander, you have to be careful about what you tell them. They'll do it exactly — no hesitation. So, I've been overly cautious sometimes; things that happen here will remain in our minds for the rest of our lives — people get killed. We will think about that for a long time. What we have to do now is make sure the boys died for something worthwhile and the guys over here continue what they are doing until this thing is won.[16]

Brownlee was evacuated to the US for further surgery on his shoulder. He became a national hero when on 20 August 1966 he was awarded the Silver Star for his actions on 2 January 1966 in the Plain of Reeds and a month later awarded a second Silver Star for his actions on 13 March 1966 on Operation SILVER CITY. Before receiving these awards he had tried to represent the attitudes of the soldiers fighting in Vietnam to correct reports in the media which portrayed them as ruthless, destructive warmongers:

> Nobody who has seen our own dead will ever forget them, or the wounded as they are brought in, or the memorial services after each operation. We do not mind the crawling in the mud, or the staying in the jungle. We grew accustomed to sleeping in wet clothes and going unwashed for weeks. But we did not get used to being shot at — Vietnam has not made us warlovers.

One of his most telling comments was about the change in attitudes to the Viet Cong by the men of the 173rd:

> The Paratroopers, all volunteers, were a swaggering lot of soldiers, confident in their ability and believing the scruffily-dressed, emaciated-looking VC were more bandits than soldiers. We now know that he is tough, fanatical and resourceful. We didn't give him the credit and we paid with blood for our ignorance.[17]

On 14 March the 2/503rd found Objective 'George' after another attack by Company C on the positions that had been the scene of

Brownlee's Company's fire fight the day before. The reinforced platoon that had fought with Company B had been one of the protection elements for the Viet Cong headquarters. Like the Diggers in the Ho Bo Woods, the Paratroopers of the 2/503rd were on top of a huge labyrinth of tunnels and fortifications. They found underground hospitals, offices and storage areas full of weapons, ammunition and medical supplies. Even a tailor's shop, complete with sewing machines and cloth for making uniforms, was found.

The next day the Paratroopers searched the first levels of an extensive tunnel system and discovered more weapons and supplies. Around them were the ominous signs of an enemy build-up. Australian patrols, aerial reconnaissance, infra-red photography and radio intercepts confirmed that the 271st Main Force Regiment had concentrated its three battalions. Platoon and company groups were seen and engaged at long range.

On 14 March Second Lieutenant Kevin Lunny's platoon observed an enemy platoon moving towards the Australian perimeter. Major Jim Tattam ordered Second Lieutenant John Dwyer to form a fighting patrol and intercept the Viet Cong. With eight men, Dwyer moved out. After advancing about 500 metres, the patrol's machine gunner, Private Lionel Baxter, saw two Viet Cong soldiers 20 metres to his left. He turned, taking aim, and signalled to his Number 2, Private 'Kit' Carson, to be ready. Baxter fired and hit both Viet Cong. Then the area in front of Baxter erupted with automatic fire as a platoon of about twenty Viet Cong advanced towards them in assault formation. Baxter was hit with several rounds about the head and shoulders and died. Carson pushed him aside and took up the blood-stained M60 machine gun and started firing.

Baxter's burst of machine gun fire had alerted the remainder of the patrol to the direction of the Viet Cong assault. They went quickly into their battle drills and returned fire. Second Lieutenant John Dwyer recalled:

> Myself and my sig[naller], 'Smoky' Dawson were up forward and were being brassed up from the trees to our front. I ordered those around me to throw grenades and then assault straight into the trees to get us out of our exposed position. Grenades were thrown, and the section, myself and the sig[naller] jumped up and made a rush for the treeline. As we dived into a protected area, there was a burst of fire to my immediate front and Private Vic Simon, who was right next to me, was 'bowled' over . . . I dived over to Simon to see if he was alive — miraculously, he had only taken one round and it had hit squarely onto the foresight of his M16 [rifle], driving it back into his chest and 'bowling' him over. Shaken, he quickly recovered.[18]

Manoeuvre was impossible for Dwyer now as Viet Cong fire pinned his men down in a small depression in the ground. The only other force

Major Jim Tattam could deploy was the Company's support section. Corporal Alan 'Robby' Robinson led the Support Section out in the direction of the sounds of the fire fight. The Viet Cong broke contact before Robinson's group arrived.

Baxter was the only casualty from this contact. On 3 December 1965 he had said goodbye to his wounded brother, Tom, at Tan Son Nhut Airport. Tom had been seriously wounded on Hill 82 with Major John Healy's A Company during Operation HUMP. They had wished each other good luck and promised to have a beer together when Lionel returned from Vietnam.[19] Lionel Baxter was the third brother of the three sets of brothers in 1 RAR to be killed.

The intensity of the patrol battle around LZ BUGS BUNNY increased throughout the day and into the night. Preece had sent Major John Healy's A Company on a three-day patrol to deny the Viet Cong use of a series of roads and tracks which ran north to south towards the base area. During the day several inconclusive fire fights had broken out between Healy's platoons and groups of Viet Cong. In one exchange, Second Lieutenant Rick Culpitt's platoon engaged a group of well-dressed and equipped Viet Cong, wounding three and killing one. The search of the body confirmed the proximity of the 271st Main Force Regiment.[20]

That night, Healy ordered Lieutenant Tony White to set a platoon ambush on a major well-used track while the remainder of the company camped nearby. Just on last light as the platoon was moving silently into position, a Viet Cong Main Force company, bunched up and carrying lights, came down the track from the north. They were preceded by a cautious group of five scouts. The Diggers waited in silence, ready to ambush the larger group they could hear moving further down the track. Hearts pounded as one of the Viet Cong scouts stopped and peered at White's northern machine gun position. As the scout raised his rifle to fire and call to his companions he was cut down by a withering burst of machine gun rounds. The remaining scouts were all killed.

There was pandemonium further north for a few seconds, and then the Viet Cong company went into an immediate, skilful and aggressive counter-ambush drill. As the Viet Cong swept towards Corporal Alcorn's machine gun position, they were met with steady M60 machine gun fire. For 20 minutes Alcorn's men, supported by the fire of the remainder of the platoon, held off the Viet Cong until Alcorn was able to return to the main platoon position. Healy recalled:

We [the rest of the company] were only 300 metres away from this intensive fire fight between Tony White's platoon and the Viet Cong but could not intervene because of the darkness and difficulty of manoeuvring against a large enemy group through thick jungle without being detected. What a show it was — long streams of green tracer from the Viet Cong's RPD machine guns, crisscrossed by long streams of red tracer from White's platoon. I ordered White to break clean as it would be only a matter of time before he ran out of ammunition and the Viet Cong would attack. I was amazed that for all the firing that went on, none of White's men were hit but it was clear from the cries and yells that a number of VC had. Probably due to the fact that White's men were stationary in prepared positions and the VC had been moving and caught by surprise.[21]

White was able to pull his men back and disengage from the Viet Cong. He and his men lay in silence for the rest of the night listening to the grisly sounds of the Viet Cong evacuating their dead and wounded less than 70 metres away.

Back at LZ BUGS BUNNY, the Viet Cong were probing the Australian and US perimeters and repeating the technique of setting up claymore mines, detonating them and then firing long bursts into the position. Corporal Lex McAulay recalled:

The VC had success in creeping up to the US perimeters and setting up a DH-10 wire link to large locally-made claymore mines which they then detonated. The Yanks would *not* put out patrols or sentries, and talked, sky-larked and played radios as well as wandering around half dressed. It was not difficult for the VC to get in close. A four-man standing [stationary sentry position] patrol from D company engaged about 10 VC creeping in, and one of the first shots hit a DH-10 [claymore mine made in China]. The resulting explosion stripped all the leaves from an area 35 paces across. Jim Tattam sent out a reaction force and I recall the trees running with blood. We found pieces of clothes and a Garand M1 buttstock. The VC had collected the various pieces of bodies on a piece of plastic and run.[22]

Throughout the night the three battalions of the Viet Cong 271st Main Force Regiment were moving into position for an attack on the 2/503rd. Reconnaissance elements had noted that each morning the battalion's three rifle companies would depart and conduct patrols in the area, leaving the battalion headquarters lightly defended. The attack was timed to occur once the companies had left. The ratio of Viet Cong to Paratroopers would be at least six to one. The Commander of the 9th Division had allocated the Commander of the 271st Regiment some precious artillery assets for this attack. For once he planned to give the Paratroopers the experience of being shelled. The 2-37 and 2-43 Artillery Battalions equipped with 75 millimetre Howitzers, 60 millimetre and 82 millimetre mortars and 57 millimetre Recoiless Rifles manoeuvred into position and their forward observers joined reconnaissance elements maintaining surveillance of the Paratroopers' position.[23]

At first light on 16 March, the Viet Cong were in position 300 metres from the Paratroopers' position. The 2/503rd did not send out clearing patrols and, after they pulled in their listening posts (two-man sentry positions), the Viet Cong crept in even closer to the perimeter. Luck began to favour the Paratroopers when their breakfast of cooked 'A' rations was late in arriving and the rifle companies remained in position around the headquarters as the sun rose higher. The Viet Cong Regimental Commander was now in an awkward position. He had over 2000 soldiers concentrated near a US airborne battalion. The longer they stayed in position the better was the chance of them being discovered from the air and being subjected to artillery and airstrikes.

Lieutenant William Vose recalled the start of the battle:

I was just finishing shaving in my helmet when through the trees I saw a chopper coming into the LZ with hot 'As' [A rations] for breakfast. As it descended to about tree top level, I heard the deep chugging sound of a HMG [Heavy Machine Gun]. At first I thought it was testfiring, but when the chopper dropped out of the sky like a rock and crashed into the trees I knew that something other than animals had been crawling around the perimeter that night. From all around me came the sounds of LMG and HMG fire, the explosive 'crump' of hand grenades with a deafening sound, and then, a fraction of a second later, the answering, death-giving sound of 600 [US] M16s and 22 M60 machine guns.

The fire of the Viet Cong heavy machine gun had been the signal for the Viet Cong to attack from the north, west and south simultaneously. However, the signal had been given prematurely. The waiting Viet Cong infantry had been told that they would attack after the Paratroopers had eaten breakfast and left the position on patrol to the east. All of these timings had been put back when the 'breakfast' helicopter did not arrive until 7.30 a.m., an hour late. Only the Viet Cong battalion poised in the north attacked. The other two battalions hesitated. The delay of several minutes for the assaults to come from the west and south allowed the Paratroopers time to organise themselves and stand ready to defend. There was also a lifesaving delay in the Viet Cong bringing accurate artillery and mortar fire to bear on the position.

Vose wrote later:

After 32 minutes the calls started coming back from the Line Companies for more ammo. With a couple of others I started gathering ammo and grenades from the Headquarters personnel and started forward for A Company . . . The rest of the morning passed quickly while I learned my way around on the line and tried to get used to the constant incoming fire, the grenades exploding all around and the ceaseless cries of the wounded and the dying.

The US position held firm despite the onslaught of wave after wave of Viet Cong. Female Viet Cong soldiers were running forward and retrieving the dead and wounded from each assault wave; they met the same fate as their male counterparts. Hand to hand fighting occurred in several places as the Viet Cong, dressed in black and green uniforms with plastic, camouflaged helmets, rushed into the first line of perimeter trenches. Individual Paratroopers rose and fired into them at point blank range, thrust with their bayonets and clubbed with their rifles. It was a gruesome, grisly business with men cursing, calling out and many screaming in agony as they felt their bodies being penetrated by hot lead or knifed with cold steel. After two hours the battle hung in the balance. The Paratroopers were running short of ammunition. At 9.30 a.m twelve helicopters crammed with ammunition flew low and fast over the Paratroopers and dropped their loads. Eight aircraft were hit, three crewmen were badly wounded, but none of the helicopters was downed. Several Paratroopers risked their lives to retrieve and distribute this ammunition.

The citation for Lieutenant John Vose read:

Upon his arrival at the Command Post, it was learned that the second and third platoons were dangerously low on ammunition, and Lieutenant Vose quickly volunteered to assist them. Lieutenant Vose moved the length and breadth of the company front under murderous fire and succeeded in resupplying the platoons with the critically needed ammunition. As the battle continued, the left flank of the company which was being defended by the weapons platoon was forced to pull back due to heavy casualties and was in danger of being overrun. Even though only six effectives remained in the platoon, Lieutenant Vose reorganized them and regained the lost ground.[24]

Later in the battle Lieutenant Vose was wounded while leading a group of men to destroy a machine gun post. He wrote:

A second later from our right front, the HMG opened up, casting death and destruction all about. Small trees, three or four inches [8 or 10 centimetres] in diameter, began falling from the impact of the projectiles. I looked to my left at Parks, the second man. He had hit the ground so fast that he had landed on his back and as I watched, he got hit nine times by that machine gun and then he just lay there. Well, with nothing else I could do, I started returning fire with my M16 and pistol. But it seemed that all I did was anger the gun and attract its attention, as it then directed its baseball-like missiles at me. I heard them woosh over my head and then they started to get lower, and they began kicking up dirt in front of me. While I turned to my left side to reload, I saw them coming, taking shovelfuls of dirt with them. Then I felt something warm in my right leg, then in my right side, then my right arm, and then I felt sick![25]

Other platoon commanders performed heroically that day:

Realizing his platoon's position was in great danger of being overrun by the assaulting Viet Cong, Lieutenant Boykin moved from one flank of his platoon to the other repositioning his men in critical points. His actions were a determining factor in repelling three consecutive Viet Cong assaults and driving the enemy back into the jungle. However, the weapons platoon of Company A continued to receive fire from two .50 calibre machine guns emplaced 40 metres to their front, and only three effectives remained in the platoon. Boykin quickly moved a relief force to the area of the hard pressed weapons platoon and positioned them to reinforce the entire line. It was evident that the direct fire from the .50 calibre machine gun position was inflicting numerous casualties upon the platoon. Lieutenant Boykin called mortar fire onto the position but failed to eliminate it. Taking two men, Lieutenant Boykin crawled forward under devastating fire to mark the position with smoke. One of the men was killed instantly and the other was seriously wounded. However, Lieutenant Boykin continued to crawl forward, finally reaching a vantage point from which he could mark the position. Because of his brave act, the Mad Bomber [Mortar Air Delivery aircraft] was able to destroy the position.[26]

By 11 a.m. the battle began to turn in favour of the Paratroopers. Over 3000 artillery and mortar rounds had fallen among the assault waves of Viet Cong, some falling as close as 30 metres from the perimeter. Seventy-three fighter ground attack sorties had been flown which had effectively destroyed any forces positioned further away in reserve. The Australian Gun Battery was prominent in this lifesaving artillery barrage. Major Peter Tedder's Gunners had fired continuously for nearly four hours, resulting in a number of critically timed missions breaking up several Viet Cong assaults. Lieutenant Colonel John Walsh, who had taken over command from George Dexter, wrote to Tedder after the battle, 'Thanks for saving our lives. I have never seen finer shooting.'[27]

At 11.40 a.m. the Viet Cong disengaged and withdrew to the south east, leaving strong delaying forces behind. These forces, supported by heavy machine guns, had the dual missions of creating time for dead and wounded to be cleared from the battlefield by harassing the Paratroopers while they cleared their dead and wounded and engaging any follow-up forces. It took some time to clear these delaying forces so the evacuation of dead and wounded Paratroopers could begin. The last of these delaying positions was destroyed four hours after the battle had finished. The Viet Cong machine gunner was found dead with his corpse chained to the tripod of his weapon — the machine gun itself had gone.

The Paratroopers had suffered seven killed and 162 wounded in this battle. Within 100 metres of their position, 265 Viet Cong corpses were counted with over 80 more bodies being found further away from the perimeter. Smith estimated that hundreds more Viet Cong dead and wounded had been evacuated. Once again artillery fire had caused many of the Viet Cong casualties. Over 150 individual and crew-served weapons were captured.

By 4.35 p.m. the 1/503rd and 2/503rd had linked up. Smith combined his two airborne battalions and placed them under the command of the Brigade's Assistant Commander, Colonel Duddy, calling the force Task Force DUDDY. After a request from Smith, Dupuy deployed two battalions of the 1st Infantry Division into AO ARIZONA under Smith's operational control to cut off Viet Cong escape routes. The aim was to search for and destroy the remnants of the 271st Main Force Regiment.

The next day Task Force DUDDY swept the areas around the battlefield of the previous day looking for Viet Cong. More bodies were found but there was no sign of the badly mauled 271st Regiment. Once again the Viet Cong had displayed their expertise in breaking cleanly from battle. However, they had been given breathing space because the Paratroopers did not move off until afternoon in pursuit. After going some distance, and picking up signs that they were closing in on the enemy, they deployed into a defensive position for the night.

Meanwhile, the patrol war between the Diggers and the Viet Cong continued. Lieutenant Bill Giles' half-platoon patrol observed a group of Viet Cong bathing from the opposite bank of the Song Be. They were fired on and at least one was killed and a number wounded. Lieutenant Tony White's platoon found a large cache of rice in the morning after their anxious night listening to the Viet Cong evacuate dead and wounded. A Viet Cong squad walked into the area of the cache and two were killed and a third died later at the hands of Second Lieutenant Rick Culpitt's platoon. There were numerous other inconclusive engagements where one or two Viet Cong would be killed and the others escape. The Diggers were effectively denying the Viet Cong access to the vicinity of LZ BUGS BUNNY and the all-important fire base located there.

At 8.15 p.m. a reinforced company of Viet Cong attacked the 2/503rd, supported by mortar and Rocket Propelled Grenade fire. This attack continued intermittently until 11 p.m. Once again the Viet Cong suffered heavy casualties from mortar and artillery fire. In the morning only five bodies were discovered, but numerous blood trails from the area told the true story of the fate of the attackers. The Paratroopers lost one killed and eleven wounded. This fruitless attack was possibly a diversion to allow other substantial forces to leave the area and evacuate stocks of weapons, equipment and foodstuffs.

That same night over 200 Viet Cong soldiers walked through one of Major Ian Fisher's D Company platoon ambushes. Second Lieutenant Bob

Davis had delegated the task of initiating the ambush to one of his section corporals. This NCO 'froze' when he saw the large numbers of Viet Cong move into the ambush area, and failed to open fire. His men waited for the signal to fire; it never came. Fisher and Essex-Clark were furious at the lack of enterprise by this platoon, however they were not lying on their stomachs in the ambush making the decision on what was a sound tactical risk and what was a suicidal decision. Essex-Clark co-ordinated a series of artillery missions based on his assessment of the Viet Cong company's direction and speed of movement. Documents captured later confirmed that the company had taken casualties.[28]

On 19 March the commander of the 9th Viet Cong Division planned one last attack on the 173rd. He concentrated two regiments for a night attack. A combination of aerial infra-red photography, Australian patrol reports, radio intercepts and other sophisticated detection techniques gave Smith the location of this concentration of troops. At 11 p.m. he ordered his five field batteries, the Big Red One's 8 inch [203 millimetre] battery and two 175 millimetre batteries to open fire.[29] The results of this fire are unknown but the Viet Cong divisional attack against the 173rd was abandoned. The Viet Cong retreated from AO ARIZONA, defeated but not destroyed.

The remaining days of the operation were quiet. As quickly as the Viet Cong had been able to concentrate two Main Force regiments and two artillery battalions, they dispersed without a trace. The Brigade returned to Bien Hoa Airbase on 22 March. The Diggers felt satisfied that their stealthy patrolling had protected the logistic and fire support base and gathered timely intelligence. The Paratroopers felt satisfied that the Viet Cong 9th Division had given their best and been defeated.

Postscript

The 2/503rd was awarded the US Presidential Unit Citation for the gallantry displayed against the 271st Main Force Regiment on 16 March 1966. The Viet Cong 9th Division was reinforced by North Vietnamese conscripts over the later months of 1966. It took some time to recover from its defeat in AO ARIZONA and did not fight as a division again until the Tet Offensive of 1968 when it was destroyed as a fighting force.

11 The last searches

For their last operations the Paratroopers fought a 'big' war, the Diggers fought a 'patrol' war, and the Viet Cong returned to a 'guerilla' war. Precedents were set for all the protagonists for the next few years. However, the North Vietnamese were on the march south. Westmoreland ordered the 173rd to Phuoc Long Province to stop them.

Naming operations after western towns continued after Operation SILVER CITY. The Diggers' last two operations were called ABILENE and DENVER. The pattern of US and Australian operations in III Corps had become established. Since their arrival in May 1965 the Paratroopers had caused an enormous amount of damage to the war-making capabilities of the Viet Cong employing the mobility of helicopters and the tactics of firepower. The Infantrymen of the Big Red One were also trained for conventional warfare and saw no reason to change the search and destroy formula developed by the Paratroopers.

The Diggers participated in these large-scale, short-term operations but maintained a small-scale, long-term attitude to finding and fighting the Viet Cong. They wanted to hunt down the Viet Cong in platoon-sized patrols, find them and attack under the most favourable tactical circumstances. The Diggers of the incoming 1st Australian Task Force were also trained in jungle patrolling operations and saw no reason to change the 'patrol and kill' formula developed by the Diggers of 1 RAR. The results of Operations ABILENE and DENVER set precedents for the way the US and Australian Armies would prosecute the war in III Corps for the next five years.

Operation ABILENE was a 1st Infantry Division operation to search for and destroy the Main Force regiments of the Viet Cong 5th Division. Dupuy hoped that, like the 9th Viet Cong Division had done with the Paratroopers, the 5th Division would decide to fight it out with his Infantrymen. He assigned the Diggers the task of protecting his divisional logistics and fire support base. He too had decided to risk taking extra

236

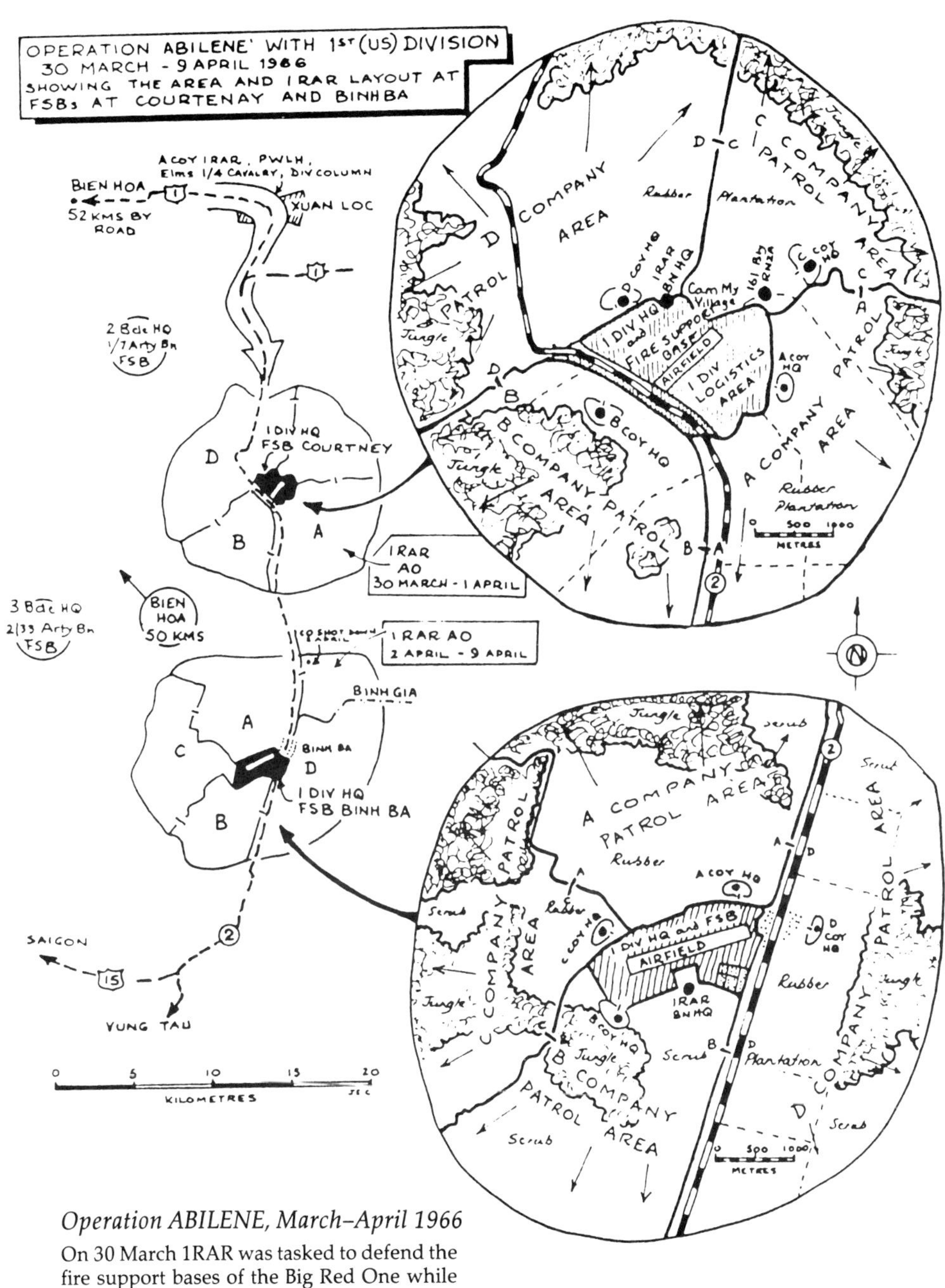

Operation ABILENE, March–April 1966

On 30 March 1RAR was tasked to defend the fire support bases of the Big Red One while its brigades searched for the Viet Cong. From 30 March to 9 April A, B, C and D Companies sent out patrols to deny the Viet Cong access to the bases.

Diggers from A Company 1 RAR mounted on an Australian APC waiting for the order to move to the Courtenay Plantation. They were protecting a 600-vehicle convoy. The man with cigarette (centre) is the vehicle commander from 1 APC Troop, Prince of Wales Light Horse Regiment.

ammunition and other stocks into the field so resupply and fire support would be more efficient. Like Smith, he had confidence that the Australians would keep the Viet Cong from attacking his base while his brigades were sweeping the surrounding areas.[1] There was one American, however, who did not think the Diggers were that good.

Brigadier General Jim Hollingsworth was the Deputy Commander of the Big Red One. He was a large gregarious man who carried a shiny pearl-handled Colt .45 revolver and smoked Havana cigars. He listened intently to Alex Preece give his briefing to the assembled headquarter staff on how the Australians would defend the Divisional logistics base. He rose and asked if the Australians could prevent the base being mortared. Preece replied that the Diggers would patrol out to mortar range and prevent the Viet Cong getting in close enough to mortar the base. 'Bullshit, Colonel, I bet you a hundred bucks that the base will be mortared and your men won't be able to stop it,' bellowed Hollingsworth. 'You have a bet, Sir,' replied Preece.[2]

Early on 30 March 1966 a 600-vehicle convoy protected by Major John Healy's A Company supported by tanks moved to the airfield in the Courtenay Plantation near the village of Binh Ba. Healy recalled that he was staggered by the size of the Divisional road column. Every type of military vehicle was represented and he imagined that when the first vehicle arrived at the Courtenay Plantation 50 kilometres away the last vehicle was still likely to be waiting to leave. Healy's mission was to secure a landing zone near the airfield and clear it of mines and booby traps before the fly-in of the remainder of the Battalion. The size of the road convoy and the ensuing fly-in of the Australians left the Viet Cong in no doubt that Phuoc Tuy Province was to be the target of a huge search and destroy operation.

The Australian platoons were dispersed quickly, confident in their abilities to find and fight the Viet Cong by day and night. A typical contact was between Second Lieutenant Clive Williams' forward section and a squad of Viet Cong early the next day. The section engaged the squad at close range in thick jungle. Three Viet Cong fell dead and two others were wounded but escaped. Another was captured suffering from severe shock.[3]

On 2 April the Divisional base was consolidated at the Binh Ba airfield. Preece ordered the Battalion to move to this area and flew above the road convoy in a helicopter piloted by Captain Bevan Smith of the Australian Reconnaissance Flight. Observing that all was progressing well, Preece ordered Smith to fly to an adjacent area. Suddenly several bullets drilled through the cockpit, shattering the knuckles of Bevan Smith's left hand. The shock of this wound resulted in Smith losing control of the aircraft temporarily. He regained his composure and proceeded to give Alex Preece his first flying lesson. Showing great coolness under stress, Preece and Smith managed to land the helicopter safely in a South Vietnamese Regional Force compound at Ngai Giao, north of Binh Ba. Both had been lucky. Several other bullet holes in the fuselage testified to how close they had been to being seriously wounded.

After the operation Major Paul Lipscombe, the Officer Commanding the Australian 161st Recce Flight, presented Preece with a plaque on which was mounted half a set of pilot's wings, bearing the inscription:

> To remind him [Preece] of a disturbing incident on 2 April 1966 when he successfully completed an involuntary flying lesson in a helicopter of 161 Recce Flt. On completion of a course in the use of the throttle and corrective control, he is to be awarded the other half of his pilot's wings.[4]

After surgery on his hand in Australia, Smith returned to flying duties and received a Mentioned-in-Despatches.

For the next two days the Australian platoons asserted their dominance of the area around the sprawling divisional base. During the day two-thirds of the battalion were out on patrol and the remainder provided the close defence of the base. At night a third were out on ambush patrols and two-thirds provided close security. Major John Essex-Clark recalled that when Dupuy visited he seemed to almost want to take cover when he realised that his base was not protected by a continuous line of fortifications and two-thirds of the protection force were kilometres away on patrol.[5]

The Viet Cong were 'sniffing' out the base but were encountering stiff opposition from the Diggers. In one contact Major Ian McFarlane's B Company mounted in the Australian APCs and chased a Viet Cong company until thick jungle forced them to abandon their pursuit. Warrant Officer Harold Smith, the Company Sergeant Major, fired from an APC moving at top speed, killing two Viet Cong and wounding another. These were the only casualties caused to the Viet Cong who had again failed to penetrate the Australian defences.[6]

The most successful tactic was the night ambush.[7] Over the next few days Lieutenant Bill Giles and Second Lieutenants Graham Bolitho, Rick Culpitt, Bob Davis and John Dwyer all conducted successful ambushes. The tally of Viet Cong dead and wounded was more than those of the two US brigades sweeping the area in search of the 5th Viet Cong Division. All of those killed were identified as Local Force guerillas. Because several were from the village of Binh Ba, Preece decided to cordon off the village and screen all of its inhabitants. A total of 28 suspects were detained, including a man who had evaded Second Lieutenant Graham Bolitho's ambush the night before. The Viet Cong stopped moving at night. The Local Force commander probably decided to wait until the Australians left, as they would inevitably do in a few days, before resuming normal operations.

Since the first few months the Diggers had become quite callous and single-minded about their task in Vietnam. Representative of their views was McAulay:

There is another village a little further south [of Binh Ba], which I think is VC. There's an old ambush there — the burnt wrecks of ARVN trucks, some in the village, some outside; VC propaganda banners on the trees either side of the village; and while I was checking passes and talking to the locals they gave me an earful of how they were being exploited by the manager etc, etc, etc. True they are, and the local VC are fighting for a promised better life, but I am not here to do that — improving their lot is up to Nguyen Cao Ky — who is better than his predecessors and a very busy man. I'm just here to exterminate VC. So tonight we're going to lay ambushes outside the said village and try and catch the young locals trying to

Unknown Vietnamese child. Civic action by the members of the 173rd was directed to give these innocent victims of war a better standard of living. The results were illusory.

right the world's wrongs. So far we have 11 VC KIA by body count. Not too bad. We're over the 120 mark now, by actual body count. Many more have been carried off. As a ratio, we kill about 4 and recover one. We are not doing too bad.[8]

The 'body count' approach to the war provided the sustaining logic for most of the Diggers. There was little intellectual and philosophical room to moralise about the political situation in South Vietnam when a bullet or a booby trap could kill or maim, and no Vietnamese could be trusted. However, there were efforts to improve the living conditions of some South Vietnamese.

Back at Bien Hoa, the Australian area of responsibility included the hamlet of Ong Huong — a typical cluster of impoverished Vietnamese clinging to a life of subsistence farming. Major Ian McFarlane received permission from Brumfield in August 1965 to provide medical and dental assistance to the inhabitants. The motive was philanthropic.[9]

Conscious of not undermining local authority, McFarlane ensured that all aid was organised and distributed through Mr Tran Van Tai, the hamlet chief. Captains Peter Haslau and Peter Naughton gave medical and dental treatment respectively. Naughton, a jovial dentist, quipped in the early days that he was probably 'drilling' more Viet Cong than the Diggers on patrol. McFarlane also ordered his Second-in-Command, Captain Peter Arnison, to make clothing, footwear, and fresh and tinned food available to the hamlet chief for distribution. These items were purchased from B Company funds.

After his second visit, McFarlane decided that B Company would 'adopt' the people of Ong Huong and systematically improve their living and educational standards. The primary motive continued to be philanthropic, but there were military advantages. Ong Huong had been a haven for Viet Cong raiders in the past. McFarlane hoped the attitude to the Australians would change and the people of Ong Huong would be less co-operative in the future. Eventually, intelligence information might flow which would enable the Australians to deny their area of responsibility on the airbase perimeter to the Viet Cong.

The Australian attitude to civic action had its origins in the Malayan Emergency where there were continuous efforts to improve the living and educational conditions of the Malayan peasants and poor Chinese squatters. The difference was that in Malaya the local police and government officials administered these programs while the soldiers provided protection and hunted the Communist Terrorists. McFarlane was taking the initiative as a soldier to establish a civic action program in the absence of a South Vietnamese Government with resources to do so.

The program was criticised by some other members as being inappropriate for an infantry battalion whose job it was to fight and not fraternise.

Resources that could have been directed to the welfare of the soldiers were directed to Ong Huong and later to other hamlets in the vicinity. Time, materiel and funds were spent building a school and a playground with swings, see-saws and climbing bars. Despite the racism of some and the professionally-based criticism of others, eventually each Australian company contributed men, time and funds to support the Battalion's civic action program. Other hamlets became beneficiaries of clothing, food, footwear and minor engineering assistance.

Implicit in the argument against civic action was that it would soften the Diggers' attitudes to killing. A battalion's job was to maintain a fierce aggression. Compassion towards the Vietnamese in the hamlets was seen as taking the edges off the killer instinct and possibly making the Diggers hesitant when fighting the Viet Cong in villages.

There was also a view that the battalion's Intelligence Officer should be the Civic Action Officer. This would keep the primary motive of civic action military and not philanthropic. The countervailing view was that the Vietnamese would soon distinguish the information-gathering motives of a program supervised by the Intelligence Officer. This view maintained that information would flow anyway if the motives were genuine and be a by-product of civic action, not the reason for it.

Captain Peter Arnison maintained the philanthropic emphasis of the Australian civic action program. He also ensured the program was not seen as patronising and condescending. The local Vietnamese Popular Forces provided labour for building projects and inhabitants were expected to assist. This co-operative approach established a sense of ownership and pride among the Vietnamese. By May 1966 the hamlet of Ong Huong had a two-room school filled with excited, chattering children supervised by two enthusiastic teachers. In that same month eight Viet Cong attempted to enter Ong Huong after dark. A group of Popular Force soldiers from the hamlet ambushed them, killing two, wounding another and capturing two weapons.

Mr Tran Van Trai wrote to Major Ian McFarlane,

Subject: Making Known the Feelings of the People of Ong Huong

We are working to make a very happy new life.
From the day the Australian Army arrived at Ong Huong to help everyone.
Also helping by giving medicines, food and clothes.
For the people are very thankful.
There will never be a moment when the people are not remembering the Australian Army.
I speak for all the people of Ong Huong.
We know that the Australian Army is still operating in the area of our village,

So we are able to live happily.
While carrying out their duties and in many battles,
And after the Communists are destroyed,
We welcome the Australian Army to Bien Hoa,
To help us build a peaceful life.
We send our warmest thanks.[10]

On 9 April Operation ABILENE ended. Dupuy's Infantrymen had found nothing and there had been no battles. The Viet Cong 5th Division had left Phuoc Tuy Province temporarily and refused to fight the Americans on their terms. The Diggers were happy with their efforts. Fourteen Viet Cong had been killed and their bodies recovered, twelve more had been wounded and captured, and 33 Local Force guerillas detained in the surprise cordon and search of Binh Ba village. In nine days they had 'closed down' Viet Cong operations in the Courtenay Plantation and Binh Ba areas. In so doing, they had fulfilled their primary mission of protecting the Divisional logistic and fire support base. With some professional satisfaction, Preece collected the wager from Hollingsworth.

The Viet Cong appeared to have returned to fighting a guerilla war in III Corps area having failed to gain decisive victories using conventional tactics against the 173rd and the 1st Infantry Division. These formations had been joined by the US 25th Infantry Division (Tropic Lightning) and the US 196th Light Infantry Brigade was inbound. Saigon was encircled by huge, sprawling US bases. There was little chance of the city falling to the Viet Cong in the near future. The stalemate around Saigon had in large measure been achieved by the rapid 'spoiling' operations of the Paratroopers and Diggers of the 173rd. They had kept the 9th and 5th Viet Cong Divisions off balance over a wide area, destroyed many supply areas, and neutralised two important headquarter complexes in the Ho Bo Woods and War Zone D. These operations must have also increased the morale of the ARVN formations in III Corps who had been taking a beating in the early months of 1965.

Westmoreland now ordered his 'strategic fire brigade' to take on the North Vietnamese units infiltrating into III Corps through Phuoc Long Province. The Paratroopers were returning to the scene of the battles of Dong Xoai twelve months earlier. For most of the Paratroopers and Diggers of the 173rd this was their last operation before returning home after twelve gruelling months in Vietnam. There were many mixed feelings as they boarded their 'slicks' and headed out to face the North Vietnamese.

Smith had decided to allocate each of his battalions several areas of operations and conduct rapid deployments over these areas in quick succession. He wanted to use helicopter mobility and the redeployment of gun batteries by air to increase the area the 173rd could dominate. This was to be an operation showing the state of the art in airmobile techniques. Smith calculated that he could keep all of his units within artillery range and reinforce any unit that was in contact with the North Vietnamese rapidly by air as had been done by the US Cavalrymen in II Corps area.[11] This plan depended for its success on the North Vietnamese being located in thick jungle and accepting the US terms for battle.

On 13 April the 1/503rd conducted an airmobile assault to capture the Song Be airfield which was not opposed. 1 RAR and the 2/503rd followed in C-123 Caribou and CH47 Chinook medium range aircraft. Preece pushed out patrols immediately and the Paratroopers conducted airmobile assaults into the northern half of the province. The quarry was the Viet Cong 271st Main Force Regiment which was reported to be taking on North Vietnamese reinforcements and refitting after its defeat on 16 March at the hands of the 2/503rd, and the 602nd and 603rd North Vietnamese Army Regiments that were infiltrating into the province. South Vietnamese units had not operated in the Song Be sector of the province since the battle of Dong Xoai in June 1965. For ten months the North Vietnamese had been maintaining a steady flow of men and supplies through the area.[12]

For the next three days the Diggers and Paratroopers were redeployed by helicopter over a wide area of the province. The pattern was for an airmobile assault in the morning, followed by a day's patrolling and concentration in the evening in preparation for another airmobile assault at dawn the next day. These manoeuvres did not result in much contact with the enemy but certainly kept any Viet Cong and North Vietnamese in the area wondering where the helicopters would deploy troops next.

On the night of 18–19 April the Diggers started to contact groups of North Vietnamese in very dense jungle after discovering several large transit camps. A North Vietnamese company commander from the 605th Battalion, 250th Regiment and his protection party were ambushed. After escaping from the ambush, the company commander had fled into B Company and been apprehended. He had been sent forward by his battalion commander to set up a battalion position for the next night. The proposed North Vietnamese position was one Preece had selected for 1 RAR on the next night. Smith decided not to deploy troops to ambush the incoming North Vietnamese but to order airstrikes on the position after dark the next day. The results of these airstrikes were not known.[13]

Another former North Vietnamese company commander was captured later the same night having become separated from his protection party in the dark and blundering into B Company's position. This officer was now on supply duties and was organising provisions for his battalion that was on its way from North Vietnam.[14]

Australian Prime Minister Harold Holt (white shirt) visited the 1 RAR Group on 25 April 1966. Looking on while Lieutenant Colonel Alex Preece (centre) shows him a map of the Bien Hoa area is Lieutenant General Sir John Wilton, Chief of the General Staff (left), and Brigadier David Jackson, newly-appointed Commander of 1 Australian Task Force–Vietnam (right).

The Paratroopers were also contacting small reconnaissance groups of North Vietnamese, and discovering transit camps and caches of rice. However, large North Vietnamese units did not appear to be in the area. They were probably deterred from continuing their infiltration south by the obvious presence of helicopters and troops.

In the late afternoon of 22 April Operation DENVER concluded and many of the Diggers and Paratroopers returned to Bien Hoa for the last time before returning home. McAulay wrote:

> The Yanks in the 173rd have done their 12 months, and many 'new' Yanks are here now. Standing staring at the legendary Aussies filtering out of the deep J[ungle], laden (by comparison) like mules, clothes torn, black with sweat, long-barrelled 'hunting' rifles and floppy hats.[15]

After twelve months the Diggers and the Paratroopers were still very different fighting forces. It had been decided some months before that 1 RAR would not be replaced as the third battalion of the 173rd and the 4/503rd Battalion had been raised. The Kiwi Gun Battery was allocated to the Australian field regiment that had just arrived in Vietnam. As if to mark the end of this unique experiment in ANZUS co-operation and the continuation of the ANZAC tradition, the Australian Prime Minister, Harold Holt, visited the 173rd on 24 April and returned to 1 RAR for ANZAC Day ceremonies on 25 April. He congratulated the Diggers on their performance and reaffirmed the Australian Government's commitment to supporting the US in Vietnam. That support was to take the form of the 1st Australian Task Force arriving in Phuoc Tuy Province.

After each of the Australian company commanders had drawn a straw from Alex Preece's hand, Major Ian Fisher was found to have the shortest one. He was now the commander of a group of 55 volunteers from his company to remain behind and assist the battalions of the Task Force on their first operation in Vietnam. Operation HARDIHOOD was conducted by the 173rd, and 5 RAR and 6 RAR during the period 16 May–8 June. The operation cleared the area around the new Australian Task Force base at Nui Dat.

On 1 June 1966, exactly twelve months after the first flights had touched down in Vietnam, the same 707 QANTAS jet began its shuttle service for the return of the 1 RAR Group. As the Diggers looked out of the buses carrying them down the roads to Tan Son Nhut Airport, they realised the Vietnam War had changed irrevocably. Where, the year before, there had been open, flat fields alongside the Saigon road there now stretched kilometre after kilometre of US camps. The air was more crowded with aircraft of all descriptions and the road traffic was thick with military vehicles. Their war was finished for the time being and was just beginning for thousands of others.

And so ended the unique association between the Diggers of 1 RAR, and 105 Field Battery RAA, the Kiwis of 161st Field Battery, RNZA, and the Paratroopers of the 173rd. In many ways this association in the first year of the escalation of the Vietnam War was a microcosm of the way the war was to be fought by the US and Australian Armies for the next few years. In 1965–66 the Diggers and Paratroopers of the 173rd Airborne Brigade (Separate) charted the course for those who would follow them. The US Army continued to fight a conventional 'big' war and the Australian Army continued to fight a counter-insurgent 'patrol' war. As history now shows, neither Army had the formula for lasting success but there are lessons that can be learnt from the 1965–66 operations of the tri-national 173rd Airborne Brigade (Separate).

Postscript

The 173rd remained in Vietnam for six more years and won battle honours at Binh Dinh, Phu Yen, Tuy Hoa, Pleiku, Dak To, Phu Bon, Phu Yen and Bong Song. When the Brigade left Vietnam in 1971 they had lost

C Company 1 RAR marching through Sydney's main streets on 8 June 1966 as part of a parade for Vietnam veterans from the 1 RAR Group, the AATTV and the RAAF. They received a tumultuous welcome home from 300 000 citizens. (Closest to the camera saluting from left to right) Captain Chris Peacock, Second Lieutenant Kevin Lunny and Second Lieutenant John Dwyer.

1533 men killed and over 6000 wounded. The 173rd was deactivated in 1972 and its members posted to the 4th Airborne Brigade, 101st Airborne Division. In 1981 veterans of the 173rd formed the Society of the 173rd Airborne Brigade (Separate) which has chapters throughout the US and had formed an Australian chapter in 1988. In 1986 the 1/503rd and 2/503rd Battalions were reactivated and are presently serving as foot infantry battalions in South Korea.

1 RAR returned to Australia in June 1966 leaving scores of its members who had not served a full twelve months in Vietnam to reinforce the battalions of the Australian Task Force. Several ex-members of 1 RAR were involved in the battle of Long Tan in August 1966. Those remaining in the unit were posted out to join recruit training battalions and reinforcement units as instructors. In these units they passed on their experiences to those who were about to serve in Vietnam. Another sizeable group was posted out to form the cadre of 8 RAR and went on to complete another

twelve-month tour of Vietnam with that unit. A further group of officers and NCOs completed a second twelve-month tour with the Australian Army Training Team—Vietnam.

A new 1 RAR, made up of Regular and conscripted soldiers, was assigned to the Australian Task Force in 1968 and completed another twelve-month tour. The battalion distinguished itself at the Battles of Fire Support Bases CORAL and BALMORAL early in their tour. After its return to Australia in 1969, 1 RAR was quickly deployed for a two-year tour of Malaysia and Singapore in 1969–71.

Since 1971 1 RAR has been located at Lavarack Barracks in Townsville, Queensland. In 1980 the Battalion was assigned to the Australian Defence Forces' Operational Deployment Force and today, like 1965, stands ready for rapid deployment again.

In recognition of their service for the period in 1965–66, the 173rd and its attached and assigned units were awarded the US Meritorious Unit Commendation and the Vietnamese Cross of Gallantry with Palm. Despite the precedents set by other Australian and New Zealand units wearing these same decorations, administrative bungling resulted in the Diggers and Kiwis of the Brigade not being included in the US Department of Army General Orders authorising these awards. In 1986 an approach was made by the US Military Attache in Canberra asking the Australian Army whether the awards would be accepted retrospectively if they were offered. The Australian Army's response was to insist that the approach be redirected through the proper government channels: the bureaucrats had won again, but hopefully only temporarily as the battle for recognition goes on.

12 The lessons

'Whether we wish it or not we are involved in the world's problems . . . '

Walter Lippmann, 1913

The experiences of the 173rd Airborne Brigade and the 1 RAR Group in 1965– 66 should not be forgotten. The US, Australian and New Zealand military forces may fight in Asia again. The operational setting in 1965 of having to buttress an anti-communist government against well-armed and equipped main forces supported by local guerillas may be repeated. At the least, forces may be committed to keep the peace during times of violent political upheaval. World and local public opinion may not permit the preemptive and timely deployment of sufficient military force. Like the interventions into Korea and Vietnam, the first units to fight may not be deployed until the beleaguered country has reached the point of political and military collapse.

Readiness

One prerequisite for military intervention is the existence of military formations fully manned, trained and equipped to fight at short notice. In 1965 the US had the Marines and the 173rd Airborne Brigade (Separate) stationed on Okinawa to deploy into Asia and the Pacific area. Australia had a poorly equipped and under-strength 1 RAR identified for deployment but not given the resources to fight in South-East Asia. New Zealand only had a newly raised four-gun field battery earmarked for overseas deployment.

In response to growing instability in South-East Asia in the early 1960s the Australian Government had purchased strategic aircraft and ships for the Airforce and Navy but had deprived the Army. This neglect resulted in 1 RAR arriving in Vietnam with World War II-issue Owen

Machine Carbines with no hitting power, boots and uniforms that fell apart during operations, underpowered, unreliable radio equipment and obsolete webbing. Fortunately, 1 RAR was not fully tested on arrival in Vietnam and had time to re-equip. Within six months five new weapons were being carried (5.56 millimetre M16 Rifle, M79 Grenade Launcher, a light anti-armour 'throw-away' missile M72, M26 fragmentation grenade and the Claymore anti-personnel mine), and new boots, uniforms and radio equipment were issued.

Future Australian operational deployment forces may not have several months to re-equip after deployment. A 'top down' mentality appears to dominate the thinking of defence planners in peacetime despite the timeless knowledge that it will be the Infantry who will bear the brunt of the fighting. The defeat of the Infantry is the defeat of an army. It is more logical to allocate resources from the 'bottom up'. The Infantry should be manned, armed, equipped and trained as a first priority and resources allocated to other supporting arms and services knowing that the Infantry can match their opponents in combat.

Major Don Kenning's Kiwi Gun Battery was not given its full complement of six guns for financial, not operational, reasons. Kenning had to use his spare gun on the firing line to increase firepower. It was the traditional associations of the Australians with the New Zealanders in general and Lieutenant Colonel Lou Brumfield's professional associations with Don Kenning in particular that kept the Kiwis from being relegated to a general support battery for the 173rd. Future New Zealand operational deployment forces should not be denied the resources to establish a credible presence alongside their allies.

Deficiencies in training resources before 1 RAR's deployment were partly offset because many members had fought in Korea and Malaya. Without these veterans 1 RAR would have been dangerously unprepared to fight in Vietnam. Most members of the Battalion had not practised 'live' firing their weapons in tactical settings and employed airstrikes, artillery and mortars until after arrival in Vietnam. This essential operational training was not possible in Australia because of a lack of ammunition and suitable training areas. In the future, combat veterans will not be available to make up for a paucity of training resources.

It was fortuitous that 1 RAR and 161 Field Battery were able to 'plug into' the US Army's logistic system on arrrival in Vietnam to overcome many materiel deficiencies. The Australians became the military beggars and thieves of Bien Hoa Airbase. Timber, defence stores, vehicles, tentage, clothing, generators, tools, building materials and other sundry items were 'borrowed' from the Americans. While some Australians rationalised that this systematic pilfering of their ally's supplies was a form of military sport and did not degrade US operational capabilities, it was shameful that they were forced to resort to such measures.

Australian and New Zealand military planners and civilian policy makers should be mindful that 1 RAR and 161 Field Battery could not have been deployed as independent military forces. They relied heavily on the benevolence and protection of their US ally. Moreover, it took Australia twelve months to deploy an independent, brigade-sized force of two infantry battalions and an artillery regiment to Vietnam and this force would not have been viable without the introduction of limited conscription eighteen months before.

Training and fighting

The Paratroopers and Diggers fought as they had been trained and generalised their past experiences to the situation in Vietnam. The 173rd tried to fight the Vietnam War as a Korean War with the addition of helicopters, and 1 RAR tried to fight the same war as a Malayan Emergency with the addition of firepower. This seemed to prove the old adage that initially armies will prosecute a new war like they fought the later stages of their last war. This situation is understandable. Williamson and his senior commanders were veterans of operations in Europe and Korea. Brumfield and his company commanders were veterans of operations in Malaya.

The first forays into War Zone D in July 1965 illustrated the differences between the training of a strategic reserve formation from a large army and that of an infantry battalion from a small army. The Paratrooopers were trained as 'shock troops' and stormed into the area of operations using all available firepower and tactical mobility. They had the attitude of 'the bigger the battle the better'. They formed large, noisy hunting parties and swept along roads and tracks looking for contact. The Paratroopers were saying to the Viet Cong, 'You know where we are, and when and where we will strike, take us on and pay the price.'

The Diggers deployed into War Zone D were intent on finding and fighting the Viet Cong under the optimum tactical conditions with a minimum of risk-taking. Australian platoons were dispersed over a wide area and instructed to patrol cautiously to discover enemy locations. They looked for tactical surprise. The Diggers said to the Viet Cong, 'You will never know where we are but we will find you and kill you.'

The US approach resulted in several sub-unit engagements and a sizeable, if inflated, enemy body count. The Australian approach resulted in little enemy contact, less damage to the enemy's infrastructure and fewer enemy casualties. For some operations they only achieved a tactical stand off between themselves and the Viet Cong.

In the future, planners should anticipate that the first units sent to fight in Asia will fight as they have been trained and will take some time to adapt to the imperatives of a new theatre of operations.

The expectation of a short tour and Westmoreland's desire to keep the Viet Cong off balance over a wide area of Vietnam contributed to Williamson's preference for short spoiling, search and destroy operations characterised by rapid mobility and firepower. He was looking for quick results. However, he was commanding an Australian battalion that had a different concept of how to operate in the jungle. To Williamson's credit he persevered with the Australians and allowed them to continue operating using their methods.

The difference in operational methods suggests that Australian units should not be placed under the operational control of US formations. Another US commander may have found the 'pussy-footing' of the Australians frustrating and cowardly, and attempted to have them conform to bolder tactics. Brumfield also exercised caution in criticising the Paratroopers for their sweeping tactics. Another Australian commander may have asserted that the obvious movement of the Paratroopers constituted tactical stupidity and the squandering of lives in enemy ambushes. Given the missions of the day, the 'bottom line' was that the Paratroopers were killing Viet Cong and the Diggers were not. Time and manpower were however on the Viet Congs' and North Vietnameses' side in 1965 and this will be so for any future Asian foe.

Duration of military intervention

The training background of the Paratroopers and the Diggers was one factor in explaining their tactical differences. Another was the perceptions of the duration of their mission in Vietnam. The Paratroopers' initial perceptions were that they would fight in Vietnam for a limited period and return to Okinawa. The Diggers suspected, in absence of official information, that they would be fighting for at least six and probably twelve months. They remembered the historical precedents of the Korean War and the Malayan Emergency where Australian battalions completed twelve-month and two-year tours.

The results of these different expectations contributed to quite different approaches to fighting. The Paratroopers were impatient for combat. The Diggers first wanted to find out more about the Viet Cong and then set the scene for combat. If a unit knows it will only have to fight for a limited period there will be a desire for quick results and risks will be taken to achieve them. Alternatively, if a unit knows it will fight for a long period, its commanders will have the patience to wait for results and create the optimum conditions for battle. Planners of military interventions need to understand this situation and rotate units more frequently to achieve quick results and a high intensity of operations. Less frequent rotation will result in delayed results and a lower intensity of operations.

Intelligence and security

Foiling both US and Australian attempts to bring the enemy to battle on favourable terms was the combination of lack of intelligence and the forewarning the Viet Cong had of the Brigade's operations. Williamson's tactical options were further restricted by the brief duration of the operations. However, he was always successful in causing damage to supply areas and base camps. He also achieved several stunning victories when he had timely intelligence on enemy locations and was able to achieve tactical surprise.

However, the Viet Cong were usually forewarned of the locations and timings of the Brigade's operations because the security of operational information was lax. Viet Cong agents had infiltrated the South Vietnamese armed services and US bases where they were employed on domestic duties. The Brigade made little effort to deceive the enemy on the timing, location and strength of their operations. The Brigade thought the Viet Cong would offer battle when the Paratroopers deployed and the winner would be decided after a conventional 'shoot-out'.

Planners of military interventions should ensure time has been spent gathering intelligence and establishing intelligence networks. The 173rd was most successful when intelligence information enabled enemy units, headquarters and supply areas to be identified. The need for intelligence information would be critical if the intervention is to be of a short duration and quick results are required.

Having gathered intelligence it is folly to squander its value by not deceiving the enemy about the timing, locations and strengths of operations and ensuring operational intentions are secure. The security of operational intentions may include denying information to Asian and other allies, and deceiving them and the media on the details of operations.

Firepower

The use of massive firepower was the most important factor in most of the Brigade's victories against the Viet Cong. On Operation HUMP in November 1965 artillery, mortars and airstrikes turned potential defeat into victory for the 1/503rd. On Operation MARAUDER in January 1966 the artillery again caused heavy casualties after the Viet Cong were forced out of their fortifications by the assaulting Paratroopers of the 2/503rd. On Operation SILVER CITY in April the Commanding Officer of the 2/503rd thanked the artillery batteries for saving the lives of his Paratroopers when they were assaulted by a Viet Cong Main Force regiment. Once again the difference between defeat and victory had been the weight of firepower.

The dependence of firepower was criticised throughout the Vietnam War because of civilian casualties and the damage done to the Vietnamese countryside. The 173rd and 1 RAR were organised and trained to use firepower and its employment was fundamental to tactical doctrine. This situation has not and will not change. Conventionally-trained US and Australian forces will use firepower if they are required to fight in Asia again. If the employment of firepower is politically unacceptable then planners should remember that the absence of artillery and fighter ground attack may result in politically unacceptable casualties. Even against a lightly-armed enemy, artillery, mortars and airstrikes provide additional security and are useful tactical tools when a force is outnumbered.

Consolidation of victory

In 1965–66 all of the 173rd's victories were not consolidated. The tunnels of the two Viet Cong headquarters complexes were not destroyed and the areas above them were not occupied by military forces. The huge body counts that won Presidential citations for the two airborne battalions of the 173rd were just temporary setbacks for the Viet Cong. Neither Main Force regiment was destroyed and North Vietnamese reinforcements soon swelled their ranks.

Operation NEW LIFE in November illustrated the way a tactical victory can even backfire if there is no consolidation of success. The expectations of restoring the La Nga Valley to the Saigon Government's control were high. The 173rd would clear the area of Viet Cong Main Force units, dominate the area for three weeks and give the South Vietnamese time to establish local political control under the protection of Popular Force units and the 10th ARVN Division. The operation was a military success for the Paratroopers and the Diggers but an eventual political disaster for the weak South Vietnamese Government who were unable to resist the recapture of the Valley.

The lessons from this consistent failure to consolidate hard-won victories are that Western military intervention in Asia is futile unless there is an effective political order to replace that of the enemy and the military strength to provide security for the population.

Morale

Morale in a military unit fighting overseas in a limited war is more difficult to maintain than in a unit that is fighting in a declared war which has strong home-country support. In 1965 the men of the 1 RAR Group were professional soldiers doing what they had been trained to do. Their morale was high because they did not think much about the politics of their deployment and were keen to test themselves in combat. This situation changed after a few months when casualties were taken and the political controversy about Australia's involvement in Vietnam increased. Australians were also divided on the issue of sending conscripts to fight overseas.

Despite knowing that they were not as well armed or equipped as their US counterparts and also realising that they were risking their lives in a war that did not have total public support in Australia, it was the absence of mail and newspapers from home and knowing that their mail was not reaching home that created the worst morale problems in the 1 RAR Group. The married men suffered the most. The provision of an efficient and inexpensive mail system may seem to be trivial compared to supplying a military force with the arms, equipment and ammunition to do its job. However, the effects on the morale of the men of the 1 RAR Group of delayed mail in the initial months after arrival in Vietnam suggest that the provision of a mail system is vital.

The overall importance of maintaining links back to the home coun-try deserves further emphasis. Decades after their twelve months in Vietnam, veterans of the 1 RAR Group have vivid memories of the entertainers that visited them at Bien Hoa. The most consistent recollec-tion was the boost to morale caused by being reminded of home. The entertainers reminded them of their culture and their society. They were able to temporarily put aside the alien Asian environment that sur-rounded them.

For the combat soldiers life became a cycle of the stress of operations and the relief of stress from operations. If a soldier maintained his links with home and family then he had something to look forward to and survive for. He was reminded of his place in a family and in a society he knew. In a way he remained civilised and responsible amidst the grim realities of being required to kill or be killed.

The award of medals while a unit is on operations is another import-ant factor in morale. Brumfield and Preece held back the list of officers from 1 RAR that they had recommended for the award of the Military Cross; eight officers were nominated with one officer nominated twice. Nominations for Captain Bob Hill and Captain Alex MacGregor had been forwarded to Australia by February 1966 because they were officers from other corps. 1 RAR officer's nominations were held back so their performances could be assessed in priority. Because of an arbitrary quota imposed on awards by the Australian Defence Department, adhering to guidelines embodied in the Imperial awards system, the 1 RAR Group was only entitled to two Military Crosses. Hill and MacGregor became the only recipients.

Awards of medals for bravery should be as close as possible to the event and a force's number of awards should not be restricted by a quota. Awards made while units are still fighting would be a potent incentive and a source of pride for recipients and their comrades.

Civic action

Conventional Western military units should not be expected to win the hearts and minds of an Asian population. The civic action efforts of the Paratroopers and Diggers were charitable and well-intended but futile. The issue of 'Airborne All the Way' T-shirts by the Brigade's civic action officer to the orphaned children of the Viet Cong killed on Operation CRIMP exemplifies the difficulty units, waging war in the midst of an Asian population, have in separating the impact of their killing and destruction and the desire to show the population that it is all for their own good in the long term.

Despite the paucity of information on the attitudes of the Vietnamese peasants to the Brigade's civic action efforts, aside from letters of thanks, the peasants must have been confused during the conduct of operations. No doubt they received information that the purpose of the operations was to kill Viet Cong. However, because many families had members in Local Force and Main Force Viet Cong units, all the Paratroopers and Diggers were doing was killing friends and relatives and damaging the rural environment. At the same time, men in the same uniforms were offering food, clothing and medical services. It was probably only the eagerness of the Vietnamese children to fend for themselves and the understandable obedience of the elderly and women that gave the impression that civic action was working.

The benefits of civic action were probably felt more by the soldiers themselves than the peasants. Like maintaining links to home, the soldiers were reminded that there were sets of values based on caring and not on killing. They were able to say that they were doing their best to kill off Viet Cong as well as improve the lot of the oppressed peasants.

The war that can't be won

THE Menzies Government has made a reckless decision on Vietnam which this nation may live to regret. It has decided to send Australian soldiers into a savage, revolutionary war in which the Americans are grievously involved—so that America may shelve a tiny part of her embarrassment.

The Government has obviously been under strong pressure from the Johnson Administration, which has desperately been seeking in these last weeks of military escalation in Vietnam to broaden the international basis of its progressively active policy.

Searching for friends, America has turned to her Anzus and Seato associates in the Western Pacific for at least a meaningful gesture of practical support.

The Australian people will therefore acknowledge the toughness of the problem Sir Robert Menzies and his colleagues have faced, though indeed they were half way already to direct commitment, being for the most part in wholehearted moral support of the dubious American cause.

Their decision is wrong, at this time, whichever way we look at it.

This is politics

It is wrong because Australia's contingent can have only insignificant military value, because it will be purely a political pawn in a situation for which Australia has no responsibility whatsoever.

It is wrong because until now the Australian people have been told—and rightly—that this country's military commitment to the defence of Malaysia against looming Indonesian aggression is as much as, if not more than, the nation can support.

It is wrong because it deliberately and coldly runs counter to the mounting wave of international anxiety about the shape of the Vietnam war and the justification and perils of America's military escalation.

Is Britain, though she backs American policy in Vietnam, sending in troops? Is India, under permanent Chinese threat, joining the fight? Is Canada, America's neighbor, embracing the South Vietnamese cause? The answer in each case is an emphatic no, allied with an urgent desire to see the Vietnam war melt into negotiations.

Seato divided

Neither of the Pacific defence treaties to which Australia subscribes can honestly be invoked to justify the Menzies Government's decision. Anzus cannot apply, because the United States is not under attack. Seato, more worthless than ever, certainly doesn't apply. Half its reluctant members, including France and Pakistan, are even leaning the other way.

There is another very strong argument against Australia's getting into the Vietnam fight just at this moment. This stems from current hopes that behind-the-scenes moves in London, Moscow and other capitals may lead to negotiations through the device of returning to the 1954 Geneva agreements on Indo-China.

President Johnson himself has implied the possibility of such an approach, and even the North Vietnamese have come up with counter-proposals of their own, conceivably related to the "essentials" of the 1954 accords. Despite the ferocity of the American bombing and the persistent ruthlessness of the Viet Cong infiltrations, some room for diplomatic manoeuvre has recently emerged.

But Australia has lined up her generations against the hatred and contempt of resurgent Asian peoples—without adding one iota of confidence or strength to the tragically embroiled American nation. It could be that our historians will recall this day with tears.

Two editorials from the Australian, *twenty years apart. The one written in 1965 condemns* (left) *and the other written in 1985 reflects* (right).

THE AUSTRALIAN

APRIL 27-28 1985

The lessons of the Vietnam experience

ON Tuesday we remember the tenth anniversary of the fall of Saigon. April 30 1975. It was a day in which the world saw the feebleness of Western resolve, in which the unreliability of the Western alliance was paid for in blood and suffering by an ally who had been denied the means with which to defend himself.

The Vietnam war divided Australian society profoundly. Ten years after the war's final episode seems an appropriate time to reflect on the lessons we might learn from our experience in Vietnam.

The moral case for our commitment to Vietnam was in essentials quite simple. South Vietnam was a sovereign nation, not fully a democracy — imperfect certainly — but a very long way from totalitarianism and embodying substantial freedom for its people.

. North Vietnam was a totalitarian dictatorship which, with the backing of China and the Soviet Union, wanted to impose its hegemony on South Vietnam. South Vietnam asked for help and we had a right to respond.

The geo-political case for our commitment was equally straightforward. The American presence in South Vietnam, in geo-political terms, can be seen as an extension of the doctrine of containment. That doctrine had it that in the interests of avoiding a global conflagration no great attempt would be made to liberate countries which had fallen to communism, but the spread of communism, inevitably by undemocratic means, would be resisted. Communism would be "contained" within its existing borders.

The case against our involvement in Vietnam was that the dispute was really a civil war, that the Viet Cong were indigenous South Vietnamese who had the overwhelming support of the South Vietnamese people in their struggle to throw off the shackles of imperialism.

Well, what is the verdict of the intervening years?

The Viet Cong

It is now clear that from the earliest days of the war the Viet Cong were infiltrated and manipulated by the North Vietnamese army. As the war went on the involvement of the North Vietnamese army grew and grew, so that when Saigon fell it was not to Viet Cong guerillas but to North Vietnamese tanks.

The success of the Viet Cong guerilla war had not been essentially military. Rather, it had managed, despite enormous military defeats, to inflict such casualties on the Americans and their allies that Western resolve waned, and in the end South Vietnam was abandoned.

Could South Vietnam ever have survived? After the Paris peace treaties the South Vietnamese were guaranteed certain amounts of aid, especially if the North Vietnamese broke the treaty. Of course the North Vietnamese broke the treaty as soon as it was signed, but an isolationist American Congress starved South Vietnam of aid. The South Vietnamese army fought with extraordinary bravery at times, even when the battle was hopeless — at Xuan Loc, for example. But no army could have maintained morale when it was abandoned by its friends, its supplies cut off, international guarantees ignored, and left to face overwhelming odds.

The events within Indo-China since the fall of Saigon provide the most comprehensive and overwhelming argument that we were right to try to help South Vietnam survive. The true degree of the Vietnamese people's support for the communist regime can be gauged by the unavoidable evidence of the million refugees who have fled Vietnam since Saigon's fall.

It is worth pondering this just for a moment. Imagine how horrific life must be to contemplate boarding a leaky boat, braving the depredations of Thai pirates, to seek a distant, dangerous and mysterious landfall.

It ought also to be remembered that the Kampuchean genocide, which has sickened the world, was carried out by Vietnam's erstwhile allies the Khmer Rouge. Vietnam did not fall out with the Khmer Rouge because of human rights, but because of the ramifications of the Sino-Soviet split. Now Vietnam maintains its own regime of terror within Kampuchea, with an army of occupation of some 200,000. It also rules Laos with an army of occupation, and has been particularly savage in its suppression of the rebellious Hmong tribesmen.

Re-evaluation

Throughout Indo-China the Vietnamese have developed an extraordinary network of re-education camps. These camps are terrifyingly savage.

All of this has led to a major re-evaluation of the Vietnam war. In the United States many former opponents of the war have admitted how wrong they were. Even many who still believe that US involvement in the war was mistaken concede their own support of the Viet Cong was naive. Even former Viet Cong members have joined in the re-evaluation. It is extraordinary that within Australia few of the 1960s protesters seem even to be aware of the grotesque human rights record of the Vietnamese since 1975. Certainly, they have lacked the courage of many former radicals in the US who have admitted their mistake.

One of the few really distressing things Australia did in Vietnam was the way we evacuated our embassy, a few days before Saigon's fall. The callous indifference to the fate of our former friends which saw us leave them behind, to face imprisonment, persecution and death, evacuating hardly any of the staff or friends of Australia within Vietnam was shameful.

It is said that from all evil some good flows. We have in recent years been privileged as a nation to offer a new home to tens of thousands of our former Vietnamese allies. These people have enriched our national life. They have found in Australia what was denied them in Vietnam — the sort of society they were striving for in their homeland.

On this day we should pay tribute to the brave Australians and Vietnamese who fought nobly in a just cause. That the cause was lost does not make it any less just. History will remember them, like the first Anzacs, as good and brave men and women.

Success and progress

The 173rd was initially deployed to protect the Bien Hoa Airbase for 60 days. The Paratroopers were then given the mission of keeping the Viet Cong off balance in the III Corps area for 120 days. They were then assigned to conducting search and destroy operations in Vietnam until further notice. By June 1966 the military situation in III Corps had stabilised and ARVN had been given twelve months respite from large-scale Viet Cong attacks. This period was not enough. The US and her allies continued to build up their forces and continued to take the fight to the Viet Cong and North Vietnamese to allow the South Vietnamese Government and its armed forces time to re-equip, train and establish political control of the population. These goals were not achieved.

With the benefit of hindsight, the US marines, the 173rd and the US 1st Infantry Division and US Cavalrymen that followed them into South Vietnam later in 1965 had done as much as could be done by Western military intervention twelve months after they arrived. The continuation of large-scale search and destroy operations did not permanently change the balance of military or political power in South Vietnam. In many ways the operational settings of 1965 and 1966 were repeated with different scales, intensities, durations and variations by US and Australian infantry units for the remainder of the war. The Viet Cong who were killed in search and destroy operations were replaced by North Vietnamese reinforcements and it was regular formations from North Vietnam, not Viet Cong formations from South Vietnam, that won the final battles in 1975.

Military intervention should not be undertaken without a clear understanding of the measurement of success and progress. The 173rd could have defended the Bien Hoa Airbase indefinitely. So, if defending the airbase was the criteria for success, then the military intervention was successful. If after six months the 173rd was still defending the airbase and this satisfied the criteria set for satisfactory progress, then the military intervention would have been deemed to have been making good progress.

The 173rd's criteria for success changed from achieving specific tactical goals, like defending the airbase, to conducting operations to keep the Viet Cong off balance through brief search and destroy operations. Success was measured in killing ratios, numbers of installations destroyed and tonnages of supplies denied to the enemy. Progress, however, became the accumulation of unrelated tactical successes and was not oriented to specific goals like handing over certain operational responsibilities to the ARVN after a period of six months. Thus, operations became an open ended commitment of trying to cause as much damage to the Viet Cong as possible.

Planners should be oriented to setting clear objectives for military intervention and defining the criteria for and measurements of success and progress. For example, some interventions like that of the US into Grenada in 1984 were short because intelligence was timely and accurate, tactical surprise was achieved, success came quickly and the progress made by local authorities in regaining control enabled the Americans to withdraw forces after a few weeks. The intervention by US Marines into Beirut in 1984 was longer but forces were withdrawn after achieving initial success in separating warring Lebanese and Palestinian factions but not having made satisfactory progress. The Grenada and Beirut models cannot be generalised to every situation but they confirm a requirement for politicians and military planners to set clear objectives.

Summary

The lessons from the experiences of the 173rd and the 1 RAR Group in Vietnam in 1965–66 are timeless. Too often they are forgotten. Hopefully Charles Wolf Jr was not right when he said: 'Those who don't study the past will repeat its errors; those who do study it will find other ways to err.'

Appendix A
Honours and awards

British Imperial Honours Decorations and Awards for Gallantry and Distinguished Service Awarded to Members of the First Battalion, the Royal Australian Regiment (Group) for service in the Republic of South Vietnam, 1965–66

COMPANION OF THE DISTINGUISHED SERVICE ORDER (DSO)

2507	Lt Col I. R. W. Brumfield (CO 1 RAR)	1113	Lt Col A.V. Preece (CO 1 RAR)

MEMBER OF THE ORDER OF THE BRITISH EMPIRE (MBE)

NZ30663	Capt G. D. Birch (161 FD BTY, RNZA)	NZ457585	WO2 M. C. Nabbs (161 FD BTY, RNZA)
NZ31351	Maj D. R. Kenning (161 FD BTY, RNZA)		

THE MILITARY CROSS (MC)

51407	Capt R. K. Hill (1 APC SQN (PWLH))	NZ30618	Capt B. A. Murphy (161 FD BTY, RNZA)
63507	Capt A. H. MacGregor (3FD ENGR TP, RAE)		

THE MILITARY MEDAL (MM)

54593	Pte W. P. Brunalli (4 Pl B Coy)	54328	Sgt C. Fawcett (3 Pl A Coy)
6280	Sgt J.W. Carnes (12 Pl D Coy)	215584	Pte R. S. Fraser (5 Pl B Coy)

37235	Cpl B. L. Le Sueur (9 Pl B Coy)	2411585	Sgt D.G. Saville (7 Pl B Coy)
214922	L/Cpl D. M. Munday (6 Pl B Coy)	53652	Sgt G.A. Smith (9 Pl C Coy)
		214633	Pte L. Waring (5 Pl B Coy)

THE MEDAL OF THE ORDER OF THE BRITISH EMPIRE—THE BRITISH EMPIRE MEDAL (BEM)

NZ802262	Sgt J.M. Benyon (161 FD BTY, RNZA)	NZ35314	S/Sgt G. B. Black (161 FD BTY, RNZA)
NZ38417	Sgt F. Bigg-Wither (161 FD BTY, RNZA)	NZ464557	Sgt E.G. Willbond (161 FD BTY, RNZA)

MENTIONED-IN-DESPATCHES (MID)

21523	Pte R. W. Bailey (4 Pl B Coy)	NZ209482	L/Cpl D. T. Morrow (161 FD BTY, RNZA)
235204	Capt M. J. Carroll (Sig Pl Spt Coy)	11509	Capt B. J. Smith (161 RECCE FLT)
215430	Pte J. P. Daly (4 Pl B Coy)		
213643	Cpl R. Evans (4 Pl B Coy)	1200116	Pte D. B. Vogele (4 Pl B Coy)
42774	Cpl R. H. Hillier (Post.) (B Coy)	NZ39754	Cpl W. G. Walker (161 FD BTY, RNZA)
216132	Cpl T. B. Loftus (6 Pl B Coy)		

US Decorations Awarded to members of First Battalion, the Royal Australian Regiment (Group) for gallantry and service in the Republic of South Vietnam, 1965–66

Bronze Star for Valour (BS(V))

2507	Lt Col I. R. W. Brumfield, DSO (CO 1 RAR) (with Oakleaf Cluster)

BRONZE STAR FOR MERITORIOUS SERVICE (BS(S))

1252	Capt T. J. Buckley (1 RAR)	11411	Maj R. B. McDonald (1 ALSC)
29113	Capt R. A. Ducie (1 RAR)	35062	Maj I.D. McFarlane (1 RAR)
31179	Maj J. Essex-Clark (1 RAR)	63507	Capt A.H. MacGregor MC (3 FD ENGR TP)
17036	Maj I. S. Fisher (1 RAR)		
23504	Maj B. J. Harper (1 RAR)	23561	WO2 H.E. Patch (1 RAR)
335092	Maj J. B. Healy (1 RAR)	1113	Lt Col A.V. Preece DSO, MVO (1 RAR)
51407	Capt R. K. Hill, MC (1 APC SQN (PWLH))		
335028	Maj J.A. Hooper (1 RAR)	28362	Maj J. J. Tattam (1 RAR)
61106	Maj P. D. Lipscombe (161 RECCE FLT)	57066	Capt A. G. Thompson (1 RAR)

ARMY COMMENDATION MEDAL FOR MERITORIOUS SERVICE (ACM(S))

37499	L/Cpl B. J. Adams (1 RAR)	29214	Sgt L. S. Annesley (1 RAR)
29839	Cpl J.A. Alcorn (1 RAR)	38110	Pte D. R. Aylett (1 RAR)
26413	Cpl A. G. M. Anderson (1 RAR)	54593	Pte W. P. Brunalli MM (1 RAR)

235267	Capt M. J. Carroll (1 RAR)	36682	Pte J. W. Kerr (1 RAR)
54010	Cpl C. W. Clifton (1 RAR)	244773	Spr T. G. Mason (3 FD ENGR
215430	Pte J. P. Daly (1 RAR)		TP)
215998	Pte B. J. Delaney (1 RAR)	1410367	Cpl F. L. Morrison (1 RAR)
213643	Cpl R. Evans (1 RAR)	22907	WO2 R. P. Pincott MBE (1 RAR)
28490	Sgt L. W. Fanning (105 FD BTY	37425	Cpl L. J. Powell (1 RAR)
	RAA)	47255	Cfn M. J. Rudge (1 RAR)
25857	Sgt D. M. Fyfe BEM (1 RAR)	215089	Pte R. H. Sloan (1 RAR)
53210	Sgt R. H. Greig (1 APC SQN	213760	Sgt B. Stokes (1 RAR)
	(PWLH))	14754	Cpl L. R. Tait (1 RAR)
12086	S/Sgt A.F. Harney (1 ALSC)	43096	Cpl B. G. Webster (1 RAR)
32070	WO1 D.D. Horsley (1 ALSC	2412088	Cpl C. F. Webster (1 RAR)
	WKSP DET)	54045	Sgt C. C. Wren (1 RAR)

AIR MEDAL FOR SERVICE (AM)

NZ31351	Maj D. R. Kenning MBE (161 FD BTY, RNZA)

Republic of South Vietnam Decorations awarded to members of the First Battalion, the Royal Australian Regiment (Group) for gallantry and service in the Republic of South Vietnam, 1965–1966

MILITARY MERIT MEDAL (MMM)

NZ37221	Sgt A. J. S. Don (Post.) (161 FD BTY, RNZA)	2412151	Pte W. L. Nalder (Post.) (1 RAR)
		212612	L/Cpl T. Ross (Post.) (1 RAR)
214479	Pte R. E. Field (Post.) (1 RAR)	37003	Cpl F. J. Smith (Post.) (1 RAR)
36542	Cpl A. H. T. Fotheringham (Post.) (1 RAR)	NZ928518	Bdr R. White (Post.) (161 FD BTY RNZA)

CROSS OF GALLANTRY WITH PALM (CG(P))

NZ37221	Sgt A. J. S. Don (Post.)(161 FD BTY, RNZA)	212612	L/Cpl T. Ross (Post.) (1 RAR)
		NZ928518	Bdr R. White (Post.) (161 FD BTY, RNZA)
214479	Pte R. E. Field (Post.) (1 RAR)		
2412151	Pte W. L. Nalder (Post.)(1 RAR)		

CROSS OF GALLANTRY WITH GOLD STAR (CG(GS))

2507	Lt Col I. R. W. Brumfield CBE, DSO (1 RAR)

CROSS OF GALLANTRY WITH SILVER STAR (CG(SS))

NZ31351	Maj D. R. Kenning MBE (161 FD BTY, RNZA)	311106	Capt P. H. B. Pritchard (1 ALSC)
		16369	Pte D. R. Venables (1 RAR)

CROSS OF GALLANTRY WITH BRONZE STAR (CG(BS))

| 335028 | Maj J. A. Hooper (1 RAR) | NZ457585 | Wo2 M. C. Nabbs MBE (161 FD |
| 32711 | Wo1 J. D. McKay MM (1 RAR) | | BTY, RNZA) |

ARMED FORCES HONOUR MEDAL (1ST CLASS) (AFHM(1ST CL))

| 23547 | Sgt W. M. Gray (1 ALSC) |

ARMED FORCES HONOUR MEDAL (2ND CLASS) (AFHM (2ND CL))

| 37867 | Pte M. A. Bourke (Post.) (1 RAR) | 36205 | Gnr T. Simpson (Post.) (105 FD BTY RAA) |
| 37010 | Pte W. T. Carroll (Post.) (1 RAR) | 54320 | Pte A. Van Valen (Post.) (1 RAR) |

Sources

Barnes, I.L., *Australian Gallant and Distinguished Service Vietnam 1962–1973* Sydney: The Military Historical Society of Australia, 1974

McNeill, I., *The Team — Australian Army Advisers in Vietnam 1962–1972* Brisbane: University of Queensland Press, 1984

Col A.V. Preece DSO, MVO (RL)
Maj D. Rothwell (RL)
Lt Col W. E. Kaine MBE
Brig I MacInnis, Military Secretary—Army
Col L. G. Williams, Army Liaison Officer, New Zealand High Commission, Canberra ACT

With assistance from:
Brig I. R. W. Brumfield CBE, DSO (RL)

Appendix B
Nominal Roll

1 RAR Group Nominal Roll

More than 1688 soldiers have been identified as having served in South Vietnam with the 1 RAR Group during its 1965-66 tour. Of these, 1055 served in 1 RAR, 525 in attached Australian sub-units and 108 with the New Zealand field battery and logistic element.

This nominal roll was compiled over a period of four years from various sources, including Army records and the memorabilia of soldiers involved. While some names may have been omitted the number will be minimal as all known sources have been consulted. Personnel not readily identifiable, and therefore not included, are those who served in the Royal Australian Signals Corps detachments tasked with providing rear link communications to Saigon and Australia; and those soldiers from the Armies of the United States of America and South Vietnam who served with the Group.

Placement of personnel into sub-units was only possible based on the memories of contributors over 20 years after the event. Where a soldier was identified as having served in more than one sub-unit his name has been included in each. Ranks shown are those worn on departure from Vietnam. Errors are regretted.

UNIT

1 RAR	1st Battalion, The Royal Australian Regiment
1 APC Tp (PWLH)	1st Armoured Personnel Carrier Troop (Prince of Wales Light Horse)
1 ALSC	1st Australian Logistic Support Company
3 Fd Engr Tp	3 Field Engineer Troop, Royal Australian Engineers
11 MC Gp	11 Movement Control Group
105 Fd Bty	105 Field Battery, Royal Australian Artillery
161 Recce Flt	161 Reconnaissance Flight, Australian Aviation Corps
161 Fd Bty, RNZA	161 Field Battery, Royal New Zealand Artillery
NZ Log Elm	New Zealand Logistic Element

SUB-UNIT

ADM	Administrative
ASC	Army Services Corps
ATK	Anti Tank
BHQ	Battalion Headquarters
CHQ	Company Headquarters
COY	Company
DEN	Dental
DET	Detachment
EME	Electrical Mechanical Engineer
ENGR	Engineers
HQ	Headquarters
MED	Medical
MOR	Mortar
ORD	Ordnance
PL	Platoon
PNR	Pioneer
QM	Quartermaster
R&C	Rest & Convalescent Centre
SIG	Signal
SPT	Support
TPT	Transport
WKSP	Workshop

RANK

LTCOL	Lieutenant Colonel
MAJ	Major
CAPT	Captain
LT	Lieutenant
2 LT	Second Lieutenant
WO1	Warrant Officer 1
WO2	Warrant Officer 2
SSGT	Staff Sergeant
FSGT	Flight Sergeant
SGT	Sergeant
CPL	Corporal
BDR	Bombardier
LCPL	Lance Corporal
LBDR	Lance Bombardier
PTE	Private
TPR	Trooper
GNR	Gunner
SPR	Sapper
CFN	Craftsman
LAC	Lead Aircraftman

CASUALTY CLASSIFICATION

BCAS	Battle Casualty (temporarily incapacitated — no wounds)	KIA	Killed in Action
		M/KIA	Missing Killed in Action — Body not Recovered
DOW	Died of Wounds	NBCAS	Non Battle Casualty (injured accidentally)
DWOAS	Died While on Active Service (other than from wounds)	WIA	Wounded in Action
F/NBC	Fatal Non Battle Casualty (killed accidentally)		

BHQ

LT COL I. R. W. BRUMFIELD DSO
LT COL A. V. PREECE DSO MVO
MAJ J. A. HOOPER
MAJ H. M. LANDER
CAPT K. R. BLANCH (PR)
CHAP 4 G. CUDMORE
CAPT J. G. DERMODY
CAPT R. A. DUCIE
CAPT C. J. G. PEACOCK
CAPT A. G. THOMPSON
LT I. M. GUILD
LT J. D. MCNAMARA
  WIA 13/10/65
LT G. J. PORTER
LT A. W. WHITE
WO1 W. J. BIRKETT
WO1 J. D. MCKAY MM
WO2 W. J. CUNNEEN (PR)
WO2 J. G. CURRIE
WO2 B. R. DUNN (PR)

SSGT A. ADAMS
SGT L. S. ANNESLEY
SGT E. E. DREGER
SGT F. J. HOBBINS
SGT J. D. O'SHEA
SGT M. B. R. SHANNON (PR)
SGT. B. TINDALL
SGT W. J. WELLS
SGT I. J. WELSH
CPL J. P. HENDERSON
CPL A. H. D. MCAULAY
CPL R. W. RICHARDSON
CPL J. SHEEHAN
CPL J. SITARZ
CPL B. R. WALKER
LCPL D. A. DUFFEY
LCPL J. F. KEARNS
LCPL E. R. C. ROCHESTER
LCPL P. J. SLATTERY
LCPL R. STEIN

LCPL N. B. WYVILL
LCPL J. D. YOUNG
PTE K. J. BAKER
PTE A. A. CHIEMENTON
PTE R. G. DALE
PTE H. T. DALTON
  WIA 11/10/65
PTE D. N. HOLLOWAY
PTE G. G. A. JONES
PTE G. H. KING
PTE D. G. LIMN
PTE G. W. P. LYON
PTE W. W. RICHARDS
PTE M. N. TALBOT
PTE B. D. TOBIN
PTE B. M. WALSH
PTE G. F. YEATS
PTE M. A. YOUNG

A COMPANY CHQ

MAJ J. B. HEALY   WIA 29/06/65
CAPT D. F. PAUL
CAPT P. B. H. PRICHARD
WO2 J. CRAMP
SSGT F. W. DEAN BEM
SGT B. KENNEDY
CPL G. W. HANSON
CPL G. B. RANSON
LCPL A. W. AHEARN
LCPL W. J. COLLINS

LCPL A. MACKAY
PTE L. F. BATTLEY   WIA
  7/02/66
PTE L. W. BOWYER
PTE W. B. DUNCAN
PTE B. FLEMATTI
PTE A. S. GAVINE
PTE R. W. GEPPERT
PTE R. J. HUGHES
PTE K. W. OLDFIELD

PTE W. L. ROSS
PTE A. SENIOR
PTE I. T. F. SKINNER
PTE J. L. SMITH
PTE G. R. STEPHENSEN
PTE B. N. TOOHEY
PTE M.J. TOY   WIA 20/09/65
PTE G. WALDIE

1 PL

2 LT E. J. CULPITT WIA 11/10/65
SGT G. H. PETERSON
CPL T. F. HAGAN WIA 12/10/65
CPL D. G. HAYES WIA 08/11/65
CPL R. G. HUCKAUF
CPL H. R. SMITH
CPL C. D. STIDWORTHY
CPL D. C. WILKINSON
LCPL A. M. ANDERSON
LCPL R. I. BAIHN
LCPL E. V. BARKER
LCPL J. S. I. FITCH
LCPL K. W. GARNER
LCPL R. H. J. PARKER
   M/KIA 08/11/65
LCPL T. ROSS KIA 12/10/65
LCPL T.C. WARBURTON
   WIA 09/10/65
LCPL B. G. WEBSTER
PTE D. P. ALLGOOD

PTE D. B. ALLWRIGHT
PTE T. G. BAXTER WIA 08/11/65
PTE C. W. BUTTERWORTH
PTE L. W. CARSON
PTE G. W. CAVE WIA 08/11/65
PTE G. W. CONSTABLE
   WIA 08/10/65
PTE C. H. COOMBS
PTE R. G. CURTIS
PTE R. F. CURTIS
PTE L. W. DALTON
PTE P. C. DIAMOND
PTE R. K. DOONAN
PTE D. R. EICKENLOFF
PTE R. JOYCE WIA 07/02/66
PTE R. LYNCH
PTE L. R. MAIR
PTE B. F. MCGRATH
PTE A. J. MCIVOR WIA 06/11/65
PTE L. S. MICHALOWSKY

PTE H. G. MIMI
PTE J. H. NUNAN
PTE R. J. PINKERTON
PTE J. O. V. PRASSER
PTE C. R. PRIOR
PTE E. RASMUSSEN
PTE C. J. RAYFIELD
PTE T. J. RYAN
PTE B. J. RYAN
PTE M. C. SCRIVENER
PTE J. L. SMITH
PTE G. R. STEPHENSEN
PTE E. J. TOWNSEND
   WIA 08/11/65
PTE R. G. UNWIN WIA 12/10/65
PTE D. L. WASS
PTE G. E. WILMOT
PTE G. B. WOODWARD
   WIA 06/11/65

2 PL

LT I. M. GUILD
LT A. W. WHITE
2LT N. E. BROWN
SGT R. J. FARLEY
CPL J. A. ALCORN
CPL J. R. BARBER
CPL G. M. FERGUSON
   WIA 09/08/65
CPL B. MOORE
CPL G. H. NEWBERY
LCPL K. A. BENIER
LCPL W. J. COLLINS
LCPL W. F. RYAN
LCPL A. E. STEEL
LCPL T. SUTER F/NBC 27/02/66
PTE R. J. AINSCOUGH
PTE L. A. BAKKER WIA 09/08/65
PTE D. C. BARBER
PTE D. L. BEYNON
PTE G. BONA
PTE R. T. BOULTON

PTE R. B. BRADFORD
PTE B. E. CHANT
PTE P. J. COTTER
PTE W. P. DEVINE
PTE P. W. DICK
PTE K. R. ELLIOTT
PTE R. E. FIELD KIA 09/10/65
PTE B. FLEMATTI
PTE M. E. GRAHAM
PTE D. M. HARTSHORN
PTE N. J. HELM
PTE B. G. HORNUNG
PTE G. W. HOUSE
PTE D. C. HOWELL
PTE J. P. HUIGENS
PTE A. J. JEFFERY
PTE R. J. J. JEFFERY
PTE M. I. JONES
PTE A. L. KUBIAK
PTE A. W. KUNDE
PTE D. R. LISTER

PTE B. F. MCGRATH
PTE L. S. MICHALOWSKY
PTE S. J. MINNIECON
PTE V. W. MITCHELL
PTE K. F. MOORE
PTE R. J. PINKERTON
PTE I. T. RASMUSSEN
PTE H. J. REED
PTE W. L. ROSS
PTE K. J. RUFF
PTE I. D. SEABROOK
PTE G. A. STEVENS WIA
   14/03/66
PTE D. D. STEVENSON
PTE M. J. TOY WIA 20/09/65
PTE T. J. TURNER
PTE G. J. M. VAN HOOF
PTE J. H. VINCENT
PTE M. WALDRON
PTE G. F. YEATS

3 PL

2LT C. O. G. WILLIAMS
SGT C. FAWCETT MM
CPL C. J. PEARCE WIA 02/04/66
CPL R. D. SEIPEL WIA 12/10/65
   KIA 07/02/66
CPL F. J. SMITH KIA 21/09/65
CPL P. C. TAYLOR
CPL C. F. WEBSTER
LCPL N.R. DARBY WIA 08/01/66
LCPL L. F. HIGGINS
LCPL L.J. IDIENS
LCPL N. S. PARKES WIA
   31/07/65
LCPL R. K. PIPER
PTE D. R. AYLETT
PTE R. W. BALDOCK
PTE W. J. L. BALE
PTE L. J. BASSETT
PTE L. F. BATTLEY WIA
   07/02/66

PTE V. CAMPISI
PTE A. C. CARLON
PTE L. B. DOMASHENZ
PTE W. B. DUNCAN
PTE R. K. ELLIS
PTE P. R. GILLSON
   M/KIA 08/11/65
PTE W. J. GREENWOOD
   WIA 02/04/66
PTE J. P. W. HANSEN
PTE D. HARWOOD
PTE I. W. HOLMES
PTE K. E. J. JARROLD
PTE L. JOHNSTON WIA
   16/03/66
PTE G. H. KING
PTE R. E. KUSCHERT
PTE G. R. LOBB
PTE C. P. MANKTELOW
   WIA 12/10/65

PTE B. L. MECKENSTOCK
PTE P. A. MIFSUD
PTE J. H. MITCHELL WIA
   19/03/66
PTE C. T. MOONEY
PTE B. J. MOYLE
PTE K. REDFORD WIA 11/10/65
PTE J. M. SHREEVE
PTE J. P. S. SMITH
PTE A. T. THIRKELL
PTE B. N. TOOHEY
PTE M. C. VICKERS
PTE R. R. B. WELLINGTON
   NBCAS 14/10/65
PTE A. B. WILKES
PTE L. S. WILLIAMS WIA
   31/03/66
PTE D. J. R. WOODFORDE
PTE H. P. ZERBES WIA 31/03/66

B COMPANY CHQ

MAJ I. D. MCFARLANE BCAS
   08/01/66
CAPT P.M. ARNISON
WO2 K. A. HALL
WO2 H. E. SMITH
SSGT D. H. TYLER
SGT R. HUGHES
CPL A. A. BAGDONAS
CPL G. J. MCINTYRE

CPL W. A. METCALFE
CPL J. R. WHATLING
CPL A. R. WOODWARD
LCPL K. J. MARTIN
LCPL E. J. MCAULIFFE
PTE I. BARKER
PTE B. L. BORRIE
PTE M. I. BURGESS WIA
   08/01/66

PTE W. B. CAWTHORNE
PTE R. B. COCKERILL
PTE B. J. HUHSE
PTE J. P. SPITZERS
PTE J. B. THATCHER WIA
   12/10/65
PTE P. A. WILKIE

4 PL

2 LT G. E. BOLITHO
SGT F. G. HAMERSLEY
CPL R. EVANS MID
CPL R. H. HILLIER MID KIA
   29/11/65
CPL L. J. MCNAMARA
CPL H. R. WEARING
LCPL L. T. E. LINDSAY
LCPL P. B. PEDDIE
LCPL W. M. RHODES
PTE F. B. ALLENDER
PTE R. W. BAILEY MID
PTE A. C. D. BAXTER
PTE K. A. BEST
PTE K. M. BIRBECK
PTE P. J. BLASKETT
PTE D. J. BRIGGS
PTE W. P. BRUNALLI MM WIA
   24/02/66

PTE D. A. W. CALDWELL
PTE C. J. CULLEN
PTE J. P. DALY MID
PTE D. O. DANAHER
PTE C. J. DURBIDGE
PTE J. T. DWAN
PTE K. L. EASON
PTE J. EATON
PTE D. J. EVANS
PTE H. E. FORNO
PTE J. R. FULLER
PTE R. E. GERHARDT
PTE G. J. GROTII
PTE F. J. HANLY BCAS 11/01/66
PTE N. W. HORNE KIA 08/01/66
PTE W. M. B. JUHAS
PTE A. P. LING WIA 17/12/65
PTE M. W. LUCHT
PTE R. G. MCLEAN

PTE B. F. MCLEOD
PTE I. D. C. MUNRO
PTE W. J. NOBLE
PTE K. W. PALMEN
PTE J. C. PEEBLES
PTE P. A. PFEFFER
PTE P. A. PULIS
PTE J. M. SCOTT
PTE R. S. SECRETT
PTE J. P. SHORTLAND
PTE D. B. VOGELE MID
PTE P. J. WATTS
PTE L. C. WHITE
PTE W. R. WILLIAMS

5 PL

2LT W. F. HINDSON
SGT T. E. PROSSER
CPL B. J. DOUGLAS
CPL F. LAWLER
CPL D. G. PARKER
CPL J. J. WHITAKER
LCPL T. H. CROSS
LCPL R. J. CURRAN
LCPL A. A. LAW WIA 19/03/66
LCPL R. L. SINCLAIR
PTE W. J. ANNS
PTE L. R. BARNETT
PTE B. G. BARTELS
PTE J. BOOTY
PTE W. S. A. BORHAM

PTE J. M. BOSS
PTE B. BRODERICK
PTE J.L. CRUICKSHANK
PTE J.H. DAVIS
PTE H.E. DENNIS
PTE B. N. EKELUND
PTE R. S. FRASER   MM
   WIA 22/09/65
PTE R. J. ISAACS
PTE D. L. JONES
PTE D. H. JUCKEL
PTE J. A. LANG
PTE R. K. MCLEAN WIA
   12/10/65
PTE R. C. O'BRIEN

PTE R. F. PEARSON
PTE J. F. PEDERSEN
PTE J. S. SEWELL
PTE J. S. SMAILES
PTE J. M. STEVENS
PTE N. A. THOMAS
PTE A. UNWIN
PTE D. WALKER
PTE L. WARING MM
PTE G. R. WILLS

6 PL

2LT C. J. MCINTYRE
2LT P. A. SIBREE
SGT R. I. BENNETT
SGT M. J. KIRBY
CPL P. T. FLEMING
CPL M. V. GREALY WIA
   19/03/66
CPL D. P. HAINES
CPL T. B. LOFTUS MID
   WIA 12/10/65
CPL G. J. MCINTYRE
CPL G. RAMMA
CPL J. J. WHITAKER
LCPL T. J. ADAMS
LCPL D. R. CAMERON
LCPL G. P. KELLY
LCPL A. A. LAW WIA 19/03/66
LCPL D. M. MUNDAY MM
   WIA 07/07/65
LCPL R. F. STAINER
PTE J. K. BAIRD
PTE G. J. BARR
PTE J. J. BARRETT
PTE R. W. BATT

PTE N. R. BEXTRUM
PTE A. B. BRENNAN
PTE G. J. CHAD
PTE R. J. CLEAVER
PTE R. B. COCKERILL
PTE G. T. COLE
PTE R. G. CROSS
PTE J. A. CROWTHER
PTE R. E. EAREA
PTE G. J. EASTLEY
PTE R. S. ELLIS
PTE W. D. FAGERLUND
PTE D. L. FORMAN
PTE A. R. FRASER
PTE B. B. GRIFFITH
PTE S. HODDER
PTE. P. F. HODGSON
PTE W. J. KELLY
PTE R. W. KLUPP
PTE B. J. LANSDOWN
PTE K. A. LINKE
PTE R. MANGANO WIA
   12/10/65
PTE B. MARWICK

PTE B. A. MEADOWS
PTE R. J. NORTHEY
PTE R. K. D. O'BRIEN
PTE K. A. O'KANE
PTE G. A. OWENS
PTE W. J. PEARCE
PTE G. T. PERKINS
PTE G. D. PIPER
PTE J. A. PORTER WIA 07/08/65
PTE J. H. PRIESTLEY
PTE B. R. REILLY
PTE W. E. SCOTT
PTE R. H. SLOAN
PTE B. J. SMITH WIA 20/03/66
PTE E. J. SOMERS
PTE W. E. STRANGE
PTE J. B. THATCHER
   WIA 12/10/65
PTE P. D. THOMPSON
PTE L. V. J. TURNER
PTE T. J. VEALE
PTE E. R. WEATHERALL
   WIA 07/07/65
PTE J. A. E. WILLIAMS

C COMPANY CHQ

MAJ J. J. TATTAM WIA 08/01/66
CAPT M. F. LE BARS
CAPT C. J. G. PEACOCK
WO2 R. E. JONES
WO2 H. E. PATCH
SSGT N. L. KRAUSE
SGT E. ADAMS
CPL O. W. BROWN
CPL D. J. HAWKINS
CPL R. W. RICHARDSON

CPL A. G. ROBINSON
CPL C. C. WREN
LCPL K. W. BROWN
LCPL D. W. EVANS
LCPL T. W. J. LUPTON
PTE P. J. ARNOLD
PTE G. K. CHISHOLM
PTE J. P. HUDSON
PTE P. J. ISRAEL BCAS 08/01/66
PTE K. R. JOHNS

PTE F. LINCK
PTE V. B. E. MELBOURNE
PTE E. J. MOK
PTE T. J. OSMOND
PTE N. H. ROBINS
   NBCAS 26/06/65
PTE P. THOMAS
PTE G. G. WEIR

7PL

2LT J. P. DWYER WIA 05/04/66
SGT D. F. SAVILLE MM
SGT R. J. H. WEST WIA 12/03/66
CPL N. H. DAVIS
CPL D. W. JENKINSON
    WIA 13/10/65
CPL G. E. PIPER NBCAS
    26/06/65
CPL A. G. ROBINSON
CPL P. C. THOMPSON
    NBCAS 26/06/65
LCPL B. J. EVANS
LCPL W. G. FRY NBCAS
    26/06/65
LCPL D. G. HAMILL
LCPL C. W. LAWLER
LCPL T. A. SMITH
PTE A. AISTHORPE
PTE F. J. ANDERSON
PTE L. J. BAXTER KIA 15/03/66
PTE M. A. BOURKE
    F/NBC 26/06/65
PTE H. A. BOYD WIA 12/03/66
PTE R. R. BROWN WIA 13/10/65
PTE A. A. BURT

PTE V. M. CAMERON
    WIA 05/04/66
PTE W. T. CARROLL
    F/NBC 26/06/65
PTE D. R. CARSON
PTE E. G. DALEY
PTE I. K. DAWSON
PTE J. A. J. DOORLEY
    WIA 12/03/66
PTE B. S. FLEMING WIA
    05/04/66
PTE. P. GODDARD
    NBCAS 10/03/66
PTE R. J. GOULDEN
    NBCAS 26/06/65
PTE W. L. HALL
PTE M. J. JAGERS
    NBCAS 26/06/65
    IA 12/03/66
PTE D. C. LEAMAN
PTE P. F. LINDWALL
PTE J. D. LOADER
PTE A. W. MACDONALD NBCAS
    26/06/65
PTE W. I. MCLEOD WIA
    12/03/66

PTE J. A. O'BRIEN
PTE V. K. OTWAY
PTE D. H. PENN KIA 10/01/66
PTE I. K. PHELPS
PTE. V. PODESTA
PTE P. J. RIDDETT WIA 09/10/65
PTE N. H. ROBINS
    NBCAS 26/06/65
PTE L. B. ROGASCH
PTE J. D. RUTLAND WIA
    05/04/66
PTE V. W. SIMON
PTE B. L. TOMKINSON
    WIA 12/03/66
PTE A. VAN VALEN
    NBCAS 26/06/65
    DOW 29/06/65
PTE D. R. VEALEY
PTE R. H. S. WEITZMANN
PTE W. A. WELDON
PTE J. P. B. WHITE
PTE H. W. WHITE
PTE J. G. WILLETT WIA 12/03/66

8 PL

LT J. D. MCNAMARA
    WIA 13/10/65
2LT W. E. KAINE
2LT K. W. LUNNY
SSGT K. J. PRIOR
SGT B. J. COLLETT
SGT A. J. J. LIGHTFOOT BEM
    WIA 08/10/65
SGT R. J. H. WEST WIA 12/03/66
CPL G. G. CRICK
CPL J. MCKILLOP WIA 08/10/65
CPL K. G. SIMONS
CPL R. W. WRIGHT
LCPL K. W. BROWN
LCPL C. W. CAVANAGH
LCPL C. J. CLARKE WIA
    13/10/65
LCPL D. W. EVANS
LCPL W. J. NELSON
    BCAS 08/10/65
LCPL B. A. SMITH
PTE W. H. R. ALLEN
    WIA 08/10/65
PTE G. V. ANDERSON
PTE J. R. ARNOLD
PTE W. BARTKIW WIA 08/01/66
PTE W. E. G. BEATTIE

PTE R. BLIGHT
PTE. R. E. BREBNER
PTE C. F. M. BROWNHILL
PTE B. F. BUCKLE
PTE G. D. CLARKE WIA
    13/10/65
PTE D. L. COX
PTE A. W. DOWNEY
    WIA 05/04/66
PTE G. L. DUNGEY
PTE D. W. EDGLEY
PTE D. J. GRIFFITHS
PTE K. R. GUDGEON
    WIA 08/01/66
PTE W. M. HALL
PTE A. R. HANSEN KIA
    25/10/65
PTE P. J. ISRAEL BCAS 08/01/66
PTE W. J. JACKSON WIA
    08/10/65
    BCAS 08/01/66
PTE S. L. JONES
PTE R. B. KELLY
PTE D. H. J. KIRKBY WIA
    13/10/65
PTE K. C. LESTER
PTE S. P. MEHARG WIA
    08/01/66

PTE A. E. MIRANDA
    NBCAS 26/06/65
PTE A. R. MORRIS
PTE R. MORTON WIA 08/10/65
PTE K. NEWMAN
PTE H. F. NOCKOLDS
PTE H. J. O'BRIEN
PTE B. ORNOWSKI
    NBCAS 26/06/65
PTE H. PANOSSIAN
PTE R. RAINES WIA 08/01/66
PTE T. P. RYAN
PTE G. J. SCHUTS BCAS
    08/10/65
    BCAS 25/10/65
PTE D. G. M. SEMPLE
PTE W. C. SHEEAN
PTE J. P. STANWIX
PTE I. R. TYERS
PTE F. W. WATSON WIA
    17/03/66
PTE J. R. WILLIAMS WIA
    08/10/65
PTE A. P. WILSON-BROWN
    BCAS 08/10/65

9 PL

2LT R. D. LOFTUS
SGT G. A. SMITH MM
CPL B. L. LESEUER MM
CPL N. H. MCGAVOCK
CPL G. E. PIPER
  NBCAS 26/06/65
CPL B. J. SNOW
LCPL G. E. BLAND
LCPL R. J. HALLIDAY
LCPL R. R. HOCKING
LCPL T. W. J. LUPTON
LCPL J. A. NELSON
LCPL T. A. SMITH
PTE R. F. BERGER
PTE L. R. BOVEY

PTE W. R. BROOK
PTE K. J. BROOMHAM
PTE M. J. BROWN
PTE W. R. BUCKLAND
PTE K. G. CHEERS
PTE R. W. CURRALL
PTE J. C. EWING
PTE P. R. FAGERLUND
  WIA 10/10/65
PTE S. HANUSZEWICZ
PTE G. M. HAUPT WIA 12/07/65
PTE J.H. KALMA
PTE W. J. KUCZYNSKI
PTE W. P. LUDZIK
PTE P. MANN

PTE R. J. MULLER
PTE I. NAGY
PTE R. T. NIELSON
PTE P. J. O'HALLORAN
PTE P. K. OAKFORD
PTE G. R. PATTERSON
PTE R. B. PAYNE
PTE M. K. PEARD
PTE A. J. REHDER
PTE F. G. STEVENS
PTE R. L. STYLES WIA 10/10/65
PTE C. F. TORRENS
PTE C. E. WHITTINGTON

D COMPANY CHQ

MAJ I. S. FISHER
MAJ B. J. HARPER
CAPT D. P. ROTHWELL
WO2 R. P. PINCOTT
SSGT K. J. PRIOR
SGT F. P. HELE
CPL L. W. BURNS
CPL I. R. COLLISON

LCPL R. E. COXON KIA 13/01/66
LCPL D. FISHER
PTE B. J. ALEXANDER
PTE C. C. CHAMBERS
PTE D. M. DUNCAN
PTE R. GILLSON
PTE R. J. HANLON
PTE H. B. HARRIS

PTE R. B. HICKEY
PTE P. G. LACKEY
PTE R. G. LUHRS
PTE W. A. ROCHE
PTE L. G. SCHMIDT
PTE L. C. SMITH

10 PL

2LT O. S. LIND NBCAS 16/09/65
SGT W. D. FROST WIA 09/01/66
SGT T. GARSON BCAS 19/03/66
CPL W. B. AITKENHEAD
CPL G. T. COOPER
LCPL R. E. COXON KIA 13/01/66
LCPL B. J. GARTSIDE
LCPL C. R. GEAPPEN
LCPL T. J. MCDONNELL
  WIA 13/01/66
LCPL M. MCINTYRE
LCPL D. T. SHERGOLD
PTE B. P. ALLEN
PTE R. J. BAILEY
PTE R. W. BAYLISS
PTE N. P. BERZINSKI
PTE A. J. CAMBEY

PTE N. J. CAMPBELL
  WIA 12/10/65
PTE A. J. COHEN
PTE W. H. CROMBIE
  WIA 19/03/66
PTE D. W. T. CUNNINGHAM
PTE K. J. DALTON
PTE W. DOBUSH
PTE R. W. EAST
PTE K. J. FINUCANE
PTE B. J. HANSEN
PTE D. J. HARDMAN
  WIA 06/07/65
PTE E. G. HAZEL
PTE R. B. HICKEY
PTE R. W. HOWARD
PTE G. F. JONES

PTE A. R. JONES WIA 12/10/65
PTE E. J. KELLY
PTE T. J. LANGFORD
PTE M. C. LINES
PTE W. E. MCCLURKIN
  WIA 08/10/65
PTE J. C. MCCOLL
PTE J. C. MONK
PTE R. A. MOTT
PTE R. P. OCKENDEN
PTE B. W. PAPWORTH
PTE B. A. THOMPSON
PTE P. J. TONKES
PTE T. D. WHITE WIA 13/01/66
PTE G. T. K. WILLIS
PTE A. J. WRIGHT

11 PL

LT W. J. GILES
2LT C. E. LEGGETT
   NBCAS 30/06/65
SSGT K. J. PRIOR
SGT M. J. JORDAN
SGT A. J. J. LIGHTFOOT, BEM
   WIA 08/10/65
CPL R. J. KELLY WIA 25/09/65
CPL F. L. MORRISON
CPL V. R. RYAN
CPL J. SCHONKALA
LCPL R. L. BIRCH
LCPL P. J. BOURKE
LCPL G. L. GRIFFITHS
LCPL N. JOHNSTON
LCPL R. W. KIRBY

PTE C. G. BEETON
PTE A. E. BRIDLE
PTE B. F. J. CARTER
PTE M. I. CLARKE
PTE S. J. COCKER
PTE C. J. P. CURRAN
PTE J. A. DONNELLY
PTE R. W. DUFF
PTE M. J. FITZPATRICK
PTE P. N. GRAMBOWER
PTE J. H. HARRAP
PTE P. W. HARROWER
PTE E. G. HARTAS
PTE W. R. HAZELL
PTE J. P. JANAS
PTE R. A. KENNEDY

PTE M. R. MADDEN
PTE B. W. MAGANN
PTE A. E. MCGEOWN
PTE J. L. MITCHELL
PTE L. F. MOYLAN
PTE M. J. MURRAY
PTE G. L. NIELSON
PTE J. C. PARKER
PTE R. W. PODSTAWKA
PTE P. RICHARDSON
PTE D. RYDER WIA 29/11/65
PTE W. F. SWEETNAM
PTE R. A. TOWNS
PTE R. G. TYRES
PTE R. F. WALTERS

12 PL

2LT J. R. BOURKE WIA 08/01/66
2LT L. E. D. COOPER
2LT R. J. DAVIS
SGT J. W. CARNES MM
CPL W. C. DATE
CPL E. G. EHLERS WIA 08/01/66
CPL G. A. E. NEWTON
CPL L. J. POWELL
CPL R. E. SMITH WIA 08/01/66
LCPL D. C. BOWLES
LCPL J. W. PRATTEN
LCPL P. K. WILLIAMS
PTE W. K. BLAIKIE WIA
   14/07/65
PTE B. J. DELANEY WIA
   08/01/66

PTE J. A. DENSLEY WIA
   07/02/66
PTE P. J. DOODY
PTE F. K. EBERLE
PTE G. J. ERHARDT
PTE L. P. FITZGERALD
PTE M. N. GOLDSMITH
   WIA 05/07/65
PTE E. A. GRILLS WIA 08/01/66
   WOAS 12/02/66
PTE A. M. GRINTER WIA
   08/01/66
PTE B. JAUDZEMIS
PTE M. A. KILBURN
PTE O. G. F. KRENKE
PTE R. H. LOVE WIA 14/04/66

PTE K. J. K. MCLEOD
   WIA 24/10/65
   WIA 27/11/65
PTE W. L. NALDER WIA
   07/07/65
   DOW 08/07/65
PTE C. J. NEWLYN
PTE L. A. PARKE
PTE B. O. PETERSON
KIA 10/01/66
PTE E. PINOLI WIA 11/01/66
PTE B. E. PRINGLE
PTE R. L. RILEY WIA 14/07/65
PTE J. G. SMIGOWSKI
PTE P. SMIT
PTE P. C. E. SNEDDON

SUPPORT COMPANY CHQ

MAJ J. ESSEX-CLARK
WO2 J. G. CURRIE
SSGT K. J. PATA
SGT F. J. HOBBINS
SGT R. G. HUENDER
CPL R. R. BATTERSBY

CPL N. B. GROUNDWATER
CPL R. J. JACKSON
CPL W. A. METCALFE
PTE R. T. BARTLETT
PTE M. LOURIGAN
PTE M. J. PATTERSON

PTE C. N. PITT
PTE J. T. ROBERTS
PTE D. R. VENABLES
PTE R. H. WALLBANK

SIGNALS PL

CAPT M. J. CARROLL MID
SGT B. H. COX
SGT V. C. J. POWELL
CPL B. J. ADAMS
CPL K. J. ALCORN WIA 08/01/66
CPL B. DAVIES
CPL P. T. FLEMING
CPL P. V. FLEMING
CPL G. R. FORD
CPL G. J. FRANCIS
CPL T. J. GAMBLE
CPL D. K. HOWELL
CPL W. M. MCFADDEN
CPL L. J. STANSFIELD
CPL B. D. STOKES
LCPL B. F. KENNA
LCPL I. PAUZA

LCPL L. G. SMITHSON
LCPL P. A. WATTERSON
PTE R. L. BOWMAN
PTE A. B. BRANDT
PTE K. C. S. BRIGGS
PTE E. M. CHALMERS
PTE W. A. COOPER
PTE D. B. ELBOURNE
PTE F. C. S. FANNA
PTE R. J. FAULKNER
PTE R. L. FLEMING
PTE F. W. GORDON
PTE J. P. HUDSON
PTE V. J. H. JACKSON
PTE A. P. JASSE
PTE L. J. LAMBERT
PTE R. LEE

PTE R. D. W. LEHN WIA
   11/10/65
PTE R. P. MCCALLUM
PTE I. C. MCLEOD
PTE A. M. MCPHERSON
PTE C. H. MCQUILLAN
PTE P. A. MILLER
PTE R. L. PADDON JONES
PTE I. K. M. PASCOE
PTE K. R. PAULSEN
PTE L. J. PEDRANA
PTE C. J. REYNOLDS
PTE W. R. SUTTON
PTE G. J. TURVEY
PTE A. B. WEDGWOOD

MORTAR PL

CAPT M. C. PECK
LT D. N. COLLINS
2LT N. E. BOWN
SGT J. E. DEAN WIA 13/10/64
SGT B. F. GRANLAND
SGT D. J. JUILLERAT
SGT K. R. PHIPPS
SGT B. STOKES
CPL J. W. BLUNDELL
CPL L. W. CHAFFEY
CPL T. H. GOSPER
CPL M. V. GREALY WIA
   19/03/66
CPL T. J. HEWITT
CPL J. KENNEDY WIA 29/06/65
LCPL J. W. MCDONOUGH

LCPL N. J. O'HALLORAN
PTE D. P. ALLGOOD
PTE W. G. CAMPBELL
PTE W. M. CHEVIS
PTE P. EDDEN
PTE R. FLEMING
PTE B. J. GIBSON
PTE A. T. GOODSELL
PTE B. D. GRAY WIA 29/06/65
PTE J. W. GUEST
PTE R. A. HARRIS
PTE A. J. HENRY
PTE P. HOLCROFT
PTE I. K. JOHNSON
PTE P. T. JOHNSTON
PTE V. G. JONES

PTE R. S. JONES
PTE G. W. P. LYON
PTE G. R. MCCORMACK
PTE R. D. MCLEOD
PTE P. E. MCMAHON
PTE M. A. MOODY
PTE W. A. MORTIMER
PTE E. L. NEALE
PTE E. H. NIDDRIE
PTE J. A. W. O'REGAN
PTE L. D. PHELPS
PTE W. R. SKEEN
PTE W. J. SPENCE
PTE J. H. WHITTON
PTE H. WILCOX
PTE R. G. WILLCOCKS

ASSAULT PIONEER PL

2LT K. A. ANDERSON
2LT H. L. GAUVIN
SGT C. G. EVANS
SGT B. STOKES
CPL G. B. BUCKLAND
CPL C. W. CLIFTON
CPL A. H. FOTHERINGHAM
   F/NBC 17/12/65
CPL T. R. MAXWELL
CPL L. C. MCDONNELL
   KIA 09/03/66
CPL W. L. O'SHEA
CPL T. G. SCHMIDT
LCPL R. R. HILDITCH
LCPL D. E. JORDAN
LCPL N. P. MCLEAN

LCPL W. J. RAMSAY
LCPL R. L. SINCLAIR
PTE R. J. ALLDRIDGE
PTE J. E. ARMSTRONG
PTE K. F. ATKINSON
PTE B. J. BENSON
PTE R. E. CLAUSEN
PTE J. A. DAWKINS
PTE J. J. FINNIGAN
PTE G. R. FRENCH WIA
   02/01/66
PTE B. A. GLOVER
PTE R. M. GOUBAREFF
PTE K. B. HANDLEY
PTE L. F. KING
PTE K. C. LAMPARD

PTE A. W. LARSEN
PTE J. A. R. MCINTOSH
PTE N. MCNAE
PTE L. E. MEIER
PTE P. R. NORMAN
PTE R. G. O'CALLAGHAN
PTE B. G. O'HEHIR
PTE E. J. PIGRAM
PTE D. A. RAYMOND
PTE J. H. RIDLEY
PTE R. F. SINCLAIR
PTE N. VIDOT
PTE F. N. VINCENT
PTE A. L. WARD
PTE S. J. YOW YEH

ANTI TANK PL

CAPT C. J. G. PEACOCK
2LT W. E. KAINE
SGT R. I. BENNETT
SGT M. J. JORDAN
SGT N. J. MANN
CPL C. W. CROCKER
CPL K. W. FORDEN
CPL D. J. A. NEWBERRY
CPL R. ORGAN
CPL T. G. SCHMIDT
LCPL W. H. BAKER
LCPL P. C. DORTER
LCPL W. J. MANI
LCPL W. J. NICHOLSON
PTE R. A. ANDERSON
PTE P. J. APLIN

PTE A. J. BATT
PTE R. J. BETTANY
PTE G. H. G. BIGGS
PTE C. S. CARRUTHERS
PTE C. J. CARTER
PTE M. J. CONSTABLE
PTE D. W. CRUSE
PTE P. B. DEVINE
PTE A. W. DOWNEY
 WIA 05/04/66
PTE G. L. DOYLE
PTE M. B. GOULD
PTE B. T. GRAHAM
PTE R. J. HUMBLES
PTE J. T. JARRETT
PTE F. KUZBA

PTE V. R. MACDONALD
PTE J. H. MELKSHAM
PTE J. A. MOYLE
PTE P. J. MURRAY
PTE T. G. NEAL
PTE E. R. PATTERSON
PTE G. G. PONTIN
PTE R. E. RICHARDS
PTE F. W. RICHARDS
PTE P. E. ROBERTS
PTE F. S. SMITH
PTE G. SOTNIKOV
PTE A. L. THOMAS
PTE J. G. ZIMA

ADMINISTRATION COMPANY CHQ

MAJ B. J. HARPER
MAJ P. G. SHARP
SENREP A. HALL
WO2 J. CHRISTENSEN
SSGT R. V. RIDER
SGT J. S. TYRRELL
CPL R. E. CONSIDINE

CPL S. L. ELLIS
CPL D. M. PATTERSON
CPL M. G. SHORT
LCPL W. J. MANI
PTE S. R. ALBRECHT
PTE P. A. BENSLEY
PTE C. F. M. BROWNHILL

PTE W. L. CHARLTON
PTE G. L. COUPLAND
PTE R. GILLSON
PTE J. R. GOLDSMITH
PTE R. A. KAISER

QUARTERMASTER PL

CAPT T. J. BUCKLEY
2LT J. F. IRVINE
WO2 A. R. ELLIOTT
WO2 L. J. STANFORD
SGT J. J. COTTERELL (EME)
SGT D. H. FYFE BEM
SGT A. J. HILL
SGT I. D. MACQUEEN
SGT D. H. TUDOR
CPL W. CARNEY (EME)
CPL T. R. MAXWELL
CPL P. F. MORAVEC
CPL D. M. PATTERSON

CPL K. G. ROGERS
CPL N. G. VINCENT
LCPL W. G. FRY NBCAS
 26/06/65
LCPL I. S. MILLER
LCPL R. MITCHELL
LCPL M. RALPH
LCPL M. P. SAUNDERSON
LCPL N. G. SMITH
PTE S. R. ALBRECHT
PTE H. E. BACK
PTE L. BAKKER
PTE W. L. CHARLTON

PTE R. E. CHISOLM
CFN J. C. EDWARDS (EME)
CFN H. GOOCH (EME)
PTE B. J. MOYLE
PTE H. J. NEWBERY
PTE J. D. NICHOLAS
CFN M. J. RUDGE (EME)
PTE C. T. SHAY
PTE L. C. SMITH
CFN R. L. TONGE (EME)
PTE D. S. WALSH
PTE P. V. WATERS
PTE D. P. WOODBURY

TRANSPORT PL

LT W. J. GILES
LT H. E. N. MARTENS
2LT C. E. LEGGETT
 NBCAS 30/06/65
SGT P. L. DICKSON
CPL W. J. MARTIN
CPL T. M. THOMPSON
CPL W. O. WHALAN
LCPL R. M. BUTLER
LCPL A. R. GEORGE
LCPL W. C. ROWE
PTE T. W. BERRY

PTE M. K. BUTLER
PTE P. CARDWELL
PTE G. K. CHISHOLM
PTE R. A. DUCK
PTE H. J. EMERY
PTE G. B. ERICKSEN
PTE S. M. FINNELLEY
PTE C. A. FRASER
PTE B. D. GANNON
PTE B. E. GORDON
PTE M. A. HOWE
PTE W. J. JAGO

PTE I. P. JOHNSON
PTE A. S. KNOTT
PTE W. L. KOETTER
PTE B. A. NEWCOMBE
PTE K. J. PETERSEN
PTE L. H. TAYLOR
PTE D. K. THOMPSON
PTE L. V. J. TURNER
PTE E. WEST
PTE L. R. WOOD

MEDICAL PL

MAJ M. A. NAUGHTON
CAPT J. D. CAMPBELL
CAPT P. HASLAU
WO2 T. P. WAHLIN
SSGT E. H. P. BROWN
SSGT N. C. GRANT
SSGT E. M. ROSS
SGT G. BEKENDAM
SGT E. R. BROMFIELD
SGT B. L. KENNY
CPL A. G. M. ANDERSON
CPL L. D. BAILEY
CPL J. R. HARPER
CPL R. H. HORE
CPL G. H. P. KENDRIGAN
CPL K. M. MICSHKE
CPL L. A. MORRISON

CPL N. J. RIDDOCK
CPL M. L. TAYLOR
CPL J. W. THORNEY-CROFT
CPL R. J. WALKER
CPL M. R. WILSON
LCPL P. ROBBINS BCAS
  08/01/66
LCPL C. W. SCRAGG
LCPL B. R. SPENCER
PTE G. M. BOYD
PTE T. H. BROMLEY
PTE R. J. BURTON
PTE C. CLARK KIA 08/01/66
PTE J. F. COLE
PTE K. L. DOYLE
PTE R. J. HARBACH
PTE L. J. HIGGINS

PTE P. J. HOLZ
PTE W. H. R. JAMES
PTE J. W. KERR BCAS 08/10/65
PTE M. E. A. KRANZ
PTE R. C. NOVICE
PTE I. C. PHILLIPS
PTE W. G. QUIRK
PTE J. REYNOLDS
PTE J. R. SEAGG
PTE L. R. TAIT
PTE A. J. TESLER
PTE P. VANDENBERG
PTE D. R. W. WARNER
PTE J. D. WATTS WIA 12/10/65
PTE M. A. F. WILSON
  KIA 08/01/66
PTE R. J. WILSON

SUBUNIT NOT DETERMINED

PTE T. R. BECHAZ
PTE A. C. BLANCO
PTE B. F. BOURKE
PTE R. T. BURSTALL
PTE R. C. CARNE
PTE R. L. CARTER
PTE W. DAVIS
PTE T. R. EDWARDS
PTE R. EDWARDS
PTE B. D. FORSYTH
PTE R. J. FOX
PTE C. J. GANNON

PTE D. G. GRAHAM
PTE D. J. HARGANS
PTE P. T. HAZELL
PTE D. W. HUDSON
PTE P. E. HULBERT
PTE M. T. HUNT
PTE E. J. JARDEN
PTE C. T. JOHNSON
PTE N. K. JONES
PTE C. R. KENNEDY
PTE J. J. MALONEY
PTE C. J. MARTIN

PTE J. MCCLELLAND
PTE I. M. MORGAN
PTE T. M. PAYNE
PTE B. G. POOLE
PTE D. J. SMITH
PTE A. F. STOREY
PTE A. M. TINCKNELL
PTE N. F. TURNER
PTE R. P. M. VIKUCKIS
PTE H. R. WILSON
PTE B. G. YOUNG

1 ALSC

MAJ P. F. T. GOWANS
MAJ R. B. MCDONALD HQ
CAPT F. J. ALIZZI ORD DET
CAPT T. I. HEESOM WSKP
CAPT D. S. HEMING WKSP
CAPT J. A. HOGGART DEN SECT
CAPT M. D. KING ENGR DET
CAPT E. R. MACKENZIE ENGR
  DET
CAPT P. J. NAUGHTON DEN
  SECT
CAPT P. H. B. PRITCHARD HQ
CAPT N. W. SPENCER ORD DET
LT D. M. HANNELL HQ
2LT E. W. SIMPSON ORD DET
2LT W. J. O'GRADY ASC DET
WO1 D. D. HORSLEY WKSP
WO1 C. H. L. SEABROOK WSKP
WO2 M. J. BROWNE HQ
WO2 C. C. CARRUTHERS ORD
  DET
WO2 S. H. CHEESMAN WKSP
WO2 S. E. EDWARDS HQ
WO2 J. K. HALES ASC DET
WO2 D. J. HENRYS WSKP
WO2 W. J. MARQUET ENGR DET

WO2 J. G. MCCLOUGHAN
  WSKP
W02 M. J. PEDERSON WSKP
WO2 D. P. PINI ORD DET
WO2 S. R. PRIOR 11 MC GP
WO2 O. A. ROBINSON WKSP
WO2 L. A. STANLEY ORD DET
WO2 H. W. TOM WKSP
SSGT L. H. ANDERSON HQ
SSGT R. T. DEVINE ASC DET
SSGT J. R. HANCOCK DEN SECT
SSGT A. T. HARNEY ORD DET
SSGT J. A. LEANE ENGR DET
SSGT D. LYNCH HQ
SSGT R. C. MEREDITH ENGR
  DET
SSGT M. R. NEYLAND ORD DET
SGT G. J. ANDREWS ORD DET
SGT J. A. ASHER HQ
SGT J. A. BATES WKSP
SGT J. H. BATES WKSP
SGT E. W. BILLINGSLY HQ
SGT R. COGHLAN ORD DET
SGT T. M. CONVERY WKSP
SGT F. H. O. HOWETT HQ

SGT W. S. JOHNSTONE ENGR
  DET
SGT L. LAMOTTE ASC DET
SGT P. A. MACKIE ORD DET
SGT B. J. NICHOLLS WKSP
SGT V. PARKIN ORD DET
SGT P. R. SEAWARD WKSP
SGT R. SIMS ENGR DET
SGT G. P. SPENCER ASC DET
SGT A. A. SPINNEY HQ
SGT D. J. THOMAS 11 MC GP
SGT B. THOMPSON WKSP
SGT H. F. VAN TONGEREN ASC
  DET
SGT B. T. WILSON ORD DET
SGT C. H. YORK WKSP
CPL P. J. BIGGS HQ
CPL L. W. CHALMERS HQ
CPL B. K. CUMMINGS HQ
CPL M. J. EDGHILL ORD DET
CPL D. E. ELDER ORD DET
CPL R. A. G. ELLIS ENGR DET
CPL R. J. FORBES ORD DET
CPL P. J. B. GALLAND DEN SECT
CPL A. R. GREEN ORD DET
CPL A. F. GROOME R&C CEN

CPL G. T. GUEST WKSP
CPL D. W. HAYES WKSP
CPL J. L. HORWOOD HQ
CPL H. J. HURIJ HQ
CPL H. D. JAGER ASC DET
CPL R. F. JOHNSON ORD DET
CPL B. A. JOHNSON WKSP
CPL D. K. KING DEN SECT
CPL B. R. KRAMER HQ
CPL J. E. LAWRENCE R&C CEN
CPL K. H. LEGGETT ASC DET
CPL M. C. LEWIS ENGR DET
CPL T. L. MAYTON ENGR DET
CPL J. F. MCADAM WKSP
CPL R. T. MCADOO ASC DET
CPL A. MCINTYRE ORD DET
CPL A. D. MCKEAN HQ
CPL K. R. MINEHAN ORD DET
CPL J. C. MUCKLESTONE WKSP
CPL H. L. MURRAY ASC DET
CPL L. J. O'DWYER WKSP
CPL M. W. OSBORNE WKSP
CPL B. A. OTWAY ORD DET
CPL B. K. PITT HQ
CPL O. M. PITTS ENGR DET
CPL H. K. ROLLS ORD DET
CPL T. W. SHARP HQ
CPL R. C. SNOW ENGR DET
CPL R. E. STANMORE WKSP
CPL J. D. TAYLOR ORD DET
CPL F. TILLEY ORD DET
CPL C. P. VAN DER AAR HQ
CPL R. F. VENESS HQ
CPL J. P. WHITE ASC DET
LCPL E. ALBRECHT HQ
LCPL G. E. BLACK ORD DET
LCPL T. J. BUTLER 11 MC GP
LCPL R. W. CARR ASC DET
LBDR M. G. CARTER HQ
LCPL R. W. B. CHURCH WSKP
LCPL N. S. G. EEKHOFF ASC DET
LCPL P. KILLEN ENGR DET
LCPL G. R. J. LYME WKSP
LCPL T. G. THOMSON ORD DET
LCPL N. H. M. WOODS HQ
PTE R. J. ALWAY ORD DET
PTE H. BAART ASC DET
PTE A. BOYD ORD DET
CFN A. J. BOYLE WKSP

PTE K. F. BRAMLEY HQ
PTE M. J. BUTLER ENGR DET
PTE R. A. CANN ORD DET
PTE P. A. CAUST ASC DET
SPR B. J. CAVEN ENGR DET
PTE T. W. CLARK HQ
PTE J. M. CLARKE ORD DET
PTE A. W. CLEMENT ORD DET
PTE M. J. W. CORRIN HQ
PTE V. P. COY R&C CEN
CFN N. B. CROMARTY WKSP
SPR W. F. R. DAUK HQ
SPR P. DAVENPORT ENGR DET
PTE B. DEWAR ORD DET
SPR S. D. DONNELLY ENGR DET
TPR W. A. DOWNIE HQ
SPR J. EAGLETON ENGR DET
PTE E. J. EGGMOLESSE ASC DET
CFN L. J. FERGUSON WKSP
PTE R. F. FOX ASC DET
PTE H. L. FREEBURN ASC DET
GNR L. GOODA HQ
PTE S. G. HALSE HQ
PTE V. L. W. HAMPSON ASC DET
SPR M. G. HARDING HQ
CFN C. A. HEINRICH WKSP
PTE L. W. HENDERSON ASC DET
SPR W. D. HIGGINS ENGR DET
PTE R. R. HILLS ASC DET
PTE R. A. HUGHES HQ
PTE T. B. INGE ORD DET
PTE W. E. JEROME ASC DET
PTE G. R. JOHNSON ASC DET
CPN T. JOHNSON WKSP
PTE J. T. JONES ENGR DET
PTE R. KITCHEN ASC DET
SPR D. E. J. KOCK ENGR DET
PTE S. KUSTURIN ORD DET
PTE V. J. LAGETTIE WKSP
PTE R. J. LAWRENCE ASC DET
PTE G. W. LEE ASC DET
PTE R. M. LEWIS ASC DET
SPR G. J. LILLYST ENGR DET
PTE A. R. LINNEY ASC DET
CFN J. A. LYDEAMORE WKSP
PTE A. B. MAAT HQ
PTE G. J. MALHERBE ORD DET

PTE P. R. MARCELINO ASC DET
SPR N. MCDERMOTT ENGR DET
PTE J. J. MELTON HQ
CFN T. J. MILFULL WKSP
PTE J. A. B. MILLS HQ
CFN C. H. MINGAY WKSP
PTE M. MOLONEY ASC DET
PTE P. G. MORGAN ASC DET
CFN R. B. NEVILLE WKSP
CFN D. E. NICHOLLS WKSP
PTE A. K. PEARSE ORD DET
PTE J. POSTEMA HQ
PTE K. G. PURDIE ASC DET
CFN G. E. RAYNER WKSP
PTE G. A. D. ROBERTSON ORD DET
PTE R. M. ROSS DEN SECT
CFN S. G. ROSS WKSP
CFN M. G. ROSSER WKSP
PTE R. N. SANDERS ORD DET
PTE C. J. J. SANDERSON ASC DET
PTE G. G. SANDIFORD ASC DET
PTE K. SHEDDON HQ
PTE J. H. SIMPSON ASC DET
CFN H. M. SIMPSON WSKP
PTE J. H. SMIT ASC DET
GNR L. F. SMITH HQ
CFN N. G. SNAPE WKSP
SPR G. W. SPACKMAN ENGR DET
PTE P. SUGDEN ORD DET
PTE B. H. SYMONS ASC DET
SPR J. W. TAIT HQ
PTE K. E. TAYLOR ASC DET
SPR J. R. THORBURN ENGR DET
PTE M. L. TILLEY ORD DET
PTE G. E. TOMS HQ
PTE J. M. VAN ROOSMALEN ORD DET
SPR K. L. G. WARNE ENGR DET
SPR A. M. WARNER ENGR DET
CFN L. A. WHITE WKSP
PTE D. J. WHITWAM ORD DET
CFN N. E. WILESMITH WKSP
SPR R. E. WILLIAMS ENGR DET
SPR E. D. WILLIAMS ENGR DET
CFN S. J. WOOLCOCK WKSP

105 FD BTY

MAJ P. N. O. TEDDER
CAPT K. W. BADE KIA 08/01/66
CAPT A. G. HUTCHINSON
CAPT A. KARAS
CAPT B. J. STARK
CAPT P. J. C. TRELEAVEN
LT J. A. R. JANSEN
LT J. C. LONG
LT R. B. MAHER
LT G. G. POUND
LT B. H. STARK
2LT G. R. MAUGHAN
WO2 J. CROOK
WO2 S. D. JAMES
WO2 D. W. MCLEOD EME DET
WO2 J. J. SOXSMITH
SGT J. H. BUHMANN
SGT W. COTTEE
SGT M. D. DUX
SGT L. W. FANNING
SGT M. J. FLETCHER EME DET
SGT J. R. HAIM
SGT R. T. HARPER
SGT L. R. HEDGE
SGT L. C. KEARNS
SGT D. W. MCDONALD
SGT I. C. MORLEY
SGT D. K. NICHOLLS
SGT N. E. WILLS
BDR O. W. BELL
BDR B. D. CANE
BDR L. D. HENDERSON
CPL W. J. HUDNOTT
BDR R. D. HUMPHRIES
BDR V. J. IRWIN
BDR I. R. JAMES
CPL P. M. KABLE
BDR T. B. KLIESE
BDR J. LILLIS
BDR J. S. MCCONNELL
CPL D. A. A. MCDOUGALL
  EME DET
CPL A. F. NELSON EME DET
BDR S. M. OXENHAM
BDR M. J. RICHARDS
BDR L. A. SANDERSON
BDR A. E. SHAW
BDR P. A. E. SPARKES
BDR C. R. SWANSON
CPL L. H. TAYLOR

BDR B VOYZEY
CPL D. A. WADDINGHAM EME
  DET
LBDR R. B. ASHMAN
LBDR G. R. BALDWIN
LBDR C. ELWELL
LBDR R. J. FERGUSON
LBDR H. A. GRIGGS
LBDR T. L. HANSON
LBDR R. R. MCINTOSH
GNR B. G. ARNOLD
GNR G. N. BADKE
GNR G. L. BAKER
GNR L. J. BARKER
GNR R. BARTKUS
GNR B. A. T. BIERTON
GNR R. C. BONNER
GNR E. J. BRADLEY
GNR P. E. BRADLEY
GNR J. Mc. BRADLEY
GNR P. R. BROOKE
GNR G. P. BROWN
GNR P. H. BROWN
GNR R. J. BULLPITT
GNR R. J. G. CARLISLE
GNR J. J. CATHCART
CNR B. D. CAVANAGH
GNR R. A. CHAPMAN
GNR J. R. CHEYNE
GNR R. W. CLIFF KIA 06/02/67
CFN R. E. CONNELL EME DET
GNR M. M. CREIGHTON
GNR T. L. CURLEY
GNR C. J. CYBULSKI
GNR W. W. FEARON
GNE P. W. FLEMING
GNR S. D. FREESE
GNR N. S. GALBRAITH
GNR K. D. GANN
GNR H. R. GARDINER
GNR C. C. GELJON
GNR J. GILLANDERS
GNR. M. GODDARD
GNR J. C. GOURLAY
CFN B. GREETHAM EME DET
CNR F. GULYAS
GNR T. H. HALF
GNR A. R. HALL WIA 12/01/66
GNR P. F. HAYLOCK
GNR A. K. HOLLOWAY

GNR F. V. HURMAN
GNR M. JANSSON
GNR J. A. J. JAUNCEY
PTE S. J. JENKINS
GNR B. M. JOHNSTON
GNR W. KONIAS
GNR A. J. LAWS
GNR D. E. LINDGREN
GNR A. E. LLOYD WIA 08/01/66
GNR W. A. LOCKE
GNR R. A. LONG
GNR T. J. LUCHTERHAND
GNR J. MALONE
GNR R. C. MATTHEWS
GNR N. W. MINON
GNR L. E. MUSSARED
GNR A. J. NALL
GNR A. D. NELSON
GNR J. W. NEVILLE
GNR P. G. O'NEILL
GNR V. PINNELL
GNR B. W. PRINTER
GNR G. W. PYLE
GNR J. C. RANDALL
GNR J. A. REYNOLDS
PTE K. L. RYAN
GNR K. J. SALOWAY
GNR E. A. SAUNDERS
GNR D. J. SCHEIWE
GNR T. SIMPSON
  DWOAS 09/12/65
GNR J. P. SMITH
GNR F. A. A. SOMMERTON
GNR A. SPANN
GNR D. J. STAPLETON
GNR B. D. STILLWELL
GNR K. G. SUMMERSFORD
GNR M. A. TERRELL
GNR P. J. WALSH
GNR R. J. WARD
GNR D. L. WATTS
GNR D. N. WHITE
GNR J. E. WICKHAM
GNR L. F. WILLEY
GNR C. M. WILSON
GNR R. J. WOODFORDE
GNR G. J. WOODWARD
GNR W. T. WRIGHT
GNR W. L. WRIGHT

3 FD ENGR TP

CAPT A. H. MACGREGOR MC
LT G. STEWART
SSGT L. G. HODGE
SGT B. SANT
CPL R. W. BOWTELL KIA
  11/01/66
CPL C. B. DENNIS
CPL J. F. FAIRWEATHER
CPL W. R. GALLAGHER
CPL G. R. GOATER EME DET
CPL J. P. OPIE
CPL L. P. RAYNER EME DET
CPL B. SAUNDERS
CPL R. J. SEDDON
CPL R. G. THORBURN
LCPL D. T. EVANS
LCPL J. T. GARNER
LCPL B. A. LAUDER
LCPL B. J. TICKNELL
SPR P. J. ASH
SPR D. C. AYOUB
SPR I. R. BARNETT
SPR I. H. BIDDOLPH
SPR R. L. BILLMAN
SPR T. M. BRADBURY

SPR A. J. BROWN
SPR P. M. CACHIA
SPR A. CHRISTIE
SPR B. M. CLEARY
SPR A. S. COLEMAN
SPR L. R. COLMER
SPR D. COOK
SPR C. W. COOLBURRA
  WIA 18/03/66
SPR W. C. CORBY
SPR J. R. COTTER WIA 18/03/66
SPR J. W. COTTRELL
SPR R. H. DONOGHUE
SPR W. O. DOUGLAS
SPR W. S. EYLES
SPR R. C. FORSTER
SPR D. W. GOODING
SPR G. C. GREEN
SPR G. C. GUEST
SPR B. J. HARFORD
SPR B. F. HAY
PTE A. M. HEASLIP
SPR J. D. HUTTON
SPR D. A. JAMES
SPR K. R. KERMODE

SPR S. W. LAW
SPR M. G. LEE
SPR M. F. LILLEY
SPR M. R. LIVINGSTON
  WIA 17/03/66
SPR F. C. MALLARD
SPR T. G. MASON
SPR M. MCGRATH
SPR K. MILLS
SPR W. A. MURRAY
SPR W. P. MURRAY
SPR D. J. PETERS WIA 17/03/66
SPR B. J. POLLARD
SPR G. R. A. REID
CFN C. N. RICHARDS EME DET
SPR D. L. ROPER
TPR D. W. SANDERSON
SPR P. T. TRICKETT
SPR A. R. TUGWELL
SPR K. W. UNMEOPA
SPR B. F. VAN HAM
PTE J. W. VANDERZON
SPR G. J. WILSON
SPR R. L. WILSON
SPR J. B. WOMBELL

1 APC TP (PWLH)

CAPT R. K. HILL MC
  WIA 28/06/65
  WIA 29/06/65
LT R. C. GUYMER
LT W. L. RUTTLEDGE
  WIA 10/01/66
SGT W. R. BENNETT
SGT A. J. BLADES EME DET
SGT R. A. GREIG
SGT E. W. KEEVERS
SGT N. J. MODYSTACK
SGT R. E. RICHARDS
SGT L. R. SYMONS
CPL K. T. ALEXANDER
CPL N. D. BEARE
CPL W. D. BIELBY EME DET
CPL R COKER EME DET

CPL B. J. DELANEY
CPL K. J. HENDERSON
CPL J. P. HOUSTON EME DET
CPL I. W. JOHNSTON
CPL A. A. MURPHY
CPL H. J. L. NEIHOFF
CPL E. T. O'NEILL
CPL J. L. TOWNSEND
CPL D. P. WOODS
CPL P. F. YEATES
LCPL R. B. HOLT
PTE K. R. BALL
TPR A. J. BEETON
TPR W. H. BINNING
TPR B. J. CAMERON
TPR A. J. DUGGIN
CFN W. J. ELLIOT EME DET

TPR I. B. ELLYARD
TPR G. F. GARNER
TPR A. E. P. GENTRY
TPR R. M. GILLAM
TPR B. HARBOUR
TPR S. E. HART
TPR S. HUCKING
TPR R. L. JOSE WIA 21/02/66
TPR P. B. KILBY
TPR J. MCLEVEY
TPR J. J. O'SHEA WIA 24/11/65
TPR G. D. SAVAGE
TPR I. M. THOMAS
TPR A. V. VEARINGS
TPR R. WARREN

161 RECCE FLT

MAJ P. D. LIPSCOMBE
CAPT N. R. PINKHAM
CAPT B. J. SMITH MID
    WIA 02/04/66
LT J. A. GUILD
LT J. A. F. PURVIS
LT H. VON MUENCHHAUSEN
2LT D. COCKERELL
2LT D. T. ETTERIDGE
WO2 C. O. SCAFE
SGT L. S. DAWBER
SGT J. ELLIS EME DET
SGT H. J. GIBSON
FSGT L. LARNEY
SGT B. J. MATEER
SGT K. W. ROBERTSON
CPL G. H. AVERN
CPL B. L. BEAN EME DET

CPL T. H. BLAIR EME DET
CPL M. BYNG EME DET
CPL P. G. CUMMINGS
CPL C. E. EBNER
CPL K. T. ELSON EME DET
CPL J. S. JORDAN EME DET
CPL I. M. MACDONALD EME
    DET
CPL K. C. RAISON
CPL W. J. RAWLINGS EME DET
CPL C. A. SMITH
CPL T. A. WINTERTON EME DET
LAC K. I. A. BELL RAAF AFch
LCPL R. COOMBS
LCPL L. S. PUKALLUS EME DET
CFN N. R. BENNETT EME DET
PTE J. BLAKEY
CFN D. N BUDD EME DET

PTE C. D. CROOK
PTE R. D. DOYLE
PTE F. T. FINNIGAN
GNR R. J. HART
CFN R. E. HODGKINSON EME
    DET
PTE R. HOLLAND
PTE R. P. HUTCHISON
PTE L. C. MCCARTHY
CFN R. MCLEANN EME DET
CFN J. A. NICHOLS EME DET
CFN D. W. O'BRIEN EME DET
PTE B. G. PEARSON
CFN O. C. REYNOLDS EME DET
PTE M. SITARZ
PTE P. VINEY
CFN R. K. WHITE EME DET
CFN H. R. WILLIS EME DET

161 FD BTY, RNZA

MAJ D. R. KENNING MBE
CAPT G. D. BIRCH MBE
CAPT G. M. CONNOR
CAPT E. J. MCKINNEY
CAPT B. A. MURPHY MC
LT K. P. MURPHY
LT G. J. WILLIAMS
WO2 I. H. CUNNINGHAM
WO2 M. C. NABBS MBE
SSGT G. B. BLACK BEM
SSGT J. R. MCMEIKEN
SGT W. G. ANDERSON
SGT V. D. COLSON
SGT B. C. COOK
SGT A. J. S. DON KIA 14/09/65
SGT J. F. DONNELLY
SGT W. F. GILES
SGT A. S. SIMEON
SGT A. B. TUSTIN
SGT E. G. WILLBOND BEM
BDR R. BIGG-WITHER MBE
BDR W. C. F. BROWNE
BDR W. J. H. COOPER
BDR J. F. DEAZLEY
BDR D. T. DONALDSON
CPL P. R. DOWNS
BDR D. S. J. DWANE
BDR R. G. EDWARDS
BDR D. C. GUNN
CPL D. M. HUTTON
BDR V. W. LITCHFIELD
BDR F. M. LUPO
CPL J. MACKAY
BDR D. MC. G. MCCORT

CPL M. J. MILLAR
BDR N.D.E. RHYND
CPL S. F. RYDER
BDR J. F. STEWART
BDR J. TAITUA
BDR J. M. R. TUAINE
BDR W. G. WALKER MID
BDR R. WHITE KIA 14/09/65
BDR A. H. WILLIAMS
LBDR D. H. CARSWELL
LBDR R. H. CURREY
LBDR C. T. EDWARDS
    WIA 14/09/65
    WIA 09/10/65
LBDR P. J. FAIRMAN
LBDR S. J. R. GREEN
LBDR O. HADDON
LBDR R. J. HANDLEY
LBDR T. H. HETERAKA
LBDR W. G. HUGHES
LBDR A. A. JOHNSON
LBDR R. K. JONES
LCPL A. O. LANCASTER
LBDR K. MANSELL
LBDR A. S. MCMATH
LBDR D. T. A MORROW MID
LCPL D. V. PORTER
LBDR J. POTTS
LBDR F. TOKO
LBDR M. WHITTLE
LBDR W. A. WILLIAMS
GNR N. J. ABBOTT
GNR N. F. ALDOUS
GNR R. J. ALISON

GNR S. T. BALDWIN
GNR W. A. BOYES
GNR P. J. BUSH
GNR C. W. CASS
GNR P. P. COLLINS
GNR C. A. COOPER
GNR K. M. DEACON
GNR R. A. EDWARDS
GNR C. M. ELLIOTT
GNR K. A. FORD
GNR W. H. FOREMAN
GNR P. A. GEORGE
PTE C. J. JOHNSON
GNR A. A. JOHNSTONE
GNR J. T. KERR
GNR M. MAKAORE
GNR T. T. MATEKUARE
GNR M. W. MAUNSELL
GNR D. G. MAXWELL
GNR C. MCISAAC
GNR C. D. MOORS
GNR D. E. NEPIA
GNR W. F. ROBSON
GNR T. F. RYAN
GNR A. D. SADLER
GNR A. T. T. SCOTT
GNR D. R. SEMB
GNR J. M. SEMB
GNR P. M. SIDDALL
GNR R. H. A SMITH
GNR A. K. TAURUA
GNR M. T. WATENE
GNR H. T. WILSON

NZ LOG ELM

CHAP4 A. MCKENZIE	SGT D. KEOWN WKSP	CPL P. MERTAR WKSP
LT P. M. REID	SGT F. PARRY WKSP	LCPL D. MCINTYRE WKSP
SSGT J. MOWER WKSP	CPL R. COLLINS WKSP	CFN MOROS WKSP

Notes

1. The ANZUS Connection

1 J. Monash *The Australian Victories in France 1918* 2nd edn, London: Hutchinson, 1920, p. 64

2 D. M. Horner *High Command — Australia and Allied Strategy 1939-45* Canberra: Australian War Memorial, 1982, Chapter 12, E. D. and A. Potts *Yanks Down Under 1941-45 — The American Impact on Australia* Melbourne: Oxford University Press, 1985, Chapters 4 and 16

3 N. Harper *Australia and the United States — Documents and Readings in Australian History* Adelaide: Griffin Press, 1971, p. 163

4 H. G. Gelber *The Australian–American Alliance — Costs and Benefits* Sydney: Pelican, 1968, pp. 31–2. In 1965 Australia had spent 3.7 per cent of Gross National Product on defence. The US had spent 8 per cent and Britain 6.8 per cent. Selective conscription for service in Australia had been introduced and discontinued in the 1950s. In 1964 another selective National Service Scheme was introduced for service in and outside Australia. This scheme provided the manpower for Australia's commitment to the Second Indochina War

5 R. O'Neill *Australia in the Korean War 1950–53 Vol. II, Combat Operations,* Canberra: Australian War Memorial and the Australian Government Publishing Service, 1985, pp. 156–8. This is the account of the Battle of Kapyong in Korea where the Australians were supported by New Zealand artillery units. Later, New Zealand artillery and infantry units joined the 28th Independent Infantry Brigade in Malaysia under the ANZUK Treaty. This brigade incorporated British, Australian and New Zealand troops

6 L. L. Robson *The First AIF — A Study of Its Recruitment 1914–1918* Melbourne: Melbourne University Press, 1970, pp. 202–3. A. H. McLintok *An Encyclopaedia of New Zealand* Wellington: New Zealand Government Printer, 1966, pp. 567–8

7 W. C. Westmoreland and U. S. G. Sharpe *'Report on the War in Vietnam' (as of 30 June 1968)* Section II, pp. 84–97. W. C. Westmoreland *A Soldier Reports* New York: Doubleday, 1976, pp. 104–8

8 E. Doyle and S. Lipsman (eds) *The Vietnam Experience — America Takes Over 1965–67* Boston: Boston Publishing Company, 1982, p. 8
9 L. B. Johnson, Speech of 17 February 1965. Quoted in *Vietnam — First Half of 1965* No. 2 of 1965, Canberra: Department of External Affairs, 1965
10 G. Pemberton *All the Way: Australia's Involvement in Vietnam* Sydney: Allen and Unwin, 1987, pp. 266–75
11 Transcript of Parliamentary Statement by the Minister for External Affairs, Mr Paul Hasluck, 23 March 1965, p. 24
12 G. Lewy *America in Vietnam* New York: Oxford University Press, 1978, pp. 43–7. This reference is used for the next few paragraphs to summarise the negotiations that went on to involve the US more substantially in the Vietnam War
13 M. Sexton *War for the Asking* Melbourne: Penguin, 1981, pp 44–5
14 Quoted in F. K. Crowley *Modern Australia in Documents 1939–70* Vol. 2 Melbourne: Wren Publishing, 1973, p. 480
15 *Australia's Military Commitment to Vietnam* Canberra: Department of Foreign Affairs, 1975, pp. 2–3
16 Quoted in Crowley *Modern Australia in Documents* p. 480
17 Westmoreland *A Soldier Reports* p. 135
18 J. Essex-Clark, interview with author, 23 December 1984
19 E. W. Williamson, interview with author, 29 April 1986
20 K. S. Holyoake, Statement of 27 May 1965, quoted in *Vietnam — First Half of 1965* Department of External Affairs, No. 2 of 1965, Canberra

2. The deployment

1 R. A. Ducie, interview with author, 9 June, 1985. T. Buckley, taped comments on the preparations and deployment of 1 RAR in 1965. J. S. Tattam, Debrief on Exercise SKY HIGH II, April 1965
2 J. Essex-Clark, interview with author, 22 December 1984. Buckley, taped comments
3 Buckley, taped comments
4 M. Naughton, letter to author, 2 July 1985. Confirmed by R. A. Ducie in interview with author, 9 June 1985
5 ibid.
6 J. Essex-Clark, letter to author, 6 May 1987
7 Exercise SKY HIGH TWO Confirmatory Notes to Verbal Orders by Commanding Officer 1 RAR, 1 April 1965. Copy No. 17. J. S. Tattam, paper entitled 'Debrief on Ex SKY HIGH TWO', April 1965. Exercise SKY HIGH TWO Preliminary Instructions, 19 March 1965
8 A. H. D. McAulay, annotations to third draft of the book 'The Quiet Professionals'. Buckley, taped comments. Members of 1 RAR did not perceive the deficiencies in resources as being extraordinary. Aside from the continuing opinion held by soldiers that more funds should be spent on national defence, most accepted the status quo as being the lot of the soldier. Major Tom Buckley (RL) (the Quartermaster of 1 RAR at the time) disagrees with the author that the Battalion was poorly equipped and did not have the resources to train for war. The deficiencies in resources at 1 RAR were not the fault of the Quartermaster. The roots of these deficiencies were in the government's appropriations for the Department of Army
9 Interviews with several veterans of 1 RAR, 9 June 1985
10 H. Gullet *Not as a Duty Only — An Infantryman's War* Melbourne: Melbourne University Press, 1976, pp. 1–2

11 A. A. Calwell, quoted in Crowley *Modern Australia in Documents*
12 I. R. W. Brumfield, interview with author, 14 June 1977
13 Doyle and Lipsman *The Vietnam Experience* pp. 14–15. This reference is used to summarise the situation in Vietnam in May
14 J. Faisie, quoted in the *Australian* newspaper, 1 June 1965
15 P. Richardson, interview with author, 26 February 1977. Richardson was a soldier in 1 RAR at the time
16 J. M. Gibson 'The Separate Brigade' *Military Review* May 1970, pp 82-6
17 E. W. Williamson, interview with author, 29 April 1986. This reference is used to describe the organisation and characteristics of the 173rd during the next few paragraphs
18 J. B. Channon and G. A. Russill *The First Three Years — A Pictorial History of the 173rd Airborne Brigade (Separate)* Brigade Information Office, 1966. F. C. Coker 'Annual Historical Summary — Troop "E", 17th Cavalry (Airborne)' January–December 1965, US National Archives, Washington DC
19 E. W. Williamson, interview with author, 29 April 1985
20 Channon and Russill *The First Three Years*
21 Interviews with veterans of the 173rd during Brigade Reunion 1986. Williamson, interview with author. Story contained in literature distributed to support the Brigade's Reunion in 1986
22 Westmoreland *A Soldier Reports* p. 36
23 E. W. Williamson, Combat Commander's Note No. 63, 5 June 1965.
24 *Sydney Morning Herald* 28 May 1965
25 *Daily Telegraph* 28 May 1965
26 G. A. Cudmore, Chaplain's Report—Operation TRIMDON—27 May–8 June 1965, June 1965, p. 1
27 D. F. Paul, told to author, 26 November 1984
28 Westmoreland and Sharp 'Report on the War' p. 95
29 J. Essex-Clark, interview with author, 22 December 1984
30 J. Essex-Clark, annotations and sketch on third draft of the book 'The Quiet Professionals'
31 ibid.
32 I. R. W. Brumfield 'RAR Vietnam Instruction — 1 RAR, 173 AB Bde, Bien Hoa Vietnam' 2 June 1965
33 J. Essex-Clark, personal diary, entry of 29 June 1965
34 C. O. G. Williams, letter to family, 4 June 1965
35 J. Essex-Clark, annotations on third draft of the book 'The Quiet Professionals'
36 Quoted in article by Don Peterson in the *Courier Mail* 24 June 1965
37 Quoted in the *Courier Mail* 14 June 1965
38 A. H. D. McAulay, annotations on third draft of the book 'The Quiet Professionals'
39 Quoted in article by Tom Tiede in the *Casper-Star Tribune* 17 August 1965
40 Quoted in Australian Associated Press release, 11 June 1965
41 Quoted from copy of document entitled 'Speech by Major General Nguyen Van Thieu, Minister of National Defence, in Welcome of the Australian Infantry Battalion on their Arrival in RVN on 10 June 1965'
42 Westmoreland and Sharp 'Report on the War' p. 109. Doyle and Lipsman *The Vietnam Experience* p. 15
43 Doyle and Lipsman *The Vietnam Experience* p. 15
44 Lewy *America in Vietnam* p. 48
45 Quoted in Doyle and Lipsman *The Vietnam Experience* p. 16

46 J. Essex-Clark, interview with author, 22 December 1984
47 J. A. Hooper, comments on third draft of the book 'The Quiet Professionals'
48 T. Loftus, annotations on first draft of the book 'The Quiet Professionals'
49 A. Ramsay, article in the *Courier Mail* 27 June 1965
50 W. E. Kaine, annotations on second draft of the book 'The Quiet Professionals'
51 W. E. Kaine, letter to author, 26 March 1985
52 J. P. Dwyer, letter to author, 11 March 1985
53 ibid.
54 Ramsay, article in the *Courier Mail*
55 Kaine, letter
56 I. Mackay *Australians in Vietnam* Adelaide: Rigby Ltd, 1968, p. 27
57 Dwyer, letter
58 The *Sydney Telegraph* 28 June 1965
59 Australian Associated Press report, 28 June 1965
60 The *Sydney Sun* 8 July 1965
61 Quoted in Lewy *America in Vietnam* p. 49
62 D. Peterson *Courier Mail* 14 June 1965

3. The first forays

 1 J. Dermody, A. Thompson, A. H. D. McAulay, annotations on third draft of the
    book 'The Quiet Professionals'. All were intelligence staff in 1965–66
 2 ibid.
 3 *Courier Mail* 19 June 1965
 4 J. B. Healy, Post-Tour Report of August 1966 '1 RAR War Diary'. Healy com-
    manded A Company 1 RAR during the period June 1965–June 1966
 5 A. H. D. McAulay, annotations on third draft of the book 'The Quiet
    Professionals'. J. Essex-Clark, interview with author, 22 December 1984
 6 I. S. Fisher, Post-Tour Report of August 1966 '1 RAR War Diary'. Fisher com-
    manded D Company 1 RAR from January 1966–June 1966
 7 A. H. D. McAulay, annotations on third draft of the book 'The Quiet
    Professionals'. J. Essex-Clark, interview with author, 22 December 1984
 8 I. D. McFarlane, Post-Tour Report of August 1966 '1 RAR War Diary'. McFarlane
    commanded B Company 1 RAR during the period June 1965–June 1966
 9 C. O. G. Williams, letters to family, 14 June and 27 September 1965
10 McAulay, annotations. Thompson, annotations. Dermody, annotations
11 Westmoreland and Sharp 'Report on the War' p. 84
12 W. E. Kaine, photograph of sign provided
13 C. O. G. Williams, letter to family, 28 June 1965
14 McAulay, annotations
15 Quoted in *Courier Mail* 14 June 1965
16 J. Essex-Clark, personal diary, entry of 29 June 1965
17 J. B. Healy, annotation on second draft of the book 'The Quiet Professionals'.
    'Record of Casualties — First Tour of Vietnam by 1 RAR May 65–May 66'. This
    was a register maintained by the Operations Sergeant and signed periodically by
    the Commanding Officer recording the regimental particulars of each casualty,
    date and nature of wounds and evacuation details
18 C. Leggett, interview with author, 28 February 1977
19 W. Nalder, quoted in the *Australian* 20 July 1965
20 Interviews with many veterans of the 1 RAR Group since 1977
21 J. Dean, comments on third draft of the book 'The Quiet Professionals'

22   The Sydney *Daily Telegraph* 30 June 1965. These bags of mail were to arrive late in July 1965
23   J. A. Hooper, comments on third draft of the book 'The Quiet Professionals'. Hooper was 1 RAR Second-in-Command during the period January–June 1966
24   Quoted in *Courier Mail* 14 June 1965
25   J. MacNamara, comments on second draft of the book 'The Quiet Professionals'. MacNamara was a platoon commander in 1 RAR during the period September–October 1965
26   J. Essex-Clark, interview with author, 22 December 1984
27   Doyle and Lipsman *The Vietnam Experience* pp. 14–16. Westmoreland and Sharp 'Report on the War' p. 107. Westmoreland *A Soldier Reports* p. 145. These sources have been used to summarise the situation in South Vietnam at the time
28   Westmoreland *A Soldier Reports* p. 139
29   Channon and Russill *The First Three Years* p. 15
30   G. Dexter, interview with author, 9 May 1986. Also 173rd Airborne Brigade (Separate) 'Debrief of Operation 17/65 (6–9 July 65)'
31   C. Cavazza, interview with author, 28 April 1986
32   173rd Airborne Brigade (Separate) 'Debrief on Operation 17/65 (6–9 Jul 65)'. ibid. 173rd Airborne Brigade (Separate), Daily Journal. E.W. Williamson, Combat Commander's Note No. 67, 14 July 1965. These sources cover the US actions on this operation
33   A. Ramsey, quoted in *Courier Mail* 7 July 1965
34   '1 RAR War Diary' entry of 7 July 1965. C. McQuillan, annotations on fourth draft of the book 'The Quiet Professionals'. McQuillan was a signaller in Delta Company and a close friend of Jaudzemis
35   P. Burgess *WARCO—Australian Reporters at War* Melbourne: Heinemann, 1986, pp. 4–7. This reference is used to describe the action from an eyewitness point of view. Other quotes are from D. Peterson, quoted in the *Courier Mail* 9 July 1965. The remainder of the story is pieced together from T. Loftus, annotations on first draft of the book 'The Quiet Professionals' and McFarlane, *B Company 1 RAR in Vietnam 1965–1966* Unpublished monograph p. 7
36   McFarlane, annotations
37   A. H. D. McAulay, letter to wife, 10 July 1965 (Eyewitness to Nalder's evacuation)
38   *Sydney Morning Herald* 20 July 1965
39   E. W. Williamson, Combat Commander's Note No. 67, 14 July 1965. Also 173rd Airborne Brigade (Separate) 'Debrief on Operation 17/65 (6–9 Jul 65)'
40   Quoted in *Australian* 5 July 1965. Also *Courier Mail* 5 July 1965
41   I. R. W. Brumfield, interview with author, 14 June 1977
42   T. Buckley, taped comments on third draft of the book 'The Quiet Professionals'. Buckley was the Quartermaster at the time and accompanied Brumfield while he pointed out to the Minister the problems the Battalion was having with clothing and equipment. Brumfield had directed Buckley to lay out items which could be used to illustrate his points on tables inside a tent. It was inside the tent and not in view of the media representatives that he made his representations to the Minister. The author does not know how the nature of these protests were made known to the correspondents who were waiting some distance away, having been excluded from coming into the tent.
43   J. Dean, comments on third draft of the book 'The Quiet Professionals'
44   W. Downing, Williamson's Aide d'Camp's Diary, entry of 4 June 1965
45   E. W. Williamson, interview with author, 29 April 1986
46   Dean, comments

47 McAulay, annotations
48 Williamson, interview
49 *Sydney Morning Herald* 24 July 1965
50 S. D. Newman '161 Battery, Royal New Zealand Artillery, History in South Vietnam' (final draft). This source covers the description of the 161st Field Battery in 1965
51 Transcript of 173rd Airborne Brigade (Separate) 'Debrief on Operation 17/65 (6–9 Jul 65)'. E. W. Williamson, Combat Commander's Note No. 67, 14 July 1965
52 Williamson, interview
53 Transcript of 173rd Airborne Brigade (Separate) 'Debrief on Operation 17/65 (6–9 Jul 65)'
54 Williamson, interview
55 Dexter, interview
56 G. Connolly, article in *Courier Mail* 14 October 1965
57 1 RAR Operation Order 6/65, Copy No. 33, 6 August 1965
58 Robinson, annotations
59 Essex-Clark, annotations
60 McFarlane *B Company 1 RAR in Vietnam 1965–1966* p. 6
61 Gleaned from a number of interviews. There was a general feeling among veterans from 1 RAR 1965–66 that the Viet Cong knew in advance of each of the operations except Operation CRIMP which followed immediately after an Operation MARAUDER in January 1966. Infiltration of ARVN Headquarters by Viet Cong agents was suspected. McAulay, annotations. McAulay remembers listening to radio intercepts of Viet Cong communications talking of the anticipated operations of the Brigade
62 McFarlane, *B Company 1 RAR in Vietnam 1965–1966* p. 6
63 C. O. G. Williams, letter to family, 11 August 1965
64 W. F. Hindson, interview with author, 10 November 1984. Also McFarlane *B Company 1 RAR in Vietnam 1965–1966* p. 7
65 E. W. Williamson, interview with author, 29 April 1986
66 Channon and Russill *The First Three Years* p. 16
67 '1 RAR War Diary' entry of 26 August 1965. *Sydney Morning Herald* 27 August 1965
68 Essex-Clark, interview

4. The Iron Triangle

1 T. Mangold and J. Penycate *The Tunnels of Cu Chi* Sydney: Pan Books, 1985, p. 33
2 J. S. McKay (ed.) *Vietnam the Second Year — 173rd Airborne Brigade (Separate) — A Pictorial History* Tokyo Brigade Information Office 1968. Also Mangold and Penycate *The Tunnels of Chu Chi* p. 163
3 173rd Airborne Brigade Operation Order 25-65 (Operation IRON TRIANGLE), Annex B Intelligence
4 Mangold and Penycate *The Tunnels of Cu Chi* p. 33
5 Westmoreland *A Soldier Reports* pp. 162–3
6 173rd Airborne Brigade Operation 18-65, Copy No. 26, 13 September 1965
7 173rd Airborne Brigade Operation Order 25-65 (Operation IRON TRIANGLE)
8 McAulay, annotations. McAulay was an Australian-trained Vietnamese linguist with 1 RAR. Before the operations he overheard a trooper from the 173rd inform a Vietnamese laundress that the Brigade was going to Ben Cat in a few days. It has

been noted earlier that Vietnamese civilians frequented the Brigade area. They would have noticed preparations for operations and are likely to have been able to ascertain the areas that were to be searched. When McAulay interviewed peasants in the area of operations they told him they had been warned of the arrival of US units. Later in this chapter it is shown that the ARVN 7th Infantry Regiment was infiltrated by Viet Cong. As a formation deployed in support of the operations it is most likely that infiltrators would have informed Viet Cong contacts of the operations. Also, as in all operations, a copy of operation orders was sent to the South Vietnamese III Corps Headquarters

9   S. Newman *History of the 161st Field Battery, RNZA* p. 19

10   G. Clarke and G. Williams, interview, 9 June 1985

11   S. Lind, interview, 18 August 1977. MacNamara and Dwyer, annotations

12   Quoted in *Casper-Star Tribune* 23 September 1965

13   Channon and Russill *The First Three Years* p. 9

14   J. Tyler, quoted in transcript of a debriefing on Operation Ben Cat I, 14–27 September 1965, held at Bien Hoa a few days after the operation was completed

15   ibid.

16   173rd Airborne Brigade Headquarters Company Daily Journal, 20 September 1965

17   C. O. G. Williams, letter to family, 27 September 1965

18   McFarlane *B Company 1 RAR in Vietnam 1965–1966* p. 9

19   Quoted in Australian Associated Press report in *Courier Mail* 27 September 1965

20   A. H. D. McAulay, letter to wife, 24 September 1965

21   '1 RAR War Diary', entry of 27 September 1965

22   I. R. W. Brumfield, quoted in *Courier Mail* 5 July 1965

23   Australian Associated Press reports quoted in *Courier Mail* 25 and 27 September 1965

24   J. Reston, quoted in *Courier Mail* 1 October 1965

25   G. Dexter, quoted in transcript of debriefing held on Operation Ben Cat I, 14–27 September 1965, a few days after the operation was completed

26   E. W. Williamson, quoted in transcript of debriefing held on Operation Ben Cat I, 14–27 September 1965, a few days after the operation was completed.

27   173rd Airborne Brigade Operation Order 26–65 (Operation IRON TRIANGLE), 5 October 1965. 173rd Airborne Brigade, Critique of the Iron Triangle Operation, 25 October 1965, p. 2

28   J. Essex-Clark, annotations on third draft of the book 'The Quiet Professionals'. The front and second rows for the 1 RAR Rugby team in 1965 were made up of the following: Corporal Terry Loftus (Prop), Sergeant Allan Lightfoot (Hooker), Captain Peter Arnison (Prop), Major John Essex-Clark (Second Row) and Lance Corporal Denis Shergold (Second Row)

29   D. P. Rothwell, tape-recorded comments on third draft of the book 'The Quiet Professionals'

30   Essex-Clark, annotations

31   G. Schuts, quoted in *Australian* 11 October 1965

32   A. P. Wilson, interview with author, 9 June 1985

33   ibid.

34   ibid. Rothwell, tape-recorded comments

35   P. G. Bourne *Men, Stress and Vietnam* Boston: Little Brown, 1970, pp. 180–1. Bourne treated two of the victims of the incident while working as a psychiatrist attached to the US Army in Vietnam

36   McAulay, annotations

37   A. H. D. McAulay, letter to wife, 8 October 1965
38   173rd Airborne Brigade 'Critique of the Iron Triangle Operation' 25 October 1965, p. 4
39   '1 RAR War Diary' entry of 8 October 1965
40   W. J. Giles, comments on third draft of the book 'The Quiet Professionals' 2 March 1986
41   W. Downing, entry in Brigadier General E. W. Williamson's Aide d'Camp's Diary, 8 October 1965
42   173rd Airborne Brigade 'Critique of the Iron Triangle Operation' 25 October 1965, p. 14
43   A. H. D. McAulay, letter to wife, 9 October 1965
44   J. Essex-Clark, interview with author, 22 December 1984 (Colonel Alex Preece MVO DSO (RL) was also in attendance). J. Essex-Clark, personal diary, entry of 9 October 1965. J. Essex-Clark, annotations on third draft of the book, 'The Quiet Professionals'. A. Thompson, annotations on third draft of the book 'The Quiet Professionals'
45   1 RAR After Action Report, 10 October 1965
46   1 RAR After Action Report, 9 October 1965
47   Newman *History of 161 Battery* p. 6
48   C. O. G. Williams, annotations on second draft of the book 'The Quiet Professionals'
49   '1 RAR War Diary' entry of 10 October 1965. '1 RAR Record of Casualties'. McAulay, annotations
50   McAulay, annotations
51   '1 RAR Record of Casualties'. Second Lieutenant Culpitt was wounded in this incident and the author has deduced that he must have initiated the first explosion, the company closed up, and the second explosion occurred.
52   A. H. D. McAulay, letter to wife, 1435 hours 12 October 1965
53   McAulay, annotations
54   W. K. S. Olds and A. E. Hartle 'One Unwary Moment' in A. N. Garland (ed.) *Infantry in Vietnam* Nashville: Jove Books, 1982, pp. 76–7
55   T. Tiede, quoted in his article in *Casper-Star Tribune* 27 October 1965
56   Garland, *Infantry in Vietnam*
57   '1 RAR War Diary' entry of 12 October 1965
58   T. Loftus, annotations. R. Mangano, interview with author, 9 June 1985
59   G. Cudmore, told to author, 18 May 1985
60   McFarlane *B Company 1 RAR in Vietnam* p. 11
61   ibid.
62   I. R. W. Brumfield, notes on key officers in 1 RAR sent to author in 1984
63   T. Hagan, annotations on the first draft of the book 'The Quiet Professionals'. Hagan was an eyewitness.
64   Article in *Courier Mail* 12 October 1965
65   Hagan, annotations
66   P. G. Sharp, letter to author, 18 September 1977
67   A. H. D. McAulay, letter to wife, 1115 hours 13 October 1965.
68   ibid.
69   McFarlane *B Company 1 RAR in Vietnam* p. 12
70   A. H. D. McAulay, letter to wife, 1115 hours 13 October 1965
71   ibid.
72   J. D. MacNamara, written comments on second draft of the book 'The Quiet Professionals'

73 A. H. D. McAulay, letter to wife 1115 hours 13 October 1965
74 McAulay, annotations
75 McFarlane *B Company 1 RAR in Vietnam* p. 12. W. Hindson, told to author, 12 August 1984
76 ibid.
77 McFarlane *B Company 1 RAR in Vietnam* p. 12
78 A. H. D. McAulay, letter to wife, 14 October 1965
79 ibid. 'The Radio Research Unit (RRU) actually an Int[elligence] mob (listen to VC radios) got a VC Battalion forming up to attack the Aussies and from the messages figured out where they were, and the Arty let them have it. Ten bodies were still there the next day and considering they carry off all casualties and equipment, they must have copped it.' McFarlane *B Company 1 RAR in Vietnam* p. 12
80 ibid.
81 173rd Airborne Brigade 'Critique of the Iron Triangle Operation' 25 October 1965, p. 2
82 ibid., p. 20
83 ibid.
84 O. D. Jackson, quoted in *Courier Mail* 20 October 1965
85 A. H. D. McAulay, letter to wife, 1115 hours 14 October 1965
86 J. Essex-Clark, personal diary, entry of 28 November 1965. Date of the battle comes from *US Army News* 19 January 1966. Essex-Clark had a personal interest in the fate of the 7th ARVN Regiment because of what he knew about them from the Iron Triangle operations
87 Mangold and Penycate *The Tunnels of Cu Chi* p. 166. Also Lewy *America in Vietnam* p. 64
88 ibid., p. 169
89 Lewy *America in Vietnam* p. 64
90 ibid., p 65. Mangold and Penycate *The Tunnels of Cu Chi* pp. 175–7

5. The bloody hump

1 173rd Airborne Brigade Operation 28–65, 1 November 1965, Annex B Intelligence
2 Cover of the Brigade's Operation Order 28–65 had a symbol showing 'May 65' on the left joined to 'May 66' by a curved line which at its apex was written '173D ABN BDE (Sep)'. It was a clear symbol that the 173rd had come to the top of the 'hump' and was on the downward stretch to May 1966
3 Combat Operations After Action Report (MACV/RCS/J3/32)
4 C. O. G. Williams, letter to family, 31 October 1965
5 A. H. D. McAulay, letter to wife, ? November 1965
6 A. H. D. McAulay, letter to wife, 24 October 1965
7 A. H. D. McAulay, letter to wife, 2 November 1965
8 Copy of citation for the Military Medal — Corporal B. J. Le Seuer
9 A. H. D. McAulay, letter to wife, 24 October 1965
10 J. Essex-Clark, personal diary, entry of 29 September 1965
11 P. N. O. Tedder, letter to author, 4 March 1986
12 ibid.
13 Newman, *History of 161 Battery*, p. 23
14 B. J. Stark, notes to author, 6 March 1986 (Stark was the Battery Captain of 105 Field Battery at the time)
15 Tedder, letter
16 Doyle and Lipsman *The Vietnam Experience* pp. 66–9

17 Rothwell, annotations
18 A. H. D. McAulay, letter to wife, 5 November 1965
19 McFarlane *B Company 1 RAR in Vietnam* p. 13
20 E. W. Williamson 'Critique of Operation HUMP' 19 November 1965, p. 3
21 Williams, annotations. '1 RAR War Diary' entry of 6 November 1965
22 I. Welsh, annotations on first and second drafts of the book 'The Quiet Professionals'
23 A. H. D. McAulay, letter to wife, 'D + 2 0715 hours' 7 November 1965
24 Translation: VC newspaper article. *Quan Giai Phong* No. 69, 30 November 1965, entitled 'Head on Battle Destroyed One Battalion of the US Expeditionary Force — Three Comrades Repulsed 15 American Assaults, Killing over 50 Enemy'
25 E. W. Williamson, Combat Commander's Note No. 85, 14 November 1965. Also J. M. Hutchens *Beyond Combat* Chicago: Moody Press, 4th edn, 1969 (Chapter 11, 'Hill 65'). Author was the chaplain to 1/503rd and was decorated for valour for his actions in the battle on Hill 65 on 8 November 1965
26 Hutchens *Beyond Combat* p. 102
27 Copy of Citation for the Medal of Honour, S5 L. Joel
28 E. W. Williamson, Combat Commander's Note No. 85, 14 November 1965
29 Translation: VC newspaper article
30 ibid.
31 R. Brownlee, interview with author, 30 April 1986. Brownlee was a fellow Captain with Daniels in the Brigade and wrote of this incident in his photograph album/diary of the period
32 2/503rd Battalion Daily Journal, entry of 8 November 1965
33 Combat Operations After Action Report (MACV/RCS/J3/32) '1 RAR War Diary' has 762nd Regiment. Entry in Williamson's Aide d'Camp's Diary has Q761 Regiment. Williamson's description in 'Critique of Operation HUMP' has only a mention of a 'main line Viet Cong Regiment of three battalions'. However, the most authoritative source seems to be Combat Operations After Action Report (MACV/RCS/J3/32) which points out that the 271st were involved on 8 November 1965 and had taken very heavy casualties which were replaced by North Vietnamese regulars.
34 Hagan, annotations. Hagan was the acting platoon Sergeant of 1 Platoon on this operation and he stated when writing his account of the operation, 'Time dims the memory but the period 6–9 November 1965 is still vivid'.
35 C. O. G. Williams, letter to family, 10 November 1965
36 Healy, annotations
37 Quoted in Australian Associated Press report, 11 November 1965
38 Notes on Healy from I. R. W. Brumfield, A. V. Preece and J. Essex-Clark.
39 Healy, annotations
40 A. H. D. McAulay, letter to wife, 16 November 1965
41 Healy, annotations
42 C. Fawcett, told to author, 9 June 1985. C. O. G. Williams, told to author, 9 June 1985. A. H. D. McAulay, letter to wife, 16 November 1965
43 Healy, annotations. Notes on relationship of Healy and Murphy came from I. R. W. Brumfield, letter to author, 11 December 1984
44 Hagan, annotations
45 Hutchens *Beyond Combat* pp. 113–14
46 Williamson 'Critique'
47 J. B. Healy, told to author, 9 June 1985. Corroborated by J. Essex-Clark
48 A. H. D. McAulay, letter to wife, 16 November 1965. The NCO concerned was a

friend of McAulay's
49 Essex-Clark, interview
50 A. H. D. McAulay, letter to wife, 1145 hours 9 November 1965
51 D. P. Rothwell *The Jesus Nut Poems* Sydney: Wentworth Books, 1973
52 J. Essex-Clark, personal diary, entry of 10 November 1965
53 A. H. D. McAulay, letter to wife, 1125 hours 10 November 1965
54 J. Essex-Clark, personal diary, entry of 11 November 1965
55 J. Essex-Clark, interview with author, 12 June 1987
56 A. H. D. McAulay, letter to wife, 13 November 1965
57 Williamson 'Critique'
58 ibid.
59 E. W. Williamson, letter to author, 17 August 1986
60 J. Reston, quoted in Australian Associated Press report, 14 November 1965
61 Doyle and Lipsman *The Vietnam Experience* p. 72
62 References for these actions come from a number of sources which include Doyle
    and Lipsman *The Vietnam Experience* pp. 70–5 and J. A. Cash, J. Albright and
    A. W. Sandstrum *Seven Firefights in Vietnam* New York: Bantam Books, 1985
63 Interviews with Brumfield, Essex-Clark, McFarland and Tattam about contrasts in
    US and Australian tactical training and methods. J. Essex-Clark, personal diary,
    entry of 13 November 1965
64 Copy of Major J. Essex-Clark's map showing the attack plan
65 Quoted in *Courier Mail* 16 November 1965
66 ibid.
67 Account given in *Courier Mail* 16 November 1965
68 A. H. D. McAulay, letter to wife, 15 November 1965
69 Mrs P. E. Gillson, letter, 24 November 1965

6.   The false harvest
 1 M. Naughton, written comments on third draft of the book 'The Quiet Pro-
    fessionals'
 2 A. H. D. McAulay, written comments on third draft of the book 'The Quiet
    Professionals'. McAulay's best friend Private Paul Slattery became Brumfield's
    orderly and had told McAulay of the requirement to assist Brumfield from his bed
    in the mornings. Also R. A. Ducie, told to author, 9 June 1985
 3 A. H. D. McAulay, letter to wife, 14 November 1965
 4 A. H. D. McAulay, letter to wife, 12 November 1965. Also J. Currie, taped
    comments on 1 RAR's Tour of Vietnam sent to author, 25 May 1986
 5 A. H. D. McAulay, letter to wife, 15 November 1965. Numerous interviews with
    veterans from 1 RAR testify to the increased tendency to drink heavily to relax
    and settle down between operations
 6 173rd Airborne Brigade (Separate), Fragmentary Order — NEW LIFE '65, 19
    November 1965. Also Garland (ed.) *Infantry in Vietnam* p. 170
 7 ibid.
 8 Garland (ed.) *Infantry in Vietnam* p. 170
 9 173rd Airborne Brigade (Separate), Fragmentary Order — NEW LIFE '65, 19
    November 1965. Also 1 RAR Operation Order 16/65, 20 November 1965. Also
    A. H. D. McAulay, letter to wife, 21 November 1965
10 A. H. D. McAulay, letter to wife, 21 November 1965
11 173rd Airborne Brigade (Separate), Fragmentary Order — NEW LIFE '65, 19
    November 1965, Annex B Intelligence. Also A. H. D. McAulay, letter to wife, 21
    November 1965. McAulay had been responsible for speaking to ARVN personnel

about the location and size of Viet Cong units in 1 RAR's area of operations

12 '1 RAR Commander's Diary' entry of 22 November 1965

13 The account of the attack on Duc Hanh is based on the following sources: Lander, annotations. J. Essex-Clark, personal diary, entry of 25 November 1965, and interview with author, 22 December 1985. J. R. Bourke, personal diary, entry of 23 December 1965. J. R. Bourke 'After Action Report' 25 November 1965. D. P. Rothwell, letter to author, January 1985. D. P. Rothwell 'Attack on Duc Hanh' *Australian Infantry Magazine* 1971. D. P. Rothwell, taped account sent to author in April 1985. Healy, annotations. W. Giles, letter to author, 2 March 1986.

14 J. R. Bourke, personal diary, entry of 23 December 1965

15 W. Giles, letter to author, 2 March 1986

16 ibid.

17 J. R. Bourke, personal diary, entry of 23 December 1965

18 Rothwell 'Attack on Duc Hanh'

19 Giles, letter

20 McAulay, annotations. Also Giles, letter

21 Quoted in *Courier Mail* or *Sun* in an article by Garry Baker, 17 December 1965

22 McAulay, annotations

23 ibid.

24 McFarlane, annotations. Copy of letter from Hung provided.

25 R. West, letter to Mr R. Payne, 12 March 1985. West was the section commander of the section involved in this incident and an eyewitness. Verified by J. P. Dwyer, the Platoon Commander and also an eyewitness, in an interview with the author, 9 June 1985

26 '1 RAR War Diary' entry of 25 November 1965

27 McFarlane *B Company 1 RAR in Vietnam* p. 14

28 'I RAR War Diary' entry of 27 November 1965. McFarlane *B Company 1 RAR in Vietnam* p. 14

29 '1 RAR War Diary' entry of 28 November 1965

30 A. H. D. McAulay, letter to wife, 28 November 1965

31 Australian Associated Press report, 29 November 1965

32 J. Essex-Clark, personal diary, entry of 29 November 1965

33 J. P. Dwyer, letter to author containing comments on second draft of the book 'The Quiet Professionals' 11 March 1985

34 A. H. D. McAulay, letter to wife, 27 November 1965. McAulay was an eyewitness to this incident

35 ibid. Also J. Essex-Clark, interview with author, 22 December 1984. Also D. F. Paul, entry in photograph album of his period in Vietnam 1965–66. (Paul was Second-in-Command of A Company for the tour)

36 McFarlane *B Company 1 RAR in Vietnam* p. 15

37 McAulay, annotations

38 McFarlane *B Company 1 RAR in Vietnam* p. 15

39 ibid.

40 Arnison, annotations. Arnison was the Second-in-Command of Bravo Company

41 A. V. Preece, interview with author, 22 December 1984

42 Preece, annotations

43 J. A. Hooper, letter to author, 19 September 1985

44 Garland (ed.) *Infantry in Vietnam* p. 173. The account of the 2/503 operations in the La Nga Valley was written by Major R. B. Carmichael and Lieutenant R. E. Eckert in an article entitled 'Operation NEW LIFE' published in *US Infantry* Jan–Feb 1967, pp. 43–7. The article was republished in the reference given and it

has been assumed that the authors participated in the operation
45 ibid., p. 174
46 McFarlane, annotations
47 Australian Associated Press report, 6 December 1965
48 C. O. G Williams, letter to family, 8 December 1965
49 Australian Associated Press report, 6 December 1965
50 Australian Associated Press report, 7 December 1965
51 ibid.
52 '1 RAR War Diary' entry of 15 December 1965. Record of Casualties
53 McKay, annotation
54 '1 RAR War Diary' entry of 16 December 1965
55 '173rd Headquarters Company Daily Journal' entry dated 17 December 1965
56 Anon., letter, 15 December 1965
57 McFarlane, paper entitled 'VC Tactics encountered by 1 RAR in Vietnam 1965–66' August 1966, p. 11. Verified by Kaine, annotations
58 J. Rowe *Vietnam—The Australian Experience* Sydney: Time Life Magazine, 1987

7. The river battles
 1 1 RAR Operation Order 17/65, 16 December 1965
 2 Preece, annotations
 3 R. Brownlee, interview with author, 28 April 1986
 4 Doyle and Lipsman *The Vietnam Experience* p. 141
 5 Lucky Starr, recorded interview with C. McQuillan and R. Payne, April 1987
 6 ibid.
 7 Don Lane, recorded interview with C. McQuillan and R. Payne, April 1987
 8 ibid.
 9 Quoted in *Courier Mail* 27 December 1965
10 H. Cox, article in *Courier Mail* 25 November 1965
11 G. Barker, quoted in article in Sydney *Sun* 14 December 1965
12 '1 RAR War Diary, entry of 27 December 1965
13 Westmoreland and Sharp 'Report on the War' pp. 113–14. Also Westmoreland *A Soldier Reports* p. 160
14 1 RAR Operation Order 18/65, Copy No. 45, 29 December 1965. Also 173rd Airborne Brigade Operation Order 30/65, Copy No. 22, 28 December 1965
15 The descriptions of the actions involving 1/503rd and 2/503rd on 2 January 1965 have been gleaned from 'Daily Journals of Headquarters 173rd Airborne Brigade (Separate)'. R. Brownlee, interview with author, 28 April 1986. E. W. Williamson 'Critique of Operations MARAUDER and CRIMP' 24 January 1966. E. W. Williamson, Combat Commander's Note No. 90, 18 January 1966. A. Hartle, Aide d'Camp's Diary, entries of 1–3 January 1966
16 '1 RAR After Action Report'
17 C. McQuillan, notes to author, April 1986. McQuillan was a signaller at Battalion headquarters and witnessed this incident
18 'Daily Journal Headquarters 173rd Airborne Brigade' entry of 2210 hours 3 January 1966
19 D. P. Rothwell, letter to author, 11 March 1985. Rothwell was an eyewitness to this incident
20 ibid.
21 The account of this attack on the hamlet has been gleaned from I. D. McFarlane, *B Company 1 RAR in Vietnam 1965–66*, 23 November 1966, and annotations on third draft of the book 'The Quiet Professionals'

22 Williamson 'Critique of Operations MARAUDER and CRIMP'
23 173rd Airborne Brigade (Separate), the Meritorious Unit Commendation. Figures taken by author from copy of recommendation sighted in the US archives, Suitland, Maryland
24 '1 RAR War Diary' entries of 1–7 January 1965

8. The Ho Bo Woods

1 A. H. D. McAulay, letter to wife, 9 January 1966
2 173rd Airborne Brigade (Separate), Operation Order 1/66, 6 January 1966
3 A. V. Preece and J. Essex-Clark, interview with author, 23 December 1984
4 Dermody, annotations
5 McFarlane *B Company 1 RAR in Vietnam* p. 15
6 E. W. Williamson 'Critique of Operations MARAUDER AND CRIMP' 24 January 1966
7 A. H. D. McAulay, letter to wife, 9 January 1966
8 J. Essex-Clark, interview with author, 23 December 1984
9 McQuillan, annotations
10 J. R. Bourke, personal diary entry made between 14 and 21 January 1966. The account of the ambush of Bourke's platoon has been constructed from the following sources: J. R. Bourke, notes to author, 4 June 1985, and interview with author, 4 February 1977. W. Giles, notes to author, 2 March 1986. I. S. Fisher 'Post-Operational Report' 16 January 1966. P. H. Graves, eyewitness account, 23 May 1967. R. Smith, letter to author, 21 December 1984. D. P. Rothwell, taped comments for author of May 1985. McQuillan, annotations
11 J. R. Bourke, personal diary, entry of 28 January 1966. Also Rowe *Vietnam — The Australian Experience* p. 45
12 McQuillan, annotations
13 M. Naughton, recorded interview with C. McQuillan, 8 June 1985
14 P. H. Graves, eyewitness account, 23 May 1967
15 M. M. Fraser, letter to Captain P. H. Graves Jr, 19 January 1968
16 McFarlane *B Company 1 RAR in Vietnam* p. 21. P. M. Arnison, interview with author, 8 June 1985
17 '1 RAR War Diary' entry of 8 January 1966
18 A. V. Preece, interview with author, 23 December 1984
19 Payne, annotations
20 'Combat Operations After Action Report (MACV/RCS/J3/32)'
21 McAulay, annotations
22 Williamson 'Critique'
23 A. Hartle, Aide d'Camp's Diary, entry of 14 January 1966
24 'Combat Operations After Action Report (MACV/RCS/J3/32)'
25 McFarlane *B Company 1 RAR in Vietnam* p. 22
26 McAulay, annotations. Kaine, annotations
27 Rothwell, annotations
28 Rothwell, annotations. A. V. Preece, interview with author, 23 December 1984
29 A. V. Preece, interview with author, 23 December 1984. E. W. Williamson, interview with author, 29 April 1986
30 '1 RAR War Diary' entry of 13 January 1966
31 Kelly, annotations. D. P. Rothwell, taped account, 1985
32 'Combat Operations After Action Report (MACV/RCS/J3/32)'
33 L. J. Mercier '173rd Airborne Brigade, Summary of Civil Affairs, Civic Action and Psychological Operations from 5 May 65–20 Jan 66', 28 January 1966

34   Preece, annotations

9.   The construction site
1   Westmoreland 'Report on the War' pp. 122–3
2   Reprint of editorial in *Playboy* magazine, May 1966. R. L. Brownlee, interview with author, 28 April 1986
3   B. Limb, recorded interview with C. McQuillan and R. Payne, 25 May 1987
4   *Sunday Telegraph* 30 January 1966. Copied at the Mitchell Library by Donna McQuillan on 19 June 1987
5   *Australian* editorial of 17 January 1966
6   1 RAR Intelligence Estimate — Operation 3/66 ROUNDHOUSE, 3 February 1966
7   J. Essex-Clark, notes on Battalion Patrol Planning. Written as a post-tour report in August 1966
8   Rothwell, annotations
9   W. J. Giles, written notes to author, 2 March 1986
10   M. Naughton, written notes to author, 25 January 1987
11   C. O. G. Williams, interview with author, 9 June 1985
12   E. W. Williamson, letter to Lieutenant Colonel A. V. Preece, 7 February 1966
13   Channon and Russill *The First Three Years* p. 3
14   A. V. Preece and J. Essex-Clark, interview with author, 23 December 1984
15   P. F. Smith, letter to Lieutenant Colonel A. V. Preece, 14 February 1966
16   J. A. Hooper, letter to author, 21 November 1984
17   173rd Airborne Brigade Fragmentary Order 5-66, 17 February 1966. 1st Brigade, 1st Infantry Division, Operation Order 6-66 (ROLLING STONE), 10 February 1966. 1 RAR Operation Order 4/66, 17 February 1966
18   G. P. Johnson 'Combat Engineers' in Garland (ed.) *Infantry in Vietnam*
19   J. Essex-Clark, notes on Battalion Patrol Planning. Written as a post-tour report in August 1966
20   Annex A to 1 RAR Operation Order 4/66 INSUM No. 9, 18 February 1966
21   A. H. D. McAulay, letter to wife, 19 February 1966
22   Reconstruction by author based on the fact that D800 Main Force Battalion were based in the area and joined the battalions of the 761st and 762nd Regiments in the attack on the headquarters
23   Essex-Clark, notes on Battalion Patrol Planning, p. 3
24   A. H. D. McAulay, letter to wife, 18 February 1966
25   1 RAR After Action Report. R. Currall, interview with author, 9 June 1985. J. Rowe *Vietnam—The Australian Experience* J. Essex-Clark, interview with author, 23 December 1984
26   '1 RAR War Diary' entries of 22–24 February 1966. J. Dermody, interview with author, 9 June 1985
27   '1 RAR War Diary' entry of 23 February 1966. J. Essex-Clark, personal diary, entry of 24 February 1966
28   McFarlane, annotations. I. D. McFarlane, *B Company 1 RAR in Vietnam 1965–66* p. 27
29   I. D. McFarlane, *B Company 1 RAR in Vietnam 1965–66* p. 27
30   A. H. D. McAulay, letter to wife, 24 February 1966
31   McFarlane, *B Company 1 RAR in Vietnam 1965–66*
32   ibid.
33   A. H. D. McAulay, letter to wife, 24 February 1966
34   '1 RAR War Diary' entry of 24 February 1966

35 A. H. D. McAulay, letter to wife, 24 February 1966
36 J. Essex-Clark, quoted in J. Rowe, *Vietnam — The Australian Experience* p. 51
37 I. D. McFarlane, VC Tactics Encountered by 1 RAR in Vietnam 1965–66. Written as a post-tour report in August 1966
38 A. V. Preece, transcript of letter provided to author

10.   The showdown
 1 G. Dexter, interview with author, 10 May 1986
 2 '1 RAR War Diary' entry of 26 February 1966
 3 Dexter, interview
 4 *Australian* 7 and 8 March 1966
 5 Westmoreland 'Report on the War' p. 124
 6 Dexter, interview
 7 173rd Airborne Brigade Operation Order 6/66, 8 March 1966
 8 '1 RAR War Diary' entry of 9 March 1966
 9 J. A. Hooper, letter to author, 19 September 1985
10 173rd Airborne Brigade Operation Order 6/66, 8 March 1966
11 McFarlane, *B Company 1 RAR in Vietnam 1965–66* pp. 28–9. '1 RAR War Diary' entries of 11 March 1966. A. V. Preece and J. Essex-Clark, interview with author, 23 December 1984
12 T. Hagan, letter to R. Payne, 8 October 1984
13 J. Dean, letter to author, 11 March 1985
14 '1 RAR War Diary' entry of 13 March 1966
15 P. Smith, Combat Commander's Note No. 1, 14 May 1966. '173rd Airborne Brigade Headquarter Company Daily Journal' entry of 14 March 1966
16 R. L. Brownlee, interview with author, 28 April 1986. Horst Faas *Denver Post* 8 March 1966
17 R. L. Brownlee, quoted in *Plain Dealer* 9 May 1966
18 J. P. Dwyer, letter to author, 11 March 1985
19 J. P. Dwyer, told to author, 9 June 1985
20 1 RAR After Action Report by Second Lieutenant R. Culpitt, 17 March 1966
21 Healy, annotations
22 McAulay, annotations
23 The description of the ensuing battle comes from P. F. Smith, Combat Commander's Note No. 1, 14 May 1966. '1 RAR War Diary' entry of 16 March 1966. W. C. Vose, letter to Willie C. Monroe, 22 May 1984, with attached essay describing his part in the battle
24 173d Airborne Brigade (Separate), General Orders No. 422, 27 September 1966
25 Vose, letter
26 173d Airborne Brigade (Separate), General Orders No. 422, 27 September 1966
27 P. N. O. Tedder, R569-1-26 'Operation Analysis: SILVER CITY (8/66)' 30 March 1966
28 J. Essex-Clark, personal diary entry of 18 March 1966
29 Tedder 'Operation Analysis' p. 3

11.   The last searches
 1 1 RAR Operation Order 7/66, 28 March 1966
 2 A. V. Preece, annotations, and told to author, 22 December 1984
 3 '1 RAR War Diary' entry of 1 April 1966
 4 Preece, annotations
 5 J. Essex-Clark, interview with author, 23 December 1984

6   McFarlane, *B Company 1 RAR in Vietnam 1965–66*, p. 31
7   '1 RAR War Diary' entries of 1–6 April 1966. McFarlane, pp. 32–3
8   A. H. D. McAulay, letter to wife, 3 April 1966
9   I. D. McFarlane, interview with author, 9 June 1985. P. M. Arnison, notes provided to author on civic action in June 1985
10 Tran Van Trai, letter to Major I. D. McFarlane, 30 December 1965
11 A. V. Preece and J. Essex-Clark, interview with author, 23 December 1984
12 1 RAR Operation Order 8/66, 11 April 1966
13 McFarlane, *B Company 1 RAR in Vietnam 1965–66*, p. 33
14 ibid.
15 A. H. D. McAulay, letter to wife, 22 April 1966

Bibliography

Official sources

'Australia's Military Commitment to South Vietnam' paper tabled in accordance with the Prime Minister's statement to the House of Representatives, 13 May 1975

Brumfield, I. R. W. 'Tasks of 1 RAR Recce and Advance Parties' 26 May 1965

Coker, F. C. 'Annual Historical Summary Troop "E", 17th Cavalry' January 1965–June 1966

Descanio, J. L. 'After Action Report (Chemical Activities) for Operation CRIMP' 17 January 1966

Dunlop, J. E. 'Organizational History Delta Company 16th Armoured' January–December 1965

Eastern Command 'March Through Sydney — Elements of Australian Army Force Vietnam' 20 May 1966

1st Brigade, 1 Infantry Division 6/66

Fisher, I. S. 'Sub-Unit Operational Analyses' 18/65, 1/66

Harper, B. J. 'Sub-Unit Operational Analyses' 17/65

Healy, J. B. 'Sub-Unit Operational Analyses' 16/65, 17/65, 18/65, 1/66

McFarlane, I. D. 'Sub-Unit Operational Analyses' 16/65, 17/65, 18/65, 1/66

MacGregor, A. H. 'Operational Analysis 3 Field Troop' 17 December–21 December 1965

Muller, F. M. 'Annual Historical Summary Troop "E", 17th Cavalry (Airborne)' January–December 1966

1 RAR Operation Orders, 4/65, 6/65, 7/65, 9/65, 10/65, 11/65, 14/65, 16/65, 17/65, 18/65, 1/66, 3/66, 4/66, 6/66, 7/66, 8/66

1 RAR 'Parade and Church Service — Bien Hoa, ANZAC Day 1966' 24 April 1966

1 RAR 'Standing Orders for Operations (SKYHIGH TWO)' March 1965

1 RAR 'Vietnam Instruction' 2 June 1965

'1 RAR War Diary' August 1965–June 1966

1/503rd Airborne Battalion, Operation Orders FRAG ORD 9/66

'173rd Airborne Brigade (Separate), Headquarter Company Daily Journals' May 1965–June 1966

173rd Airborne Brigade (Separate), Operation Orders 1/65, 18/65, 28/65, 29/65, 30/65, FRAG ORD 19 November 1965, 1/66

Rothwell, D. P. 'Sub-Unit Operational Analyses' 16/65

Tattam, J. J. 'Sub-Unit Operational Analyses' 16/65, 17/65, 18/65, 1/66

Tedder, P. N. O. '105 Fd Bty, RAA, Unit Operation Analysis Operation MARAUDER 1–7 January 1966, and Operation CRIMP' 9–14 January 1966

——'Operation Analysis: SILVER CITY (8/66)' 30 March 1966

'2/503rd Airborne Battalion Daily Journals' May 1965–June 1966

US Department of State 'Aggression from the North — The Record of North Vietnam's Campaign to Conquer South Vietnam' February 1965

Westmoreland, W. C. and Sharp, U. S. G. 'Report on the War in Vietnam' US Government Printing Office, Washington

Williamson, E. W. 'Critique of OPORD 17–65' 27 July 1965

—— 'Critique of Operation HUMP' 19 November 1966

—— 'Critique of Operation MARAUDER and CRIMP' 24 January 1966

Unpublished sources

Bourke, A. R., The History of the 105th Field Battery, 1978

Bourke, J. R., selected extracts of personal diary while serving in Vietnam

Brumfield, I. R. W., letters to author, 11 December 1984 and 4 January 1986

Carroll, M. J., Battalion Communications in Vietnam, 1966

Cudmore, G. A., Chaplain's Report—Operation TRIMDON: 27 May–8 June

Dermody, J. G., letter to author, 9 September 1977

Downing, W. A., letter to author, 12 May 1986

Dwyer, J. P., letter to author, 11 March 1985

Essex-Clark, J., personal diary while serving in Vietnam 1965–66

—— Notes on Battalion Patrol Planning, 1966

—— The First Tour 1965–1966, 1985

—— Airmobile Operations, 1986

—— Notes on Planning and Controlling 1 RAR Operations in South Vietnam (May 1965–May 1966), 1986

—— The Dynamics of Command, 1986

Fisher, I. S., Viet Cong Tactics Encountered in South Vietnam and Suggested Methods of Countering Them, 1966

Foote, R. C., Soldiers March 8th June 1966, undated

Fraser, M., letter to Captain P. H. Graves, 19 June 1967

Hagan, T. F., letter to C. H. McQuillan, 8 October 1984

Harper, B. J., Notes on Establishment and Operation of A Echelon, 1 RAR — South Vietnam, 1966

Haslau, P., Summary of Health Problems Encountered by 1 RAR During Their Tour of Duty in Vietnam, 1966

Healy, J.B., Tactical Lessons Learnt in Vietnam, 1966

Hill, R. K., A Summary of Lessons Learned from Operations with APCs in Vietnam 1965–66, 1966

Hooper, J. A., letter to author, 3 September 1985

McAulay, A. H. D., extracts of letters written while serving in Vietnam 1965–66

McFarlane, I. D., Notes from Vietnam, 6 June 1966

—— B Company 1 RAR in Vietnam 1965–1966, 23 November 1966

MacNamara, J., extracts of letters written while serving in Vietnam 1965–66

Naughton, M., letter to author, 2 July 1985

Newman, S. D., History of 161 Battery Royal New Zealand Artillery in Vietnam, 1985

Peacock, C. J., letter to author, 26 August 1977

Peck, M. C., Some Notes on Fire Support in Vietnam 1965–1966, 1966

Rothwell, D. P., letters to author, 25 January, 27 April and 11 November 1985

Sharp, P. G., 1 RAR Operations in South Vietnam 1965, 1977

Smith, P. F., Combat Commander's Note No. 1, 14 May 1966

—— letter to Lieutenant Colonel A. V. Preece, 14 February 1966

Tattam, J. J., Debrief EX SKY HIGH TWO, April 1965

Tedder, P. N. O., letter to author, 4 March 1986

Thieu, N., Welcome to the Australian Infantry Battalion, 10 June 1965 (copy of a transcript)

Vose, W. C., letter to W. C. Monroe, 22 May 1984

Westmoreland, W. C., letter of Commendation to Chairman, Chiefs of Staff Committee, 30 May 1966

Williams, C. O. G., extracts of letters written while serving in Vietnam 1965–66

Williamson, E. W., letter to Lieutenant Colonel A. V. Preece, 7 February 1966

—— Combat Commander's Notes, June 1965–February 1966

—— Aide d'Camp's Diary, 1965–66

Zasloff, J. J., Political Motivation of the Viet Cong: The Political Regroupees, RM-4703/2-ISA/ARPA, Rand Corporation, Santa Monica, 1968

Newspapers and press services

Australian Associated Press

Brownlee, R., scrapbook of the *Casper-Star Tribune*

Burgess, M., scrapbooks of the Brisbane *Courier Mail*

Cotterell, J. S., scrapbooks of the Sydney *Daily Telegraph*

Paul, D. F., scrapbook of newspaper cuttings and photographs

The *Australian*

The Brisbane *Courier Mail*

The *Bulletin*

The Sydney *Daily Telegraph*

The *Sydney Morning Herald*

The Sydney *Sun*

Books and monographs

Barnes, I. L.
Gallant and Distinguished Service Vietnam 1962–1973 Melbourne: The Military Historical Society of Australia, 1974

Bartlett, N. *1776–1976 Australia and America Through 200 Years* Sydney: Ure Smith, 1976

Bourne, P. G. *Men, Stress and Vietnam* Boston: Little Brown, 1970

Brass, A. *Bleeding Earth—A Doctor Looks at Vietnam* Melbourne: Heinemann, 1968

Burgess, P. *WARCO—Australian Reporters at War* Melbourne: Heinemann, 1986

Burns, R. D. *The Wars in Vietnam, Cambodia and Laos 1945–1982*
—— *A Bibliographic Guide* California: ABC–CLIO Information Services, 1984

Channon, J. B. and Russill, G. A. *The First Three Years — A Pictorial History of the 173rd Airborne Brigade (Separate)* Brigade Information Office, 1966

Crowley, F. K. *Modern Australia in Documents 1939–70* Vol. 2, Melbourne: Wren Publishing, 1973

Dexter, D. *Australia in the War of 1939–45: New Guinea Offensives* Canberra: Australian War Memorial, 1955

Doyle, E. and Lipsman, S. (eds) *The Vietnam Experience—America Takes Over 1965–67* Boston: Boston Publishing Company, 1982

Fairbairn, G. *Revolutionary War and Communist Strategy* London: Penguin, 1968
—— *Revolutionary Guerilla Warfare — The Country Side Version* London: Penguin, 1974

Fishel, W. R. (ed.) *Vietnam — Anatomy of a Conflict* Illinois: 1968

Frost, F. *Australia's War in Vietnam*, Sydney: Allen & Unwin, 1987

Garland, A. N. (ed.) *Infantry in Vietnam — Small Unit Actions in the Early Days: 1965–66* New York: The Battery Press, 1982

Gelber, H. G. *The Australian-American Alliance — Costs and Benefits* Sydney: Pelican, 1968

Gullett, H. *Not as a Duty Only — An Infantryman's War* Melbourne: Melbourne University Press, 1976

Harper, N. *Australia and the United States — Documents and Readings in Australian History* Adelaide: T. Nelson, 1971

Hay, J. H. *United States Department of Army Tactical and Matereil Innovations* Vietnam Studies Series, Washington: US Army, 1974

Henderson, W. D. *Why the Viet Cong Fought — Control in a Modern Army in Combat* Connecticut: Green Wood Press, 1979

Horner, D. M. *High Command — Australia and Allied Strategy 1939–45* Canberra: Australian War Memorial, 1982

Hutchens, J. M. *Beyond Combat* Chicago: Moody Press, 4th edn, 1969

Lewy, G. *America in Vietnam* New York: Oxford University Press, 1978

Lucas, J. G. *Dateline: Vietnam* New York: Award House, 1966

Mackay, I *Australian in Vietnam* Adelaide: Rigby Lts, 1968

McAuley, A.H.D. *When the Buffalo Fight* Melbourne: Bantam, 1987

McKay, J. S. (ed.) *Vietnam the Second Year — 173rd Airborne Brigade (Separate) — A Pictorial History* Tokyo: 1968

Mangold, T. C. and Penycate J. V. G. *The Tunnels of Cu Chi* Sydney: Pan Books, 1985

Matloff, M. (ed.) *American Military History, Army Historical Series* Office of the Chief of Military History, Washington DC: US Army, 1969

Monash, J. *The Australian Victories in France 1918* 2nd edn, London: Hutchinson, 1920

Mulligan, H. A. *No Place to Die: The Agony of Vietnam* New York: William Morrow, 1967

O'Neill, R. J. *Vietnam Task* Melbourne: Cassell Australia, 1969
—— *Australia in the Korean War 1950–53* Vol. II, Combat Operations, Australian War Memorial, Canberra, 1985

Pemberton, G. *All the Way — Australia's Involvement in Vietnam* Sydney: Allen and Unwin, 1987

Pike, D. *Viet Cong* Massachusetts: MITP 1966

Potts, E. D. and Potts A. *Yanks Down Under 1941–45 — The American Impact on Australia* Melbourne: Oxford University Press, 1985

Race, J. *War Comes to Long An — Conflict in Vietnamese Province* Los Angeles: University of California Press, 1973

Robson, L. L. *The First AIF — A Study of Its Recruitment 1914–1918* Melbourne: Melbourne University Press, 1970

Rothwell, D. P. *The Jesus Nut Poems* Sydney: Wentworth Books, 1973

Rowe, J. *Count Your Dead — A Novel of Vietnam* Melbourne: Angus and Robertson, 1968

——*Vietnam-The Australian Experience* Sydney: Time Life Magazine, 1987

Stanton, S. L. *Vietnam Order of Battle* Washington DC: U.S. News Books, 1981

Stone, G. *War Without Honour* Brisbane, Jacaranda Press, 1966

Summers, H. G. *On Strategy: A Critical Analysis of the Vietnam War* Los Angeles: Presidio Press, 1982

Thompson, R. *No Exit from Vietnam* London: Chatto and Windus, 1969

Thompson, W. S. and Frizzell, D. D. (eds)*The Lessons of Vietnam* Brisbane: University of Queensland Press, 1977.

Walt, L. W. *Strange War, Strange Strategy* New York: Funk and Wagnalls, 1970

Westmoreland, W. C. *A Soldier Reports* New York: Doubleday, 1976

Articles

Anon. 'Head on Battle Destroyed One Battalion of the US Expeditionary Force' Translation of Viet Cong newspaper article

Breen, R. J. 'Problems of an Expeditionary Force — First Battalion, The Royal Australian Regiment in 1965' *Defence Force Journal* No. 60, September–October 1986

Brown, A. C. 'The Viet Cong Blues — A Report From War Zone D' *Bulletin* 14 August 1965

Gibson, J. M. 'The Separate Brigade *Military Review* May 1970

Lipski, S. 'The Diggers Of Bien Hoa' *Bulletin* 23 April 1966

McFarlane, I. D. 'Civic Action' *Australian Army Journal* No. 218, March 1967

MacGregor, A. H. 'Engineers on Operations in Vietnam' *Australian Army Journal* No. 219, August 1967

Rothwell, D. P. 'The Attack on Duc Hanh' *Australian Infantry Magazine* 1971

Sharp, P. G. 'Battalion Resupply — Vietnam Style' *Australian Army Journal* No. 210, November 1966

Interviews/tapes

Alcorn, K. J., 28 February 1977
Arnison, P. M., 8 June 1985
Benson, B. J., 26 February 1977
Brownlee, R., 28 April 1986
Brumfield, I. R. W., 14 June 1977
Buckley, T., 1986
Burke, J. R., 25 February 1977 and 4 June 1985
Cavazza, C., 28 April 1986
Crick, G. G., 28 February 1977
Cudmore, G. A., 11 September 1984
Currie, J., 1986
Dermody, J., 9 June 1985
Dexter, G., 9 May 1986
Ducie, R. A., 9 June 1985
Essex-Clark, J., 23 December 1984
Evans, C. G., 28 February 1977
Fawcett, C., 9 June 1985
Fletcher, L., 1987
Hagan, T. F., 25 February 1977
Hansen, J. P., 28 February 1977
Hilditch, H. R., 28 February 1977
Hindson, W. F., 11 September 1984
Lane, D., April 1987
Limb, B., 25 May 1987
Lind, S., 18 August 1977
Lunny, K. W., 14 October 1984
McFarlane, I. D., 9 June 1985
McNamara, J. D., 9 June 1985
Neilson, G. L., 26 February 1977
Pinkerton, R. J., 28 February 1977
Pratten, J. W., 28 February 1977
Preece, A. V., 22–23 December 1984
Prior, C. R., 26 February 1977
Richardson, P., 26 February 1977
Rothwell, D. P., 1986
Starr, L., April 1987
Welch, I., 9 June 1985
Williams, C. O. G., 9 June 1985
Williamson, E. W., 29 April 1986
Wilson, A. P., 9 June 1985

Reviewers of author's drafts

Arnison, P. M.
Bourke, J. R.
Brumfield, I. R. W.
Buckley, T. J.
Currie, J. G.
Dean, F.
Dean, J.
Dermody, J. G.
Dwyer, J. P.
Essex-Clark, J.
Fisher, I. S.
Giles, W. J.
Healy, J. B.
Hooper, J. A.
Horner, D. M.
Kaine, W. E
Lander, H. M.
Loftus, T.
McAulay, A. H. D.
McFarlane, I. D.
McKay, J. D.
McQuillan, C. H.
Naughton, M. A.
Payne, R.
Preece, A. V.
Rothwell, D. P.
Tattam, J. J.
Thompson, A. G.

Photographic sources

155	J.A. Hooper
162	R.L. Brownlee
163	GTV 9 Melbourne The Third Generation
166	Australian Army Public Relations
168	Australian War Memorial
170	O.S. Lind
172	Channon and Russill
182–3	The Clark Family
188	J. Essex-Clark
190	A.H.D. McAuley
193	Channon and Russill
198	US Army Public Relations (R.L. Brownlee)
199	W.E. Kaine
205	Channon and Russill
207	GTV 9 Melbourne 'The Third Generation'
216	G. Dexter
218	New Zealand Army Public Relations
219	Australian War Memorial
223	J. Essex-Clark
224	Australian Army Public Relations (J. Essex-Clark)
225	R.L. Brownlee
238	Australian Army Public Relations (J. Essex-Clark)
241	W. Downing
246	Australian Army Public Relations
248	Australian Army Public Relations (A.V. Preece)

Index